T0244482

Cast a Diva

Cast a Diva

The Hidden Life of Maria Callas

Lyndsy Spence

Put a human note into your story, please do. Because I am rather human at times.

Maria Callas

Front cover: Europress/Shutterstock
Back cover: Fotocollectie Anefo

First published 2021
This paperback edition first published 2022

The History Press
97 St George's Place, Cheltenham,
Gloucestershire, GL50 3QB
www.thehistorypress.co.uk

© Lyndsy Spence, 2021, 2022

The right of Lyndsy Spence to be identified as the Author
of this work has been asserted in accordance with the
Copyright, Designs and Patents Act 1988.

All rights reserved. No part of this book may be reprinted
or reproduced or utilised in any form or by any electronic,
mechanical or other means, now known or hereafter invented,
including photocopying and recording, or in any information
storage or retrieval system, without the permission in writing
from the Publishers.

British Library Cataloguing in Publication Data.
A catalogue record for this book is available from the British Library.

ISBN 978 1 80399 026 2

Typesetting and origination by The History Press
Printed and bound in Great Britain by TJ Books Limited, Padstow, Cornwall.

MIX
Paper from
responsible sources
FSC® C013056

Trees for LYfe

Contents

Acknowledgements

I am grateful to the following individuals and organisations: Adam A.R.; Aine Lagan; April Ashley; Beinecke Rare Book and Manuscript Library; Colin Jones; Columbia Rare Book and Manuscript Library; Cosimo Capanni; Daphne Dennis; Dimitris Pyromallis; Dr Brigitte Pantis; Dr Michael Paroussis; Elizabeth K. Mahon; Floria Di Stefano; Graziella Chiarcossi; Joe Oliver; Isabella Giacovazzo; Lainie Reed; Laura Mobley Greenwood; Maria Callas Alumni Association of the Music School of Kalamata; Mark Beynon; Nadia Pastorcich; Nathan Coy; New York Public Library; Nicos Haralabopoulos; Nuri Lidar; Pietro Dall'Aglio; Professor Mario Giacovazzo; Renzo Allegri; Sara Allouche; Serge Mafioly; Sound Archive at Stanford University and Vanessa Porras.

A note on images: all images are from the private collections of Cosimo Capanni, Dimitris Pyromallis, Nicos Haralabopoulos, Nuri Lidar, Renzo Allegri and Sara Allouche.

Author's Note

After a season bursting with prima donnas, it is clear there is nobody like our Maria. You have 'It', call it 'charm', call it 'magic', call it 'Maria'.

Dorle Soria, 1961

Maria Callas was the greatest opera singer of the twentieth century, and to this day, she is unrivalled – *La Divina Assoluta*. But in her private life, her voice, unless she was singing, was seldom heard. She confided in those whom she trusted, not for sympathy – she was too proud – but in a bid to be understood. Dismissing her troubles, they said Callas was too strong, and undermined her suffering. I wanted to give Maria, the woman, a voice.

1

Displacement

I will storm the Gods and shake the Universe.

Medea, Euripides

The story of Maria Callas does not begin with her birth but the sadness which preceded it. 'I've had to help myself,' she said. 'Since I was a child, I knew I had to help myself.'[1] A replacement child, she was to alleviate her mother's grief after her 2-year-old son, Vasily, died in the summer of 1922. The cause of death was either typhoid or meningitis; the symptoms of both illnesses were much the same: a fever and a rash. Having consulted with an astrologer and the *phatoe* – a device similar to the Ouija board – her mother believed the unborn baby would be Vasily reincarnated.

Some claim that trauma is inherited from our forebears and their experiences shape our DNA. At the time of Maria's conception, which was calculated by messages from the spirit world, her parents, George[2] and Litsa[3] Kalogeropoulos,* lived in the close confines of their apartment above his pharmacy, unable to share their grief. As the only pharmacist in the small town of Meligalas, in the Peloponnese, his vocation provided a comfortable life for his wife and eldest child, Yacinthy, which included two maids and a cook. There was also a handyman, Christos, a handsome young soldier and Litsa's favourite servant. To Christos, she spoke for hours, exorcising her regret, 'My father was a general, God rest him. And I … I married a pharmacist.'

Litsa was five months into her pregnancy when George sold the pharmacy and bought three passages to America. Infuriated, she said that only paupers

---

* A note on Greek surnames: the feminine and masculine spelling of surnames are used in their correct context, therefore the spelling may vary.

emigrated and did not consider the political situation: during the population exchange between Greece and Turkey, there was an influx of more than 1 million refugees. Furthermore, Vasily's illness and subsequent death were embedded in his psyche, and it was common knowledge that the refugees had brought with them an epidemic of viral diseases. Instead, she claimed it was due to his affair with the mayor's daughter, who became pregnant. Years later, she wrote to Maria, 'Your good father is notoriously two-faced and a hypocrite, and he comes out on top. I shall tell you a great secret of your father's, which I have been keeping to myself all these years.'[4]

On 2 August 1923, the family arrived in New York and were greeted by flags flying at half-mast and newspaper headlines of President Warren G. Harding's death. A superstitious woman, Litsa burst into tears and called it a bad omen.[5]

There were 50,000 Greeks living in New York, and they, particularly the lower classes, were considered 'a menace to the American [working] man'.[6] Attempting to fit in, George simplified their name to Kalos and changed Yacinthy's name to Jackie* after an immigration officer mispronounced it. Their new home was a modest apartment at 87 Sixth Avenue[7] in Astoria, Queens, and they had only one friend,** Dr Leonidas Lantzounis, an orthopaedic surgeon who had left Meligalas with $15 in his pocket. Soon, George's optimism declined, and his salary from teaching Greek at a high school could not pay their bills, and within months they ran out of money.

It was into these circumstances that Maria was born, on 2 December 1923, at the Flower Fifth Avenue Hospital in Manhattan. Disappointed that her baby was a girl, Litsa turned her head to the window and for four days refused to look at her. She had wanted another blonde-haired, blue-eyed boy and instead was presented with a daughter with raven hair and black eyes.

Although George had a similar response, he suggested they name her Cecilia, but Litsa refused and chose Sophie. They eventually agreed on Maria, but throughout her childhood she was called Mary or Marianna.[8]

Furthermore, the day of Maria's birth was uncertain: Litsa said it was the third, George argued it was the fourth, but Lantzounis, who had driven her to hospital and became the child's godfather, claimed it was the second. She was registered as Sophie C. Kalos, with her birth date as 3 December, but other documents listed it as the second.[9]

---

* From herein Yacinthy shall be called Jackie.

** George's brother, Demetrios Kalogeropoulos, had emigrated to New York before him. His name and address, given as 'NY', was listed in their emigration papers. However, they seem to have become estranged.

Maria liked the fourth, as it was St Barbara's Day, the patron saint of artillery – an appropriate prophecy for her life. As Maria grew older, she resented Litsa's recollection and viewed it as a sign that she was unwanted. Whether it was intentional or not remains unknown, for Litsa embellished her memories of the day with a record-breaking snowstorm, although meteorological records indicate the weather was dry but cold. In her memoirs, she wrote, 'I could hear snow slapping against the window like the palm of a wet hand, and across the avenue I could see white sheets of snow sweeping through Central Park.'[10]

In some ways, Litsa's behaviour could be explained by her grief and, perhaps, postnatal depression. Before going to New York, she considered leaving George and returning to her mother in Athens, but thinking she was pregnant with a son – the highest status for a Greek mother – she forgot her plan and stayed with her husband. In America, however, she was isolated and lonely, with only Jackie, then 7 years old, for company. Therefore, the arrival of Maria shattered her illusions and placed her precarious mental health under further strain. 'It is a cruel thing,' Maria later said, 'to make a child feel unwanted.'[11]

Maria's earliest memories were of upheaval as she moved nine times in eight years,* to cheaper apartments in neighbourhoods in upper Manhattan, and she attended as many elementary schools.** It offered her little opportunity to make friends, as Litsa disapproved of their working-class neighbours and would not let her daughters invite others to the apartment. Their final address was 561 West 180th Street in Washington Heights. Half a century before, it had attracted rich New Yorkers who had built their European-style castles on its rocky terrain, and in the late 1920s, it was a leafy suburb with open spaces, medieval-style architecture, and a large Greek community.

Differences that had been tolerable in Greece were now magnified in New York. Litsa resented George's origins as the son of peasant farmers whom, she said, had no ambition. She chided him for his position as a sales assistant in a pharmacy and his modest salary, which barely covered their expenses. From her perspective, she deserved better and claimed to have aristocratic lineage: her (dyed) blonde hair was proof of such noble bearing.

She was a fantasist – her father, Petros Dimitriadis, had been an army general in Constantinople, who, after being invalided, gambled with disastrous results to increase his pension. Their home was sold to pay his debts, and in 1913, Litsa and her family moved to a rented house in Athens. It was rumoured she had

---

* 240 West 34th Street; 465 Columbus Avenue; 64 West 135th Street; 520 West 139th Street; 609 West 137th Street; 569 West 192nd Street; 561 West 180th Street.

** P.S. 228M; P.S. 9; P.S. 43; P.S. 192M; P.S. 189; P.S. 164.

only married George because she was pregnant and her real ambition was to be an actress. Her behaviour, such as her heightened sexuality – or what Maria called 'her shameful conduct'[12] – pointed to a chemical imbalance.

However, George was not blameless, he ignored the difficulties he would face in learning English and the high cost of living. He was jealous of Litsa, whose provocative behaviour attracted the male gaze, if nothing else, and reacted furiously if she spoke to another man. When everything seemed hopeless, Litsa swallowed poison and was found by Maria and Jackie, on the apartment floor, vomiting after having her stomach pumped.[13] George committed her to a psychiatric ward at Bellevue Hospital, a public institution with 500 beds for the city's mentally disturbed. Using his connections, namely Leonidas Lantzounis, the incident was not reported to the police (as Litsa had broken the law by attempting suicide and would have faced two years in prison).

At a young age, Maria became aware of the cyclic changes to her mother's behaviour – possibly hormonal, 'Hormones make our characters,' she later said[14] – and how it corresponded to the phases of the moon.[15] However, far from understanding, George offered no support and called his wife 'that crazy woman'.[16] There were great highs, which preceded Litsa's dark moods, during which time she would be imaginative and playful. On their weekly outings for chop suey at a local Chinese restaurant, she pretended the inexpensive meal was a stately banquet, and at home, she taught the girls how to tango and foxtrot. Nevertheless, Maria knew she could not trust those fleeting moments when Litsa was 'the most magical person on earth'.[17]

As in Greek culture, the man was head of the family, but the woman was head of the house and raised the children as she saw fit. For as long as Maria could remember, Litsa poisoned her mind against George, lamenting him for being lazy, poor and unambitious. He was vain and self-centred; he dyed his hair and moustache black; he lied about his age;[18] and he seldom interacted with his daughters. Sometimes he asked Maria and Jackie questions about school, but they were too embarrassed to engage with him.

At a young age, Maria knew her father was a womaniser, but she did not resent him, for she would also look for love and attention wherever she could find it. She remembered how her father loved Greek music and played it on their phonograph, but Litsa would charge into the room and turn it off, replacing it with operatic arias. As her parents fought, Maria sought comfort from Jackie and looked for the reassurance that neither parent offered. However, Jackie was equally unhappy and, at the age of 10, contemplated suicide.

Litsa wanted to control her children in every way, from insisting they wear hats, even though Jackie, in particular, hated it, and hitting them if they disobeyed her. The two girls shared a bed, and if they left it unmade, Litsa would take their clothes and throw them in the hallway of their apartment. If she suspected they were lying, she would put pepper on their lips; she had also used pepper to stop Maria, then a baby, from crying.

Only once did George intervene, when Litsa hit Jackie over the head with an umbrella, and on another occasion, he criticised her parenting style, 'I had several times to say, "It's not good to treat daughters this way".'[19] His new job as a travelling salesman took him away from home, which was a welcomed respite from his responsibilities toward his family. Nevertheless, Maria idolised him and thought they shared the bond of victimhood. 'I always sided with my father,' she said. 'I was his favourite when I was a child … or maybe always.'[20]

All her life, Maria believed Litsa suffered from undiagnosed schizophrenia; a secret she could not share.[21] There were traits of instability in Litsa's family: one of her brothers committed suicide at 21, and her sister became a nun at the age of 12 and died of cancer five years later – both were religious fanatics, prone to extreme behaviour. Sometimes, Litsa fuelled her unhappiness by attending church and returning home embittered by the affluent families there. The narcissism, the highs and lows, and the swift changes in Litsa's character certainly pointed to a borderline personality problem. 'They don't do enough for mental illness these days,' Maria later said. 'All this stress on cancer, but they don't spend enough money for the mentally sick.'[22]

Five years after arriving in New York, George obtained a licence to practise pharmaceuticals. With no money to open a pharmacy, he asked Leonidas Lantzounis for a loan of $10,000 – which he made no effort to repay – and opened the Splendid Pharmacy at 483 Ninth Avenue at Thirty-Seventh Street, in Hell's Kitchen. Also helping herself to Lantzounis's loan, Litsa took the children to her rich cousin's home in Tarpon Springs, Florida, where they stayed for six months. Years later, Maria recalled the days swimming in the sea and playing with her cousins as the happiest period of her childhood.

Returning to New York, Maria was hit by a car after running across the road to greet her sister. 'I'm seized by sudden tender impulses,' she said, 'and feel ashamed of them immediately afterward.'[23] Dragged to the end of the street, she escaped with minor injuries and a concussion. However, Litsa claimed it altered her behaviour: she had grown moody and viewed her sister as a rival, perhaps a feeling inspired by their mother declaring Jackie more beautiful and competent. To attract attention, whether good or bad, she interrupted Jackie's piano lessons by climbing under the pianola and working the pedals with her hands. Soon, she was also taking lessons, which George considered a waste of money.

Four months later, the American economy crashed, and George was forced to close his pharmacy. Far from being sympathetic, Litsa berated him for losing his business and blamed him entirely for the Wall Street Crash. To make ends meet, they rented a room to a Greek-Turkish couple, Callespe and Otto Canar, and humiliated by their circumstances, Litsa claimed the lodgers were her servants.[24]

Having become obsessed with bettering her circumstances, she saw in her daughters the ability to earn money. Around that time, Maria began to imitate the opera records that Litsa borrowed from the library. The first recording she heard was *Tosca*, although she called the heroine 'a clown … I don't like her very much'.[25] She taught herself arias from *Carmen* and learned the piano score and lyrics to 'La Paloma', her untrained voice attracting a small crowd beneath the opened window. A Swedish neighbour overheard her singing and offered to give her free voice lessons for two months.

Determined to turn Maria into a child star, Litsa was desperate to find a good voice teacher, although she could not afford it. 'It's a big destiny and it's terrifying,' Maria said. 'Mine is a big destiny.'[26] To pay for the $10 lessons, Litsa tried to pimp Jackie out to their landlord. However, Jackie refused and found work as a dressmaker's model, her salary going into the household. Maria turned to her three canaries and studied their throats, mimicking their muscle control and pitch.

Then, Litsa considered it a good omen when she saw a newspaper advertising a children's talent contest hosted by Jack Benny for WOR radio station. Accompanied by Jackie on the piano, Maria sang 'La Paloma' and 'A Heart That's Free' and won the second prize – a Bulova watch – the first prize went to an accordion player. There were further radio performances, and while Maria enjoyed the attention, she came to resent Litsa forcing her into a singing career. She could not recall a favourite toy, nor did she play as the other children did. Instead, she had to memorise arias and practice her scales. 'Children should not be given this responsibility,' she later said. 'Children should have a wonderful childhood. I had not had it. I wish I could have.'[27]

A theory exists that Maria applied for talent shows under the names Anita Duval and Nina Foresti, as her father disapproved of her singing on the radio. There is a recording from 1935 of Foresti on *Major Bowes Amateur Hour*,

introducing herself in a Mid-Atlantic accent and singing 'Un bel di' from
Madama Butterfly. The judges rated the performance as a 'D' and noted a 'faint
possibility for [the] future'. According to Maria's former secretary and friend,
Nadia Stancioff, she admitted to using aliases: 'When I was a kid, I took part in
a singing competition ... I called myself Anita Duval ... Afterwards, I switched
to Nina Foresti. I thought that sounded more like an opera singer!'[28] It contra-
dicts what Maria told another friend: 'The *Butterfly* piece is not true – I always
called myself by my own name.'[29]

Evidence proves that Nina Foresti was the stage name of a young Italian-
American woman named Anita Duval, who gave her address as 549 W. 144th
Street in Washington Heights. In Foresti's application (dated 11 March 1935)
for *Major Bowes Amateur Hour*, she wrote:

> My musical studies were begun when I was four years old. I studied piano
> [for] many years but as my family was in very comfortable circumstances,
> my music was not considered seriously. I was sent to finishing school, studied
> languages and singing all as social accomplishments only. One day in 1930,
> upon our return from a cruise, we found our 'comfortable circumstances'
> had vanished so I have been giving piano instruction. However, I always
> loved to sing so I continued my vocal studies and have sung in concerts and
> made my debut as Nedda, in *Pagliacci*, but as an amateur. My voice is admired
> but opportunities are so few and I find that corner – from amateur to profes-
> sional – a very difficult one to turn.[30]

Duval/Foresti was born Annette Duval in Pennsylvania in 1915, to a rich
family who lost their fortune in the Wall Street Crash. Graduating from school,
she sang on the newly established radio network, WCDA[31] and in 1928, performed as Nedda in *Pagliacci* with the New York Opera, as mentioned in the
Easton Lafayette:

> Next Tuesday night, October 24, the long-awaited performance of the New
> York Opera Company will become a reality on the stage of the Orpheum
> Theatre ... *Pagliacci* will be presented under the supervision and general
> direction of Maestro dell-Orefice, former coach of Enrico Caruso ... The
> role of Nedda will be played by Nina Foresti, talented American singer.[32]

After appearing on the *Major Bowes Amateur Hour*, she resumed her position
at the department store, Strawbridge & Clothier. What remains interesting is
the inclusion of Duval/Foresti's 'Un bel di' on Maria's recordings for EMI, and

that Duval/Foresti never revealed her identity nor sought to correct the error. Given that her opera career petered out in 1935, perhaps she enjoyed being associated with Maria, knowing that her voice has been heard by millions.

In those days, Maria sang arias suited to accomplished singers, and many believed it contributed to the vocal problems from which she later suffered. Dismissing this, she claimed she had matured early, and it correlated with her vocal development. 'You see, I had my first menstruation when I was ten,' she said, shocking those who asked about her precocious talent.[33]

Conflicted between the girl and the artist, Maria's formative years were marred by an internal struggle to accept her looks, despite her voice warrant-ing her praise. She entered a period of self-loathing: she hated her dark looks, her acne and myopia which forced her to wear thick glasses. Her mother and sister criticised her weight, although medical reports discredit any suggestion that she was overweight: at the age of 11, she weighed 119lb and was 5ft 3in tall. Two years later, her height was recorded as 5ft 7in, perhaps causing her to be self-conscious as she was now as tall as her father.[34] Only when she sang did she feel loved.

Toward the end of 1936, Litsa made plans to return to Greece so Maria could study music at the Athens Conservatory. She also claimed that her father's ghost had appeared, ordering her to leave George. Later, she said it was 'for love of Jackie ... my daughter was homesick for her country'.[35] Unsurprisingly, George did not object to their leaving – Jackie sailed first – and fell to the floor, crossing himself, 'At last, my God, you have pitied me'. He remained in New York, relieved to be separated from his wife and free of his responsibilities toward his children.

Maria remained oblivious to her parents separating. Litsa promised they would return in a year, after she had completed her studies. She did not enrol in high school, and in the months leading up to their departure, she worked in a music shop to save money for their trip.

On 20 February 1937, Maria and Litsa sailed to Greece on the SS *Saturnia*, with their meagre possessions and three canaries. After two days of seasickness, they emerged from their cabin, and Litsa began to promote Maria's talents, telling everyone she was a soprano on her way to Athens to begin a promising career. She sang 'La Paloma' and 'Ave Maria' in the tourist-class lounge, which earned her a small income in tips.

The captain, who was making his inspections, invited her to sing at church on Sunday. However, she refused but agreed to perform at a party in the first-class dining room instead. Accompanying herself on the piano, she wore a simple blue dress with a white collar, powder on her face to cover her spots and, as she would do later, removed her glasses before singing. Finishing with *Carmen*, she took a carnation from a nearby vase and threw it to the captain, who picked up the flower and kissed it. Reciprocating the gesture, he gave Maria a bouquet of flowers and a doll, the first she had ever owned.

Maria's first experience of Greece was the balmy climate and scent of Daphne, and the rundown port of Patras, with passengers scrambling to collect their luggage and pass through customs. It was late when they checked into a cheap hotel before catching the morning train to Athens. She had never seen an old wooden carriage and was not bothered by the uncomfortable seats or mediocre dish of overcooked lamb with too much gravy. Looking out of the window, she seemed mesmerised by the primitive landscape of the Peloponnese: the old fortress, the peaks of the Chelmos mountains, and the coves of the Ionian Sea.

In the fourteen years since Litsa had left, everything remained the same, but for Maria, an American-born girl with New York slang and broken Greek, everything had changed. A new identity was founded. 'In Greece,' she said, 'I again became Maria Kalogeropoulou.'[36]

2

Destiny

No one ever admits
he was born in poverty.
There's not a beggar
who, to hear him, doesn't
come of high lineage.

Madama Butterfly, Puccini

Maria arrived in Athens feeling sullen and anxious, something which Jackie attributed to her being alone with their mother. It was clear to them both that Litsa was experiencing a manic episode. The signs were evident: her fast-paced speech and enthusiasm to introduce Maria as a rising star and demanding that she sing for her unsuspecting relatives. 'Please tell her to stop,' Maria pleaded, despite knowing they were powerless. Sensing Maria's distress, her grandmother, Frosso, embraced her and put her at ease.

Throughout the years, Litsa had spoken of her wealthy relatives. However, the reality of their grandmother's situation was apparent to Maria and Jackie. They had known poverty in New York with the rich and poor often separated by one street, and the Great Depression with men jumping out of windows and sleeping in doorways.[1]

A woman of slender means, Frosso lived with her two unmarried daughters, whose modest civil servant wages contributed to the household, as did her late husband's army pension. Despite her limited income, Frosso paid for their nightly visits to tavernas, during which Maria consumed several helpings of tyrópita (cheese pie) and bread soaked in sugar and water. This fondness for starchy foods inflamed her acne and gave her a rash on her face, 'probably due to some indigestion'.[2]

One night, Litsa told Maria to sing for her brother, Efthimios, who had friends at the Athens Conservatory. She went to the piano and, accompanied by Jackie, she sang 'La Paloma', her shyness and nerves making her voice uneven. Polite exchanges followed, interrupted by Litsa asking her relatives to pay for Maria's studies. Although embarrassed, they declined and said the child's voice was nothing special. To ease the tension building between Litsa and her siblings, Frosso suggested she return to her husband in New York. The others advised her to enrol Maria in high school and to forget about an opera career. An argument followed, and they moved out of Frosso's home and into rooms at a boarding house on Ithakis Street.

A month later, they moved into a furnished house at Terma Patission, remaining there for the summer. However, George's monthly payments of $100 stopped and they had to survive on handouts from Frosso. In dire straits, they found a cheap unfurnished apartment at Harilaou Trikoupi, which had no electricity, and they slept on the floor. Ashamed of their situation, Litsa warned the girls to tell no one.

Maria, in particular, felt the indignity of their circumstances. There was no one in whom she could confide; she barely spoke Greek and, isolated with her mother and sister, she was homesick for her father. '[Litsa] really imposed her will on the girls,' Maria's cousin, Titina Koukoulis, said. 'With one look she withered them into submission.'[3] Dismissive of such claims, Litsa wrote, 'I might add that children enjoy feeling abused (I did myself).'[4]

Having become a passive bystander to Litsa's plans, instead of going to school Maria was told she would sing. 'My mother was commanding the family. So, I had to act accordingly,' she said. 'It was no trouble for me because I didn't really enjoy myself playing with children.'[5] Only in hindsight did she resent her mother's decision. 'I was only thirteen. What could I have done? Protest? To someone with my mother's forceful temperament?'[6]

However, when Litsa tried to enrol Maria in the Athens Conservatory, 'they laughed in her face … What were they to make – they said – out of a thirteen-year-old girl?'[7] So, Maria went to the conservatory, knocked on the door of Loula Mafta and sang 'La Paloma'. Her heavy voice drew criticism from an onlooker, who remarked, 'She sings like a man … as if she had a sweet stuck in her throat'.[8] Afterwards, Mafta said, 'This isn't the place for you. Go to an elementary teacher first, learn music, and then come back to be taught by a singing teacher.'[9]

Despite the rejection, Maria's life had taken on a semblance of normality and she spent her days with her great-aunt and cousins, who taught her to ride a bicycle. This was a trivial rite of passage, but to Maria, such experiences were alien. Sometimes she was invited to tea parties, but Litsa insisted on chaperon-ing and 'flew off the handle at the slightest provocation'.[10]

Having tolerated Litsa for months and considering her 'the shame of the family', her aunt reproached her, and the visits came to an end.[11] Although Maria suffered from the fallout, she had other responsibilities, and Litsa told her, 'I didn't bring you into this world for nothing ... I gave birth to you, so you should maintain me'.[12] Reminding Maria of her duty, Litsa added, 'Think back a bit, what I went through for you, the beautiful youth I sacrificed.'[13]

Determined that Maria's voice would be heard, Litsa took her to a taverna at Perama that was popular with amateur opera singers and talent scouts. Singing 'A Heart That's Free', she was congratulated by Yannis Kambanis, who was a student of Maria Trivella, a teacher at the National Conservatory. Several weeks later, Maria sang 'La Paloma' for a spellbound Trivella, who afterwards announced, 'But this is talent!' Litsa, however, was frank. 'As regards to the fees,' she said, 'please be very lenient and make them as moderate as you can.'[14]

Thinking Maria was 'beautiful and likeable' and perhaps sympathising with her forceful mother, Trivella agreed to teach her for free.[15] Every day, she went to Hoffman Street for an hour's singing lesson, and she stayed for lunch, as Trivella sensed that Litsa struggled to put food on the table.

The recognition of Maria's talent failed to compensate for the unhappiness she felt. She turned to food to suppress her feelings, particularly the guilt she felt for breaking up her family. Litsa had used her as an excuse to leave George, and in doing so, she believed she ended her parents' marriage. Pining for her father, she imagined he was unhappy without her, but there was no contact between them. The census shows he was living in San Francisco and work-ing at the Golden Eagle pharmacy. However, by 1942, he was in Washington Heights and working as a travelling salesman. She had no way to contact him: she knew of no mailing address, and furthermore, there was no telephone con-nection between Athens and New York.

Within months, Maria had gained a significant amount of weight and found no sympathy from her sister or mother, who accused her of being greedy. Hiding her feelings, she made excuses for overeating. 'In order to sing well one needs to be hefty and blooming, I stuffed myself, morning and night, with pasta, chocolate, bread and butter, and zabaglione. I was rotund and rosy, with a quantity of pimples which drove me mad.'[16]

The fact was, she had no self-control and felt inferior to Jackie, who was encouraged by Litsa to wear make-up and stylish clothes. Preoccupied with her looks, Jackie never failed to compare herself to Maria: her slim waist, her smooth complexion, her chestnut hair. As Maria was not yet fluent in Greek, Jackie translated the insults from onlookers who, she said, compared them to Laurel and Hardy.

With her resentment mounting, Maria became aggressive. 'As she got heavier and heavier,' Jackie recalled, 'I could no longer hold her at bay and I started to surrender in case she wrestled me to the ground.'[17] Furthermore, she was frequently reminded of her size – 'You've put on weight,' Jackie said, 'don't you think you should diet a little?'[18] – and was made to feel unattractive and unworthy of love.

During that period, the question of enrolling at the National Conservatory arose but Maria was two years too young. Trivella and Litsa both agreed to alter her age to 16 on the application form, despite Efthimios's warning, 'Don't push her too fast – she's still only a little girl.'[19] As they arranged Maria's future, she stood to one side, invisible.

'I suddenly wondered just what did she want,' Jackie recalled. 'What on earth was going on inside her?'[20] To her mother, Maria said, 'If I manage to get a scholarship, I will keep on studying music. But if I do not get it, I will stop and do something else.'[21]

The decision, however, rested with Manolis Kalomiris, the conservatory's founder and director, and Yorgos Karakantas, head of its opera school. In particular, Karakantas was impressed and encouraged Kalomiris to offer her a scholarship. Her confidence boosted, Maria said, 'The fact, therefore, of winning scholarships represented for me a firm guarantee that my parents were not deluded in believing in my voice.'[22] It was a conflicting statement, for her father had thought singing lessons were a waste of money, and the National Conservatory was partly founded on the ethos that it would support artists from poor backgrounds, regardless of their talent.

During that period, Litsa became estranged from her family, having argued with her mother and brother about money. It fell to Jackie to provide for them, and each day Litsa escorted her to the real estate offices of Mr Polikala, hoping she would meet a rich man and become his mistress. After days of sitting in the lobby, Jackie was introduced to Harry and Milton Embirikos, scions of a wealthy shipping family. A dinner invitation followed, and afterwards Litsa encouraged Jackie to go for an unchaperoned drive with Harry, hoping it would give him the wrong impression. A week later, Harry invited her to Zonars, a café in Athens, but she found Milton waiting for her, a ploy that had been devised by the brothers.

Having succeeded in her plan, Litsa gave Jackie an ultimatum: become Milton's mistress or starve to death, for they had no money and risked being evicted from their apartment. Instead, Jackie suggested they appeal to the American Consul for repatriation to America, as George would be financially responsible for them. 'Do you only think of yourself?' Litsa said. 'Maria has to have her lessons and you're the only one who can help.'[23] So Jackie offered herself to Milton, and in exchange, he paid the rent on their new apartment at 5 Marni Street and bought a piano for Maria.

Although benefiting from the arrangement, Maria remained conflicted. She was furious with Litsa for – as she viewed it – selling Jackie's virginity to keep a roof over their heads. Having lost respect for her sister, whose status was no longer *parthenos* (a virgin), she yelled, 'I'm going to get to the top, but I don't know what you are going to do. Right now you're selling yourself to Embirikos!'[24]

Although she disapproved of Milton, she accepted his invitation to *La traviata* at the Olympia Theatre and was hypnotised by the production. It changed nothing, however, and she could not accept the part Milton played in ruining her sister. She also loathed Litsa's casual relationships with men, particularly her affair with her younger sister's fiancé.

Regardless, Maria retained an air of innocence and, when studying a libretto, she asked, 'What does it mean by "honour"?'[25] The director laughed and told her to ask her mother. Somehow, she had remained naïve, and years later, she pretended the topic of sex was off-limits at home; she had been raised the old-fashioned way. It was lies, as Litsa had a sordid obsession with the sex lives of her young daughters – including Maria, who, despite her youth, looked older than her years and lecherous men took advantage of this.

Given the atmosphere at home and her mother's lack of protection, she retreated into herself, neglecting her appearance and doing her best to remain untouched. 'She never poured out her soul to me in times of mutual confidence,' Litsa recalled. 'But I believe she was frank and honest whenever I asked her the questions a mother usually asks daughters who are visibly nubile.'[26]

Although Maria was ashamed of her mother and sister's living arrangements, she was also resentful that the opposite sex did not find her attractive. She was afraid of men, yet she wanted to wield her feminine power: an inner conflict which exerted itself as jealousy. The young men who studied at the conservatory made unkind remarks about her figure, calling her an 'eyesore … at the beach, in her bathing suit, she was a terrible sight'.[27] Telling her she was ugly, they gave her a complex about her strong features, 'larger than life as though designed specifically for the stage'.[28]

Her competitive nature repelled many, particularly her arrogance: she studied acting with Yorgos Karakantas but disliked his methods and preferred to teach herself. 'I am used to fighting, though I don't like fighting,' she said, years later. 'My only weapon is my voice. If I don't have my weapon, it's ridiculous I fight. It's just plain suicide.'[29]

During that period, Litsa reaped the spoils of Jackie's affair with Milton, and they moved to a spacious, top-floor apartment at 61 Patission Street. For the first time, Maria had her own bedroom, having grown up sharing a bed with her sister. However, Litsa took in a lodger, Marina Papageoropoulou, whose young nephew often stayed with her, and so Maria lost her room. With no privacy, she came to resent Litsa, especially when she intruded on her lessons and tried to sing along. 'So I am always on the defensive. I get aggressive,' Maria later said. 'Since my childhood, I've been aggressive. Do you blame me?'[30] Their arguments were the subject of neighbourhood gossip: Litsa's shrill voice echoing through the street below, and Maria's mangled accent, which a friend called 'Manhattan street twang, Italian musicality, girlishness, a touch of diva resonance, a kind of Greek harshness'.[31]

In the spring of 1938, Maria sang in the conservatory's annual concert at Parnassos Hall and snubbed her peers who declared her conceited and overly ambitious. 'When we are young, we are owed everything,' she said. 'That's the thoughtlessness: life has a duty to give us all the chances in the world. I wasn't afraid of anything. I couldn't have cared less.'[32] However, Yannis Kambanis later reformed his opinion and wrote, 'I take great pride in your triumphs, as believe me, this was exactly what I foretold many years ago and now it has come to fruition.'[33]

Confident in her abilities, Maria asked Trivella to enter her for the proficiency test. Out of the fourteen students, she was placed fifth and given a distinction, narrowly missing the prize money of 500 drachmas awarded to the first four. 'That was no voice,' a member of the audience remarked, 'it was a whole orchestra!' Afterwards, Litsa went to Trivella and told her to give Maria a diploma, but she refused as her voice needed more work.

Far from being encouraged by Trivella's plans, Litsa felt she was moving too slowly in helping Maria to establish a career. So, taking matters into her own hands, she contacted the Greek-American Society of Athens and promoted her American-born daughter. On 4 July, Maria made her public debut at the Rex Theatre to celebrate American Independence Day, performing as Marianna Kalogeropoulou.

The following April, Maria was given the part of Santuzza in the conservatory's production of *Cavalleria rusticana* at the Olympia Theatre, alternating with Hilde Woodley, who sang in the first performance. On the day of the performance, Maria awoke with a toothache: swollen and in pain, she feared she could not sing. 'I've always had to pay for all my triumphs immediately without fail,' she said.[34] However, she was spurred on by her classmates' jealousy, and some claimed she slapped an individual who criticised her distorted face – an exaggeration, for she risked being expelled from the conservatory. 'Everything went well,' she said of her first leading part.[35]

A month later, she sang in the conservatory's annual concert, performing a duet from *Aida* with Kambanis, whom she disliked. Fifteen years her senior, she resented how Trivella favoured him and how he had won the respect of their fellow students and teachers. She then performed in a concert with eighteen other students and participated in a final concert for the conservatory at the Olympia Theatre, although none of the students were given solos. She became tired of the repetitiveness and longed for a challenge, but Trivella warned it would damage her voice. Although she was encouraged by winning the first prize and 500 drachmas in her first two proficiency tests, Litsa reminded her, 'It was no thundering triumph.'[36]

Inspired to leave Trivella, Maria said, 'I am impatient when I am asked to conform to standards of work and behaviour, which I know are inferior.'[37] Many described Trivella as a teacher of limited means, whose students screamed and made unpleasant sounds to reach the high notes.

To an outsider, Maria appeared ungrateful to Trivella, who had also taught her conversational Greek and French. 'I began studying with a teacher, probably of Italian origin, Maria Trivella,' she later wrote. 'Barely a year later, however, I succeeded in achieving my aim and moved on.'[38]

Deeply hurt, Trivella said, 'I worked with her not only with the care and experience of a teacher but the love and devotion of a mother.'[39]

To understand Maria's behaviour, one must consider the strength of her survival instincts. 'She always kept after me,' Maria said of her mother, 'until I was nothing more than a goddamned singing machine.'[40] On the day of her first proficiency test with Trivella in 1938, she had devised a secret plan with Litsa, which took a year to reach fruition. She learned that Elvira de Hidalgo, a famous coloratura soprano, although retired from the stage, taught at the Athens Conservatory. The day after the proficiency test, Litsa introduced herself to de Hidalgo, telling her Maria could benefit from her teaching.

However, before Maria sang a note, de Hidalgo scrutinised her appearance: her bad skin and wire-framed glasses, the black pinafore with a white collar, worn-out sandals, and a white cap on top of her braided hair. Singing 'O patria mia' from *Aida*, de Hidalgo thought to herself, 'Now that is someone'[41] and agreed to give her free lessons.

Years later, de Hidalgo said, 'She had a certain look in her eyes and an interpretative style because she didn't know much Italian and she was singing in Italian. That struck me. She watched me the whole time, with that mouth, that large mouth, and her eyes which spoke to me.'[42]

As Maria had one year to complete before gaining her diploma at the National Conservatory, Litsa advised her to proceed with Trivella and later enrol in the Athens Conservatory. So, after finishing her daily lessons with Trivella, Maria often attended de Hidalgo's classes, arousing suspicion from the students, who were curious about the 'big fat girl'.[43] Most of the lessons, however, were at de Hidalgo's home, which she shared with her former pupil and lover, Lakis Vassilakis. This was hardly an ideal environment for a young girl, but given the arrangement between Jackie and Milton, and Litsa and her gentlemen callers, she was not in a position to judge.

Unlike Trivella, who encouraged Maria to sing through her nose, as was the technique in French opera, de Hidalgo was trained in bel canto. 'The bel canto is not beautiful singing, it's a sort of a straight-jacket that you're supposed to put on,' Maria explained. 'You have to exactly learn to form your sentences, learn music, which is essential, good taste, which is essential. Founded in the eighteenth century, it required perfect breath control and vocal embellishments – trills, intervals, scales, runs, legati – a whole, vast language on its own.'[44]

Before her exam at the Athens Conservatory, in September 1939, Maria dined with Trivella, who remained oblivious to the deception. If she failed, she told herself she would return to Trivella and the National Conservatory. 'She makes her own rules,' Litsa later said, 'and builds her own excuses for everything she does.'[45]

However, before her audition with its director, Philoktitis Oikonomidis, they questioned her motives and disapproved of her replacing Trivella, who, although not a great teacher, was respected by others. Sitting before Oikonomidis and a panel of teachers, Maria nervously bit her nails and waited for her name to be called. She sang 'Ocean! Thou mighty monster', her voice hypnotising de Hidalgo, and then returned to biting her nails while the examiners discussed her performance. Despite their personal feelings, she was granted a scholarship. The gamble had paid off.

Maria failed to recognise the duplicity of her actions. Many of de Hidalgo's students and colleagues thought it underhanded, and eventually, the news reached Trivella. 'My only weapon – a very powerful and fair one – is always to be prepared,' Maria said. 'They say I always win. These are my means: work and preparation. If you consider those means harsh, then I really don't know what to say.'[46]

Refusing to be treated as a consolation prize, Trivella suffered deeply from Maria's betrayal. 'I shall always be grateful to Trivella for what she did for Maria,' Litsa wrote, a decade later. As for Maria, she seldom acknowledged her first teacher and credited de Hidalgo with discovering her talent. 'As a young girl,' she said, 'that means at thirteen years old, I was thrown into her arms.'[47] She gave Trivella a parting gift, however – although the significance of the gesture was unrealised at the time. It was an autographed photo, inscribed in English: 'To my darling teacher to whom I owe everything.'

3

Survival

Mortal fate is hard. You'd best get used to it.

Medea, Euripides

As Maria was taking her first steps toward studying at the Athens Conservatory, Europe was descending into a world war. It remains doubtful whether she paid attention to the news, for her time was spent listening to opera records and reading libretti, loaned to her by Elvira de Hidalgo. There had been one warning, in the summer of 1939, when Maria, Litsa and Jackie, like other Athenians, watched the Hellenic Army's anti-aircraft exercise with search-lights and flares and heard the sounds of gunfire. Thrilling and terrifying in equal measure, although Benito Mussolini, Il Duce of Italy's National Fascist Party, promised he would not invade Greece, despite his invasion of Albania in April. Moreover, Britain and France pledged to maintain Greece's neutrality in the war.

Later, when the Italians were imminent, Maria used it as motivation to hurry her studies. As Jackie recalled, 'This panic to get on before we were engulfed by some nameless horror made her increasingly impatient.'[1]

In the autumn of 1939, Maria began her studies at the conservatory as one of de Hidalgo's thirty students, registered as Marianna Kalogeropoulou. She had to repeat her theory lessons from the National Conservatory, as they were not recognised by the Athens Conservatory. Furthermore, she had to correct the habits she had learned from Trivella, who made her sing low notes in head voice, thus forcing her voice down, instead of in chest voice. The most significant problem was a wobble, noticeable in her passaggio – the breaks between registers – which de Hidalgo thought were undeveloped in comparison to the rest of her voice. 'While the rest were saying that you were a dramatic soprano at sixteen,' de Hidalgo said, 'I made you sing *La Cenerentola* and practise the scales as a soprano.'[2]

However, many believe that de Hidalgo, who began her career at 16, caused Maria to strain her vocal cords by singing a wide repertoire of different vocal types (fachs) and ranges, such as mezzo-soprano, dramatic soprano and coloratura soprano. Some thought her voice was unattractive, but she was not afraid to sing in an ugly tone, if the part called for it:

> I don't want my singing to be perfect. The composer asks for particular colours: dark, sometimes. It's all in the music. And when it's not written, it's like when you read a letter; you have to read between the lines. Perfection isn't about reciting, it's about understanding the atmosphere and the thousands of colours that make an interpretation out of a music sheet.[3]

The question remains unanswered: was de Hidalgo a good teacher? According to her students, she was an opera expert and a good singer, if not great, and demonstrated how to sing a part and how to act. Comparing herself to a sponge, Maria absorbed de Hidalgo's instructions. She would imitate her technique, the position of her voice and how to act on the stage. 'Now you see I was right when I told you not to listen to anyone because with my method one day you would be able to sing any opera,' de Hidalgo wrote to her in 1949.[4] From the perspective of Maria, who idolised de Hidalgo, she was brilliant, 'Not only could she teach a girl to sing but she saw what she could sing best.'[5]

Aside from their student–teacher relationship, it was evident that Maria was searching for a mother figure, and in de Hidalgo, she found someone who could nurture her talent and give her confidence. Or, to quote Aristotle, 'Those who educate children well are more to be honoured than they who produce them.'

Perhaps thinking of de Hidalgo's influence, Maria later said, 'We mothers, and I say "we" because I am a woman, though I've never had children. We are responsible for this youth of the future. We have the obligation to support them, to give them courage and strength, this is our goal, our duty as a woman.'[6] Years later, de Hidalgo told her, 'I consider you as my daughter.'[7]

Given her troubled relationship with Litsa, it is interesting that Maria was drawn to a woman who had similar traits to her mother. Both de Hidalgo and Litsa were charming and bad tempered; they were fixated with money and impressed by grandeur; and they embellished their stories with fantastical details. Arriving in Greece in 1930 to sing at the Olympia Theatre, de Hidalgo fell in love with its co-owner, Panayis Karandinos, and moved in with him while still married to her French husband, Armand Bette. She lied, however, and claimed to have arrived in Athens before the war and, as such, had become stranded.

Although Maria respected Litsa's position and authority – 'I have great respect for my mother, especially because she's called *mother*'[8] – she did not love her. So, music was placed on a pedestal, and her feelings for de Hidalgo and opera were much the same. Could Litsa have sensed their similarities and felt jealous of the woman who had become the central figure of Maria's life? It seemed likely, for around that time, Litsa complained if Maria sang too loudly in the apartment, telling her, 'We've had enough, our heads are spinning, we can't hear ourselves think.'[9] In her memoirs, Litsa had the final – albeit deceptive – word, '[Maria] did not love de Hidalgo as she had loved Trivella.'[10]

Surprisingly, (or perhaps not) de Hidalgo was a fascist sympathiser and admired Mussolini, whose bust she displayed on her piano, next to an image of Puccini. There is no evidence to suggest that Maria took an interest in politics – 'We have enough to do just being artists without also being politicians'[11] – and, when she arrived in Greece in 1937, it was under the nationalist regime of Ioannis Metaxas. Perhaps Maria viewed de Hidalgo's fascist ideology as being similar to her approach to opera: the authority of her teacher complemented her discipline toward music. In many ways, she was subservient to things that she deemed bigger than herself. 'What I wanted to be was a servant of art. All I ever wanted is to serve art.'[12]

The devotion Maria had for music was an antidote to the hostility she endured from her fellow students. 'Who is that rag-doll?'[13] one of them asked de Hidalgo. During the months when she had secretly attended de Hidalgo's lessons, she befriended Zoe Vlachopoulou, a lyric soprano eleven years her senior, whose parents were opera singers. They each had studied at the National Conservatory before going to the Athens Conservatory; Vlachopoulou graduated from the former in 1933 and the latter in 1939, having been awarded a gold medal. As they were both from impoverished backgrounds, they could not afford the streetcar and had to walk home. 'Music,' Maria said, 'is born from distress or from poverty or from physical pain.'[14]

At the time of Maria's official enrolment, Vlachopoulou had graduated from the conservatory and Maria, the only poor female student in her class, was conscious of her lowly origins. Her peers laughed at her appearance and she tried to disguise her background from the other girls, who wore stylish clothes and studied opera for pleasure, their lessons paid for by rich fathers.

Jackie and Litsa were unsympathetic. They blamed Maria and warned that her size and unkempt appearance would invite mockery.[15] However, some of her male contemporaries found her attractive, with one remarking:

> Yes, she may have been rather fat, rather slatternly and thick in the leg, but she certainly excited interest in men. She didn't do it deliberately: it was just her manner, the way she moved. She had a good waist, and when it was held in, it emphasised her bust.[16]

Reflecting on their criticism, she said, 'To tell the truth, even as it was I didn't know my looks.'[17]

At times, de Hidalgo 'spoke quite sharply' to Maria and ordered her to lose weight, as she had difficulty kneeling and falling during her acting lessons.[18] Bursting into tears, Maria asked, 'What do I have to do to make you say I am getting on all right?'[19]

Once, she had asked Maria to wear her chicest outfit and was exasperated when her protégée appeared in a red skirt and blouse and a hat that resembled a baby's bonnet. Tearing the hat from her head, de Hidalgo threatened to stop her singing lessons if she did not improve her appearance. It inspired Maria to work twice as hard – she could learn a score in two weeks – and she never took for granted that she was de Hidalgo's most talented student. She remained at the conservatory until six o'clock, watching the others sing, and returned home with de Hidalgo to dine with her and practise some more. In return for the free lessons, it was rumoured that Maria cleaned her house and walked her dog, something that de Hidalgo denied.

At the end of the academic year, Maria performed in several concerts for the conservatory. After the first, the treasurer praised her performance and told de Hidalgo that she would soon be singing at the Metropolitan in New York. 'Don't exaggerate,' de Hidalgo replied, knowing there was work to do. For the annual student concert,* she sang the leading part in Puccini's one-act opera, *Suor Angelica*. The nun's habit, de Hidalgo remarked, would 'cloak the fat' she had not managed to lose.[20]

'You were terrific,' her classmate, Ypatia Louvi, said.

'Well, I worked hard, I really slogged at it,' Maria replied.[21]

---

* Interestingly, in the original programme, Jackie (credited as Tzáky Kalogeropoulou) is billed as Rose in *Lakmé*, though she was not one of de Hidalgo's students and instead studied piano lessons at the conservatory. It serves as an indication of Jackie's interest in opera, despite her claiming that she did not have a voice.

Alarmed by her response, Louvi suggested she would become a great artist if she lost weight.

Four days later, Maria signed a year-long contract with the Greek National Opera, founded in 1939 as a division of the National Theatre. According to de Hidalgo, she took Maria to a hairdresser, manicurist and dressmaker, before presenting her to its manager, Kostas Bastias. 'You have to give this girl a job, pay her a salary, engage her as a chorister but she must not sing,' de Hidalgo said. 'She must have an income and only study, no singing. We must protect this treasure or she will waste her time singing for soldiers for a crust of bread.'*[22]

The contract was negotiated by de Hidalgo, who asked for 1,500 drachmas a month (100 drachmas were deducted for tax), and an additional 50 drachmas for each performance above ten per week. It was also agreed that Maria would not sing immediately, as part of de Hidalgo's negotiations with Bastias was to hire her on paper. In reality, she helped in his office and continued to study at the conservatory. 'It was evident that Mr Bastias has brains, ears, and nose,' Maria said. 'In other words, he can smell something of value.'[23]

Despite Maria receiving an income, Jackie denied that she contributed to the household, stating that she spent her money on lipstick and confectionery. Or on what de Hidalgo called her three passions in life: music, pastries and ice cream.

On 28 October 1940, the Italian Army invaded Greece from Albania; however, the Greek Army succeeded in forcing the Italians back and halting an invasion until the spring. It signalled the beginning of the Greco-Italian War, which began at 4.30 a.m., with the prime minister, Ioannis Metaxas, King George and Crown Prince Paul signing a general mobilisation order. Before signing the document, Metaxas crossed himself and said, 'God save Greece.'

Two hours later, Maria was awoken by the sound of air-raid sirens. Curious about the demonstrations, she followed the crowds to Omonia Square, where newspapers, hastily printed hours before, were fuelling patriotism and army recruitment lists were pinned to the walls. Hostilities toward the Italians in Athens began immediately, with attacks on their schools, cultural offices and

---

* Elvira de Hidalgo confused the timing of Maria's original contract with the Greek National Opera with her latter contract during the German Occupation. However, many times she did sing for a 'crust of bread'.

the headquarters of the Italian airline, Ala Littoria. For two days, the country descended into chaos: travel was restricted, schools were closed and military hospitals were formed. Two weeks later, the first British servicemen arrived in Athens and calm was restored.

Before, when there were rumours of war, Maria spoke of returning to New York, but her attachment to de Hidalgo stopped her from leaving. Now, she was forbidden to travel outside of Athens without a special permit, as she was not a Greek citizen. A month later, she understudied Nafsika Galanou in the part of Beatrice in *Boccaccio* and sang in several matinees and one evening performance. Galanou, however, loitered in the wings, loudly criticising her weight and calling her 'that American bitch'. Although Maria fled to her dressing room in tears, it taught her to fight back. 'I cannot be taken too abruptly,' she said, 'because then I become truly wild.'[24]

Two months later, on 6 April 1941, the German Army invaded Greece, and the country entered the Second World War. On that morning, Maria went to the conservatory and Litsa queued with Athenians, who panic-bought canned food. Later that evening, the port of Piraeus, 7 miles south-west of Athens, was bombed. However, the centre of Athens, like Rome, was considered an unfortified city and was not targeted by enemy bombs, although its surrounding areas were. As the air-raid sirens wailed, Maria, Jackie and Litsa descended the 120 steps to the basement. Overcome with nerves, Maria vomited, as she would do, after each air-raid warning.

Around that time, they planned to leave for Cairo which, until that point, maintained its neutrality in the war. Waiting on the gangplank, they received news of a battleship's sinking – a bad omen. Litsa convinced them to forget their plans and return home. Besides, Jackie recalled years later, Athens was a 'better prospect for [Maria's] career'.[25]

Perhaps this was recounted with bitterness, for Egypt, Cairo in particular, had a thriving entertainment industry and its most famous singer, Umm Kulthum, a trained contralto, was someone whom Maria admired and regarded as an 'incomparable voice'. Either way, they were trapped in political chaos: the prime minister had committed suicide, the king fled to Cairo, and the Germans had allied themselves with the Italians and defeated the Greek Army. Within days, the Swastika flag was flying over the Acropolis.

In the early days of the occupation, Maria did not attend the conservatory and instead took her lessons at de Hidalgo's apartment. Every day, she arrived at lunchtime and left before the curfew and blackout at ten o'clock. On her way home, she passed German soldiers – the same soldiers she and Jackie had spat on from the roof of their apartment.

She returned to the conservatory in June to take her examinations with de Hidalgo, and received distinctions. Interestingly, she did not attend her theory examinations with Philoktitis Oikonomidis, whom she considered an inadequate teacher. This was a mutual feeling – he thought her argumentative and disliked her.

Although the timeline is unclear, there was a reason she stopped going to the conservatory. One night, she stayed late to study, when a teacher, whose identity is unknown, saw that she was alone and entered the classroom. He assaulted her and tried to rape her, but she managed to break free and run home. In tears, she told her mother what had happened. 'A pity he didn't manage it,' Litsa said, 'then we would have made him marry you and that would have been that.'[26]

The response mirrored society's views, hearkening back to ancient times when it was deemed worse for a young girl to be seduced than it was to be raped.[27] She did not report it to the conservatory, for aside from the assault, she would have risked exposing her true age (then under 18) and thus being expelled. From an authoritative point of view, who would have believed her? She had witnessed at first hand the clique-like atmosphere within the conservatory. They, both students and teachers, had openly insulted her appearance, calling her fat and ugly, and the boys teased her for looking 'so awful we took no notice of her'.[28] More than ever, her limited world felt isolated and unsafe.

In July, the Nazis took control of the National Opera and Maria, who continued to be remunerated as an absent member of the chorus, lost her contract and her income. A month before her dismissal, she had borrowed 3,000 drachmas from the theatre, but in wartime and, with the subsequent hyperinflation, money was of little value and most things were unaffordable.

In November, she was secretly reinstated when de Hidalgo was able to convince the conductor, Walter Pfeiffer, to let her understudy Francésca Nikita in the part of Konstanze in Mozart's *Die Entführung aus dem Serail*. The secrecy was due to her colleagues' jealousy. She said:

> I was so young, they couldn't understand why I was chosen for certain roles. I suppose I could explain that very easily: it was just that I was always ready. Instead of gossiping and going around trying to get parts from other people, I just studied and was ready when the good time came.[29]

The events of the winter of 1941–42 was remembered by Maria as 'wounds that had not yet healed'.[30] She did not speak of her suffering except to recall the shortages of food, and the weather. 'The population had already been reduced to starvation for several months. It had never been so cold in Athens: for the first time in twenty years the Athenians saw snow.'[31] There was no fuel to heat their apartment, but Maria was luckier than most, as she had a tweed coat – the same coat her classmates had mocked, due to its fraying cuffs – and Litsa was a good dressmaker and fashioned things from fabric she had brought from New York.

A country that depended on the importation of its food was rationed beyond its expectations. Before the war, 30 per cent of the population was undernourished, and in 1941–42 the average caloric intake was 750–900.[32] As the winter advanced, there were 300 deaths per day in Athens: dead bodies accumulated in the street and were collected by a wagon. Graveyards were overflowing with unburied coffins and corpses wrapped in sheets. No fewer than 30,000 people died of starvation, amounting to 5 per cent of the population. In desperation, people ate horse and donkey meat, and Litsa implied that some turned to cannibalism. A report by the Red Cross stated, 'No organisations of public assistance or social welfare could have managed to save all those who suffered from famine.' The following year, 60,000 Greek Jews, predominantly from Thessaloniki, were sent to concentration camps and their belongings sold on the black market.

During the early days of the British blockade and the Nazis' strategic plan to starve the Greeks, Maria lived on boiled cabbage and tomatoes, sourced from the surrounding rural areas, having begged farmers to share their crops. It was also claimed that she salvaged food out of bins. Litsa, who had warned Maria not to return home unless she had something to eat, said they consumed nothing but bread; the starch worsening Maria's acne and weight problem.

One day, Milton arrived at their apartment with food procured from the black market: olive oil, potatoes and cornflour. 'I can't forget the incredulous stupefaction with which my mother, Jackie, and I looked at those precious goods,' Maria recalled, 'almost fearing that through witchcraft they could disappear at any moment.'[33]

Both Litsa and Jackie denied that Maria was responsible for their survival. However, in 1949, Litsa wrote:

> I know, my little [Maria] that Jackie carries on about having sacrificed herself for us. Shame on her! What are you to say then, you who were feeding your family at sixteen? I am not saying that she did not save us through that man. But it would have been better had she supported us by her work and in dignity, like you.[34]

In her memoirs, Jackie dismissed any claims that Maria had suffered hardship during the occupation. 'If proof were needed one has only to look at photographs of [Maria] taken at the time: an overweight girl with pimples,' she wrote. 'You don't get like that if you're starving.'[35]

Their hunger was enough to make them abandon their patriotism and liaise with the enemy. 'Everyone had compromised in order to survive,' Jackie said.[36] That is, everyone who, like Litsa, had a talent for duplicity.

Their first experience of collaboration had occurred, not with the enemy, but with Litsa's friend, a Hellenic Air Force officer, who asked her to conceal two British officers in her apartment. Although the men were smuggled out several days later, the women faced execution if they were caught. It was not an exaggeration: two teenaged boys faced the death penalty for removing the Nazi flag from the Acropolis.

The concealment of the British officers led to an encounter with Italian soldiers, who came to search the apartment. As there was evidence of the past inhabitants, Maria distracted them by singing 'Vissi d'arte' from *Tosca*, the clarity of her voice betraying her nerves as the Italians brandished their pistols. Claiming Maria had sung for their lives, the Italian soldiers forgot their mission and left. The following day they returned, not to arrest the women but to congratulate Maria and to give her bread and macaroni.

To refuse the food would have been patriotic, but hunger was a greater incentive. From the perspective of Athenians, it was treacherous, for not only were civilians starving, but foot soldiers in the Greek Army were paid less than a penny a day and lived on a diet of bread, raisins, tea and cognac. Naturally, Litsa saw an opportunity to gain what she needed most – food and security – even if it meant being on intimate terms with the enemy.

The Casa d'Italia (the Italian Cultural Institute of Athens) was located in Patission Street, and everywhere Maria turned she was surrounded by Italians. She also encountered them at de Hidalgo's apartment, as her teacher entertained the officers. During that period, Maria learned Italian as a better way to understand the libretti but declined to study at a fascist school. Within two months, she was conversing with the soldiers in their native language.

Rumours circulated that Nazi limousines were parked outside her apartment and that the Kalogeropoulou women were spies. An individual at the conservatory went a step further, calling Litsa the 'arch-bawd of all Greece' and insinuated her home was a brothel and its inhabitants were prostitutes.[37]

In the spring of 1942, Maria was invited to perform in concerts organised by the Italian Institute of Thessaloniki. Accompanied by Litsa, four singers and a pianist from the National Opera, it took three days by train to reach Thessaloniki, a port city on the Thermaic Gulf. Some 300 miles north of Athens, its landscape was heavily bombed by the Regia Aeronautica Italiana, and its local trade was replaced with designated brothels for the Nazis, as most Greek prostitutes had venereal diseases. On the streets, invalided and amputee servicemen begged for food, and a soup kitchen was founded by French nuns to feed starving children. Nazis often appeared on balconies, eating in front of the people below and throwing inedible things, such as stones from olives, onto the pavement, taking sadistic pleasure in watching them fight for it.

For one month, Maria and her colleagues lived in a hotel and were paid in food: pasta, coffee, sugar, bread and butter. 'Sometimes I thought of my family in Athens, eating sawdust bread and ersatz everything else,' Litsa said, 'but I don't remember being overcome with guilt because I was eating food that tasted like food while they were not.'[38] This was a misleading statement, for Litsa's elder sister, Sophie, had an admirer who was serving as an officer in the Greek Army and he sent a shipment of non-perishable food to Athens, hidden in a house on Ipponaktos Street. Curious about the stash of food, Litsa sent Maria to visit her aunts and grandmother, and she returned with a small sack of ingredients to make bread and pasta. As she walked home, she was at risk of being attacked by hungry Athenians who were so desperate for food they ate wild grass and weeds and fought dogs for scraps.

Returning to Athens, Maria accepted an engagement singing at a nightclub, rumoured to have been a brothel, near Omonia Square. It was frequented by German and Italian officers, whose currency was food. After the war, de Hidalgo reflected on the situation and claimed she had worried about Maria's virtue and her voice, but at the time, she did not hesitate to introduce her to the Italians who led to such engagements. No doubt, Maria's contacts were beneficial, particularly her friendship with Major Attilio De Stasio, an inspector for the Italian Fascists in Greece, whose office was at the Casa d'Italia, who had organised the concert in Thessaloniki. Some say Maria had fallen in love with him, although she remained silent on the matter of her wartime friendships, except to say, 'In essence, the Italians were always good to me.'[39]

The most significant wartime affair was between Litsa and Colonel Mario Bonalti, a middle-aged man from Verona. He later visited their apartment, and Maria disapproved, making a scene about her mother cavorting with the enemy. The colonel was one of many who passed through their apartment, bringing parcels of food and climbing into Litsa's bed. Sometimes, Maria was at home and felt a sickening knot in her stomach, knowing what her mother was doing. It was not sympathy for Litsa, but disgust: survival was one thing, but selling one's body for mutual satisfaction was another.

One day, she came home from the conservatory and found her mother playing cards with several Italians, they were smoking and laughing, and ignored her as she walked to her bedroom. The daily visits lasted for a year, until September 1943, when Mussolini resigned, and the provisional Italian Government surrendered.

Although much had transpired between Maria and Litsa that nurtured feelings of resentment, it was during the occupation that Maria grew to hate her mother. She could not blame Litsa for making her sing for the enemy, as de Hidalgo had exploited those connections and it meant she did not starve. Instead, she resented Litsa for encouraging her to liaise with the Italians on a personal level, to offer them something other than her voice, in exchange for money. In tears as Litsa turned her out of the apartment, Maria learned that crying to the Italians evoked their sympathy and they gave her money for nothing in return. It seems incredulous, as young girls sold their bodies in exchange for morsels of food, that she remained untouched.[40]

Her claims can be validated by the Fascist view of prostitution, which, although considered degrading, was regulated by the Italian Government and accepted (although criticised) by the Catholic Church as a way of allowing men to satisfy their sexual needs and to prevent women from being raped.[41] Had Maria succumbed to Litsa's demands, the Italians would have no longer paid for her voice and instead used her for sex, thus 'degrading' her status. Either way, Maria came home with money and Litsa happily took it, assuming she had earned it through prostitution. For this, Maria never forgave her.

The summer of 1942 brought an element of stability to Maria's life; she sang the part of Floria Tosca in the National Opera's first staging of *Tosca*. From May until its premiere at the end of August, she practised every day with de Hidalgo, learning the part in both Italian and Greek, as the authorities had demanded. 'I never was a strong horse,' she said, exhausted. 'I'm a racehorse, rather delicate and sensitive. Damn it!'[42]

On 27 August, the Greek production of *Tosca* premiered at the Summer Theatre, to an audience of German and Italian soldiers. Singing opposite the famous tenor Antónios Deléndas, his heavy frame repulsed Jackie, who said, 'The two of them were hardly likely to make a pretty sight.'[43] Equally critical,

Litsa wrote, 'When he and Maria sang impassioned duets I sometimes had to close my eyes.'[44] Despite the applause, Maria felt insecure and criticised her performance: 'I always demolish what I do when I perform.'[45]

Despite the success of *Tosca*, it was several months before Maria was given a leading part.* She accepted anything the National Opera offered her, as it included payment in money instead of food. In the New Year of 1943, she was given the leading part in *La Gioconda*, but the production was cancelled. A month later, she sang in the chorus of *O protomástoras*, an opera by Manólis Kalomiris, which ran from 19–27 February, and again from 2–20 March. The following day, she participated in a concert at the Sporting Cinema to raise money for school meals for poor children; there was also a benefit concert to aid impoverished Egyptian students in Athens. In July, she revived her part in *Tosca* opposite Deléndas; however, the show was cancelled on the 23rd, when the Germans closed the theatres.

The following summer, George's sister, Tassia, who had read about Maria's success in *Tosca*, invited the women to her home in Andania, a village on the outskirts of Meligalas. They would have declined had it not been for the certainty of fruit and vegetables, a rarity in Athens, for the Italians paid Maria only in quantities of dried pasta. When they arrived, Jackie went to find her childhood home, which had remained abandoned since their departure in 1923. The surrounding area resembled another place ravaged by war, with its desperate people and derelict buildings. A few days later, they returned to Athens.

Several months later, Maria and Litsa went to Thessaloniki, where it was hoped she could replicate the success of *Tosca*. During their month-long visit, they stayed with Litsa's cousins, Dimitris and Koralia Moundouris, whose 12-year-old daughter, also named Maria, was studying piano at the Thessaloniki Conservatory. 'We paid no hotel bills, but we did not eat the fine food the Italians fed us the year before,' Litsa recalled.[46] Her friend, the Commander-in-Chief of Macedonia who was collaborating with the Nazis, arranged for Maria to give two recitals at the White Tower Theatre, in exchange for food parcels. On both occasions, Maria, who wore her cousin's pink polka-dot evening gown, sang Rossini arias to an audience of around fifty German soldiers. However, disappointed by the poor response, they left for Athens.

---

* She sang in concerts at the Casa d'Italia, an engagement which lasted until the following April. In January 1943, she participated in a concert to mark the 150th anniversary of Rossini's birth. There were two more concerts in April and May, to commemorate the *Natale di Roma* (the birthday of Rome) and a Fascist celebration in which the guests were greeted by the guard of the Fascist Youth of Greece.

Looking to the future, Maria left the conservatory before gaining her diploma. The decision was supported by de Hidalgo, who continued to give her private lessons. 'Maria was more than just a singer,' she said. 'She was a complete artist.'[47]

Performing was the only consistent thing in Maria's life and, on 12 December 1943, she sang in a concert at the Rex Theatre to raise money for victims of tuberculosis. The infection was a scourge on Greek society, with some 3,000 beds taken up by patients in state-run and private clinics centred around Athens. As a precaution against tuberculosis, Maria consumed beaten egg yolks and sugar, when she could source such ingredients. It seemed that Litsa, like many Greek mothers, originally fed the concoction to her. Maria said of her early weight gain, 'I became fat because I was treated to a diet of scrambled eggs, which probably caused some kind of hormonal imbalance. My mother never really looked after me.'[48]

During that time, Maria began a romance with Takis Sigaras, whom she had known since 1942. He was 32, the son of a millionaire textile owner whose business had been requisitioned by the Germans, but he was now successful in his own right. During the occupation, he appeared to be a glamorous figure. He drove a black Adler and owned a firearms licence, exempting him from the curfew enforced by enemy soldiers.

Toward the end of 1943, they had grown close, experiencing what Sigaras called an 'amorous friendship', but Maria made it known that she cared only for her career – a view which contradicted an earlier remark, 'I am a woman, that's what matters!' He gave her money for the hairdresser and took her to expensive restaurants, paying the inflated bill with a briefcase of banknotes.

Those gestures confused Maria. She enjoyed male attention but did not want to be obligated to return the favour – a trap she saw Litsa and Jackie willingly enter. Nevertheless, she continued to accept his invitations to dinner and parties.

Their social life came to a halt when Sigaras's rich female friends openly gossiped about her background and insulted her appearance. After those encounters, they went for drives through the suburbs and to the seaside, parking the car so Maria could sing to him. He disliked opera, comparing it to nothing more than screaming – an insult, for she thought it was a romantic gesture. Although she let him kiss her, she declined Sigaras's request to consummate their relationship. 'She simply didn't want it,' he said. 'She wouldn't let you.'[49]

In the spring of 1944, the Nazis controlled the National Opera and the programmes were derived from German operas. 'The only time the [opera] functioned professionally was during the occupation, under the Germans,' Maria said. She did not resent their influence and instead embraced their regimental administration, for it reflected her work ethic and lack of sympathy toward those who could not adhere to long hours. She was now the highest-paid soloist in the company, confirming her status of prima donna, but she maintained that the money went entirely to Litsa. 'You know what my life was,' she wrote to a friend. 'How I worked like a dog in order to support my family.'[50]

Under the new regime, she sang the part of Marta in d'Albert's *Tiefland* at the Olympia Theatre and simultaneously rehearsed the part of Santuzza in *Cavalleria rusticana*. The German authorities suggested sending Maria and her colleagues on tour to Vienna, but they declined. Perhaps the world war, which continued in Europe, and the first stirrings of a civil war in Greece posed a risk to members of the company and their ability to return home. As the tour was aborted, Maria assumed the leading role of Smarágda in Manolis Kalomiris's adaptation of *O protomástoras*, which premiered on 30 July at the Herodes Atticus Theatre, an amphitheatre at the base of the Acropolis.

The greatest drama, however, played out between Maria and Anna 'Zozo' Remoundou, a leading soprano at the National Opera, with whom she shared the parts of Santuzza and Smarágda. It was agreed that Maria would sing in the first night of *Cavalleria rusticana*, a gesture which infuriated her colleagues: they thought the privilege belonged to Remoundou, who was older, more experienced and a favourite of Kalomiris, the general manager of the National Opera. Therefore, it seemed fair that Remoundou sang in the premiere of *O protomástoras*, but this was marred by the announcement that Maria would sing in additional performances.

Working against Maria was her forthright speech, which many found disrespectful and arrogant, especially the female employees, who resorted to flattering the hierarchy of the theatre. She approached Kalomiris with her concerns about Remoundou and found him an unsympathetic listener, partly because he had not forgotten his former student's desertion of the National Conservatory, nor her treatment of Trivella. During their exchange, Kalomiris threatened to report her to the committee which meant she would lose her licence to perform, but for unknown reasons, he changed his mind.

Those encounters with both Remoundou and Kalomiris did not hinder her career, and in June she began rehearsals for *Fidelio*, singing the part of Leonore, the lead female soprano who pretends to be a man. Giving Maria even greater satisfaction was learning that Remoundou, who wanted to sing at the premiere of the opera, was to perform as Leonore in only three additional shows in September.

On a hot August night, Maria opened in *Fidelio* at the Herodes Atticus Theatre, and the audience gave her a standing ovation. 'For the first time she was unreservedly magnificent,' Jackie said, contradicting Litsa's claim that 'sometimes [Maria's] high notes would turn shrill; sometimes she was tired …' The shrillness was particularly noticeable during *Cavalleria rusticana*, an indication of the strain she was inflicting on her voice by singing too many roles in various ranges.

Nevertheless, Maria warranted attention from the press and public. She was now recognised in the streets of Athens and the locals considered her a star. She also attracted the interest of a young Nazi officer named Oskar Botman, who had fallen in love with her voice and sent her flowers.

In terms of their involvement with Greek women, social historians argue that most German soldiers obeyed the Third Reich's racial purity laws, although it did not detract from their punishment of local women, often resorting to sexual assault and rape. It should be noted the Germans disapproved of the way Italians mixed war and sex. In turn, the Italians thought the Germans were barbarians. Furthermore, the Greek soldiers taunted the Germans by calling their women whores.

Litsa maintained that Botman was infatuated with Maria but offered little detail, except to write, 'I wonder if Maria ever thinks of this young enemy officer who admired her … or has she forgotten him as she has forgotten so much of her Athenian past.'[51]

In June, Maria was cast as La Principessa Fedora Romazov in the second performance of Giordano's *Fedora*,* with Mireille Fléri singing at the premiere. As Fléri was a close friend of Remoundou, this undoubtedly gave her a sense of victory over Maria, whom she disliked. Fléri's husband, Nikos Glynos, a tenor, claimed Maria's success was due to her sleeping with the Germans. Retaliating, Maria shouted at Glynos, telling him that she was there 'under merit, and merit alone'. They appeared before Kalomiris, who attempted to resolve the matter, but Glynos hit the desk and called Maria a dirty slut.[52] In her statement of the incident, she wrote:

> That cur called me a whore and said that I fucked Italians and Germans, and that was why I had the highest salary in the company. In tears, I told him to go to hell, but he became even more violent and hurled vulgar abuse at me, trying to hit me at the same time.[53]

---

* The programme was interrupted by the first phase of the Greek Civil War in December 1944 and, therefore, Maria did not sing in *Fedora*.

In a letter to Kalomiris, Maria stated that she could not work with 'bad-mannered, obnoxious, vulgar colleagues', and she threatened to resign from the National Opera. However, she remained with the company, despite the hostility toward her. The encounter between Maria and Glynos was not an isolated case and she was to suffer similar abuse from others, who accused her of having an unfair advantage. Instead, she internalised the injustice and told herself that one day, she would be the greatest singer in the world.

4

Liberation

Yes! Hope which always deludes!
It flickers like flame,
and is not flame!
Sometimes it rages!
It's feverish, impetuous, burning!

Turandot, Puccini

On 11 October 1944, the Germans marched out of Athens, and two days later, British and American soldiers arrived. To celebrate, Maria, Jackie and Litsa went to the roof of their apartment and tore up the worthless occupation money, throwing it onto the pavement below.

However, this false sense of security was not to last: the National Liberation Front (EAM) and the National People's Liberation Army (ELAS), under the influence of the Communist Party of Greece, seized control of Italian weapons and fought against the occupation forces and the non-communist resistance group, National Republican Greek League (EDES), with 2 million members.[*] The British Prime Minister sent troops to support the Greek Prime Minister George Papandreou's National Unity Government and the demobilisation of the EAM/ELAS forces.

During the early days of the liberation, Maria sang at the Argentina Club, a nightclub in Omonia Square, frequented by British and American servicemen. There, she met Lieutenant Raymond Morgan, a 24-year-old Welshman, who had served with the Royal Corps of Signals in Italy, Tel Aviv and Cairo.

---

[*] Among the members were Litsa's sister, Pipitsa, who was arrested, and her brother, Filon, who she falsely claimed was hanged.

Hearing her speak English, he took the opportunity to talk to her, as he had not 'seen an English girl, let alone spoken to one, since Cairo many moons before'.[1] Then he realised she was American, but did not care because she was 'good looking … much of her appeal lay in her unaffected warmth'.[2]

The following day, they walked in Omonia Square and on further outings they frequented the Acropole Hotel or Jimmy's Bar. Although they were not in love, they were jealous of one another. She knew he loved (and would later marry) Maro Sarigiannis, the daughter of Major General Ptolemaios Sarigiannis, whom she dismissed as a snob. On their final evening together, she heard a lone voice shout, 'Kappa, Kappa, Epsilon' – the initials of the Communist Party of Greece.

The winter of 1944 would become the worst period of Maria's life. Without the Italians, she struggled to source food. She queued for hours at soup kitchens, hoping to buy a loaf of bread, only to return home empty-handed. 'No matter how much money they gave you, you could never find food on the market – or on the black market, where no money was enough,' she said.[3] She never forgot an incident when a young man collapsed in front of her and died of starvation.

At the National Opera, several of her colleagues were members of the EAM and sought revenge on those who had collaborated with the enemy. The punishment was severe. The EAM/ELAS executed people in the street and hung their bodies from trees, and shaved women's hair and raped them to inflict shame. One morning, she was met by a crowd of EAM sympathisers, who verbally attacked her, calling her a traitor. Her colleague, Elvira Mataranga, struck her so fiercely she lost an earring, prompting her to run away before others followed. A month later, the National Opera temporarily closed and the EAM members organised a Festival of Freedom, but her name was absent from the programme. 'The administration granted me three months of vacation,' she later said.[4] In reality, she was not welcome under its new regime.

Through her connections, Litsa found Maria a job at the British General Headquarters (GHQ), working for the British Information Service as a translator in the office for the distribution of secret mail. Unable to afford transport, she walked 2.5 miles to her office at Syntagma Square and returned home to share lunch with Litsa before walking back. The routine continued until 3 December, when the police and British forces opened fire on an EAM/ELAS rally, killing thirty protestors, mostly youths, and injuring hundreds more. Advised to remain at the GHQ, she refused and asked to be driven home in an army Jeep, as her neighbourhood was now in the Red Zone. 'Having occupied such a delicate post as that of distribution of secret mail,' she recalled,

'I would undoubtedly be a victim of communist reprisals and subjected to inevitable torture.'[5]

During the first days of the conflict, Maria telephoned Morgan at his barracks and asked him to rescue her from Patission Street, but under the glare of his brigadier, he ended the call. The janitor of their apartment sided with the communists and led a group of snipers onto the roof, but they were killed by the British, who shot from the street below. Every morning, he chalked on the fire escape door, 'We will kill Maria first, knocking out her brains with a sledgehammer, second we will kill Mama, third Jackie.'

However, starvation was a greater threat. They were reduced to a box of beans, the last of their rations, but Maria suffered an allergic reaction and was violently ill. Their downstairs neighbour, Dr Ilias Papatesta, a tuberculosis specialist, shared his food with them until his rations were depleted.

The sort of man whom Litsa found attractive, Papatesta had money and social standing, but he resented her for bringing enemy soldiers to their building during the occupation. In him, Maria found someone necessary to her survival. 'I might have died of starvation if I hadn't had the help of my friend, Papatesta, who brought me some of the little food that he had at his disposal.'[6]

As the years progressed, she would form similar bonds with older men, perhaps to compensate for her lack of a father figure and the emotional neglect she had suffered from both parents. However, not everyone was charitable in their view of Maria's attachment to Papatesta, who was almost twenty years her senior, although he maintained his feelings were paternal. The neighbours gossiped, and Jackie accused them of having become lovers, although Maria said she was not interested in casual affairs.

Around that time, Litsa concealed her friend, General John Dourendis, the Minister of the Interior, who came to the apartment at four o'clock in the morning, having escaped from the communists who wanted to kill him. The oppressive situation was made worse by his complaining about food and the lack of coffee. 'Stop it! Keep quiet! Leave my mother alone! Leave us alone!' Maria shouted. A week later, Litsa asked him to leave, as they were afraid of being executed for hiding a military officer. 'I don't believe they would have spared us,' she said, 'even if Maria had sung *Tosca* to them as she had done for the Italians.'

Although dangerous, it offered them a respite from their daily lives which, by then, had grown desperate. There was no fuel to heat the apartment and no electricity. They lived in semi-darkness throughout the day, having to keep their curtains drawn for fear of being shot at, and they burned rags soaked in benzene to keep warm. One night, their canaries made a shadow against the curtains and a machine-gun fired through the window, killing the birds. On another occasion, desperate for fresh air, Maria opened the front door and found a dead American soldier slumped against it. She screamed with horror, but there was nothing she could do except close the door.

Twenty days had passed when a boy, disguised as a coal vendor, knocked on the door and ordered Maria to return to the GHQ. She was at risk of arrest or execution while she remained in the Red Zone but, thinking it a trap, she spoke brusquely to him and turned him away. However, he returned and offered information only she would know. She put on all the clothes she could wear and set off for Syntagma Square in the White Zone (British), walking through the debris of broken glass and barbed wire, wondering if, at any moment, a bullet would kill her. Two days later, the boy returned for Litsa, and in her memoirs she recalled joining Maria at the GHQ, where they were given food and the simple luxury of washing with hot water.

On Christmas Eve, Maria and Litsa went to the hotel where Jackie lived with Milton, in the Red Zone. Thinking their faces were haggard and their bodies misshapen from the layers of clothing they wore, Jackie asked after the canaries, and Maria burst into tears. However, she was cheered by the news that Winston Churchill and his Foreign Secretary, Anthony Eden, had arrived in Athens to a hero's welcome. Joining the crowds in Syntagma Square, she caught sight of Churchill as he gave the famous victory sign and climbed into his car.

The women remained at the hotel until February when the fighting stopped, and returned to their apartment, relieved it had not been looted.

In the New Year of 1945, a semblance of peace was restored when the British Army and the Greek Government forced the EAM/ELAS to retreat. But Athenians continued to suffer from food shortages and decent housing, as half a million refugees fled to the city, having been bombed from their homes in the surrounding countryside. The cinemas, theatres and nightclubs reopened, and Maria resumed her contract with the National Opera, now under the management of Theodoros Synadinos, whose left-wing politics appealed to those who sided with the EAM/ELAS. Many resented his appointment, as several members of the National Opera were killed in the crossfire or had been taken hostage by the communists in the mountains and only survived by eating snow.

In March, the National Opera cast Maria in two productions of *Tiefland*. As with the 1944 performance, her leading man was Evángelos Maglivéras, a famous Greek baritone who was fifteen years her senior. During the latter production, they began an affair. Some accused her of being awed by his stagecraft and using him to advance her career; others were surprised to see her hugging and kissing him. '[I am] not going to bed with one and then the other, on the contrary saying "no" to everyone,' she said. 'It's a miracle that I made a career.'[7]

Despite Maglivéras being married and having a mistress who bore him two children, it would be unfair to cast Maria as a homewrecker. There was no secrecy surrounding their affair; she visited his home and was on friendly terms with his wife, Artemis, and mistress, Kalliopi, who forgave his infidelities. Accepting that men were polygamous, she considered being in love 'a purification of the soul' and so it excused adulterous behaviour.[8] Therefore, she did not think marriage was important, providing a man and a woman loved one another without ulterior motives.

'Sexual freedom, or lack of it, had never been one of my problems,' she remarked. 'Besides, I have always been an old-fashioned romantic.'[9] She followed her instincts and not social mores. 'I am a very simple woman and I am a very moral woman. I do not mean that I claim to be a "good" woman, as the word is – that is for others to judge.'[10] Although men such as Maglivéras were married, she was always faithful. 'A woman doesn't have several men. That's not my conception of a woman.'[11]

Two months later, Maria travelled with Litsa to Thessaloniki for two concerts* at the Third Army Corps Club, at D'Espérey Street. Again they stayed with her cousins, the Moundourises, who, perhaps to distract from the grim surroundings, asked Maria to sing 'Ave Maria'.

Like Athens, Thessaloniki was destroyed by the EAM/ELAS conflict, and there had been arrests, public executions and civilian murders. The first concert, held on 9 May, coincided with Nazi Germany surrendering and the subsequent Victory in Europe, but Greece would still face a Civil War in 1946. A week later, on 17 May, Litsa hired the White Tower Theatre, and Maria gave a recital.

The remainder of the visit was spent rehearsing for her later concerts, with a young pianist, Tonis Yeoryiou, whose wife, Eleni, was embarrassed by Litsa's

* Maria sang in *A Nite of Stars*, a concert arranged for American servicemen at the United States Air Force base in Ellinikón, outside of Athens. There was also an afternoon concert for British troops. Interestingly, she was billed for the first time as Mary Callas, perhaps simplifying her last name for the English-speaking audience, but reverted to Kalogeropoulou for latter engagements.

advice: 'It's all very well to have a husband, but have a lover as well. That way, when you quarrel with your husband, you'll have something to fall back on.'[12] Maria, who was present, ignored her mother, but the Yeoryious noticed the change in her personality when Litsa was present.

Returning to Athens, Maria resumed her affair with Maglivéras and was troubled when he asked her to become his mistress. She declined his offer and asked to remain his friend: an undefined term, as her definition of friendship included affectionate gestures and levels of intimacy. A letter sent two years after their affair ended proved she looked for his approval, as though he were still her lover, 'I have lost quite a bit of weight and (if I may say so) I am quite a bit prettier. My legs have slimmed down a lot and I am very pleased'.[13]

Several months later, they parted on bad terms and, having exchanged bitter words, she said, 'You are right to accuse me of perhaps not having behaved with absolute sincerity toward you (if those feelings of yours were sincere!).'[14] She knew they were each committed to different things: he to his family, and she to her career:

> You had so many obligations and I could never live happily, even though I loved you, to the detriment and the misery of two women who have done me no wrong. But I did not stop considering you my best friend and loving you as such. I do hope that you don't hate me much, and that you love me as you did before!'[15]

It was Maglivéras who wished for something more, but Maria was not prepared to take him from the women in his life. 'You are the finest of men but you are not free,' she told him.[16] Even if he was, she claimed her answer would have been the same. As to the depth of their involvement, a clue might lie in a comment she made years later. 'I can't have sex with anyone unless I love with both my head and my heart. That's a sad thing, but that's how I am.'[17]

The ending of their affair coincided with her leaving the National Opera. Since the occupation, the Greek economy had collapsed, and it was necessary to not only reduce the size of the company but to cut wages. A system was implemented, rating singers from AA to D, their earnings reflecting their status. Maria was demoted from AA to A/B, and her monthly earnings were reduced from 40,000 drachmas to 35,000. However, she claimed her demotion was due to her colleagues, who wanted to settle old scores. Zozo Remoundou, Mireille Fléri, and Nikos Glynos went to the prime minister and warned that the entire company would strike if Maria remained its prima donna. Refusing to believe the story, Litsa claimed Maria would have 'scratched their eyes out had they tried it'.[18]

Maria learned the news from her uncle, whose contact at the National Theatre said, 'Miss Kalogeropoulou has not had her contract renewed. She has played too active a part in the last months of the occupation.'

Days later, when Synadinos sent for her, she announced she was leaving for America and said, 'Let's hope that you won't have to regret this one day.'[19] It was an impulsive response, but she hoped he would reconsider his offer. 'I'm proud, and my pride makes me fight,' she said. 'The two halves of my brain fight it out. One half says, you have to fight. The other half says, that's terrible, you should be ashamed. It's an awful struggle and it's exhausting.'[20]

Thinking her career was over, Maria turned to de Hidalgo for advice. 'You must start in Italy,' de Hidalgo told her. 'That is why you learned the language. When you have become somebody in Italy the rest will follow.'[21]

She disagreed with de Hidalgo and they had 'a regrettable rift'.[22] In recent months, their close relationship had been tested by their personal lives. Maria had insulted her by taking singing lessons with Maglivéras, and de Hidalgo was deeply unhappy after her young lover, Lakis Vassilakis, left her for another woman.

Instead, Maria listened to Litsa, who inflamed her anger toward the National Opera. 'I had gloomy visions,' Litsa recalled, 'of her spending her life in Athens singing repertory with no greater reward than local fame and the applause of her faithful admirers.'[23]

Lacking guidance, Maria turned once more to de Hidalgo and asked for letters of introduction, but de Hidalgo suggested she ask Maglivéras. However, she did write one letter, to Rosa Ponselle's teacher, Romano Romani, and unbeknownst to Maria, warned him that she was 'a very clever schemer'.[24]

Since Maria's earliest days in Athens, she spoke of returning to America after her studies were completed. Unknown to Litsa, Maria was secretly corresponding with her father from as early as 1942 – the year he applied for US naturalisation – and had sent him photographs of herself in *Tosca*. Their communication was briefly interrupted by the German invasion but soon resumed when the blockades were lifted. Although he gave his address as 660 West 180th Street, George used the mailing address of 308 Audubon Avenue, perhaps to thwart his wife's demands for money.[25] In turn, Maria might have asked him to write to her via Dr Ilias Papatesta's address, for she knew Litsa would intercept any mail sent to their apartment. Most significant was his recent letter in which he reminded her that she was an American citizen and enclosed $100.

It strengthened Maria's feelings towards her father, and she found his words encouraging and perhaps showing a measure of his love. It also dispelled the stories, told by both Maria and Litsa, that she later arrived in New York without knowing her father's address and that he, by chance, had read the passenger list in his Greek newspaper and went to the dock to meet her. Actually the homecoming had been arranged on both sides, months in advance.

Resenting Maria's admiration for him, Litsa snapped, 'You and your father! I told you, I don't want to hear another word about that!'[26]

The biggest obstacle, however, was her lack of funds, as she was not earning money, and due to inflation $100 was not enough to sustain her. She told people her trip to America was cancelled and she no longer wished to leave Athens. With that in mind, she begrudgingly accepted the National Opera's offer to sing the leading part of Laura in Karl Millöcker's operetta, *The Beggar Student*. In doing so, she signed a year-long contract, due to expire on 31 May 1946, and accepted the second-rate terms and conditions and lower pay of 35,000 drachmas.

On 4 August, she went to the American Embassy and swore an oath of allegiance and applied for a passport, the cost of which was paid with a repatriation loan from the American Government.[27] She said nothing of her plans, and the National Opera remained oblivious to her intentions; after all, had they not betrayed her first?

Then, on 3 August, Maria leased the Rex Theatre, the setting of her first public appearance in 1938, and held a farewell concert, using the ticket sales to raise money for her trip. Presumably, the nature of her concert was kept a secret until the last moment as the National Opera could have sued her for breach of contract.

In her memoirs, Litsa recalled that Maria dressed like a prima donna, wearing a white gown and a black velvet bolero trimmed with sequins, and was optimistic about her departure. Whereas, in reality, she wore a simple white dress, and acquaintances observed she was depressed at the thought of leaving and spoke of being forced to look for work after the National Opera had ousted her. Furthermore, the ticket sales were not enough to cover her travel expenses, and neither Litsa nor Jackie offered to help, for, although they had Milton's allowance, the wartime inflation continued.

Instead, Maria went to Takis Sigaras, with whom she was on good terms, and asked him to pay for her ticket, as he knew the manager of Thomas Cook and had helped another female acquaintance. Now she had a clear plan and would leave on 15 September.

However, the National Opera was not oblivious, and they replaced Maria with Anthi Zacharatou, a member of the chorus with whom Theodoros

Synadinos was having an affair – she would later marry his son. Given the past hostilities between Maria and her colleagues, she was surprised to learn they protested on her behalf, worried that Zacharatou's influence would see them losing leading parts.

Finally, Maria was invited to sing against Zacharatou before a final decision was reached. Furiously taking to the stage, she sang an entire cadenza in one breath and defeated her nemesis, who was demoted to her understudy. The backstage drama, as the part of Laura changed hands, was played out in the local newspapers, and every night the open-air theatre was packed to capacity. Unfortunately, her last performance was cancelled as storm clouds formed over Athens – an omen, perhaps.

Two days before she left for New York, she walked into Synadinos's office and tore up her contract, shouting, 'Shame on you! Shame! Shame!'

On the day of her departure, Maria told Litsa and Jackie not to accompany her to Piraeus, from where she boarded the MS *Gripsholm*, an ocean liner built for the Swedish American Line, and later used as an American repatriation ship.[28] She also claimed that her mother and sister refused to go to the port, as they 'would not be able to stand the commotion'.[29] After a farewell dinner given by Dr Ilias Papatesta, she left with three or four dresses and not a cent in her pocket.[30]

However, her impoverished state was an exaggeration, for the money from her farewell concert bought a new wardrobe, her meals on board were included in the tourist-class ticket, and she had applied for a loan of $700 from the American Government, presumably to help establish herself in New York.

From all accounts, it was a comfortable but uneventful crossing, as the ship had spacious tourist-class cabins and a saltwater swimming pool where, owing to its Swedish origins, it was rumoured passengers swam without bathing suits. When the captain of the ship asked her to sing at a farewell party, she declined, saying that opera could not be sung under those circumstances.

The uncharacteristic response might have been influenced by her parting with de Hidalgo. The night before she left, she telephoned her teacher. 'My last words are for you. I will always think of you with gratitude. Tell me you forgive me.'[31]

Warning that she was making a grave mistake, de Hidalgo said, 'You must not leave.'[32]

Those words weighed heavily on her mind, but it was too late to change course, and she told her naysayers she would sing at the Metropolitan Opera. 'I'll go there every day and sit on the doorstep. One day they'll get fed up with me and give me an audition.'[33]

As though to convince herself, Maria dwelt on her reasons for leaving, claiming she had no future in Athens. There was also the aftermath of the occupation, leaving Greece a desolate place of poverty and chaos. The political instability would lead to the second phase of the Civil War in 1946. 'There's always a beneficent God to help those who travel the straight and narrow and never do any harm to anyone,'[34] she said, certain the hand of fate was upon her.

5

Rejection

Here's a very strange affair.
How and why did she come here?

La sonnambula, Bellini

'Finally, I've come to my beloved America and I'm really very happy,' Maria said, after she arrived in New York on 9 October 1945.[1] That morning, at Pier 57 in Lower Manhattan, George waited for her. The last image she had sent him was from *Tosca* in 1942, and she looked for her father, hoping she recognised him from her memory. 'I really don't know how to describe the limitless relief with which I drew myself to him,' she said of their reunion, 'hugging him as though he had been raised from the dead, and crying on his shoulder for joy.'[2]

In person, however, the image she held of George did not correspond with reality. She told him about the occupation, and Jackie and Litsa entertaining the enemy soldiers. 'You should have got out of the house and left the two of them to deal with the Italians on their own,' he replied, unsympathetic to her suffering. Then it became clear why he had sent $100 and asked her to come home – he wanted her to be his housekeeper. Although she said nothing to her father, she was disappointed by his behaviour. In a letter to her godfather's wife, she wrote, 'I was so looking forward to seeing my father and returning to America but it isn't at all the way I expected. I've had quite a shock.'[3]

Altering the reality of her circumstances, she tried to convince others and, in doing so, hoped to deceive herself. 'He treated me like a queen,' she said of George, 'making up for everything I had suffered.'[4] In a letter to Evángelos Maglivéras, she wrote, 'My father literally adores me and I lack nothing. I have shopped for everything, I have plenty of pocket money of my own. I have also acquired two fur coats! He refuses me nothing.'[5]

She also realised that George had taken their family friend and his upstairs neighbour, Alexandra Papajohn (Papayianni), a 44-year-old spinster, as his mistress. Not wanting 'to share his affection with that Papajohn woman', she took a room at the Hotel Times Square, on the corner of Eighth Avenue and 43rd Street.[6] Its cheap dwellings catered to single men, but there was also a floor reserved for women.[7] 'I'm having a wonderful, lovely time,' she told Maglivéras.[8] However, it was the opposite, for the rundown hotel was on the fringes of Hell's Kitchen, then a notorious slum and red light district.

The future looked bleak, and to settle her fears she created her own sense of reality. 'I'm proud,' she said. 'I don't like to show my [true] feelings.'[9] It was not a question of self-preservation, but desperation: the contacts she had formed in Athens were worthless, and Romano Romani, the only teacher to whom Elvira de Hidalgo wrote a letter of introduction, refused to help – perhaps a response to de Hidalgo's warning that she was 'a very clever schemer'.

Falling into a meaningless routine, she spent her days going to the cinema and dining at kiosks, eating ice cream and hot dogs, which increased her weight to 218lb. Instead of admitting defeat, she continued to fool Maglivéras, telling him, 'The musical season hasn't started here yet, so I'm busy buying clothes and seeing people.'[10]

That winter, she found a job at Asti's, an Italian restaurant in Greenwich Village, whose waiting staff were professional opera singers and would perform on a small stage for the patrons. She also worked as a nanny to a child named Donatella, whose parents were Nelly and Sergio Failoni, a conductor and former assistant to Arturo Toscanini at La Scala. On Saturdays, she helped Louise Taylor, a retired opera singer and voice teacher, in her studio on East Ninth Street.

Through Taylor, Maria was introduced to Edward Johnson, the general manager of the Metropolitan Opera, who arranged an audition with the conductor, Paul Breisach. 'Exceptional voice,' Breisach remarked. 'Ought to be heard very soon on stage.'[11]

Afterwards, she auditioned for Gaetano Merola, founder of the San Francisco Opera Company, but he thought her too young and inexperienced, and his advice followed that of de Hidalgo. 'First make a name for yourself in Italy and then I'll sign you up.'

In turn, she replied, 'Thank you very much, but when I've made my career in Italy, I'm certain I will no longer have any need of you.'[12]

At the end of December, she auditioned a second time for the Metropolitan Opera, singing for Johnson and the conductor, Frank St Leger. 'Good material,'

Leger said, 'but needs work on her voice.'[13] They criticised her upper and lower registers, which they considered weak in comparison to her middle range. This was a blow to her confidence, and she asked, 'But who in America knows poor little Greece? And who can lend an ear to a twenty-one-year-old girl? I realised very quickly, with bitterness, that I would have to start all over again from the beginning.'[14]

In the New Year of 1946, Maria met Louise Caselotti, an Italian-American mezzo-soprano who was renowned for having sung the part of *Carmen* more than 400 times. For Maria, it seemed like fate: Caselotti's husband, Eddy Bagarozy, was the brother of the late Armand Bagarozy, director of the Columbia Opera Company in New York, and he had ambitions to found his own opera company.

Every day, she went to their apartment at Riverside Drive and was given free singing lessons by Caselotti, who criticised her technique and claimed de Hidalgo had taught her bad habits in Athens. They told her she was a dramatic soprano who had damaged her voice by singing in the ranges of lyrical and coloratura. Maria never questioned their advice nor did she realise she was being manipulated by Caselotti, whose last engagement was in 1943.

She was grateful for their friendship and had fallen in love with Bagarozy – 'My treasure', she called him[15] – and the affair took place under the gaze of Caselotti who, like her husband, viewed Maria as a commodity and encouraged the seduction. It was then, after they had become sexually involved, that Bagarozy suggested he become her agent, thus allocating him 10 per cent of her future earnings. 'With kindness,' Maria said, 'people can get anything from me, can make me foolish.'[16]

During that period, she heard from Johnson who, according to Maria, invited her to sign a three-year contract with the Metropolitan Opera, offering her *Madama Butterfly* and *Fidelio*. She refused without hesitation.[17] She thought herself too heavy for the part of Butterfly, and she refused to sing a German opera in English. Years later, Johnson told a newspaper:

> We were very much impressed, and recognised her as a talented young woman. We offered her a contract but she didn't like it – because of the contract, not because of the roles. She was right in turning it down – it was frankly a beginner's contract. But she was without experience, without repertory.[18]

However, could Bagarozy have influenced Maria's decision? It seems likely, for she had become emotionally dependent on him, provoked by his mistreatment of her. She could never escape the long shadow of her abusive childhood and was, therefore, conditioned to seek out people with similar traits to her mother. In Bagarozy, she had found a partner who was kind one moment and cruel the next. 'Force yourself,' she once implored him, 'to remember the beautiful moments we shared, and not the ugly ones.'[19] In rejecting Johnson's offers, she was committing herself to Bagarozy's revival of the Chicago Opera, renamed the United States Opera Company, despite having no money or a solid business plan.

Throughout the years, Bagarozy was involved in corrupt deals* and took advantage of other people's success. His latest scheme was to rename Maria 'Marie Calas' and promote her as a mystery Greek soprano, whose identity, he told the press, would be revealed in due course. With the help of Sergio Failoni and Ottavio Scotto, an Italian impresario, he convinced European singers to work without payment, misleading them to believe American financiers were in place. The production was Puccini's *Turandot*, and Maria was cast as the princess whose suitors faced death if they failed to solve her three riddles. Perhaps fuelled by jealousy, Caselotti accused Maria of lacking the femininity of the heroine and pleaded in vain for Bagarozy to change the production.

Toward the end of 1946, Maria received a letter from Litsa demanding $750.[20] In Litsa's memoirs, she claimed Maria begged her to come to America, as she missed her. That was not true: she was impatient for her to begin a singing career, thinking it would make them rich. Predicting that George lacked the ambition to guide Maria's future, Litsa knew she would soon fall into a routine of cooking and cleaning – a wasted life, in her opinion. As Maria 'didn't have a dime' and George refused to help, she asked her godfather for a loan.[21]

On 27 November, Litsa sailed on the *Queen Elizabeth* to New York and mother and daughter were reunited, not on Christmas Eve, as Litsa recalled, but in early December.[22] There remains little doubt that Maria wanted to fulfil her childhood ambition of having a loving family under one roof. She had since left the Hotel Times Square and had moved in with her father, perhaps anticipating Litsa's arrival.

---

* From 1935 until 1942, Bagarozy was a board member of several unsuccessful ventures, including the Glo-Ba Mining Company, for which he was sued by his associates, and was the vice president of the Differential Wheel Corporation.

However, their reunion was volatile from the moment Litsa entered the apartment. It began with Litsa criticising Maria's weight and putting her on a diet. 'In forty days Maria was no longer the fat daughter who had kissed me,' Litsa said. 'She was almost as thin as I was.'[23] Then, Litsa threw Alexandra out of the apartment and hurled her clothes out of the window. Momentarily, the Kalogeropoulou women had won, but George, deprived of his mistress, demanded that his wife share his bed. Angry words were exchanged. Litsa threatened to commit suicide and barricaded herself in Maria's bedroom, where she remained. Thinking Maria had been exposed to her father's immoral ways, Litsa took her to the Church of St Spyridon, but instead of seeking religious indoctrination, Maria prayed to the icons for a successful career.

In the New Year, Maria went to Chicago to make her opera debut with the United States Opera Company but the opening night, scheduled for the sixth, was postponed for two weeks. Not only had Bagarozy failed to secure investment from his financiers, but the American Guild of Musical Artists had given him three weeks to raise a large deposit to protect the salaries of the members of the chorus. To pay off his debts, he sold his wife's jewellery, his car and his house on Long Island. However, it was not enough: he declared himself bankrupt, the company folded and there was a benefit concert to raise money for the singers' return tickets to Europe.

Arriving back in New York, Maria resumed her job with Nelly and Sergio Failoni, and attended an interview at Macy's. As fate would have it, the artistic director of the Verona Festival, Giovanni Zenatello, was in New York to audition sopranos for *La Gioconda*, conducted by Tullio Serafin. Before meeting Maria, he debated who to engage for the leading part: Herva Nelli, an Italian-American soprano, or Zinka Milanov, a Yugoslavian dramatic soprano who had since left the Metropolitan Opera.

Failoni urged him to listen to Maria and, accompanied by Caselotti on the piano, she sang 'Suicidio!' and 'Casta diva'. Before she could finish the second aria, Zenatello, a former tenor, applauded and embraced her. Calling her the '*perla nera*' (the black pearl), he said, 'It was not so much an audition, but a revelation.' He offered her a contract of $60 per performance, although it did not include expenses, despite her having to be in Verona for a month before the rehearsals began. By comparison, Zenatello had also engaged Richard Tucker, an American tenor making his European debut, and agreed to pay him $1,500 for six performances.

Agreeing to the terms of the contract, Maria knew she could not afford to buy a ticket to Italy. Furthermore, her father was furious and said her time was better spent looking for a husband to support her. What use was a beautiful voice, he asked, if she failed to earn a living. As before, she asked her godfather for help, and he gave her $1,000. 'Nobody else but you helped me and gave me courage then,' she told him. 'I'll never forget it.'[24]

Appealing to her sense of economy, Bagarozy suggested he use his contacts to buy a cheaper ticket. He bought tickets for Maria, Caselotti and a female friend, and promised to wire the remaining money to her in Verona. Four days before she left, he pressured her into signing a contract, appointing him as her agent for ten years, which entitled him to 10 per cent of her earnings. Later, she realised she had been swindled.

On 17 June 1947, the Soviet passenger ship *Rossia* sailed from New York Harbour. The three women shared a small cabin and lived on boiled potatoes and butter. Some believe that Caselotti was sent over to collect her husband's 10 per cent, and in the interim, she hoped to revive her singing career. Twelve days later, the ship docked in Naples and they continued to Verona on a crowded train, a journey which took a day and a half, sharing one seat between them.

Maria's first sight of post-war Verona reminded her of Greece; the buildings were reduced to rubble and all ten of its bridges, including the Ponte Pietra, were bombed. She moved into the Hotel Accademia, co-owned by Zenatello and his relatives, in the Via Scala, which had survived the German bombs.

Later, she recalled, 'I was very tense and at times my worst fears were not so much for my work, but for life itself.'[25] She was 23, alone in a foreign country and with only $70 to her name.[26] Furthermore, she had no winter clothing, as she could not afford to buy any, and her parents did not offer to help. Only Litsa gave her something, a self-absorbed letter containing life advice, such as 'honour thy mother and thy father' and, reading between the lines, to send money home. 'All my mother's love naturally didn't help much,' Maria said.[27] When Maria's cardboard suitcase, held together with string, arrived at the hotel, she pretended the contents had been stolen. 'It's hard to believe, but it's true,' she said, ashamed of how little she owned.[28]

At the hotel, food was expensive and sometimes they ate 3 or 4 ounces of meat and string beans; other times they were served peaches and watermelon. Further marring her arrival was the reception toward her. A local newspaper asked, 'Why have they brought us a Greek soprano? Haven't we got enough Italians to sing opera?'

A few days later, her colleagues joined her at the hotel: Nicola Rossi-Lemeni, Renata Tebaldi and her mother, and Richard Tucker and his wife, Sara. Unlike Maria, Tucker had negotiated a favourable contract, which not only included his expenses in Verona (including sightseeing) but paid for a brief stay in Rome. Hoping to inspire friendship, Tucker called her Mary, which she disliked, perhaps reminding her of her unhappy childhood.* His first impression of her was 'partly cunning and wily, and partly girlish and naïve … one moment she could be timid and nearly helpless, and, in the next, unpromisingly demanding'. He said, 'I liked Maria, but she could be a pain in the ass.'[29]

Twenty-four hours after arriving in Verona, Maria and her colleagues were honoured with a dinner given by Giuseppe Gambato, the assistant director of the Verona Festival, at his restaurant, the Pedavena. Unbeknownst to her, she had piqued the curiosity of Giovanni Battista Meneghini, known as Titta, a 52-year-old brick manufacturer who courted visiting opera singers, hoping to represent them as an agent and, in vulgar terms, cash in.

Gambato, his friend and landlord (he rented a room above the Pedavena), told him of Maria, whom he said was exceptionally gifted and, physically, his type. 'I looked at the girl,' he recalled. 'She made an impression on me … she was full-breasted, her shoulders were powerful, and she had black hair and intense eyes.'[30] He had also heard of Maria through his brother-in-law, Dr Giovanni Cazzarolli, a physician who had performed a medical examination on her before. Years later, Titta claimed he was coerced into meeting her, although Maria remembered it differently. She passed her plate to him, and speaking in fluent Italian, said, 'Sir, if you don't mind I would like to offer you my cutlet.'

The following afternoon, Titta arrived at the Accademia to collect Maria for a sightseeing tour of Venice.[31] They went to the Piazza San Marco. 'Oh, how beautiful!' she exclaimed, and thanked him for inviting her. After dinner, they drove to Vicenza, where they went to the Piazza Garibaldi and she confided to him the problems concerning her family and how *La Gioconda* was her last chance at a singing career. He kissed her and she misunderstood the gesture as love. 'I loved the way he smiled, it was so open, and you can't explain love at first sight,' she recalled. 'It was as though God sent him to me because I was so alone.'[32]

---

* Throughout Maria's life, her mother and sister called her Mary.

Two days later, Titta took Maria to dinner at San Vigilio on Lake Garda and proposed the following, 'It's six months until the first of the year. During that period I will take care of the necessities – hotels, restaurants, wardrobe, everything. You will concern yourself with only singing and studying with the *maestri* that I choose for you.' After six months, they would evaluate their arrangement and, if they both agreed, Titta would become her manager. The next day he sent her a note:

> An enchanting evening, dreamlike and oblivious in loving peace and spir-
> itual contact with the elect soul of a sweet young creature. Maria! Your
> name, your face, your eyes thrill and enchant me like a sweet dream. You
> inspire goodness in me and I make a gift of my soul to you. I embrace you
> with all my heart.[33]

She studied with Ferruccio Cusinati, the choral master at the Arena di Verona, who thought her upper register was shrill and compared it to the sound of a ship coming into port.

Although Titta had proposed a business arrangement, Maria viewed it as a symbolic gesture of his feelings for her. She considered their meeting one another as fate, although cynically, she was also determined not to lose him. 'I considered him something of a screen for me, to protect me from the outside world,' she said.[34] In turn, she had nothing to offer him except herself – 'I thought I needed affection' – and within days, had gone to bed with him.[35]

This was a daring stance for the period and the setting, for in a Catholic country her behaviour was considered scandalous and she was without grounds if she were to become pregnant out of wedlock. As in Greece, women were second-rate citizens and society was ruled by patriarchal laws. (Even by the 1980s, 30 per cent of Italian men still expected their wives to be virgins.) Therefore, Maria's behaviour was irresponsible in every sense of the word: she had no money to return home, and it remains doubtful if her father would have helped her. At that point, George had forsaken responsibility toward his adult daughters, thinking it time they found husbands.

One might argue that Maria was securing her future, for perhaps she thought Titta would marry her eventually, particularly if she found herself in trouble. Despite her intentions being pure, she was also naïve, and in throwing herself at him, she risked losing it all.

Thereafter, he gradually lost interest, but she was preoccupied with rehears-als for *La Gioconda* and gave an optimistic interview to a reporter:

Since I was a child in the United States and Greece, your Arena, so majestic and so welcoming, always seemed like a dreamland to me, populated by the festive public. When I saw it a few days ago, for the first time, I was taken by sincere emotion.[36]

Intrigued by the 'American soprano', as the press referred to her, she was also interviewed by *L'Arena*, whose prose adopted an artistic licence:

Maria Callas is bound with an unwavering passion to her memories. It was her family that discovered her voice; she was a vivacious and graceful child with a sweet and strong voice that rang out in the upper register like a nightingale in the season of love calling out in the mysterious peace of the forest …

Maria Callas is a sweet and sensitive person. She is in love with Italy, its cities, and its villages that are dotted among lakes and seas like the beads of magic rosaries … This American singer is particularly taken with our city.

Maria Callas, who speaks with a soft and languid voice took her leave from us expressing once again her appreciation for our city and that she would be happy to live in Italy forever.

On the final day of the rehearsals, she fell through a chute on the stage and hurt her ankle. However, she insisted on continuing, and by the third act it was swollen, and she could not put her foot on the ground. A doctor was summoned but it was too late to do anything except bandage her leg and order her to rest.

Later, she claimed Titta sat by her bedside until dawn – perhaps this was how she wished it to be. His visits and letters abruptly stopped three days before the opening night and she was confused by the sudden change in their relationship. Until then, they had written to one another every day, and he responded with tokens such as, 'My soul did not support the idea of separation, however brief, which comes to me ever more unbearable.'[37] He also sent flowers to her hotel room and, according to Maria, spoke of marriage, which, at first, frightened her, as she thought it too soon to commit to a man she barely knew.

'I don't think I love him,' she told Sara Tucker. 'But he wants me to stay here, he wants me to marry him.'[38] As with her father and Bagarozy, she was overcompensating for his behaviour and inventing scenarios to meet her expectations.

Although Titta was preoccupied with his factory and commitments[*] to his mother and siblings, whom he cared for like a father, he received criticism from his friends, who said, 'Don't you see that she's built like a potato, like a sack? Can't you see how ugly she is, how clumsy?' His eleven brothers, younger than he, warned him that Maria was a gold-digger and only his widowed mother, Giuseppina, and sister, Pia, accepted her, thinking her 'shy, afraid, and rather fat'.[39] Nobody mentioned his looks and how he barely reached her shoulder, nor did they critique his paunchy frame and aquiline features.

Others, such as Sara, also thought Maria was 'grossly overweight, she moved awkwardly on the stage', and criticised her make-up and her clothing. 'She used all the wrong colours and hues, disfiguring the same features that would later make her famous.'[40] This may have been fuelled by jealousy as throughout Maria's life, she provoked strong reactions from people who, in their own way, felt inferior to her talent.

In 1947, she was not thin but she was not overweight either. Her hourglass shape and height made her a striking, if imposing, figure and her dark hair, parted in the middle, and almond-shaped eyes gave her a Middle Eastern look, perhaps validating the rumours that her father had Turkish ancestry.

In Titta, Maria believed she had found a protector against the world and the cruelty of others. However, as if to destroy her confidence and, therefore, make her dependent on him, he admitted he had slept with her out of pity and not love. He was not alone in his harsh treatment of women for, as with her father's generation, he expected them to be submissive – or, as the old Italian proverb stated, 'A woman is like an egg. The more she is beaten the better she becomes.'

Two days later, on 2 August, *La Gioconda* opened at the Arena di Verona before an audience of 25,000. Everyone worried about Maria as she moved across the cavernous stage, aware of her injured leg. In the audience that evening was George Lascelles (the future Earl of Harewood) who, in 1951, would become the director of the Royal Opera House in Covent Garden. Impressed by her performance, he said, 'I knew that what we were hearing was quite out of the ordinary: a penetrating, vibrant voice of great power and, when required, flexibility, at the service moreover of a strong stage and musical personality.'[41]

---

[*] As a young man, he wanted to pursue journalism but instead studied at the Commercial High School in Venice, which prepared him to take over the family business. However, the arrival of the First World War interrupted his studies and he enlisted as a field artillery officer, earning three military awards, and assumed his studies after the war. His father died a year later, and he found himself head of the family.

L'Arena wrote that her singing was 'passionate, rich in tone, vibrant' and the *Corriere del Mattino* called her 'a fiery Gioconda … [who] may shape into a gem one day'. Much of the acclaim, however, was reserved for Tucker, Rossi-Lemeni and Tebaldi. After four performances, which amounted to a fee of $80, Caselotti was waiting to collect her husband's commission.

Maria had been invited to sing *La Gioconda* at Vigevano, a town in northern Italy known for its shoemaking industry. Having declined, she then changed her mind, but it was too late – the part had gone to another soprano. Although disheartened, she was encouraged by Serafin's advice to study with Emma Malojoli, who could help her smooth the rough edges of her voice. 'She lacks only one thing,' Serafin wrote to Malojoli, 'she needs to be more Italian. I am convinced once this "nationalisation" is completed, we will have found the artist we have been looking for all these years.' Although Titta declined to send Maria to Malojoli, he was curious about Serafin's belief in her talent and 'considered himself her Pygmalion, her guardian angel'.[42]

After fulfilling her contract with the Verona Festival, Maria spoke of returning to New York. 'I don't like it here,' she told Sara, 'and I think I can do much better for myself in America.'[43] Responding to her qualms, Sara reminded her that she was poor, restless, and confused about her future, and advised her to remain in Verona and accept Titta's conditions.

Perhaps Maria wanted to reconcile with Bagarozy, both professionally and romantically, for she wrote to him, 'I feel for you what I felt when I left.'[44] In another letter, she wrote, 'Maria does not change the way other people do. Even though you treated me very brusquely in the months before my departure, I didn't say anything, and I continue to be faithful to you.'[45]

Bagarozy did not respond, and she had run out of options. Therefore, in mid September, Maria resumed her arrangement with Titta, who came to her hotel and stayed the night. The following morning, she wrote, 'You proved your love for me yesterday … I had suffered so much and was happy that you stayed with me like that. I would have felt so awful if you had left last night. I wanted to be in your arms, to feel you near to me as I have felt you before.'[46] In time, Titta would ignore Maria the woman, and exploit Callas the artist.

6

Transition

I can't take such fatal blows.
Oh, how much better to die!

Il trovatore, Verdi

After the Verona Festival ended, Maria found herself without a job, money and a home. 'I knew I had failed. All that work and all those years for nothing,' she said. 'I understood why people kill themselves.'[1] Her visa was due to expire at the end of September, but she delayed making a decision and penned two letters to Titta, one of which she destroyed. In the surviving letter, she wrote:

> Yesterday I decided to leave because it seemed that you were bored with me. Yes, I was decided but I had so many excuses not to make all the preparations … and so much hope that you would not want to see me leave, that I only packed half my baggage.[2]

Sensing his indifference to both herself and the agreement they made, she said, 'If you were more shrewd you would have realised that I was waiting for nothing other than a gesture of yours, a word, to make me stay.'[3]

He suggested they go to Venice and apply to the American Consulate for an extension on her visa, but it could not be issued until she settled her debt of $700 with the American Government, which he paid.[4] She moved out of the Accademia Hotel and into his room above the Pedavena. Feeling as though she were indebted to him, she said, 'I am all yours, even my tiniest feeling and slightest thought. I live for you.'

Considering the period, their cohabitation was shocking, and locals gossiped about 'the American' who was living in sin. Perhaps she thought he would marry her, and in doing so, she would forsake her career to be Signora Meneghini and devote herself to raising their children. 'A deeply felt love,' she said, 'is worth more than a lousy career that leaves you with nothing more than a name.'[5]

During the brief time they had known one another, Maria became entirely submissive to him. 'Please excuse the change in my nature,' she wrote to Eddy Bagarozy, 'Battista doesn't like it when I tell jokes.'[6] However, Titta found her overbearing, and she addressed him, 'My dear love', 'My adored and sublime love', 'Dear, dear, adored darling', 'Only you', 'My reason for living'. Her desperation was evident, and such behaviour hearkened back to Athens when she slept on the floor and was almost made homeless. Perhaps she feared Titta would turn her out onto the street, and therefore, she had to overcompensate for his kindness. She told him, 'I am the friend of your heart, your confidant, your support when you are tired, everything I can do at that moment. I would like to be so much more but I don't know how. I shall try to be what you deserve.'[7]

There was no sentimentality on Titta's behalf. 'When I first met her, she was fat, clumsy, dressed like a dog. A real gypsy. She didn't have a cent and didn't have the least prospect of making a career for herself.'[8] In terms of sending her to work, he 'wanted to get it done quickly, let her go out and sing because I can't get her out from under my feet'.[9] He took her to Milan to audition for Mario Labroca, the artistic director of La Scala. She sang 'Casta diva' followed by 'O patria mia', but Labroca interrupted the second aria and said he did not have an opening but would keep her in mind. Privately, he told Titta, 'She's not worth anything. Send her back to America whenever you want. It'll be in your best interest.'[10]

A month later, they went to the Agenzia Lirica Concertistica, a talent agency run by Liduino Bonardi, who reminded Titta that the opera season was over and the theatres were closed; a patronising response, which infuriated him. On their way out, they met Nino Cattozzo, the director of the Teatro La Fenice, who told Maria that Tullio Serafin needed a soprano for *Tristan and Isolde*. Later that afternoon, Serafin auditioned Maria, who sight-read the score, and afterwards confessed she did not know it. Nevertheless, Serafin offered her contracts for *Tristan and Isolde* and *Turandot*; both were to be staged in Venice with a fee of 50,000 lire per performance. Despite the approval of Serafin, she was yet to convince Titta of her success. 'By nature,' she said, 'I consider I'm not worth much.'[11]

At the end of October, Maria went to Rome to study with Serafin. She had little money and for hours she walked in the rain, searching for a cheap room until she found one. It had a shared bathroom and damp on the walls. 'I hope I don't catch a cold,' she wrote to Titta, who remained in Verona.[12] As she could not afford proper meals, she lived on eggs and salad, telling him she would not bother to eat unless it was necessary. Looking for his sympathy, she received none, and wrote, 'Today my leg hurt me. It hurt so much at one point that I wanted to cry … Then I had a headache, one of those horrible ones which every now and then afflict me.'[13]

Responding to her letters, he did not acknowledge her suffering and wrote only of his daily routine and reminded her to respect Serafin. It provoked her to write:

> Who makes me happy? I make everyone happy … while my feelings count for nothing. I see that you are in love with Callas the artist. You forget my soul … I wanted a little more Battista and Maria in [your letter], not Meneghini and Callas.[14]

Regretting her outburst, in another letter, she said, 'I will try to reach my goal because, above all, it will make you happy'. She hoped to restore the familiarity of her earlier letters, telling him, 'You will be my warmth in Verona … not the way you're thinking … and then again, maybe yes!'[15]

Each afternoon, Maria studied for two and a half hours with Serafin, who was impressed with her progress. 'Serafin made me,' she later said. 'He gives me his soul, because, musically speaking, I respond to him, to perfection.'[16] She was troubled, however, when he made a pass at her while she rested between lessons. Afterwards, she informed Titta, 'He won't dare do that any more!'[17]

Presumably, when they met again at the beginning of December, the incident was forgotten. Two weeks later, she went to Venice to begin rehearsals for *Tristan and Isolde* and was greeted by hostility, as many were upset that Serafin had not engaged an Italian soprano. 'That means they are also against me,' she told Titta.[18] Nevertheless, her debut at the Teatro La Fenice was a success, and a month later, she opened in the first of five performances of *Turandot*. The reviews were favourable, though she never read them. 'We singers are nothing, art is so immense.'[19]

Despite Maria's success, she received no offers from the major opera houses. Her letters from that period, as she toured the theatres in provincial towns, provide an insight into her dynamic with Titta. From Udine, where she was performing in *Turandot* on 11 and 14 March, she wanted to prove to him she could succeed. '[The journalists] kept me up until after midnight,' she wrote. 'They complimented me on my good looks....'[20] She longed for him to respond, and when he did not, her tone became desperate:

> Did you eat, sleep, and work well? Did you think a little of me? I didn't lie to you on the phone. I am really not very well. Even as I spoke, I felt my heart break. You know how I feel when I am far away from you.[21]

In Trieste, where she was singing in Verdi's *La forza del destino*, she realised a few 'disgusting creatures' wanted to embarrass her – they said that, although she was successful in her previous parts, in a Verdi opera she was a disgrace.[22] A month later, during *Tristan and Isolde*, in Genoa, she was displeased by the lack of rehearsals and her costumes which had 'such a smell of sweat (not disinfectant) that they make me nauseous'.[23]

She complained, in a letter to Titta, of feeling 'a little rundown and enervated because of [my period]'.[24] By her own admission, she suffered from migraines and believed the changes in hormones affected her voice;[25] a valid observation, for studies have proven that a drop in oestrogen creates fluid on the vocal folds resulting in the larynx becoming hoarse.[26] 'I am a woman,' she said, 'something that one forgets very often. Being a woman means all the good things there are, and all bad things as well.'[27]

Around that time, she resumed contact with Elvira de Hidalgo. In a contrast to the vulnerability of her letters to Titta, to her former teacher, she was full of bravado, 'Now they say I am the Verdi voice. Poor fools. [The critics] say that it is impossible for a powerful voice to sing Verdi. Well, in the end, I won and that's all that matters.'[28]

Responding to Maria's letter, de Hidalgo wrote:

> Brava, my Maria. I would have loved to be present at your triumph. Now you are tranquil and happy, you have won, as you say, the battle didn't last long. Think about the others, the humiliations and tears before achieving one-third of what you have. You must thank God, smile on good fortune, be courteous to everyone ... [29]

In private, however, Maria struggled with an inferiority complex. After performing in *Turandot* in Pisa and Rome, she confided to Titta, 'Audiences applaud me, but I know, inside myself, that I could have achieved so much more.'[30] She found her career unfulfilling and claimed that art was only a small part of her life, despite the ambition that had raged inside of her. 'What else can I do, if I didn't have an interest in life, such as my work?' she later said. 'I'd have found something else. I'd have had children.'[31]

Every thought centred on Titta; she claimed she did not want or need other friendships, and if he wanted her to, she would give up singing. In his absence, she felt 'tremendously empty ... so, so empty.'[32] Such feelings intensified her love for him. 'I kiss you ardently, and, dear, you do not know how much I desire you to madness.'[33]

Those feelings were not reciprocated by Titta. He no longer felt enthusiasm for her career, nor did he respond to her incessant letters and phone calls. 'My God, Battista, what anxiety,' she said of his silence and begged him to 'love me just a third as much as I love you ... if I could offer my life itself for you, to prove how much I adore you, I would do so willingly'.[34]

Instead of being flattered by her devotion, he was repelled: he had little experience with women, despite his age, and viewed the visiting sopranos as a commodity. Naturally, he played the part of a gentleman and squired them around Verona, but after the festival he never saw them again. Maria was different; she had nothing to lose and believed that he could save her from a bleak future. Her emotions consumed her, and she longed for a glimmer of approval or a token gesture, neither of which he offered. She told him, 'Everything I do, I am convinced I am doing it badly, and then I start feeling nervous and discouraged. Sometimes I get to the point of wanting death to release me from the torments and the anguish that constantly afflict me.'[35]

In a moment of clarity, Maria confided to Serafin that she was disappointed with Titta and her career and wanted to return to America. 'One must pay attention to our self-esteem,' she once said. 'It's not arrogance, it's pride.'[36] At the time, Serafin was the only one who foresaw her success. He telephoned Francesco Siciliani, the artistic director of the Teatro Comunale Florence and the May Music Festival, and told him, 'I've met an artist and she wants to go to America. She wants to leave Italy and if I can't make her stay, then she won't be staying in Italy.'[37] Although the programme for the Comunale's opera season was fixed, Siciliani listened to Maria, and announced, 'She's not going to America, she's coming to Florence, to begin in Italy, a shining career.'[38]

Before Maria's debut at the Comunale, in *Norma* and *Aida*, she went to Rome to study the part of *Norma* with Serafin. 'I have never seen Maestro so happy,' she wrote to Titta, 'but I am not, however, because I always ask too much of myself.'[39] She was concerned about her costume; she had to wear a sheer dress which exposed her waist, and she became fixated with finding the perfect reddish-blonde wig, the details of which she conveyed to Titta. Physically, she did not feel well, and she also worried about her voice, thinking the three weeks spent with Serafin could not prepare her for the part. Despite knowing it was a milestone in her career, she could not enjoy her achievements, and said:

> I would like my voice to do what I want at all times. But it seems I am asking too much. The voice is a thankless instrument … In fact, I would say it is rebellious and does not want to be ordered about, or perhaps I should say dominated. It always wants to break free, and I suffer for it.[40]

On 30 November, Maria opened in *Norma* at the Comunale, inaugurating the operatic season in Florence. The most important moment of her career, thus far, was marred by symptoms of appendicitis, but she ignored the pain and continued with the performance. Afterwards, Serafin went to her dressing room and, with tears in his eyes, he said, 'Maria, you're great.'[41]

He later recalled the audience's baffled response to her interpretation of 'Sediziose voci', which she purposely sang in an uneven voice. It was not criticism: her technique was new to Italian audiences who were used to lyricism and, therefore, a beautiful sound. *Il Nuovo Corriere* wrote, 'Her schooling is rather different from what we are accustomed to hearing, as indeed her vocal colour is unusual … This young artist is already versed in the most demanding traditions of Italian bel canto.'

Returning to Verona, Maria was hospitalised for ten days following an appendectomy. She was forced to withdraw from *Aida*, scheduled to open on 23 December, allowing her to spend Christmas with Titta. They had spent long periods apart and, although her letters spoke of passionate reunions, in the flesh, however, he was aloof and often rebuffed her advances.

Perhaps his attitude was not unusual for the era; their living arrangement was considered sinful and Maria felt ashamed of this hidden life, especially now that his family knew of their cohabitation. In particular, his brothers hated her and openly called her a whore. Despite their strong opposition, she expected him to defend her, but he did not, thus deepening her insecurities. She had never forgotten the humiliation her parents had brought upon her with their casual attitudes to sex, and though her feelings for Titta were pure, she was viewed as immoral. In a letter, she told him:

> I want the best of the best … I want, in short, to have the best of everything. Even my clothes: I want them to be the best possible to be had. I know that all this is not possible and it torments me greatly. Why? Help me, Battista. I don't think I'm exaggerating, its the way I am.[42]

Although exhausted from her recent ill health, Maria sang the part of Brünnhilde in Wagner's *Die Walküre*, conducted by Serafin, at La Fenice. 'Callas was perfect,' *Il Gazzettino* wrote, echoing the response of the Venetian public.

Behind the scenes, an influenza epidemic threatened the programme and its leading soprano, Margherita Carosio, became ill. There was no understudy to replace Carosio as Elvira in Bellini's *I puritani*, nor could Serafin find another singer good enough for the part. 'Maria can do it,' his wife, Elena Rakowska, a retired soprano, told him. She would have eight days to learn a new part, and furthermore, she would have to sing in two operas simultaneously. The parts were of different repertoires and contrasting vocal demands: one was Wagnerian, the other bel canto. 'The show must go on, even if the protagonist dies,' Maria later said. 'It's a question of duty, not of ambition.'[43]

The following morning, Serafin arrived in Venice and telephoned Maria, asking her to meet him in the music room of the hotel. She refused, saying she needed half an hour to wash and dress, but he considered it a waste of time and told her to come immediately. Waiting for her was Serafin and his colleague, Nino Cattozzo, who asked her to sing an aria from *I puritani* – the only one she knew, having learned it the night before. Half-asleep and self-conscious about her unkempt appearance, she reluctantly agreed and was offered the part of Elvira.

With Serafin's encouragement, she learned the part in six days, before the first dress rehearsal, which coincided with her final performance in *Die Walküre*. In terms of the characters' psychology, Brünnhilde was a Norse warrior maiden and Elvira was the fragile daughter of a Puritan leader who descends into madness.

Three days later, she opened in *I puritani* to an audience of Carosio's fans who formed a claque and expected her to fail but were met with a triumphant performance. 'Even the most sceptical readily acknowledged the miracle that Callas performed,' *Il Gazzettino* reported. With her usual reserve, she said, 'Yes, it went well but I've still got a lot of studying to do.'[44]

Afterwards, Maria went to Palermo to give two performances of *Die Walküre* at the Teatro Massimo. She wrote to Titta of the cold weather and how the management treated her 'as if I were a goddess'.[45] The boastful remark was for his benefit; she wanted him to know that others valued her, and perhaps she longed for him to be jealous. Nevertheless, she complained about the chaotic rehearsals – at least thirty workers remained on the stage throughout, and the orchestra played badly due to the conductor talking and paying no attention to the musicians. 'I am accustomed to perfect, orderly rehearsals, so you can imagine how I feel here, in the midst of this debacle.'[46]

Writing to Titta, she told him of her headaches and her colleague, Giulio Neri, singing the wrong notes. Furthermore, a review claimed, 'Maria Callas … did not succeed in being a barbaric Walküre.' Calling the critic an imbecile, she said, 'Here they seem to expect people on the stage to pull their hair out. I am quite angry about this.'[47] Her tone suggested she wanted to forget the provincial contracts and focus on engagements in Venice, Rome and Florence, which she considered worthy of her artistry. However, Titta, who could not resist the lure of money, accepted quantity over quality, and such was her schedule that she spent little time at home.

From Palermo, she went to Naples for *Turandot*, a critical success, with the *Roma* writing, 'Maria Callas is a most unusual singer. In softer passages, her voice is beautiful and insinuating, yet her high notes are metallic and piercing. She has a nightmarish upper extension – awesome, sinister, and inexorable.' While there, she was studying the part of Kundry from Wagner's *Parsifal* before joining Serafin in Rome for five days of rehearsals. 'It's amazing how this young girl, working on her own, understood and mastered both the text and the music in such a short time,' he recalled.

He waited until the last rehearsal to direct the scene in which Maria's character, Kundry, kisses Parsifal (played by Hans Beirer, whom she thought 'such a gorgeous man'), but she was too shy to do it. To break the tension, Serafin walked onto the stage and kissed Beirer, saying, 'Listen, Maria, if I can kiss him surely you can too.'

On 26 February, Maria made her debut in *Parsifal* to favourable reviews. *Il Messaggero* wrote, 'Maria Callas is a highly gifted singer who is well-versed in the exigencies of the stage.' The day before the final performance, on 8 March, she sang in a concert for Radio Audizione. She also signed a contract with Cetra Records, who proposed she record three of the arias she had sung on the radio, with complete operas to follow. Responding to Maria's success, de Hidalgo wrote:

> You see, Maria, I was not wrong, and the steps you took in Athens, without my consent did you no service, only slowed down the speed of the success you have had in Italy … Even though a bit late, the dream we had has been realised.[48]

The achievements in Maria's career failed to compensate for the unhappiness she felt in her private life. 'I wasn't content,' she recalled. 'I wanted, in fact, the warmth of my own home and the tranquillity that every woman derives from a happy marriage.'[49] She pleaded with Titta to marry her, thus making their living arrangement respectable and fulfilling her dream of having a family. As divorce was illegal, he worried about maintaining her for the rest of his life.

During that period, Jackie wanted to begin a career as a concert pianist and came to Verona. Having arrived unannounced at the hotel where Maria and Titta now lived, she was surprised to find them sharing a bed. Over lunch, Maria confided to Titta's sister, Pia, 'Can't you see the state I'm in? I can't go on.'[50]

Siding with Maria, Pia told Titta, 'Maria is in a bad way. Either you decide yes [to marriage] or leave her free.'[51] He muttered a weak 'yes,' and she responded by crying, palpitating and taking bites of the soup, fish, meat, salad and ice cream.

Later, when they were alone, Jackie scrutinised Maria's weight, and she replied, 'Titta likes me like this.'[52] She was prepared to alter her looks to please a man, prompting Jackie to write, 'If you were as big as [Maria] and had no intention of doing anything about it, then here was the perfect mate.'[53] Fifteen days later, Jackie, whom Maria accused of being lazy, was no further along in her career and announced she was leaving. 'As you wish,' Maria said, knowing what remained of their bond had been severed during the war.

Although Titta had proposed to Maria, he continued to avoid the subject of marriage. He explained that his parish priest at the Chiesa dei Filippini, the poorest church in Verona, warned it was impossible: she needed documents from America, and he required permission from the Vatican to marry a non-Catholic. Nevertheless, Maria obtained the necessary documents, but he told her the curia refused to sign them. Continuing with his excuses, he told her of the difficulties they faced: the opposition from his brothers, whom she claimed wanted to push her down the stairs, and the (slight) theological differences between the Catholic and Orthodox churches. It bought him time, until mid April, when she prepared to sail to Buenos Aires for a three-month engagement at the Teatro Colón.

Twenty-four hours before she was due to depart, she gave him an ultimatum. 'If you don't marry me, I won't sing again.' Later that afternoon, on 21 April, they were married in a store cupboard in the Chiesa dei Filippini, surrounded by broken pews and religious debris. 'I had been deprived of the joys and fantasies dearest to the female heart: the wedding preparations, the gifts, the flowers,' she recalled. 'No preparations, no gifts, no flowers. Only great love and an exalted simplicity.'[54] For Titta, however, it was a marriage of convenience.

After the ceremony, Maria sent her parents a telegram, written in Italian: '*Siamo sposati e felici* [We are married and are happy].' As neither spoke Italian, they ignored the message. It would be several months before she received their letters, the first arriving from George, a fantastic document filled with lies, 'You must be sure that I was, I am and will be the best husband. I always loved, love and will love my wife and I wish that my children be loved by their husbands like I loved my wife.'[55]

However, Litsa soon made her feelings clear:

> You decided to marry so soon, too soon. You should at least have opened your heart before deciding, asking my opinions even through our correspondence, out of courtesy and as a duty to the mother who bore you, if only as a point of form. But you went and married without further thought and without showing the superiority of your character even to your husband himself.[56]

Their marriage was unconsummated, and Maria promised Titta they would be 'bursting with love' when she returned.[57] In a letter, sent afterwards, she asked, 'Do you think about that night?!!!'[58] Titta, however, was relieved by their long separation and not being able to fulfil any obligations he had toward her. A few hours later, she was alone on a ship to Argentina, having bid a tearful goodbye to him at the port in Genoa.* She was, until the final moment, determined to stay in Italy and pleaded in vain for Serafin to release her from her contract, to allow her to go home to her husband. It would be her last engagement, she decided; her marriage would occupy the ambition she once had. Serafin reminded her that the tour hinged on her name and there was no choice but to proceed. 'Who would have known,' Maria later said, 'that I was to become Callas.'[59]

---

* Members of the tour included Mario Del Monaco, Fedora Barbieri, Nicola Rossi-Lemeni and Mario Filippeschi, who each brought with them a loved one. Tullio Serafin travelled with his wife, Elena Rakowska, daughter, Vittoria, and granddaughter, Donatella.

7

Success

No one who goes against her can win.

Medea, Euripides

During the three-week crossing to Argentina, Maria grew depressed and conveyed her feelings in daily letters to Titta. 'I am alive only when I am with you,' she told him.[1] She reproached him for allowing her to leave and warned, 'I hope that you will never again permit me to go so far from you.'[2] Confirming her traditional views of marriage, she referred to herself as his property and warned that 'no woman would ever be able to love you as I know how to love you'.[3] After two weeks at sea, she received his telegram which made her 'cry like a baby from joy'.[4]

On 13 May, the ship docked in Rio and the directors of the Theatro Municipal invited her to dinner and offered her *Norma*, but she refused, as she did an offer from the opera house in Montevideo. Afterwards, she wrote to Titta and asked him to send a letter to both herself and Serafin, forbidding her to extend the tour. 'Now, if you truly want me to return, you must help me,' she said. 'I can't live without you. It's time you understood that.'[5]

He wrote instead to Elvira de Hidalgo and told her of Maria's offers to sing in Brazil and Montevideo. Surprised by Maria's refusal, de Hidalgo wrote, 'I understand your desire to return to Italy to be with your spouse … but the artist often needs to make some minor sacrifices. And I think you'll agree with me on that.'[6]

In Buenos Aires, Maria was impressed by the European-style architecture, wide streets and the enormous cars. Her feelings changed, however, as time progressed, and she complained about the smog and criticised President Perón's political regime. 'All the fascists of the universe are here,' she wrote to Titta, unaware of his past Fascist connections, which soon came to light.[7] Gripped by feelings of hopelessness, she said, 'You are my reason for living. I adore you so much that I want to die in your arms.'[8] He did not respond to her letters, provoking her to write, 'I feel alone and abandoned.'[9]

On 20 May, she opened in *Turandot* to a responsive audience, although the critics detected a nervousness in her voice. The flaw was, perhaps, the result of influenza. Before the next performance, she remained in bed, drinking hot milk and cognac to cure herself. She dwelt on her unhappiness; she disliked her colleagues (apart from Serafin and his wife), particularly Nicola Rossi-Lemeni, of whom she said, 'If I ever have the chance to prevent anything important for him. I shall do so willingly.'[10]

Self-pity turned into paranoia and she felt that her colleagues took pleasure in her suffering, as they were 'all afraid, poor things … they know they pale to nothing next to me'.[11] She was unable to perform on the first night of *Aida* on 27 May and was replaced by the Argentine soprano, Delia Rigal.

At the rehearsal for *Norma*, the orchestra applauded her duets with Fedora Barbieri. 'It seems I bother some people a lot,' she wrote to Titta, 'I like to provoke people.' Five days later, she said, 'The day of the great test, of the greatest lesson in singing I intend to give everyone … God who is good and great has given me revenge.'[12]

After a successful opening night in *Norma*, her father wrote, 'You make me an even more happy and proud father of his girl. Yes, my [Maria], you are my pride, my joy and my happiness and I wish that you always triumph and the best wishes for all your life.'[13]

After the fourth and final *Norma*, on 29 June, she gave a single performance of *Aida* on 2 July, taking over from Rigal. 'It was a triumph, I got back the respect I deserve,' she said.[14] A week later, she sang in a concert to commemorate Argentina's Independence Day and was pleased that the First Lady, Eva Perón, had excluded Rigal from the programme.

The management of the Teatro Colón offered Maria *I puritani* for the 1950 season but she declined, calling Buenos Aires 'a long period of torture'.[15] Impatient to return home, Maria bought an aeroplane ticket and warned Titta not to fly to meet her, in case of a crash. 'It doesn't matter if something happens to me,' she told him, 'but it would destroy me if something happened to you. If we must die, it's better that we die together.'[16]

Learning that she could not transfer her fee out of the country, she bought fur coats for herself and her sister-in-law, Pia. She also sent $100 to her

mother and an alligator wallet to her father. Resenting the gifts, Litsa wrote
to George:

> Write to her at once and mention that terrific present she gave you, that
> wallet. And it would be a good thing if you put it in an envelope and sent it
> to her by registered post with a letter saying, 'As you have done so much for
> your family, have your wallet back, you may need to sell it.' If you don't do
> that, you're a fool.[17]

On 14 July 1949, Maria arrived in Rome and was met by Titta, who took her
to Venice for a belated honeymoon. Several days later, they moved into their
new apartment above his office at 21 San Fermo. The renovations had been
completed while she was in Buenos Aires. She bought a ladder and a toolbox
and, assisted by their maid, Matilde, she hung Titta's antique pictures on the
walls and moved furniture around the rooms. In the afternoons, she shopped
for kitchen appliances – 'mousetraps', she called them – bought in bulk and
seldom used.

A new hobby was cutting recipes out of magazines and newspapers and
glueing them into scrapbooks. She recreated the recipes but rarely ate, for
her dietary staple was steak tartare and raw vegetables. She loved the ritual
of setting the table with her best silverware and china and serving Titta the
dishes she had made from her recipe collection. It gave her a false sense of
domesticity and she began to think of children. When she asked if she could
have a baby, he replied, 'That would make you lose a year of your career.'[18]

In September, she reluctantly left their home and went to Perugia to sing
the part of Erodiade in Alessandro Stradella's oratorio *San Giovanni Battista*, at
the San Pietro, a church and abbey dating from the eleventh century. To her,
the engagement was unimportant, as she was preoccupied with thoughts of
her husband and their future together, although he continued to deprive her
of a child. The oratorio was recorded for the radio, and during the intermission
the cast listened to the playback of the first part. She later said, 'You wouldn't
have an idea how hard I cried. I didn't want to continue. I was desperate. I am
horrified by myself ... I don't like myself as a voice.'[19]

In December 1949, she went to Naples for three performances of Verdi's
Nabucco at the Teatro di San Carlo, an opera which she called 'a big bore',
despite achieving unparalleled success in the part of Abigaille. Displaying
her vocal prowess, at the end of the Act Two cabaletta, 'Salgo già del trono
aurato', she ascended a flight of stairs and emitted a high C while seated on
a throne.

As there were five days between the second and third performances, she thought of flying to Verona to see Titta, but he rejected the idea and she remained in Naples. 'I don't know what to do,' she wrote to him. 'I feel very isolated and alone here.'[20]

On the day of the opening night, she informed him, 'I have to report again – still no baby! Menstruation arrived on the eighteenth, right on schedule, together with a headache worthy of our worst enemies. We shall have to be patient.'[21]

The disappointment in her private life could not be lessened by a successful career, particularly when it was for Titta's benefit. In a rare moment of rebellion, she asked him, 'So what's the point?'[22]

Despite Maria's reluctance to continue singing, she fulfilled the contracts made for her months in advance. At the beginning of 1950, there was *Norma* in Venice, followed by simultaneous performances of *Aida* in Brescia and *Tristan and Isolde* in Rome. In March, she sang in a concert in Turin, including in her repertoire for the first time excerpts of *La traviata* and *Il trovatore*.

While singing in *Norma* in Catania, she accepted an invitation from La Scala to perform *Aida* at the Milan Fair on 12, 15 and 18 April 1950. She was disappointed to learn that she was substituting for Renata Tebaldi, who had been taken ill. Furthermore, her debut at La Scala passed without fanfare. The Milanese public, accustomed to the purity of Tebaldi's voice, was disturbed by the dark timbre she brought to the part. The *Corriere Lombardo* wrote:

> I did not care for Maria Callas … She obviously possesses temperament and a fine musicality, but her scale is uneven. She seems to improvise differently, from note to note, the method and technique of her vocal production. She does not have clear diction and she also forces her high notes, thereby jeopardising the security of her intonation.

Responding to such criticism, Maria said:

> It is a matter of loving my kind of voice, or not. Some people say I have a beautiful voice; some people say I have not. It's a matter of opinion. Some people say I have a unique voice and some people say it's all a big lie. That's also a matter of opinion. The only thing I can say is people who don't like me can just not come and hear me because when I don't like something, I don't bother about it.[23]

Backstage, she received an equally cold reception from the management, particularly its superintendent, Antonio Ghiringhelli, who she suspected hated her. After her performance, nobody congratulated her, although she overheard Ghiringhelli loudly complimenting her colleague, Rafaelle de Falchi, as he passed her door. 'All the Milanese saw was this overweight Greek lady,' recalled Franco Zeffirelli, who watched from the stalls. His observation was echoed by members of the audience, who compared her ankles to an elephant's legs and loudly asked, 'Why is she so fat?' She left La Scala without a contract, and one week later, performed *Aida* in Naples.

Toward the end of 1949, Maria had received embittered letters from her mother, accusing her of neglecting her family. Although she told her mother she wanted to have a baby and retire, Litsa reminded her, 'You belong to your public, not to your husband.' In a letter, dated September 1949, Litsa wrote:

> As you know well, anything that you may write to me unrelated to your career is indifferent to me, and for this you should love me all the more, because I am such a glory-seeker and want to know everything that happens in your career. You don't inform me where you have sung and when, to make me happy; I feel ashamed as news reaches me now and then from strangers.[24]

Although she was shocked by the tone of the letters, Maria was afraid when Litsa demanded to live with her. 'There is always room for Mother.'[25] When Maria failed to respond, Litsa added:

> You even allow Battista to feel that you don't care about your relatives, which is a hair-raising thing to come from my child. How I wish – Maria, it is my soul that speaks to you now – that you were still the [Maria] of 1945! I would have wanted you to be kinder, more generous, more tender. I would have liked you to be Maria the good and caring, and your fame to give me joy. You rose to fame very young, you made your own money, you don't need a man any longer. If you become sweeter and more human, you will live better and God will protect you doubly. My soul is sad and my heart aches for you when I think that you have cast me aside despite your promises, you have broken the family bond. But marriage ought to bring people together than divide them.[26]

In an attempt to mend their relationship, Maria invited Litsa to join her in Mexico City, where she was to perform in four operas from 23 May to 27 June 1950.

At the beginning of May, she flew to New York with her colleague, Giulietta Simionato, and they stayed at George's apartment.* Finding the heat and noise unbearable, she confided to Simionato, 'I want to go back to Titta.'[27] She was shocked to find her parents in poor health and struggling financially. In a letter to Titta, she said George was working at a pharmacy – in 1949 he was working for the New York City Prisons on Rikers Island – but Litsa claimed he 'spends his time dallying in cafeterias … sometimes he works, sometimes he doesn't'.[28]

Furthermore, she was surprised to find her mother in the hospital with acute iritis and no medical insurance to pay the bill. 'Why does sickness always come to poor people who aren't in a position to sustain the expense?' she asked Titta.[29] She visited Litsa in hospital, who later recalled:

> When Maria walked into my room, I barely recognised her. She seemed as cold as ice … As Maria sat by my bed, she began to thaw, and I caught flashes of the daughter I had always known. Then without warning, she would turn reserved and chilly again – a true prima donna.[30]

The change in Maria's temperament was due to Litsa's news: she wanted to divorce George and, again, broached the idea of living with her in Verona. Horrified, Maria asked, 'How can you abandon him now, when he's old and sick?'[31] Nevertheless, she worried about her mother's eye infection, which 'does not help her peace of mind', and asked Titta 'not to speak about these matters with anyone'.[32]

Although she was ashamed of her mother's behaviour, she portrayed Litsa in a new light. 'As with all good mothers, she thinks of her children rather than herself,' she wrote to Titta. 'But she does not get along with my father …'[33] It was not lying, as such, but a form of self-preservation against the reality of her situation. She soon dropped her guard and spoke of her fear of Litsa moving to Verona. 'May God forgive me … under no circumstances am I willing to compromise my happiness and my right to be alone with you a little. We deserve that, don't we?'[34]

---

* In her memoirs, Litsa wrote that Maria and Giulietta Simionato stayed in her old bedroom at George's apartment and that he treated the women to lunch and dinner at the St Moritz Hotel. But in a letter to Maria, written in 1951, she contradicted herself and asked her to pay her father back for putting them up at the St Moritz. It was highly unlikely George could have afforded a hotel bill.

In the meantime, Maria was nervous around Simionato and offered her beer and other cold drinks.* 'She no longer knew what to do to make me feel at ease … in the end I accepted a 7-Up,' Simionato later recalled.[35] Having drunk half of it, Simionato began to vomit, but Maria remained calm and smelled the bottle. 'Strange,' she said, 'it actually smells like oil.'[36] Afterwards, she learned that her mother kept pesticide in a 7-Up bottle and, panic-stricken, she contacted her godfather and asked for help. He warned her that if Simionato died, she would be accused of poisoning her as there was no other witness to claim otherwise. 'Don't tell anyone,' she begged Simionato. 'Otherwise, the newspapers will write that I wanted to kill you.'[37]

On 14 May 1950, they arrived in Mexico City after what Maria called a distressing flight, as her legs were swollen 'badly enough to cause alarm'.[38] The climate and altitude caused her shortness of breath and heart palpitations, and contributing to her ill health was her chronic insomnia, with which she often remained awake until 8.30 in the morning. She suffered from recurring symptoms that she could not explain: low blood pressure, eczema, aching bones and fluctuating weight, for which she received electric massages. 'I move about like a cretin … I have also physical problems which take their toll,' she informed Titta, who assumed her problems were psychological.[39]

Her mind was also on Litsa, who remained in hospital, and she hoped her mother could join her in a few weeks' time. 'But will that be good for me?' she asked. 'Will she be able to help me? Who knows!!'[40]

Longing for Titta's sympathy, she said, 'I am as alone as a stray dog.'[41] Complaining of her schedule, she added, 'My dear, is it not you who always sends me on tour for that famous something known as pride?'[42]

The first performance of *Norma* was on 23 May, and Maria complained of it being 'at a time when I know I won't be at my best'.[43] Regardless, the critics called her 'a supreme soprano with an astonishing extension of voice … we shall never again hear another comparable *Norma* in our lifetime'.[44] Encouraged by the response, the manager, Antonio Caraza-Campos, asked her to sing an E flat at the end of Act Two of *Aida*, which debuted three days later. As it was not written by Verdi, she refused, but changed her mind after the tenor Kurt Baum held onto his top notes longer than necessary. Before the second act, she asked the conductor for his permission, as it would mean projecting her voice louder than the soloists, the choir and the orchestra. 'They went berserk over *Aida*,' she wrote to Titta. 'After another ten curtain calls,

---

* In a letter to Titta, Maria said it was George who gave Simionato the drink. Perhaps she did not want him to think she was careless.

I had to go out alone. My colleagues almost spit blood.'[45] Baum warned she would never sing at the Metropolitan, and then later apologised for his outburst. 'It's obvious,' she remarked, 'that he's afraid of being too brazen in his confrontations with me.'[46]

The second performance of *Aida* coincided with Litsa accusing Maria of 'leaving her to die in economical straits'.[47] When they were reunited in mid June 1950, Maria did not mention the contents of her mother's letter and Litsa thought her 'formally, sometimes ostentatiously, kind, as she might be to a distant relative, a cousin perhaps whom she had known for years and was fond of only at arm's-length'.[48]

One evening, Litsa overheard Maria sobbing and was surprised when she confided her longing for a child. Therefore, a letter sent several months later, made Litsa's words seem all the more cruel, 'Don't you know that, until her death, a mother will only care for the life and the happiness of her children and nothing else? If you think differently, my Maria, never become a mother.'[49]

Facing 'the most trying period'[50] of her life, Maria asked Simionato to dine with them, or else she and her mother would 'tear each other's hair out'.[51] One day, the three women were together when Litsa kissed Maria, who pushed her away and said, 'Don't mother! I am no longer a child.' Simionato, whose mother had died when she was 16, was outraged. 'If *I* were your mother, Maria, I'd give you a good slap.'[52] A short time later, Simionato changed her opinion, having witnessed Litsa's demands on Maria: she wanted her to give Jackie a diamond ring and a fur stole. Pushing Litsa out of the room, she slammed the door in her face, telling Simionato, 'I can't stand that woman; she has ruined my life!'[53] Then, she fell into an armchair and sobbed like a child.

Before leaving for New York, Litsa asked Maria for a monthly allowance, and would have succeeded had Maria not found her bank statement, showing she had hidden away thousands of dollars. Instead, Maria gave her $1,000 and paid her debts, as well as George's, and bought her a mink coat. She also repaid the loans her godfather had given her in 1946 and 1947.

To avoid the subject of Verona, Maria paid for Litsa to extend her stay in Mexico. Realising it was a farewell gesture, Litsa wrote:

Do you know what cinema artists of humble origins do as soon as they become rich? In the first month, they spend their first money to make a home for their parents and spoil them with luxuries; and they send their mothers for six months to a school to learn manners, how to appear and behave, in order to present them in their homes. You have nothing like that to fear. At least I can't imagine you do. What have you got to say, Maria?[54]

Back in Verona, there was no end to Maria's domestic troubles, particularly with her brothers-in-law, who visited Titta's office below their apartment. One day, she lost her footing on the staircase and fell to the ground, but Titta's brother, instead of helping her, said, 'So good for nothing that she doesn't even know how to walk down stairs.'[55] Soon after, she and Titta moved into a top-floor apartment of a palazzo, overlooking the city's bell towers and tiled roofs. She was further troubled by letters from Litsa, who continued to harass her for money, as did her sister. Afraid she would suffer a nervous breakdown and would, therefore, be unable to sing, Titta intervened and wrote to Litsa:

> I have felt for some time that the letters Maria has received from home have been upsetting her and making her angry. To prevent this from happening any more, with consequences that could be disastrous, I have decided to write to you myself. I took your last letter to a Greek [here Litsa adds, 'A whopping lie,' insinuating that Maria herself had read them to him], who translated it for me. To my great displeasure, I saw that the letter was malicious, vindictive, and offensive, and those things cannot be written by a good mother. You are full of vindictiveness which my wife does not deserve, and I return your insults to you. I also have to think of my wife's health and her dignity, seeing that she can't expect that from you. I warn you, if you write another letter I will have it translated and I will not give it to Maria. But I hope that does not happen. Think carefully, Signora, about every sentence you write. Remember, Signora, I have obligations to the family that I have made with her and to any children we may have. And I will not allow our life to be spoiled by anybody. And I shall send your letters back with the same effrontery as you show in writing them. You are a woman who has lived her life, and I do not think Maria will forget her responsibilities and her family … Be very careful not to behave in a vulgar way, and do not utter any threats. You would do better to consider your station – Maria is up to her ears in her work – and not to say whatever comes into your head.[56]

It provoked Litsa, who had since moved to Athens, to write to her estranged husband:

> If he happens to write to you too (for as you see he is a real swine), you must send us his letter and [Jackie and I] will send you a letter in Italian to put him in his place. I have told them that to me Maria is dead, and as for him, I consider him a stranger and shall simply ignore him. Never in my life did I imagine she would so degrade her family in the eyes of those Italians.

Write to her at once and tell her that it was wicked of her to get her family involved and worse still to get that Italian to insult her mother, and tell her to pay you back the money you spent for her, and never again say that you have a daughter. She once said that we were exploiters. Write and tell her to rejoice in her money, wallow in it, and enjoy her life with the Italians. It is appalling, absolutely unheard-of anywhere in the world that anyone should make four people unhappy for no reason. If you get a letter from her, put her in her place. And send it to us.[57]

Toward the end of September 1950, Maria auditioned for Arturo Toscanini, at his home in Milan, for the part of Lady Macbeth. As with Serafin, Toscanini recognised the versatility of her voice and was disappointed to learn that Ghiringhelli, whom he called 'an arrogant ass', prevented her from signing a contract with La Scala. 'I want Lady Macbeth to be ugly and evil; her voice should be hard, stifled and dark,' Toscanini remarked. 'Yours is the voice I can use.'[58] Several days later, she received a letter from Ghiringhelli, 'I have learned with great satisfaction of your meeting with Maestro Arturo Toscanini. In accordance with what he has already indicated to you, I ask you to please confirm your availability for the months of August–September of next year.'[59]

Responding to Ghiringhelli's letter, she made herself available. However, he ignored her letter and telephone calls. She later discovered that Toscanini's rival and the musical director of La Scala, Victor de Sabata, used his power to sabotage *Macbeth*.

In the meantime, she performed in Rossini's comic opera, *Il turco in Italia*, in October 1950 – its first revival in 100 years – at the Teatro Eliseo in Rome. Watching one of the rehearsals, William Weaver, a translator of Italian literature, was surprised to see 'a [tall] matronly woman in a rather bulky fur coat' who, to his surprise, was Maria.[60] She introduced Titta as 'my husband, the industrialist'.[61] Before taking to the stage, she removed a large topaz ring, 'the size of a calling card', and asked director Gerardo Guerrilla's girlfriend to look after it.[62] Weaver recalled, 'She was perfectly capable of getting laughs when she wanted. Suddenly the quiet matron I had met earlier sounded – and even looked – like a mischievous schoolgirl. Her plumpness also became part of the joke.'[63]

In the New Year 1951, Maria was suffering from a throat infection and jaundice. Despite her illness, she performed in the Verdi celebrations in Florence and Naples, beginning with *La traviata*. During the rehearsals, Serafin remarked on her weight and dowdy appearance, claiming she was too heavy to portray the tubercular Violetta.

Although his criticism was from an artistic perspective, his words awoke the complexities of her youth. 'I prefer to have people like me for my simplicity,' Maria replied, embarrassed, for she wanted to be elegant.[64] Instead, she conformed to what Titta found attractive and dismissed Simionato's advice to shave her legs, claiming her husband did not want her to.

Some of her colleagues joked at her expense, saying she had the gait of a drunken sailor. Another recalled a performance of *Tosca* and how she slammed her leading man to the ground with such a force that the stage shook. 'Impossible,' she said. 'I'm supposed to stab him, not wrestle him.'[65]

During that period, Maria experienced conflict with Erich Kleiber, who had conducted her in *I vespri siciliani* at the May Music Festival in Florence. He disapproved of her absence at a Monday morning rehearsal, even though she was not required until the afternoon and had gone to Verona for the weekend. His sarcastic comments regarding her professionalism were met with silence, until he remarked, 'I expect not only sensibility and artistic sincerity, but also basic education.'

Putting down her score, she said, 'Now, enough. You can sing *vespri* yourself.' Several hours passed and she threatened to leave for Verona unless he apologised. 'I don't like being bullied,' she later said. 'I appreciate good manners and I don't like yelling or being yelled at.'[66]

It was a memorable production: in the first *I vespri siciliani*, she thrilled audiences and critics with a high E in the 'Bolero' aria. After the third performance, Ghiringhelli visited her dressing room, bringing with him a contract for La Scala. She would agree to the contract on her own terms, one being that she sang *La traviata*. 'They expected me to beg for a role,' she said. 'I would rather have died.'[67] A verbal agreement was made with a promise to resume negotiations in the future.

Amid the triumphs of her career, Maria continued to receive letters from Litsa, demanding money. 'After all, she does have a husband,' Maria told her godfather. 'If she didn't spend money on trips maybe she would have some more to live on.'[68] Enraged, Litsa wrote:

> You write to me that I ought not to worry about you and lead my own life.
> Why, my daughter, are you being silly? To lead what life? You, of course, do
> not care if I mop floors and live in a cemetery. Shame on you!

You write twice that you are not rich but only well-off; then you ought not to have thought of marriage. And next time don't write that your house is so small that it has no space for your mother. How dare you? Did it not hurt your hand to write such a thing?[69]

Responding to her mother, Maria offered to send money, but Litsa declined, asking instead that she pay off her debt to her father, 'which he thinks is 2,000 dollars', from when she lived with him in New York.[70] Having failed to provoke Maria, Litsa wrote that she considered her dead.[71]

Seeking comfort from Titta, she thought of him and the hope of a baby as her only solace. However, he had since relinquished his share of the family business to become her full-time manager, increasing her fee to 400,000 lire. Unbeknownst to Maria, he viewed her not as his wife but a valuable product and was prepared to sell her to the highest bidder.[72]

8

Prima Donna

Already I'm covered with all the tinsel
Of the stages of frivolous theatres.

La Gioconda, Ponchielli

At the beginning of Maria's relationship with Titta, she viewed intimacy as a *prova d'amore* and, in her own words, expected affection. Deprived of love, she waited until he was asleep before wrapping herself around him, the way a child would hold onto a dog or a favourite toy. She, however, took her vows seriously and asked only for his respect and loyalty, which, she learned, was expecting too much. In a letter written in 1960, she said, 'All that I can say is that I tried my best during more than eight years to make this marriage function … I didn't have a particularly happy face before, am I right?'[1] Instead, strangers gave her affection, and her husband loved the image she represented, particularly the rewards of her success.

In the summer of 1951, she was accompanied by Titta to Mexico City to inaugurate the opera season with *Aida* and *La traviata*. In Mexico, a critic from the *Excelsior* wrote:

> God wanted to lavish his gifts on Maria: she is a beauty of majestic and distinguished comportment; she has the maximum degree of grace for acting, elegance for dressing, and temperament for attracting and moving, and, above all, a voice for singing. And what a voice! How well justified is the title *Soprano Assoluta*.

From Mexico, she went to Brazil to make her debut at the Theatro Municipal in São Paulo. Arriving with swollen legs, her health further declined during the dress rehearsal for *Aida*, forcing her to withdraw from the production. It was an ominous beginning, confirmed by the news that Renata Tebaldi was to open in *La traviata*, with the second performance reserved for Maria.

'I assure you – and I beg you to believe me – that I didn't fret about that,' Maria later said.[2] First, she sang in a single production of *Norma*, under the familiar baton of Serafin and opposite Nicola Rossi-Lemeni. Two days later, she was again conducted by Serafin, in *La traviata*, singing for the first time with Giuseppe Di Stefano.

In Rio de Janeiro, Maria was to experience several unpleasant episodes. The first occurred when a waiter delivered breakfast to her hotel room and, finding her alone, he attempted to sexually assault her. She pushed him away with such force that he gashed his head on a door handle. Afterwards, he was taken to hospital and the police came to interview her. It was she who was viewed as the violent perpetrator, although no further action was taken, and she moved hotels.

The second was the disintegration of her friendship with Tebaldi, whom she referred to as 'my dear colleague' – and their feud was no longer a fictional account in newspapers.[3] It began when Barretto Pinto, manager of the Theatro Municipal and married to the richest woman in Brazil, asked them to participate in a benefit concert for the Fundação Cristo Redentor. Tebaldi proposed, and Maria agreed, they would not sing encores. Although Maria kept her word, Tebaldi did not, and sang an encore of 'Vissi d'arte'. 'I gave this gesture only the importance that one would give to the caprice of a child,' Maria said.[4]

According to Tebaldi, their feud began over dinner with their colleagues when Maria mentioned her unsuccessful performance of *La traviata* at La Scala. Tebaldi refused to discuss it, but Maria advised her not to sing as many operas: 'This is not good either for you or the audience.'[5] Attempting to silence Maria, Titta kicked her under the table, but she turned on him, 'Leave me alone. You are *stupido*, you don't know and don't understand anything in these matters. Leave me alone, do you hear me? And don't you dare to interrupt me.'[6]

Afterwards, Tebaldi denied they were ever friends: she and Maria had been two polite strangers before the Brazilian tour. Perhaps aware of Maria's insecurities regarding her weight (she now weighed over 200lb) and her swollen legs, Tebaldi said, 'Madame Callas in life is not a beautiful woman, but on the stage, she appears beautiful.'[7] Their feud would earn them the title 'the Angel and the Devil', with Maria being cast as the latter, and their fans were divided into two categories: 'Tebaldiani' and 'Callasiani'.

During Maria's time in Brazil, she also came to mistrust Pinto, who demoralised her work. In *Tosca*, while singing an aria in the second act, someone in the audience shouted, 'Elisabetta Barbato' – referring to the Italian soprano renowned for her *Tosca* at the Theatro Municipal. The following day, Pinto delivered the news that Maria could no longer appear on subscription nights and her *Tosca* was redundant. If he cancelled *La traviata*, she told him, he would still have to pay her.

'All right,' he answered. 'But I warn you now that no one will come to hear you.'[8]

Nevertheless, her two performances of *La traviata* were successful, and to punish her, Pinto gave the remaining *Toscas* to Tebaldi. Speaking of Tebaldi, Maria said, 'She is as nasty and as sly as they come.'[9]

Storming into Pinto's office, Maria demanded her money.

'For the performance you gave,' he said, 'I shouldn't pay you anything.'[10]

In a blind rage, she lifted a bronze inkstand and intended to hurl it at his head, but his colleague restrained her and threatened to call the police.

'Presumably, Madame Callas's marksmanship was not good and that Pinto had sufficient sense of humour and presence of mind to lay her across his knee and give her a sound spanking,' Tebaldi remarked. 'He might have rendered her a good service and Madame Callas might have learned more appropriate behaviour.'[11] Several hours later, a messenger arrived at Maria's hotel room, delivering her fee and two plane tickets to Italy.

After Maria's return to Italy, she was surprised to find Ghiringhelli, Luigi Oldani, the General Secretary of La Scala, and a lawyer calling at her home unannounced. After polite introductions, Ghiringhelli spoke of money. However, she reminded him of their verbal agreement to include *La traviata*, and he consented on the vaguest of terms. Faithful to Tebaldi, Ghiringhelli was reluctant to usurp the prima donna of La Scala and advised Maria to accept the contract without the guarantee of *La traviata*. 'Let's continue this conversation next year,' she said, before seeing them to the door. Ten minutes later, they returned and invited her to open the season.

During the interim, Maria and Tebaldi's paths were to cross in Bergamo, where they alternated in *La traviata*, although Tebaldi had been taken ill after the first performance and Maria substituted for her. For Maria, there was no competition, and having listened to a recording of Tebaldi, she was overheard saying, 'Beautiful voice, but who the hell cares?' In turn, Tebaldi thought Maria had 'a voice, well-trained, but not great'.[12]

Undoubtedly, Ghiringhelli's favouritism toward Tebaldi, who had opened La Scala after its post-war renovation, was difficult for Maria to understand. It was not due to jealousy or hatred on Ghiringhelli's behalf, but a combination of greed and ignorance: he came from a rich leather-manufacturing family and, like Titta, he marketed voices the way he would his goods. However, he had no appreciation for music or performers, unless they could earn money. Although Ghiringhelli respected Tebaldi's ability to sell out La Scala, he would cast her aside for a greater phenomenon: Maria Callas.

On 25 November, Maria went to Milan to rehearse *I vespri siciliani*, conducted by Victor de Sabata, who, at first, was frustrated by her refusal to watch him. 'Maestro, why don't you look at me?' she answered. 'Your eyesight is better than mine.'

Respecting her instincts, he said, 'Maria, if only they knew how good you are, they'd love you even more.'

The evening of 7 December was one she would never forget: on that night she conquered La Scala. The *Corriere della Sera* wrote, 'The miraculous throat of [Callas] did not tremble from prodigious extension and sounds, especially in the low and middle keys, singing with a phosphorescent beauty, agility, and technique rarely to be heard.'

After her sixth performance, she went to Parma for *La traviata* and returned to Milan on 3 January for her final *I vespri siciliani*. Once again, she asked Ghiringhelli about *La traviata* and, unsatisfied with his response, she bombarded him with telephone calls, demanding to know when it would be scheduled. 'We are working to overcome difficulties,' he repeatedly said, although she did not believe him.

A week later, she left for Florence to do *I puritani* with Serafin but continued to dwell on *La traviata* and was determined to receive a final answer from Ghiringhelli. 'He thinks he can give me the runaround,' she said to Titta, 'but he will regret it.'

As an ultimatum, she refused to perform *Norma* on 16 January unless Ghiringhelli complied. However, he ignored her threat and sent a letter to finalise the rehearsal dates. Then, realising she would cancel their agreement, he wrote, 'I reassert that every matter involving Signora Callas will always be settled in a spirit of genuine cordiality.'[13]

Three days before her opening performance of *Norma*, she went to Ghiringhelli's office and said, 'It is pointless to waste time chitchatting. You promised to let me do *La traviata*, and only for that reason did I agree to sing *I vespri*.' Finally, he admitted he could not produce the opera, and she threatened to walk out of La Scala, which Titta sensed would harm her career. Instead, they reached an agreement that Ghiringhelli would stage *La traviata* the following year, and he paid her 1.4 million lire for the four non-performances.

Between 16 January and 7 February, Maria gave six performances of *Norma* at La Scala. Her portrayal of Bellini's druid priestess inspired the critics to call her 'Italy's finest dramatic lyric soprano but also an actress of exceptional gifts':

> She electrified the audience by her very presence even before singing a note. Once she began to sing, each phrase came out effortlessly ... her agility was breath-taking. Hers is not a light voice, but she negotiated the most difficult coloratura without batting an eye, and her downward glissandi made cold shivers run up and down the hearer's spine. There was occasionally a slight tendency to shrillness and hardness on the high notes, although her pitch was faultless.[14]

Afterwards, she gave four performances of *Il ratto dal serraglio*, which *Opera* called 'yet another triumph'. She was to repeat two performances of *Norma* but sang in one and cancelled the other due to illness.

At the end of April and throughout May, she alternated between Bellini's *I puritani* in Rome and Rossini's *Armida* in Florence. During a rehearsal for *Armida*, several dancers appeared on stage and began to mime what Maria was singing. 'What's going on behind me?' she asked Serafin. He explained, 'It's the dancers; it's the staging.' She responded, 'Certainly not! Either I sing or they dance. But not both.'[15] In their review, *Opera* wrote, 'She must be one of the most exciting singers on the stage today.'

During that time, she began informal negotiations with Rudolf Bing to appear at the Metropolitan in New York. Hearing of her success during the 1950 season in Buenos Aires, he wrote, 'The Colón was a big house, if she had filled that one, she could probably sing anywhere.'[16] He considered her for *Aida* and *The Magic Flute*, but felt that 'she does not look well and is an uninteresting actress', and asked Erich Engel, of the Vienna State Opera, 'Does the beauty of her voice make up for all these defects?'[17]

Letters were exchanged between Maria and Bing, as Titta could not speak English. She asked to open the 1952 season and for $700 per performance and travelling expenses, which included Titta's fare. Responding to her terms, Bing suggested a fee of $400 as she was then unknown in America, informing her that she would have to stay in New York for three weeks of rehearsals and twelve weeks of performances, returning in the spring for a tour. Agreeing to the schedule, she made a counter-offer of $600, which he refused, but offered $500 per performance for the following season, if he engaged her.

Three weeks later, she made her terms and conditions known: ten days of rehearsals, two return tickets to Italy, and in addition to *Aida*, she asked for

Norma, I puritani, La traviata and *Il trovatore*. As for the latter season, she said she would discuss it with him in person. Considering her ungrateful, he revoked his offer.

In the spring of 1952, Maria met Bing after a performance of *I puritani* in Florence. He was repelled by her 'monstrously fat and awkward' appearance, claiming she had 'a lot to learn before she can be a star at the Met'.[18] They had an amicable discussion, but neither was willing to compromise and no offer was made. After several months, Bing wrote once more, offering her *La traviata* and was certain she would accept. Weeks later, she informed him that she would not be going to New York due to the American Government declining Titta's visa, as they considered him unemployed. That was not true: he was refused entry on the grounds of his past subscription to the National Fascist Party. However, she held contempt for America's treatment of opera, saying:

> Good things are produced, sure: but too often the commercial criterion wins over the artistic. There is a certain slapdash attitude in organising operas. If the podium isn't taken up by a good director, a maestro with the backbone and temperament of your great Toscanini, the performances are affected by the wantonness of a performer trying to impose his or her personality. The United States gives fame and prosperity to singers, but it will not enhance their artistic sensitivity: in fact, it leads to compromise.[19]

Toward the end of May, Maria and Titta left for Mexico City, an engagement that lasted two months. She invited her father, with whom she was on good terms, to meet his son-in-law and to see her perform on stage. Although George had once considered singing a waste of time, after her success, he changed his mind. 'The only time we quarrel is when he brags about me,' Maria said.[20] He wrote to her:

> I take pride in being one of the happiest fathers in the world. I often remember you telling me, 'Father, if only I were offered the opportunity to prove who I am in my art, you will see!' Indeed, I boast because you have proven that you were and are deserving from every point of view.[21]

Although she was pleased to see her father, she was disappointed by the latest developments in her parents' marriage: Litsa had gone to America to sue George for maintenance payments, and a judge ordered him to pay her $25 a week. She understood his reluctance to support his estranged wife, but she also resented his affair with Alexandra Papajohn. Still, she worshipped her father from afar and ignored his faults. 'Unfortunately,' she said, 'parents exaggerate in their love and become selfish.'[22]

Despite the issues in her personal life, the problems in her career took precedence. The programme was challenging: as well as singing *Tosca* and *La traviata*, she had to learn *Lucia di Lammermoor* and *Rigoletto*. As the highest-paid singer in the history of the Opera Nacional, the management refused to make concessions. Singing opposite her in all five operas was Giuseppe Di Stefano, a Sicilian tenor who she had met in São Paulo, and to whom she was attracted. Impressed by her vocal range, Di Stefano later said, 'I was astonished and said to myself, "She sings like a man".'[23]

After her debut in *Lucia di Lammermoor*, she was called back to the stage sixteen times. However, three days later, and with the first performance of *Rigoletto*, her confidence declined. There had been insufficient rehearsals and she asked the management to substitute it with another opera, but they refused. In a review for *Musical America* it was called 'a pedestrian performance' and 'not an ideal part'; the critics and audience were accustomed to light voices and not the heavy interpretation Maria brought to Gilda, a young virgin who sacrificed herself for love.

After the final performance of *Tosca*, which concluded the season, Maria was given a standing ovation lasting 40 minutes. The orchestra introduced her with a drum roll and played 'Las Golondrinas', a traditional Mexican farewell song, and the chorus and audience serenaded her. Moved by their warmth, she knelt onstage and wept.

Before leaving, she was introduced to Dario Soria, who managed Cetra-Soria, the North American branch of Cetra. 'Don Dario, she is the greatest artist we ever had,' Antonio Caraza-Campos said. 'You must record a complete opera with her.'[24] Her contract with Cetra was nearing its end and Titta advised Soria that she would sign with Columbia, a division of EMI. Nevertheless, it was agreed she would fulfil the remainder of her contract with Cetra and record *La Gioconda*, which was also distributed by Soria's label.

The details of future contracts were insignificant to Maria, and once more she broached the subject of retiring. She wanted to try for a baby, and if successful she would retire. Instead of refusing, as he had in the past, Titta sent her to his brother-in-law, Dr Giovanni Cazzarolli, for a medical examination. As she was under 30, the doctor said she had plenty of time to conceive; however, she did not mention her husband's reluctance to help.

It was as though the fates did not want her to be happy, for during that period she received letters from Jackie and Litsa asking for money. 'After all,' Maria said, 'it's about time each one arranges their own life as I did mine.'[25] On Maria's name day, in August, Litsa wrote:

> You seem to have grown tired of me, but I, as a mother, do not grow tired of the children I brought into the world, especially you, whom I have worshipped as a god, and more …
>
> I am a straightforward person, unhypocritical, and I lose out; your good father is notoriously two-faced and a hypocrite, and he comes out on top. I may never see you again before I die, but I shall write and tell you about a great secret* of your father's, which I have been keeping to myself all these years. I hope your triumphs continue, and I hope you stay well.[26]

Although Maria's response to Litsa was destroyed – or, perhaps, did not exist – Jackie recalled that Maria advised their mother to jump in a river and drown herself. Litsa, however, said the words were written to Jackie, who was 'so angry she couldn't speak and her teeth chattered'.[27] In her memoirs, Litsa claimed that Maria wrote, 'Money is not like flowers, growing in the gardens … I bark for my living. You are a young woman and you can work. If you can't earn enough to live on throw yourself out the window.'[28]

Given Litsa's natural ability to exaggerate, she might have embellished the letter with insults. The true nature of the letter was perhaps thus: she thought her mother was able-bodied and relatively young and, therefore, could earn a living. It was not a stretch of the imagination, but Litsa preferred to cast herself as the victim. 'It's the cheapness of their souls I cannot stand!' Maria said.[29]

What infuriated Maria was Litsa's scheme to promote Jackie as an opera singer. First, Litsa consulted with the *phatoe* and mediums, whom she said predicted greatness for Jackie. Then she convinced Jackie to write to Maria, asking for help. Or had Litsa taken the initiative and written on her behalf? In a letter from Litsa to George, she said, 'Your son-in-law said in his letter that it is too soon for Jackie to ask for her sister's hospitality. "We have had her to stay with us before, some years ago."'[30]

In her memoirs, Jackie mentioned her visit to Verona in 1949, but not her later attempts to establish herself in Italy with the help of Maria. Instead, she wrote to Maria, reminding her that she 'owed a great deal to Mother's obsessive

---

* The 'great secret' was George allegedly fathering a child with the daughter of the Mayor of Meligalas.

promotion of her talents' and that, as a Greek, 'our whole ethos is to stand by our families no matter what'.[31] Sensing the hypocrisy in Jackie's sentiments, Maria told her to mind her own business.

'For me, it was the end,' Jackie said. 'In some ways, it was a relief. Maria had gone. She was now far beyond anything we could cope with.'[32]

In November 1952, Maria was invited by Sir David Webster of the Royal Opera House, Covent Garden, to give five performances of *Norma*. She felt the weight of her responsibility, for Bellini's opera, last performed in London by Rosa Ponselle in 1929, had been revived just for her:

> I was terrified by the idea of being unable to live up to expectations. It's always like that, for us artists: we labour for years to make ourselves known, and when fame finally follows our steps everywhere, we are condemned always to be worthy of it, to outdo ourselves so as not to disappoint the public, which expects wonders of its idols.[33]

Furthermore, she was singing opposite Ebe Stignani, a mezzo-soprano who first appeared at Covent Garden in 1937 and was a favourite of the British public. 'God, how she can sing,' Maria said after their first duet.[34] In the cast was Joan Sutherland, a young Australian soprano who sang the part of Clotilde. She recalled that Maria was 'easy to work with and appreciatively considerate of others'.[35] As they stood together in the wings on the opening night, Maria turned to Sutherland and said, 'God, I should've done a pee before I came up. This is a great long scene … ah well!'[36]

Regardless, she held a high D for twelve beats, inspiring critics to call her 'the most exciting singer on the stage today'.[37] *Opera* wrote, 'Callas held her audience in abject slavery.' Contradicting the praise, Ernest Newman, the musicologist and critic for the *Sunday Times*, announced, 'She is not a Ponselle.'

On 7 December, Maria returned to La Scala for *Macbeth*, conducted by de Sabata instead of Toscanini. During Lady Macbeth's sleepwalking scene, at the end of which Maria sang in pianissimo, members of the Tebaldi claque blew whistles. The *Corriere Lombardo* wrote:

> Perhaps no other opera can be considered as tailor-made for Callas as *Macbeth*. This should have been remembered by those two or three who,

with prearranged whistles, tried to harass the singer after the great sleepwalk-ing scene, thereby transforming what would have been enthusiastic applause into a triumphant interminable ovation.

As a gesture of friendship and hoping to end their feud, Maria watched Tebaldi's rehearsals from the director's box. Finding it unnerving, Tebaldi complained that Maria was trying to intimidate her. However, Maria stated otherwise, 'I shall always find something to learn in the voices of all of my colleagues … And I who have tortured myself hour after hour in search of continuous improvement shall never give up listening to the singing of my colleagues.'[38]

It was considered bad manners, and Walter Legge, artistic director of EMI, claimed to see through the guise of friendship, '[Maria] could be vengeful, vindictive, malicious in running down people she was jealous of or had taken a dislike to, often without reason'.[39] In her defence, Nicola Rossi-Lemeni spoke of her habit of watching her colleagues and asking for their advice, 'I can say one thing. How very humble she was … She was always afraid she had sung badly, that it wasn't as good as she wanted; her ambition was such that she was never satisfied with herself.'[40]

Maria went to London to perform in *Aida* to commemorate Queen Elizabeth II's coronation and complained about the threadbare costumes, tired sets and mixed reviews from the critics. 'She is at her worst in *Aida*,' the *Statesman* wrote, 'gulping through "Ritorna vincitor".' Her colleague, Michael Langdon, recalled, 'The thing I remember most about her in those early days was her delicious sense of humour. She and Simionato were always going off into peals of laughter.'[41] He recalled the ballet sequence of the triumphal scene with Maria and Simionato sitting at his feet, conversing in Italian without moving their lips. Overhearing the phrase 'Marks & Spencer', he realised they were discussing the price of their underwear.

During that period, Maria did test recordings for Walter Legge, who remarked, 'I had found a fellow-perfectionist as avid to prove and improve herself as any great artist I have ever worked with. She was always so critical.'[42]

On one occasion, she called over the microphone, 'Walter, is that all right?'

He replied, 'Maria, it's marvellous, you can go on.'

She said, 'I don't want to know if it's marvellous, is it good?'[43]

Having first heard Maria's voice on a Cetra recording in 1949, Legge declared, 'At long last, a really exciting Italian soprano!'[44]

It was in 1951 that he and his wife, the German soprano Elisabeth Schwarzkopf, had visited Tebaldi in Rome, and he, unbeknownst to his hostess, went to the opera to see Maria in *I puritani*.* After the first act, he telephoned Schwarzkopf to join him, but she declined: she was listening to a broadcast of Maria and 'neither wild horses nor the promise of supper at Passetto's could drag her from hearing the second half'.[45] At the end of the performance, he went to Maria's dressing room and offered her an exclusive contract with EMI.

The negotiations lasted for a year, and when Legge asked Maria to sign her name, Titta explained they had a superstition that prevented them from signing a contract until two weeks after it had been mutually agreed. He was given *parola d'onore* that the signed copy would be sent to London within fifteen days. However, three weeks passed before Legge sent a colleague to Verona to obtain her signature, but by this time Titta wanted EMI to increase their terms. The demands were met, and Maria signed the contract without informing Legge that she had several months remaining on her Cetra contract. 'Hers was the brilliance of the diamond, not of the sun,' he said, 'she could blind without warning.'[46]

In the autumn of 1953, she met once more with Dario Soria who, along with his wife, Dorle, was launching a new American label, Angel Records. He said:

> If Angel Records started in glory it was mostly because of Maria Callas. It was fascinating to work with her but not always easy. She knew her worth and what she wanted. What she wanted was to be the first in everything. When asked about her fee, she said: 'I am not interested in the money but it must be more than anyone else.' She asked for the most but she gave the most. She was completely dedicated to her work.[47]

Despite Maria's demanding schedule, she felt unfulfilled as an artist and had, on several occasions, clashed with Serafin. This restlessness could be attributed to the changes in her professional and private worlds: although she strove for perfection in her work, she was yet to correlate her vocal genius with her physical being. Self-conscious of her size, she once said, 'Who would want to drag all this around?'[48] She recalled her idol, Maria Malibran, the famous nineteenth-century soprano, whose father admonished her for being overweight after giving birth: 'How can you present yourself on stage with all that fat?'

There had been unsuccessful attempts to lose weight; she had electric massages and salt baths, she fasted and ate raw vegetables. It had become a problem:

---

* In his memoirs, Legge erroneously wrote that it was *Norma*. However, in 1951, her only production in Rome was *I puritani*. She performed *Norma* in 1953.

after performances in which the acting required her to fall and kneel, her legs were covered in bruises, as she often hit the stage too hard. She was also breath-less and perspiring too much and found it difficult to manoeuvre in her heavy stage costumes. At that time, she doctored her professional photos to make herself appear thinner: the photographer used nail scissors to trim around the image, thus reducing her size, and photographed it against a black background.

The criticism was painful, particularly when her colleague, Tito Gobbi, dared her to stand on the scales and was shocked by the results. Then she removed her shoes, coat and handbag, but it did not change. Her denial about her weight mirrored what others thought of her: some called her obese, while some, when she was dressed in her corseted stage costumes, thought she was 'never really fat ... she was a big woman ... Junoesque, heavy; but she knew – even then – how to move'.[49] Titta was far more blatant and called her 'a kind of clumsy, encumbered whale'.[50]

Throughout much of 1953, Maria adhered to a strict diet and lost 26lb. After her initial weight loss, she struggled to shed additional pounds and was advised by Elena Rakowska to consult with Professor Coppa, a specialist in women's health. Having relayed her symptoms, she told him of her hormonal imbalance and metabolic issues, which began in her teens and were diagnosed but never treated. He said, 'If you are sick, it is in your head. You artists are a little crazy.'[51]

However, Titta claimed she suffered from a parasitical infection – a common side-effect of eating raw meat – and several weeks after her consultation, she expelled half a tapeworm. The other half was removed by medication. It would appear the parasite caused an inflammation of her digestive system, making her body overproduce cortisol, which acts as a fat-storage hormone. After one week, she lost 6lb, which reduced her weight to around 170lb, and several more pounds followed.

Until then, she had immersed herself in the vocal techniques of opera. Now she wanted to physically embody its heroines. She said, 'You can't portray a beautiful young woman if you're enormous.'[52]

A forthcoming production of *Medea* at La Scala was her incentive: she wanted a sharp chin 'for expression in certain very hard phrases, cruel phrases or tense phrases'.[53] The director, Margherita Wallmann, thought she resembled 'a caryatid on the Acropolis ... her physical state served her well for *Medea*; she gave the character something of an antique quality'.[54] The sexual frustration from her marriage was also channelled into the part, and those 'unfulfilled passions found expression in her singing'.[55] Maria said, '[Medea] was not born to be a woman; she was not a woman. She betrayed what she was supposed to be: a sorceress.'[56]

Before the opening night, the conductor, de Sabata, withdrew and Maria suggested Leonard Bernstein, a young American conductor whose recent radio broadcast had impressed her. It would be Bernstein's first opera and he would be the first American to conduct at La Scala. Several telegrams were sent between Ghiringhelli and Bernstein: he had never heard of *Medea* and, although he admired Maria, he initially declined, as friends warned she was difficult to work with. She telephoned him and, after a long conversation, he agreed to conduct the production.

Perhaps Ghiringhelli's decision to stage *Medea* was also inspired by Tebaldi's performance of *La Wally*, which had opened to mediocre reviews. Attending the opening night, Maria smiled at Tebaldi and applauded enthusiastically, but her gestures were ignored, and her nemesis refused to reconcile. The following evening when Maria sang in *Medea*, a member of the Tebaldi claque blew a whistle and was chased from the theatre. According to Franco Zeffirelli, 'The world of opera was changed … there was BC and AC, before and after Callas.' Afterwards, she was surrounded by her fans at the stage door and, after signing autographs, she tried to disperse the crowd by saying, 'If you really love me, you'll let me go home and get some rest.'

For Tebaldi, who considered herself 'La Scala's own creation', her position was clear, and she resigned after the season. She said, '[Maria] seems to succeed in everything she desires. She wanted money – she married a rich man. She wanted clothes and jewellery – she has them now. She wanted to become thin, and she did. She wanted La Scala, and she succeeded.'[57]

L'Europeo wrote, 'If these were better times for music, Maria Callas would be the most famous woman in Europe.' For now, at least, she was the reigning queen of La Scala.

9

Metamorphosis

No, it's simply a question
of letting ourselves be taken by the waist
and listening to a compliment.

Carmen, Bizet

At the beginning of Maria's career in Italy, she was advised by Serafin to invest in beautiful costumes, for while she was not singing the audience needed something to gaze at. 'She has an innate courtesy to her audience which makes her wear her costumes for their pleasure.'[1] However, as with her opera heroines, she would create an image for the public to admire, on and off the stage.

Three years before, she had tried to improve her appearance and visited the atelier Biki of Milan, founded by Elvira 'Biki' Bouyeure, the step-granddaughter of Giacomo Puccini. Its director, Luis de Hidalgo, the brother of Elvira de Hidalgo, had seen her on stage and asked to dress her, but he lost his nerve when she entered the boutique.

In person, he was startled by the contrast between the prima donna and the woman standing before him, perusing a rack of clothing and scrutinising the prices. 'Don't waste your time on that one,' Biki remarked, horrified by Maria's shapeless suit, flat shoes and plastic earrings. Then, she asked her, 'How much do you weigh? More than 100 kilograms? Before returning to me you must lose weight as fast as possible. At least thirty kilos; no less.'

In early 1954, Maria visited a Swiss clinic run by Dr Paul Niehans, a pioneer in living cell therapy, who injected her with dried hormone extract[*] to

---

[*] Possibly TRH (Thyrotropin-releasing hormone), but Niehans was known to use cells from lamb foetuses.

stimulate her endocrine system, reducing her weight to 165lb. Unsatisfied with her progress, she sought a different treatment from Niehans in which iodine was injected into her thyroid gland. It was also rumoured that she went to another Swiss doctor for additional injections and was therefore overdosing on iodine, resulting in an overactive thyroid. Despite the risk to her health, the results were to her liking: she now weighed 140lb and her measurements had decreased from 45–35–47 to 37–28–37.[2]

Although Maria was satisfied with her new figure, she began to make other changes to her appearance. Evidence suggests she resorted to plastic surgery to tighten the skin around her arms.[3] Arm lifts (or reductions) had originated in the 1920s and were popular in the 1950s due to the trend for strapless evening gowns; the procedure was simple and advanced, with an incision made in the armpit. She would also have an eye lift and she later capped her teeth to close the gap at the front. However, she disliked her legs, which she felt were out of proportion to her slender body and consulted with plastic surgeons, who refused to operate due to her issues with fluid retention.

Having achieved her goal, Maria returned to Biki and demanded a new wardrobe from the couturier, who had once said, 'If I had to dress a woman like that I'd become crazy.'[4] Biki entrusted Maria to her son-in-law, Alain Reynaud, who had received his training from the Parisian fashion house of Jacques Fath. Having considered her style to be in bad taste, he was also sensitive to her feelings and realised she had suffered years of unkind remarks. He called her transformation a miracle. He was struck by her hands and how they had changed from 'heavy, bone-free, like pieces of rubber' to long and slender.[5] Following his advice on colours, silhouettes and accessories, she learned the rules of fashion as though it were a libretto.

During that period, Maria and Titta sold their apartment in Verona and moved to Milan, buying a small house at 44 Via Buonarroti. Its interior design of antique furniture and paintings and gold draperies was compared to a brothel with pretensions to class.[6] There was a large back garden with a pond, and she filled it with goldfish and turtles, gifts from fans who knew of her love for animals. To maintain what she called perfect harmony and perfect order, she employed a housekeeper, cook, maid and gardener. 'Her life took a sybaritic pattern,' *Time* wrote:

> In the morning she usually sang at the piano. Afternoons, she visited her
> dressmaker or her beautician, taking treatments worthy of a courtesan: cream,
> oil and electric massages and rubdowns, face packs and facials of every kind.
> When shopping, she added a wardrobe that already included twenty-five fur

coats, forty suits, one-hundred-and-fifty shoes, two-hundred dresses, and at least three-hundred hats. She never has gloves washed, just tosses them away after a few wearings.[7]

Maria was not only slim but carried herself with confidence: the woman was now at one with the artist.

After a flirtatious exchange with Giuseppe Di Stefano, she asked if he liked her new figure. 'No,' he responded, claiming he was disgusted by it. The response was typical of Di Stefano, who was known for his 'sudden flare-up of uncontrollable passion and desperate temper', often directed at Maria during their collaborations.[8] She tolerated his insults and delighted in his boyish charm, finding a companion for her repressed sense of humour, as Titta did not like her to tell jokes.[9] However, at the time, her view of marriage was puritanical, and she shared a bed only with her husband, even though he did not find her attractive. 'Fleshy women appeal to me more,' Titta said, who, unknown to Maria, visited overweight prostitutes at a brothel.[10]

In January, Maria and Di Stefano performed in *Lucia di Lammermoor* at La Scala. Conducted by Herbert von Karajan, his instincts matched her interpretation of the part. 'Lucia's world is different,' she said. 'Melancholic and emotional. Especially at the stage of madness, you understand that in her.'[11] He did not try to direct the climactic Mad Scene but instead allowed her to control it without the gimmicks of a murder weapon and fake blood. 'No kilts and sporrans for Callas,' Walter Legge had warned him.[12] At the end of the Mad Scene, they showered her with red carnations. After taking twelve curtain calls, she burst into tears, thinking she had performed badly. 'I always demolish what I do when I perform,' she said.[13]

In Berlin, she repeated the performance and also wept. 'It has happened to me once that I return home after a show and – while I was applauded – start crying bitterly because I did not succeed … in serving the composer's intentions as I felt.'[14]

After performances of Gluck's *Alceste* and Verdi's *Don Carlo*, many began to wonder if Maria's slimness had compromised the range of her voice, as she no longer had a large diaphragm to support it. Perhaps the vocal issues were due to her age. Now in her early thirties, she had been singing demanding operas since her teens, and the strain on her vocal cords was beginning to show.

'If you want to appreciate me, you must hear me often,' she said. 'I know I vary, that the voice varies, but I am always trying to do something and only sometimes will it be successful. If you don't come often, you won't catch the good performances.'[15] Critics detected it in her studio recordings, but she dismissed their theories. 'I had my greatest recordings when I was skinny as a nail.'[16]

That April, she spent ten days recording *Norma*. It was an unpleasant experience, as she was coming down with the 'flu. There was also an offer from Legge to sing the mezzo part in 'Requiem'. The lead soprano for the recording was his wife, Elisabeth Schwarzkopf. She declined: it was prima donna or nothing. No longer would she make concessions – she respected opera and, in turn, demanded respect from her colleagues.

At the Arena di Verona, she sang in *Mefistofele* but the first performance ended after Act Two due to stormy weather. She was also rehearsing *Aida,* but after disagreeing with its conductor, Fausto Cleva, she walked out. 'Is that the way you do it?' she asked him. 'Well, that's not the way I do it.' She terminated her contract and never again performed at the Arena. 'I was always requiring things for a performance, never for myself,' she later said. 'It was always for the opera, the stage, so the public would enjoy it even more.'[17]

Although Maria's recordings had made her an opera star, her physical transformation turned her into an international celebrity. 'It was like Andersen's fairy tale,' Rudolf Bing said, equating the media's interest to ticket sales.[18] He wrote once more, inviting her to perform at the Metropolitan and offered her $800 a performance on the condition she travelled alone. She wanted more money and would not travel without Titta, and thus she declined. 'If you cannot afford Callas,' Titta told Bing, 'you should put her out of your mind.'

However, she would make her American debut with the newly established Chicago Lyric Opera, who offered her $2,000 a performance and paid her expenses. It was an ambitious undertaking on behalf of its young founders: Nicola Rescigno, a conductor; Larry Kelly, an accountant; and Carol Fox, an amateur soprano, who realised their talents were of greater use behind the scenes. Naturally, given Maria's past experiences with Bagarozy, she was reluctant to accept, but after a meeting with Fox* she signed a contract.

In October, Maria arrived in Chicago to a blaze of publicity which 'put Chicago's new and improved opera company into international orbit'.[19] The press waxed lyrical about her American upbringing as the child of

---

* Maria was on first-name terms with Larry Kelly, who would become a close friend, but she always referred to Carol Fox as 'Miss Fox'. To reflect their dynamic, she will be referred to as Fox.

impoverished immigrants who had found fame and fortune abroad. Denying she had grown up in poverty, she later said her family was 'living in the best manner my father could have [provided]'.[20] She invited George to Chicago and was photographed greeting him as he stepped off the plane, and rather tellingly, he peered into the camera lens as she embraced him.

Opening in *Norma*, Maria sang opposite Nicola Rossi-Lemeni and Giulietta Simionato; critics wrote of her duet 'Mira, o Norma' with Simionato as 'something which we can tell our grandchildren about'. But it was her physical appearance that garnered the most press. 'She is as thin as a twig and beautiful within the tragic masque – with a tinge of inner-serenity. She has presence and style.'[21]

In *La traviata*, she sang with Tito Gobbi and wore costumes designed by Biki; the red bow on her ballgown matched the shade of her Elizabeth Arden lipstick. In *Lucia di Lammermoor*, she caused pandemonium and gave twenty-two curtain calls. The *Chicago Tribune* wrote, 'There was an avalanche of applause, roars of cheers growing steadily louder and a standing ovation, and the aisles were full of men pushing as close to the stage as possible.'

One such man who pursued her from afar was Bagarozy. He recalled their 1947 contract and demanded $100,000 in unpaid commission. She was advised by Rossi-Lemeni to settle with Bagarozy, as he had also fallen victim to his schemes in New York and paid $4,000 to terminate their contract. Influenced by Titta, she refused, as Bagarozy had not acted as her agent. 'It's a sacrifice to put up with the stupidity of others and yourself, because, alas, we can all be stupid,' she said, perhaps thinking of the mistake she had made as a young woman.[22] Her response to Bagarozy was indicative of her naïvety, especially after he filed a lawsuit in New York and threatened to sell her love letters to the newspapers.

In many ways, she suffered by not having a publicist and always answering questions in a forthright manner. 'I have to be honest,' she would often say, although it gave the American press a licence to manipulate her words. She never courted the press and had to be prompted by Dorle Soria to send thank-you notes, particularly to the music critic, Emily Coleman,* 'for all the wonderful things she has done for you',[23] in *Newsweek* and *Theatre Arts*:

> You know how devoted she is to you, and it would mean a great deal to her to have a note in your own handwriting. Besides, from a purely professional

---

* After 1954, Maria befriended Coleman, who remained devoted to her. 'You are a dear friend and it's good to know it,' she wrote in 1962.

point-of-view, since you are coming back to Chicago next year, I know you would not want to hurt her feelings.[24]

Now, she was as recognisable as any Hollywood star, 'She stood up, twirled about in an imitation of a model, or what she fondly believed was an imitation of a model … She said, "Surprise!" Here was a suave, utterly feminine, in a sense, freshly seductive figure.'[25]

On speculating how she lost the weight, it was believed she had swallowed a tapeworm in a glass of champagne. The practice of consuming pills made from tapeworm eggs had been around since the Victorian era and experienced a revival in the 1950s, with quack medical companies marketing chewing gum that contained the eggs. Unbeknownst to Maria, Titta repeated the rumour to a reporter from *Oggi*:

> I can tell you with certainty that the instrument of this impressive feat was a rapacious tapeworm swallowed with an iron will in a glass of champagne. I know that something so revolting as this intrusive parasite is hardly compatible with the everyday life of a diva but that's what happened.[26]

In interviews, Maria hinted that she had experienced an unpleasant condition which, in her words, was shameful:

> Something had gone wrong with me and I couldn't explain it. Doctor's couldn't explain it. All of a sudden, I found the cause … can't say it, it's not very pleasant. I cured the cause … not by medicine, I never did take any medicine, except if I have a headache – as all women do, sometimes … they take an aspirin. I watched a bit my diet, that is true, but I think it was mostly that I was supposed to grow thin and I had the good fortune to really grow thin.[27]

Nevertheless, she was flattered by the attention – a departure from the unkind remarks that were printed in the past. An Italian journalist had once written, 'As far as feminine charms were concerned Maria Kalogeropoulos had very few. Delicate health, thick ankles, obesity, and a marriage of convenience.'[28]

However, she was suspicious of those who tried to exploit her image. 'Now the public will think that I'm even doing business with my body,' she said. Two such individuals were Gino Coen, an engineer of the Pantanella pasta mills, and Titta's brother-in-law, Dr Giovanni Cazzarolli, who used her image to promote 'physiological pasta', claiming it had made her lose weight. The testimonial, written by Cazzarolli, read, 'I certify that the marvellous results obtained in the diet undertaken by Signora Callas was due in part to her eating the physiological pasta produced in Rome's Pantanella mills.'

In retaliation, Maria ordered her lawyers to file a lawsuit against the Pantanella Mills, but it was a lengthy case and one which, in terms of publicity, was not in her favour. Its president, Prince Marcantonio Pacelli, was the nephew of Pope Pius XII and, therefore, Maria was advised to accept Pantanella's settlement outside of court. However, she refused. 'I'll see this to the end,' she said, before calling Coen a fraud. Finally, in 1959, the court ruled in her favour.

In late 1954, Maria returned to La Scala to collaborate with Luchino Visconti, a film-maker and scion of one of Milan's oldest aristocratic families. 'I really admired Maria, I was truly captivated,' he said, having followed her career since *Parsifal* in 1949.[29] For years he waited for an opportunity to direct her in an opera, but Ghiringhelli prevented him from entering La Scala due to his affairs with men and wartime involvement with the Italian Communist Party.

As Maria held considerable influence at La Scala, she asked for Visconti to direct her in Spontini's *La vestale*. 'Maria has timing in her blood,' he said, 'it is absolutely instinctive.'[30] In a sense, they were both playing a part into which they were not born: she with her humble background and ability to portray a queen, and he with his non-conforming lifestyle that contradicted his aristocratic upbringing. Some spoke of her in a derogatory way, although she was never ashamed of her origins:

> Be careful when you say 'ghetto' ... music comes from there. I've almost never seen a great musician who had an upper-class background. There's something good about ghettos because if you come from there it makes you want more. It makes you say, 'One day I'll be someone.' It gives you a will to better yourself, to achieve: 'Today I am worth nothing but tomorrow I will be, and they'll listen to me.'[31]

Having grown envious of their friendship, Titta told Visconti that several television producers wanted to film *La traviata*. Visconti was furious; he thought television, with its small screen and limited production value was sacrilegious to Verdi's opera. 'How can Maria be allowed to be seduced by a project so absurd and fraught with danger?' he asked Titta. 'My God! My God!'[32] Furthermore, Titta was unamused by the light-hearted moments between the two, particularly when Visconti teased Maria for being near-sighted and led her around the stage with a scented handkerchief of Penhaligon's Hammam Bouquet.

Despite their friendliness, Visconti treated her abruptly and was overheard saying, 'Shut up, *conne*.* Sing, which is the only thing you are able to do.'

Responding to his vulgarity, she said, 'When you talk that way, you turn my stomach.'[33]

There were times when Maria had the upper hand, and Visconti would stroke her long hair, telling her it reminded him of his mother's. She followed him with a lovesick devotion, which Bing called 'the girlishness, the innocent dependence on others that was so strong a part of her personality when she did not feel she had to be wary'.[34] Sometimes, her behaviour was mistaken as flirtatious. 'I am sometimes silly,' she told her friend, Leo Lerman, who then observed, 'This was flirting, I enjoyed this game very much. I had played it many times before. So had she.'[35]

Despite a generous budget and Maria singing opposite Franco Corelli, *La vestale* was a critical failure. The libretto was at fault and not the visuals that Visconti and the set designer, Piero Zuffi, had created, taking their inspiration from the neoclassical paintings of Andrea Appiani the elder, with three-dimensional sets of marbled pillars, and antique silver on the tables. She did, however, receive thunderous applause from the audience on the first night when she approached Toscanini in his box and presented him with a red carnation.

The artistic fulfilment that Maria had achieved with Visconti was lost on her next production. She was to sing in *Il trovatore* with Mario Del Monaco, but five days before the opening night, he feigned an attack of appendicitis. Or, as Maria predicted, perhaps he did not want to be upstaged. He demanded Ghiringhelli replace it with Giordano's *Andrea Chénier*, as the tenor's part was significantly larger than the soprano's (she had one aria and two duets). On the opening night, during her aria 'La mamma morta' in the third act, the Tebaldi claque hissed,** only to be outdone by Maria's cheering fans.

The invisible presence of Tebaldi did not threaten Maria: she enjoyed the rivalry and, likewise, her nemesis agreed it was 'good for business'. When Larry Kelly asked her to open the Lyric's 1955 season, she proposed that Tebaldi sing on alternative nights, 'Then your auditorium will have the chance to compare us and it will ensure even more success for your season.'[36]

> [Tebaldi] is a vocalist of a certain repertoire. I consider myself a soprano – one who does what they used to do, once upon a time. If the time comes when my dear friend, Renata Tebaldi, will sing, among others, *Norma* or

---

* French slang for 'bitch'.

** In the 1970s, the hissing was omitted from the live recording.

Lucia or *Anna Bolena* one night, then *La traviata* or *Gioconda* or *Medea* the next – then, and only then, will we be rivals.[37]

The patterns of Maria's youth were apparent in her insecurities, and when she was unhappy in her private life, she lashed out at others. Although she was yet to admit it, she had outgrown the petite bourgeoisie life she shared with her husband. She was often embarrassed by Titta's behaviour; he was no longer her protector but a hindrance. He could demand the highest fee while her fame permitted it, but she was ashamed of how he harassed the rich patrons of La Scala and was not oblivious to their looks of disgust. At times, the hostility from her colleagues was provoked by his meddling in her affairs, often lying and turning her against them.

Admittedly, she gave a better performance when she was angry. 'You know that she can be a beast when she wishes,' a friend observed, 'but oh those prima donna smiles, wiles, and graces.'[38]

One incident, in particular, happened during the recording of *Aida* with Richard Tucker.* She was unable to command her voice and fell into a dark mood. On the ninth day, she recorded several takes of 'O patria mia' and, unhappy with the results, she spoke harshly to Serafin and rebuffed Tucker when he complimented her. Then, as Tucker sang 'Pur ti riveggo', she paced behind him. The sound of her high heels was detected by the microphone and the engineers had to stop the recording.

'I want everyone in this theatre to realise that the music of *Aida* is *very* sacred to me,' she said. 'For me to make a recording of this sacred music, I must have complete cooperation in this theatre. No one must distract me at any time!'[39] She pointed to a box where the philanthropist Fredric R. Mann and his family were sitting and demanded they leave, or she would. 'Sometimes she has to make trouble in order to sing well,' Serafin remarked to Tucker. 'Sometimes she needs to fight – it is her nature.'[40]

In the New Year of 1955, Maria was preparing to open at La Scala in Bellini's *La sonnambula*, directed by Visconti and conducted by Leonard Bernstein. It was delayed by two weeks due to her suffering from exhaustion and having a large boil on her neck. 'Callas is still abed with her *furunculo*, being a

---

* In 1955, Maria made recordings of *La sonnambula*, *La vestale*, and *Rigoletto*, conducted by Serafin; and *Madama Butterfly*, conducted by Karajan.

real old-fashioned prima donna,' Bernstein wrote to his wife.[41] When they met, at their first reading of the libretto, she moved him to tears with her interpretation of Amina, an orphaned peasant whose engagement to a rich farmer is threatened after villagers accuse her of committing adultery.

During the rehearsals, which lasted until four o'clock in the morning, Visconti wanted her to channel Marie Taglioni, a prima ballerina of the romantic era. He taught her how to move like a dancer, and to adopt the fifth position when standing still. In the sleepwalking scene, she used breath control to create the illusion of falling from a broken plank; her sudden exhalation caused the audience to gasp. 'She was a magician of the theatre,' costume designer Piero Tosi said. 'She knew all the tricks.'[42] In comparison, Bernstein called the production 'slightly camp', particularly the sight of Maria in a peasant's dress and covered in moonstones, singing her final aria on the stage apron, with the great chandelier ablaze and carnations flying from the boxes.[43]

In her next opera, *Il turco in Italia*, directed by Franco Zeffirelli, she complained of the empire waist costumes. 'All that dieting and you give me a waistline up here,' she said.[44] Having been cast in the mould of a tragedienne, she now struggled to relate to the comic part of Donna Fiorilla, although audiences responded to her deliberate overacting and silliness toward the Turk (Nicola Rossi-Lemeni), who dazzled her with his jewels. Although it was not in the original libretto, Zeffirelli drew on Maria's love of jewellery and covered Rossi-Lemeni in ruby rings, and by the end of their courtship, it was Donna Fiorilla who was wearing the jewels.

At the end of May, Visconti realised his dream of directing Maria in *La traviata* at La Scala. For three weeks, he and the conductor, Giulini, worked with Maria, creating their vision of Violetta, which differed from the Rome production of 1953, in which she wore the heavy crinolines of the 1850s. Instead, Lila de Nobili's costumes were modelled on the narrow silhouettes of the late eighteenth century, with bustles and trains in shades of maroon, gold and black – the colours denoting the phases of Violetta: courtesan, opulence, death. Striking the balance between realism and magic, the sets drew inspiration from the La Belle Époque, its Chinese vases and silk screens were, to the discriminating eye, brushstrokes. The realism, however, was found in Violetta: she sang in a tired voice and her rigid movements conveyed rigor mortis, as death consumed her, and she died with her eyes open.

During the rehearsals, Maria disagreed with Visconti's direction of the final scene: he wanted her to put on a hat before losing her strength and collapsing into the chair. Maria disagreed: she believed it was unrealistic, and said, 'The hat is the very last thing you put on before leaving the house. Violetta wouldn't have got that far.'

There was further tension between the cast, whom Maria described as listless, particularly Di Stefano, who sang the part of Violetta's lover, Alfredo. He clashed with Visconti and disliked his direction, thinking he paid more attention to the details than to the singing. 'It's a lack of respect for me, a lack of regard for you also,' Maria remarked to Visconti, who told her to forget about him.

After the first performance, she took a solo curtain call, and Di Stefano walked out of the production and was replaced by Giacinto Prandelli. 'No one is indispensable,' she said of his absence.[45] She was accustomed to fighting with her male colleagues: Mario Del Monaco started a rumour that she had kicked him in the shins to prevent him from taking a solo bow. 'I think that people who spread such stories should be ashamed of themselves,' she said.[46] In her defence, the singer, Nicola Zaccaria, said, 'Maria Callas, of course, had a very strong personality. This personality suited her very well in everything that she could do. Some people felt antagonistic when faced with her personality, and so some hostility was created.'[47]

Much of the discord came from the Tebaldi claque, who had sent anonymous letters to Maria, warning her that she would be whistled. Nothing occurred on the first two nights, but on the third she noticed many critics in the audience, who had been invited by an anonymous letter writer, promising it was 'a chance to have some fun'. When she made a provocative movement with her pelvis – perhaps a nod to Violetta's origins – as she leaned against a table, someone shouted, 'This is a scandal!' Their words distracted her and the production came to a halt.

'The audience's slightest reaction affects us. At times one feels oneself to be enormous, larger than the theatre. At other moments, one is small, tiny, one feels ashamed, one would like to run away, one is terrified.'[48] Turning to her colleagues in the wings, she said, 'They are hissing up there like snakes. They are after my blood.' She composed herself and sang to her detractors in the gallery, prompting the audience to applaud.

During its revival in January 1956, the Tebaldi claque continued to disrupt the performance and someone threw a bunch of radishes onto the stage. Owing to Maria's near-sightedness, she mistook the radishes for roses and kissed them. However, she realised her error and displayed them to the audience, who applauded louder than before. A misjudged insult, perhaps, for radishes were so valued by the ancient Greeks – it was also believed they cured consumption – that replicas were made in gold.

In October 1955, Maria arrived in Chicago, unaware of the tempest that awaited her. She opened the Lyric's season with *I puritani*, conducted by Nicola Rescigno, singing with Rossi-Lemeni and Di Stefano. The excitement of her arrival was typical of American publicity, something she could not fathom. They called her the European Marilyn Monroe, and one critic wrote, 'I adore the woman; I am a slave in her spell.'[49]

Claiming to dislike the attention, Maria said, 'It astonishes me, it irritates me. I don't put myself on exhibit. I live in seclusion. I am wild, very.'[50] Carol Fox accused her of being 'too Hollywood' and resented the demands which Dorle Soria, acting as her unofficial publicist, made on her behalf, such as, 'Don't forget that Papa Callas is coming to Chicago and must be taken care of.'[51] There was an Angel Ball, organised to celebrate Maria's opening at the Lyric, and Soria sent Fox a lengthy guest list, full of last-minute changes to the seating arrangements.

Still, the blaze of publicity continued, and the *New York Times* critic, Howard Taubman, wrote:

> Miss Callas is the 31-year-old soprano who is credited with having restored the ancient lustre to the title of prima donna … Tonight, they were waiting for her with palpable excitement. When she stepped out on the stage in the second scene of the first act, there was such an ecstatic greeting that the show was stopped dead in its tracks. Thereafter she could do no wrong. Chicago is that way about her. And you can't blame Chicago.

The arrival of Rudolf Bing vexed Fox, who viewed him as a rival. He came to obtain Maria's signature on a contract that they had discussed in the spring, having offered her *Lucia di Lammermoor* and *The Magic Flute*. However, she complained of his choice of conductor, Fausto Cleva. When Bing refused to replace Cleva, she declined to sing *The Magic Flute* in English.

On the second night of *Madama Butterfly*, she learned that process servers, acting on behalf of Bagarozy, were waiting outside the theatre and avoided them by leaving in a freight lift and spending the night at Fox's mother's apartment. After her final *Madama Butterfly* with Di Stefano, she was ambushed in her dressing room by the county sheriff, who pushed the court summons down the front of her kimono, therefore making the bodily contact that was legally required. She told the sheriff and his ten police officers, 'I will not be served! I have the voice of an angel! No man can touch me!'[52]

The Lyric's press agent, Danny Newman, had arranged for photographers to wait backstage and they captured her following the sheriff, screaming multi-lingual abuse in his wake.[53] Bursting into tears, she warned, 'Chicago will be sorry for this. I will never sing here again.'

To Dorle Soria, she wrote, 'I could not [have] been treated worse ... Only one thing you should keep in mind: don't trust them! When I write to you the details you will freeze in horror.'[54]

However, Maria suspected Fox was behind the sabotage and had allowed the process server and policemen to go backstage, and had collaborated with Newman in an attempt to humiliate her. Having confronted Fox with her suspicions, she also accused her of breaching the terms of their contract and implied she would sue the company. Turning to Maria, Fox screamed, 'Get out of my theatre, you dirty Greek bitch!'

The career that had been her first love would soon demand more than she could give. Nevertheless, a critic wrote, 'Maria Callas is still a star ... skip the rest.'[55]

10

Scandal

Fever of jealousy.
Now I sink exhausted
In the darkness!
I am reaching the end …

La Gioconda, Ponchielli

In Milan, Maria instructed her American lawyer, Walter Cummings, to counter-sue Bagarozy who, in his legal statement, claimed he had spent $85,000 launching her career.[1] Further complicating matters, he had sold her contract to Zenith Management, who was suing her for $30,000; an estimated 10 per cent of her earnings from 1 November 1954 – the date in which he relinquished his rights – until 27 October 1955.

In her statement to the United States District Court, she said, 'I know I was stupid to place my trust in Bagarozy, but I was young and I imagined he would feel sorry for me after the collapse of the opera season in Chicago.' She accused him of obtaining her signature through 'fraud and duress', as he refused to give her a ticket to Italy unless she signed the contract.[2] However, Bagarozy claimed it was Maria's idea to sign the contract as a way to reimburse him. His brother, Guy, reiterated this and said she would have 'made a deal with the devil, or even sacrificed her own mother, to achieve her artistic goals'. Refuting her statement, Bagarozy told reporters:

Having engaged in this cat and mouse game, Miss Callas now takes the position of someone who is being harassed and annoyed and I am made out to be an interloper or Johnny-come-lately who is trying to latch onto the success of a fabulous performer.

Amid the legal entanglements, Maria opened in *Norma* at La Scala. The premiere, five days after her 32nd birthday, was a gala evening in honour of Giovanni Gronchi, President of the Italian Republic, and for the occasion the theatre was decorated by Pierre Balmain.

She sang with Mario Del Monaco who, during the rehearsals, told Ghiringhelli there would be no solo curtain calls. After del Monaco's first-act aria, he devised a plan to undermine Maria and arranged for the Tebaldi claque, led by the ageing tenor, Ettore Parmeggiani, to give him an ovation. Titta reproached Parmeggiani, and del Monaco responded that the Meneghinis did not own La Scala, nor could they control the audience. Afterwards, the claque hurled vegetables toward the stage, and despite Maria's insolence in receiving them, she went to her dressing room and cried.

The audience now expected a scandal: she had become known as the tigress of opera and warned, 'I'll do everything I can so as not to dismount my tiger'.[3] They were disappointed by her next opera, *Il barbiere di Siviglia*, a production so bad that Giulini conducted with his head down so as to not make eye contact with the stage. There was also *Fedora*, set in Imperial Russia, and her interpretation of Princess Fedora divided the musical circles of Milan. Some thought her brilliant, and others thought it a waste of her talent.

In June 1956, Maria went to Vienna with La Scala to perform in *Lucia di Lammermoor* at the Vienna State Opera, under the baton of Herbert von Karajan.[*] On the opening night, the President of Austria, Theodor Körner, was in attendance, and after her performance, the audience applauded for twenty minutes. The excitement she generated was somewhat overlooked by critics, even her most ardent supporters; in particular, Claudia Cassidy of the *Chicago Tribune* found that 'her voice just simply doesn't respond'.[4]

The lapse in Maria's voice was due to her disenchantment with Karajan, who allowed an encore of the sextet that preceded the equally taxing Mad Scene. Infuriated, she kept her back to him during the scene. Years later, she asked, 'Now, tell me, what was it you did when I was so bitchy and turned my back on you in the Mad Scene? I knew you were clever. But the accompaniment was so perfect. I decided you were not only a genius; you were also a witch.'[5] It was simple: he had watched her shoulders to determine her breath control, and that was his 'cue for attack'.[6]

---

[*] Months before, Maria had sung *Lucia di Lammermoor* in Naples and complained that her conductor, Francesco Molinari-Pradelli, lacked the artistry of Karajan. She wrote to Walter Legge, 'I simply can't hear the opera without [Karajan]. Tell him I miss him and it is a shame we don't work more together.'

Following *Lucia di Lammermoor*, Karajan wanted to stage La Scala's production of *La traviata* at the Vienna State Opera for the 1957 season, thus replacing Giulini. It provoked a furious response from Visconti:

> I am dismayed by your news. I thought of Giulini who, through so much love and dedication, personally contributed to the success of this production of *La traviata*. Does it not seem to you to be a great slight to this maestro – unfair and tactless?[7]

The production with Maria was abandoned due to contractual differences with the management regarding her fee, which Titta had increased by 30 per cent. Instead, Karajan staged it with Virginia Zeani, the Romanian-born soprano who had also replaced Maria in a 1952 production of *I puritani*. The result was unsuccessful. 'As the saying goes,' Visconti wrote, 'he who speaks last speaks best.'[8]

In the meantime, she was disappointed when Serafin conducted EMI's *La traviata* with Antonietta Stella singing the part of Violetta. Legally, Maria could not participate in the recording, as a pre-existing clause in her contract with Cetra prevented her from recording the opera until 1957. At the time, however, she thought Serafin could have waited and blamed him for the lost opportunity. The press wrote of a feud, portraying her as ungrateful toward the elderly man who had launched her Italian career:

> Her decision automatically eliminates him from his old job as conductor for her opera recordings and the old man is finding that other singers are now mysteriously unable to sing under him. Says he: 'She is like a devil with evil instincts'. Says La Callas: 'I understand hate: I respect revenge. You have to defend yourself. You have to be strong, very, very strong. That's what makes you have fights.'[9]

Although Maria denied a feud, confidential documents between Walter Legge and his EMI colleagues revealed the truth, 'Callas flatly refused for the future to record any opera with Serafin and insists that the Company shall take the responsibility for the change of plans, and that Serafin is never to know that it is she who refuses.'[10]

In the summer of 1956, Maria and Titta went to Ischia. She spent her days by the sea, snorkelling and playing with her poodles, Thea and Toy, whom she had recently acquired. 'So much cuddling,' Titta said of her devotion to the dogs. Detecting the jealousy in his voice, she asked, 'Whom should I be cuddling? My colleagues?'[11]

There, she received news from her lawyer regarding Bagarozy. He planned to exhibit three letters* that she had sent him from Verona in 1947, asking for advice regarding her career and detailing her intimate feelings for him, despite being courted by Titta. 'In the hope of always being considered your Maria,' she wrote to Bagarozy in August 1947, and in October, when she was living with Titta, she wrote, 'Okay, I'm ending this long, long letter with a big kiss on both cheeks and … one on your sweet, tempting mouth, but I'm afraid I would be unfaithful to Battista, for that would be too dangerous!'[12]

On the eve of Maria's Metropolitan debut, Bagarozy threatened to sell her letters to the press and Titta knew scandal was on the horizon. Her lawyer consulted with the Metropolitan's legal representatives and it was understood that the company would protect her from Bagarozy and any process servers. Writing to Rudolf Bing, she complained of having to pay 'someone whose contribution to my career and my artistic development is not the weight or the value of a grain of sand'.[13] The Metropolitan offered to deposit her fee into her Swiss bank account but Titta declined, asking for it in cash, and Bing, who 'hated [him] to death',[14] paid him in $5 bills.

At the airport, she was met by Francis Robinson, the Metropolitan's assistant manager, and a lawyer, both of whom escorted her to and from her hotel and attended her press interviews. 'Madame Callas, you were born in the United States, you were brought up in Greece, you are now practically Italian. What language do you think in?' a reporter asked.

She said, 'I count in English.'[15]

Her hostility toward the press was due to a *Time* investigative article. The reporter had travelled to Athens to interview Litsa, but Jackie refused to comment and thought her mother had spoken too freely, thus influencing the reporter to adopt a biased view against Maria, 'who was just a naughty girl who needed a smack'.[16]

Denying her mother's claims, Maria said, 'They say my family is very short of money. Before God, I say why should they blame me? If someday I need help, I wouldn't expect anything from anybody.'[17]

However, unbeknownst to Maria, the 'most cooperative sources'[18] were Dario and Dorle Soria, who had assisted *Time*'s researcher:

---

* See Chapter 5 for further excerpts from Maria's letters to Bagarozy.

I wish to extend sincerest thanks for your generous assistance during the preparation of our current cover story on Maria Callas. We are indebted to you for all the time you gave not only during the past ten weeks, but over a period of years to dig up facts about Callas.[19]

Before the *Time* article was published, the artist Henry Koerner went to Milan to paint her portrait for the cover. He compared her to a New York career girl and decided he hated her, but derived pleasure from making her suffer during their long sittings. The photographer, Horst P. Horst, also found her difficult, and during their session in his New York apartment 'you could cut the air with a knife'.[20]

Cecil Beaton, who photographed her, said, 'Miss Callas looks less like a singer than a smart woman playing bridge for high stakes. When she speaks Italian, she is an artist, but the myth is shattered the moment that Brooklynese* pours forth.' It contrasted with the experience of Henry Sell, the editor of *Town and Country*, who met Maria backstage at the Metropolitan:

Golly, wouldn't it be FUN to be RICH and madly in love with her! What a wonderful ride through the stormy nights and sultry days … Anything on her is a masquerade … I know the photos** that can catch her as she should be caught … She is inner-lighted.[21]

Attempting to counteract the *Time* article, William Weaver, who had first met her in 1950, wrote an article entitled 'Just Plain Maria':

Fortunately for her admirers, she has never been and never will be 'just plain' anything. She is something far more thrilling than an opera star. To the stranger, meeting her for the first time, she may not seem immediately loveable; but the more one knows her, the more one admires her infinite courage and devotion to her work.[22]

During the rehearsals for *Norma*, the humidity of the Indian summer affected Maria's voice and she began to feel unwell. One of her admirers, Marlene Dietrich, had prepared beef tea and delivered it in a thermos flask. 'Mmm, it's

---

* Ahead of Maria's New York debut, many newspapers reported that she was born and raised in Brooklyn. The New York census for 1956 lists a Maria Callas living in Brooklyn.

** 'Our babe certainly can give out with a strong LOOK,' Sell said of the photographs.

good, it's delicious. Which stock cubes do you use?' Maria asked. Recalling the incident, she said, 'How was I to know she was such a *hausfrau*?'[23]

They had met once before, introduced by their mutual friend, Leo Lerman, who remembered Maria looking at Dietrich's endless legs and smiling, causing Dietrich to laugh. 'There was a finishing-school atmosphere,' Leo recalled. 'They fell to chatting.'[24] Dietrich told her, 'But, liebling, you should really not have such hair. But liebling, I know exactly the right hair for you.' Putting her hand on Maria's shoulder, Dietrich crooned, 'I will help you.'[25]

At their second meeting, Dietrich invited Maria to recuperate at her apartment but she declined. 'Oh no, I wasn't going to get involved in that set-up. I didn't want my name associated with that lady-lover.'[26]

At the first performance of *Norma* on 29 October, Maria was overcome by nerves and gave an uneven rendition of 'Casta diva'. She was further unnerved by Zinka Milanov's[*] arrival during the intermission and the audience's thunderous applause as the diva walked to her seat. Despite this, she respected Milanov, who debuted in *Norma* at the Metropolitan in 1943, and remarked, 'I was afraid she could see straight through me. She was gracious, but still, I was quite intimidated.' Later, Milanov said:

> Callas, to put it simply, took advantage of possibly cheap publicity stunts and major and minor scandals. Those advanced her career. But they did not detract from the fact that she was an excellent singer, a special singer. Her career was quite short but good. By the time she debuted at the Metropolitan, her voice was already not at the standard audiences expected.[27]

Although Bing claimed Maria was not in the best voice, she was spurred by Milanov's stunt and sang with ferocity. 'When my enemies stop hissing, I'll know I've failed,' she said. 'They only make me furious, make me want to sing better than ever to drive the rudeness down their throats.'[28] At the end, she was showered with roses and, moved to tears, she presented them to her colleagues.

'For me, she is exciting and deeply moving – her sense of design, her never-failing animal-like absorption in the instant – that spiral of inner activity which

---

[*] According to Bing, after the second performance of *Norma*, someone from Milanov's claque threw radishes onto the stage, which Maria mistook for tea roses. She made no mention of the incident, and presumably she never picked up the radishes. However, Maria denied this. 'If I had received vegetables in homage in America, too, I would calmly tell you about it, as I did with regard to *La traviata*.'

is rare and devastating to watch,' Martha Graham, the dancer and choreo-grapher, wrote.[29] The critics remained ambivalent:

> It is more restrained in action, more deliberate and yet somehow less impos-ing ... She is treating her voice more kindly now and no longer is putting it through the torturous paces in the interest of emotional expression which, in Chicago, made one fear for its safety ... There is now a certain monotony in the quality ... what she does may not always enrapture the ear.[30]

Five days later, Maria was to give her second performance at a matinee, but sent word from her dressing room that she had a cold and was unable to sing. Bing found her with Titta and a doctor; the overture had begun to play, and he convinced her to go on, saving the Metropolitan from, what he called, a riot.

Noël Coward, who watched from Bing's box, admired Maria as an actress but was 'not so mad about her voice ... she delighted him'.[31] He attended three times and wrote in his diary, 'She completely captured me. True, her high notes were a bit scratchy but she is a fine singer, beautifully controlled and in technical command of every phrase.'[32] There was an ovation, 'the like of which I have seldom heard ... it was fascinating to see how her quality triumphed with that vast, prejudiced, over-knowledgeable audience'.[33]

In the next production, *Tosca*, the critics were unanimous in their praise:

> Act II was hair-raising, Callas entered Scarpia's den looking like the Queen of the Night ... When it was over the audience came back to reality and howled like the West Point cheering section while Maria Callas curtsied, hugged herself and blew kisses through fourteen long curtain calls. Giuseppe Campora doggedly appeared* with her every time, although toward the end he began to look rather tired of keeping up with Callas.[34]

Although Visconti had warned Maria against performing opera on television, she sang the second act of *Tosca* on *The Ed Sullivan Show*. In her review for the *Chicago Tribune*, Claudia Cassidy wrote:

> I had not expected to find it butchered to a jigsaw of fifteen minutes, mis-erably crowded on a clumsy stage, and so horribly photographed that the

---

* It was against the rules of the Metropolitan to take solo curtain calls. However, after the opening night of *Norma*, Mario Del Monaco forgot his earlier hostility and pushed her onto the stage alone.

lovely Callas was turned haggard as a witch. She sang like a changeling too. I would not have believed 'Vissi d'arte' if I had not seen it coming out of her mouth, a shrill, shaky ghost of alluring Callas song … But there it was, just a dud. Not a spark, not a gleam, just an inexcusable blunder.

Two days later, the Metropolitan Company staged a single performance of *Norma* at the American Academy of Music in Philadelphia. Referring to her as 'Maria-You-Know-Who', the *Musical Courier* wrote, 'Callas is a human being; not a goddess. She certainly sang like no goddess.'

The critics' hostility peaked in *Lucia di Lammermoor*, her final production for the Metropolitan. 'What it all boils down to is that either one falls under her spell of this artist's fascination and willingly accepts her limitations in exchange for it – or one does not,' *Musical America* wrote. In a similar review, the *New York Times* compared her high notes to desperate screams but found her interpretation of the role 'interesting, and, occasionally even thrilling … Miss Callas again showed herself to be a remarkable singer, but she also showed that her striking physical resources have their limits'.

In the second performance, her colleague, Enzo Sordello, held a note too long which made her look short of breath. '*Basta!** You will never sing with me again,' she hissed.

Sordello replied, 'And I will kill you.'

Afterwards, Maria went to Bing and demanded he fire Sordello, or she would leave the production. For Bing, the solution was clear: he found Sordello argumentative and uncooperative, and he cancelled the remainder of his contract. However, Bing did not correct the reporters who wrote of her kicking Sordello and calling him a bastard – he exploited the '*basta*' remark – and was solely responsible for the termination of his contract.

The reviews had become more than criticism, and the columnists used their platform to attack her. Elsa Maxwell, an elderly gossip columnist who loved Tebaldi and hated Maria, called her 'a devious diva' and 'an egocentric extrovert'. Several days later, Maria attended a benefit for the American Hellenic Warfare Fund at the Waldorf Astoria and encountered Maxwell. 'Miss Maxwell,' Maria said, 'you are the one woman in New York I do want to meet, because … you are honest.' At the end of the evening, Maria flashed the smile of a sorceress and asked, 'I will ring you, if I may?' For Maxwell, a lesbian, it was love at first sight.

* Italian for 'enough'.

Days later, Maria gave her final performance* of *Lucia di Lammermoor* without Sordello. However, she continued to be harassed by him – he tore up her photo in front of reporters and booked a ticket on the plane taking her back to Italy. Flanked by photographers, he approached her and offered a festive greeting before suggesting they shake hands. 'First, you must apologise,' Maria said, but he refused, so she shrugged her shoulders and walked away. 'I don't like this man taking advantage of my publicity,' she told the reporters.

In the New Year of 1957, Maria returned to New York to attend a ball at the Waldorf Astoria in aid of the Hospitalised Veterans Service of the Musicians Emergency Fund. A member of the women's committee wrote, 'We thought it would be a stunning idea to ask Madame Callas to appear in a tableau at our Imperial Ball as Theodosia, Empress of Byzantine, or Poppea, Empress of Rome.'[35] Instead, she attended as the Egyptian Empress Hatshepsut, wearing a gold lamé gown and Harry Winston emeralds worth a million dollars. The guest of honour was the Aga Khan, but at the helm was Elsa Maxwell, who wrote in her column, 'It seems Maria and I are going to be friends'.

Four days later, Maria gave a concert in Chicago for the Allied Française in aid of Hungarian relief. At the first rehearsal, she clashed with the conductor, Karl Böhm, after he disagreed with the tempo for 'Ah! non credea mirarti' from *La sonnambula*, resulting in him walking out. 'I have severe standards. More severe for my own work than for anyone else,' she said. 'I will accept no artistic compromise that might lead to a poor performance.'[36]

Many were unnerved by her calm demeanour, although she was preparing for battle, having created 'the ideal emotional climate to trigger … that impetus she craved for big events'.[37] She asked for Fausto Cleva to replace Böhm, and he was engaged at the cost of her reputation, for the press now portrayed her as a tyrant. Of the concert, Claudia Cassidy wrote, 'It was not beautiful, for it was forced to a degree altogether perilous to the human voice so mistreated … It was a triumph for Callas, unless you value her so highly you want her restored to her incomparable best.'[38]

Following an absence of four years, Maria went to London to give two performances of *Norma* at the Royal Opera House. 'They have gone crazy and thank God all the bad talk has calmed down,' she said. 'Probably they exaggerated too

---

much and the people understand.'[39] It was a reprieve from the negativity she had experienced in America, and the English reporters spoke of the excitement her performances had generated.

On the opening night, she 'was practically canonised by the audience' and received a six-minute ovation.[40] In the second performance, she and Ebe Stignani gave an encore of the cabaletta to 'Mira, o Norma', causing pandemonium, as it was the first encore given in a quarter of a century at Covent Garden.

Many critics thought her voice had declined. *The Times* reported, 'It cannot be said that the voice itself has become more beautiful … the singer's sense of pitch was apt to stray in either direction.' *Opera* agreed, 'Her voice proved less rich than before, with occasional shrillness and a new hard edge.' However, *Musical America* wrote, 'Miss Callas's voice was in fine fettle, and apart from the now accustomed sour note and occasional off-pitch singing, we found her better than ever.'

Before leaving London, Maria recorded *Il barbiere di Siviglia*, conducted by Alceo Galliera, which, along with her appearances at Covent Garden, were almost sabotaged by England's quarantine rules regarding dogs. She refused to go without her poodle, and Walter Legge wrote, 'If La Divina makes it a condition of coming to London to bring her dog with her, then we are bitched.' Refusing to be held ransom to her demands, Legge suggested she smuggle her dog through customs at her own risk, but in the end, she travelled without it.

After a period of overwork and intense scrutiny, Maria began to experience a change in her outlook. She viewed Titta from a new perspective, although she internalised her feelings and suffered due to his greed for money and inability to deal with the press. 'Glory went to his head. Glory goes to other people's heads,' she said. 'Not my head. Glory terrifies me.'[41]

The dynamic between Maria and her father was also changing:

My dear Maria, it has been fifty days since I heard from you, not even a few words to let me know how you are. You can't use the excuse that you're always so busy because it wouldn't take more than five minutes of your time, or Battista's, to send even one cutting from a London newspaper to let me have your news. However, I hope that you are well, even if you don't write to me.[42]

There were further conflicts: the *Time* article was of interest to the Italians, who viewed her treatment of Litsa as sacrilegious – a contrast to Tebaldi's devotion to her mother. After its publication, Tebaldi wrote a letter to the editor, responding to Maria's alleged comment, 'When I'm angry I can do no wrong. I sing and act like someone possessed [but Tebaldi wilts]. She's got no backbone. She's not like Callas.'[43] In response, Tebaldi said, 'I have one thing that Callas doesn't have: a heart.'

Although Maria claimed that Tebaldi 'does not interest me at all … the only thing that interests me is my husband, first of all, my health, second of all, of course, and myself …'.[44] Letters written in 1957 prove otherwise, and she asked her friends to report on any gossip relating to Tebaldi. 'You try and find out from honest people who might know and let me know.'[45]

To Dorle Soria, she accused Tebaldi of having had 'fame on the expense of being my rival … isn't her agent smart – whomever it is?' She speculated that Tebaldi's mother, who had suffered a heart attack, as having 'nothing special wrong with her'* and called it 'a beautiful piece of publicity … I'm surely fed up with all this nauseating poor Renata business. I think it really has gone too far. God does not like such methods for publicity and weapons against me'.[46]

The troubling episode was punctuated by Bagarozy's case, which was eventually settled out of court in the autumn of 1957. A letter to her American lawyer, Walter Cummings, demonstrated the frustration she felt toward Bagarozy and the fear he could destroy her, both 'morally and financially'.[47] She asked, 'Who guarantees me all this [defamation and financial] damage: Bagarozy?'[48]

The date of the court hearing coincided with Maria's concert in Dallas and the opening of La Scala's season. 'I can't miss contracts like that. You realise the scandal that comes out of each of my cancellations by illness – imagine for a lawsuit,' she wrote to Cummings. 'It's out of the question! My name and career [are] at stake.'[49] Therefore, to avoid another scandal, Maria implored Cummings to 'find a way out … I cannot live in this ridiculous way'[50] and offered Bagarozy 'a modest payment'** to return her letters. The only redeeming part of the Bagarozy scandal was that he died less than a year later and was eradicated from her life.

Not everything could be settled with money, and the game of cat and mouse that Titta had initiated with the press was closing in on her. No longer could she run away from her past, nor could she fight Litsa's attacks

---

* Two weeks later, Tebaldi's mother died of heart failure.

** Maria never disclosed the amount she paid to Bagarozy, except to hint it was around $15,000.

with silence. Capitalising on the tabloid interest, Litsa revived her scheme to launch Jackie's career and contacted the Metropolitan. As part of her plan, she found an elderly Greek-American couple, the Zarras, to sponsor Jackie, and they went to New Jersey to meet their benefactors, who turned out to be impoverished fans of Maria. Failing to become a singer, Jackie left for Athens and Litsa remained in New Jersey, living off their kindness. There was further embarrassment for Maria when she learned that George had begun divorce proceedings.

Maria was protective of her private life and paranoid about gossip so, perhaps to counteract the negativity, she dictated her life story to Anita Pensotti, a reporter from *Oggi*, who banned Titta from the sessions, as his presence was stifling. The concluding paragraph, although narrated with her usual bluntness, only inflamed the scandal, 'I know that my enemies are lying in wait for me; but I will fight, as much as humanly possible, not to disappoint my public, which loves me and whose esteem and admiration I don't want to lose.'[51]

Returning to La Scala, Maria and Visconti collaborated in several productions. The first, *La sonnambula*, was described by *Musica e dischi* as 'popular delirium … we had the best Callas one could wish'. The next, Donizetti's *Anna Bolena*, was last staged in 1850 and revived in 1956 in Bergamo, a year before she assumed the part of Anna. Visconti and Nicola Benois designed the set; the shades of black, grey and white reflected the macabre fate of the heroine. For the part, Visconti covered Maria in jewels and dressed her in blue gowns and robes inspired by Holbein's portrait of Anne Boleyn, and Giulietta Simionato, who played Jane Seymour, wore red.

During one of the rehearsals, Maria approached Simionato and patted her on the shoulders, and without thinking, Simionato turned around and slapped her across the face, leaving her stunned. Then she turned and walked to her dressing room, her cheek ablaze with Simionato's scarlet imprint. Recalling the incident, Simionato said:

> Maria had beautiful but heavy hands, and had the bad habit of patting the shoulders as a sign of affection … Those pats did tremendous pain. I complained every time she showed me her affection that way; she laughed, because she didn't realise the harm she was doing to me.[52]

For half an hour, Visconti and Titta conferred between the two women until, eventually, Maria forgave Simionato. The opening night was a gala event and the *Corriere della Sera* wrote, 'Everything makes of her an Anna who can have no rivals today.'

The third production* was Gluck's *Ifigenia in Tauride*, based on Euripides's Greek tragedy. As with *La traviata*, Visconti attracted controversy when he altered the period of the opera, bringing it forward to the nineteenth century – the era of Gluck's composition – with rococo sets. Although Maria trusted his direction, she argued with him over her portrayal of Ifigenia, 'It's a Greek story and I'm a Greek woman, so I want to look Greek onstage,' she said, but followed his orders to play her as a 'Tiepolo fresco come to life'. *Opera* wrote, [She had] noble dignity of bearing and authoritative command of the stage … her singing caused none of the momentary discomfort that has sometimes seemed to go with her slimmer figure'. The *Corriere della Sera* dismissed it as 'an admiring, exclamatory vacuum, a vacuum of concentric reflectors – around the art of Callas'.

In the summer of 1957, Maria agreed to sing in two concerts at the Athens Festival and offered to do it for free. However, the organisers were offended and said it was not a charity.** Given their response, she asked for 270 million drachmas, thinking they would decline. Instead, they agreed, but she continued to hesitate until the festival's director, Achilleas Mamakis, reputedly said, 'All right, then, don't come, but it's a pity they won't be able to see you as you are now.'[53]

Vanity prevailed, and she signed the contract to perform at the Herodes Atticus on 1 August, a decision which troubled her father: 'Maria, I saw in the Greek newspapers that you've signed a contract to appear at the [Athens] Festival. This has really upset me, because if you do, you will regret it – I am afraid that that crazy woman will create scandals and harm you.'[54]

The scandals were created by Philoktitis Oikonomidis, the general manager of the Athens State Opera and a member of the Athens Festival. In a far-fetched statement, he wrote he did not know Maria, nor had he heard her sing in Athens, and he objected to her fee. He leaked stories to the Greek newspapers, claiming that her fee was paid at the expense of the taxpayer and, therefore, the public should have a say – he did not mention her suggestion to sing for free – and that her mother and sister were banished to America at the government's expense. The latter was untrue, for Litsa had remained in

---

* The opera season concluded with President Gronchi bestowing on her the honorary title of *Commendatore* for her services to Italian opera. She then went to Zurich, to give a concert, and to Cologne for a revival of La Scala's *La sonnambula*.

** It was a similar response to the one given to her recent donation of 1 million lire to the poor of Milan, which Italian newspapers said was done to upstage Tebaldi, who had given a benefit concert at the Manzoni in Milan.

New Jersey and Jackie was living in Athens, but neither she nor Maria wanted to reconcile.

Many Athenians who remembered her as Marianna Kalogeropoulou, cast their minds back to the war and bitterly recalled her singing for the enemies while others starved. They were further enraged by her imperious greeting over the airwaves:

> I would like to say hello to my dear people, the people who heard me when I lived in Greece at the time when we all suffered together [through] the good years and the bad ones … Many people have done injustice to me in the press. These things have nothing to do with me. Mr Mamakis has brought me here so that the dear people could hear me – people whom I have known and they have known me. I have no political aspirations whatsoever. I am sad because they got me involved in those things. Artists must not do that … because we should have no political aims; we belong to people. I belong first and foremost to the Greek people. I am married to an Italian, the whole world praises me, but my blood is Greek, and no one can nullify that.[55]

Before Maria left for Greece, she was suffering from nervous exhaustion but ignored her doctor's advice to recuperate. The conditions in Athens could not have been worse: the climate was hot and airless, the winds were strong, and when she reached her hotel, the Grande Bretagne, she was disturbed by the noise of a neighbouring shipyard. After her arrival, she developed an inflamed vocal cord, and at the first rehearsal she was hoarse. She asked the organisers to find a substitute, but they would not consider it. 'Don't worry about it,' they said, 'we'll inform the audience and they'll understand.'

Despite this, she refused to sing with a compromised voice. The public responded badly, and it was rumoured that she had refused to perform unless King Paul and Queen Frederica attended her concert. At her daughter's expense, Litsa said:

> At once she flew into one of her characteristic rages, ordered her bags to be packed and telephoned the airport for reservations on the first plane out. Diplomats of the Athens Music Festival intercepted her on her way to the airport and promised that the Prime Minister and members of his Cabinet would appear to applaud her art on the 5 August if she sang. She sang.[56]

While it was true that Maria had packed her bags and wanted to leave on the first plane to Italy, Titta convinced her to stay and to sing at the second concert.

Undoubtedly, he wanted to collect her fee, regardless of her suffering. In an attempt to salvage her reputation, she spoke candidly in a radio interview:

> Maybe I was a bit tired or I might have caught a mild influenza. I can't think of everything, and I have strived very much [to do this]. After all, I am willing to bear the consequences … I am sad about it, and wished to sing, but I would not have sung well; I am certain that you would not have liked that. I wish to give my best to you who love me, and whom I love as well.[57]

At the beginning of the concert, someone from the audience shouted 'shame!' before she performed her first aria, but a strong police presence deterred further disruption. Her voice silenced her critics and excited the audience, whose applause could be heard miles from the Herodes Atticus. Someone requested an aria from *Norma*, but she declined as she had no chorus to sing 'Casta diva', but she obliged the prime minister when he asked her to sing the second part of Ophelia's mad scene from *Hamlet*.

From her seat, close to the stage, Elvira de Hidalgo wept with pride, and backstage Maria was embraced by her first voice teacher, Maria Trivella, to whom she had sent a ticket. 'I want to come to that little house, to see that little house where I started,' she said to Trivella, although she did not visit in the end. When she was invited by the festival organisers to return in 1958, she said, 'Never again.'

Two days later, Maria returned to Milan, feeling enervated and exhausted. Her doctor warned she was on the verge of a nervous breakdown and insisted she rest for a month, or risk being hospitalised. In nine days, she was to appear with the La Scala company in *La sonnambula* at the Edinburgh Festival, but the management refused to accept the doctor's certificate, declaring she was 'capable of working miracles'.[58] Against medical advice, she went to Edinburgh to perform in what she thought would be four performances, but Ghiringhelli added a fifth and, out of principle, she refused to do it. On the opening night, her voice was bad and the poor stage lighting compromised Visconti's aesthetic. Backstage, she wrapped herself in silk scarves and complained of having cold hands, which she placed in hot water.[59] The second evening followed a similar course, and in the third performance her voice threatened to crack. On the fourth evening, however, the critics found her in excellent form.

After the fourth performance, Maria considered her contract fulfilled and packed her bags for Italy. The director of the festival, Robert Ponsonby, went to her hotel and demanded an explanation; he was under the impression she had one more performance. She presented her original contract, stipulating the four performances, and said she was leaving. For several hours, Ponsonby exchanged telephone calls with Ghiringhelli who, in a final attempt to salvage La Scala's reputation, asked her to cite illness as the reason for her absence. Consenting to a doctor's report, it informed the public, 'Maria Callas left the festival because of her precarious health', and Renata Scotto replaced her.

On the night of the fifth performance, Maria was in Venice attending a party given in her honour by Elsa Maxwell. It coincided with the International Film Festival and the press were indignant in their coverage. 'I like relaxation with my friends. Must I stay home like a nun?' she railed. 'If I stayed home all the time, I would be frustrated and nervous.'[60] Over four days, she was photographed singing, dancing, drinking and smoking, and sunbathing on the lido. In the photographs, Titta disappeared into the background, while an older Greek man sat next to her, listening to her converse and watching her sign autographs: his name was Aristotle Onassis.

At Maxwell's ball at the Hotel Danieli, Maria danced with Onassis but found him ugly, and his over-attentiveness unnerved her. She asked if he minded dancing with her, for she was so much taller. Not so, the billionaire shipping magnate and owner of Olympic Airways answered; at that moment, he felt 10ft tall.

But it was Maxwell's gossip column that overshadowed the events and caused Maria infinite damage: 'I have had many presents in my life, but I have never had any star before give up a performance in an opera house because she felt she was breaking her word to a friend.'

In Milan, Maria consulted with Professor Carlo Trabattoni, a specialist in mental health disorders, who diagnosed a nervous breakdown. She was warned to rest or risk being hospitalised and, perhaps thinking of Litsa's breakdown in 1929 and her period in Bellevue, she heeded Trabattoni's advice. There was more to her ill health than she divulged, for around the time of her Metropolitan debut, she had visited Max Jacobson, known as 'Doctor Feelgood', who treated celebrities with injections to increase their stamina. The highly addictive injections were mixed with vitamins, amphetamines and methamphetamines, which strained her nervous system and marked the beginning of her dependency on stimulants; first to get through her demanding schedule, to which Titta turned a blind eye, and later, to cope with life.

Instead of admitting the truth – that she had suffered a nervous breakdown – she claimed to have Asian flu,* which did not evoke sympathy from those

---

* A global pandemic in 1957–58, which killed 1 million people.

baying for her blood. She also expected Titta to act as her press agent, but he remained silent, hoping for maximum coverage. Then, she cancelled her contract with the San Francisco Opera and her three post-season performances at the Shrine Auditorium in Los Angeles and one at the Fox Theatre in San Diego.

The opening night was two weeks away, and she had initially sent a telegram informing Kurt Adler, the general director, that she could not sing due to health reasons, and asked to postpone her appearance for a month. 'We are sure that our Californian climate would do you good and you could sing all of the planned performances in full health,' Adler wrote to her. 'It would be reasonable to come a bit earlier to relax.'[61]

Declining his invitation, she attempted to salvage their agreement by offering to appear in *Macbeth* during the second half of the season, which Adler initially agreed to but then changed his mind. Attempting to control the damning reports, Dorle Soria wrote to Maria:

> It might be nice if you wrote to the president of the San Francisco Opera Association, and the various people … telling them how sorry you are that you could not come to San Francisco … and that you hoped to be able to sing in their beautiful city and magnificent opera house, or words to that effect.[62]

However, Maria's next move created a public relations disaster. On the day that she was due to inaugurate the San Francisco opera season, she began a six-day recording session of *Medea* conducted by Serafin for Mercury Records in Milan. In her defence, Maria claimed she had an outstanding agreement with Mercury, and she had not broken her contract with the San Francisco Opera but had wished to postpone it until she was fit to travel. Exasperated, Soria hoped Henry Sell could influence her:

> Please, dear Maria, clear the air by confirming the story that, although too exhausted to travel to San Francisco, [you] were also during that period to record *Medea*. Gossip world swirling with many coloured-up stories. Solid confirmation or denial by you is seriously indicated.[63]

Her initial reaction was to say, 'I do not intend to justify myself. I have too much pride to ask for pity, and besides, I have no use for it.'[64] In a telegram to Sell, she wrote, '*Medea* recorded before San Francisco contract. Influenza had me bedridden from 25 September till 15 October. Am feeling better now. San Francisco treatment most unjust and discourteous.'[65]

It was too late to counteract the negative press. Hedda Hopper, the Hollywood gossip columnist, warned that the San Francisco Opera would never again invite her.* Responding to the criticism, Maria stated that her nervous tension was caused by the newspapers, dishonest people and jealous colleagues. Incidentally, she did not receive a response from Hopper, which she considered bad manners. In a letter to an admirer, who implored her to write a statement to silence her critics, she wrote, 'I need comfort and the assurance that it's worthwhile singing because I assure you things got a little too difficult. I don't know why I attract all this nastiness from people but I can assure you that I certainly don't deserve it.'[66]

At the end of November, Maria travelled to Dallas at the behest of Larry Kelly, who had since broken from Carol Fox and the Lyric and founded the Dallas Opera Company. The original offer from Larry was to have her singing the three female parts in *Tales of Hoffmann*, which prompted Maria to joke, 'My dear, would you pay me three fees?' Instead, they agreed she would sing in two concerts to inaugurate the Dallas opera season.

Arriving in Dallas, she was met by Larry and his friend, Mary Carter, and was taken to an airport diner for lunch. 'I think she enjoyed it. She wasn't that particular,' Mary, who was to become her confidante, recalled. 'Once we went to Disneyland, and she loved the corn dogs and cotton candy.'[67] On another occasion, after a rehearsal at the Metropolitan, Maria and Mary went for lunch at the Automat, followed by a shopping spree in Woolworths.

Although underweight and bearing the strain of her recent ill health, Maria gave a dramatic performance. Backstage, she was unnerved by Elsa Maxwell's presence and refused to be left alone with her. Months before, Maxwell had reputedly made a pass at her in her dressing room at La Scala. She had even dedicated her book, *How to Do It, Or the Lively Art of Entertaining* to Maria. In it, she wrote, 'Callas is completely alone in her field ... She is without question the greatest creative artist in opera, the most fantastic talent, that I have ever known.'

Sensing the change in her beloved's nature, Maxwell had begun to sharpen her poison pen, but her threats (and abuse of power) evoked no response from Maria – an unusual stance, for many maintained a friendship out of fear. On the flight home, they ignored one another, except for a brief squabble, after which Maxwell said, 'You destroyed my love that day.'

---

* Hedda Hopper took credit for the San Francisco Opera hiring Maria. 'I did my bit, in turn, by introducing Maria to some people sitting directly across from us who were members of the board of the San Francisco Opera. "Why don't you get her to open your season?" I prompted.'

Their disagreement was overheard by a flight attendant, who leaked the story to *Time*, whose article, although unpublished, had insinuated the women were lovers. 'If *Time* magazine asks about it, you must deny everything categorically, as I did,' Maxwell warned her. However, Maxwell later wrote to her:

> I felt compelled to write and thank you for being the innocent victim of the highest form of love that a human being can have for another. It is I who terminated it or, more precisely, you who helped me to end it. It brought you no happiness and, apart from a few marvellous moments, it brought me only profound misery. I do not mean to reproach you for anything, except for not crushing my feelings before it was too late … I stood up to your enemies, Maria, of which you have many![68]

After Maria's unpleasant episode with Maxwell, whom she called 'a fat old son of a bitch', she returned to La Scala to perform in *Un ballo in maschera*, conducted by Gianandrea Gavazzeni and directed by Margherita Wallman. 'It has to be a success,' she said. 'Why must I have to fight all the time?'[69] She had not forgiven Ghiringhelli, who had promised, but failed, to release a statement about the Edinburgh Festival. Thus, she was in a fighting spirit, as portrayed in her interpretation of Amelia, and *Opera* claimed, 'There is only one Callas'.

Five days later, Maria went to Rome to rehearse *Norma* at the Piazza Esedra, an unheated space made all the more uncomfortable by the cold December weather. A bout of influenza was going around: Fedora Barbieri, who was to appear as Adalgisa, became ill and left the production before the first dress rehearsal.

On New Year's Eve, Maria sang 'Casta diva' live on a Eurovision television broadcast, and afterwards toasted the New Year with a glass of champagne at the Circolo degli Scacchi nightclub. The following morning, she awoke with a sore throat; Titta sent for a doctor and informed the management of the Teatro dell'Opera that a substitute would have to be found. 'Nobody can double Callas,' was the response and, furthermore, it was being broadcast to the nation. Twenty-four hours later, she felt considerably better and agreed to perform on the opening night, a gala event in honour of the president.

As the first act progressed, her voice almost cracked on 'Casta diva', provoking someone in the audience to shout, 'Why don't you go back to Milan, you have already cost us a million lire.'[70] During the intermission, which lasted for one hour, pandemonium broke out and the audience shouted and whistled. She decided not to return for the second act, even though Wallman told her she was a great actress and could convey *Norma* without the full capacity of her voice. It was Titta, however, who made the final decision and refused to allow her to continue. As a last resort, the management asked her to walk onstage and faint, but she refused to deceive the audience.

Over a loudspeaker, it was announced that the remainder of the opera was cancelled 'for reasons beyond their control'. The audience roared from the theatre and an overzealous mob gathered outside the stage door, preparing to lynch her. 'This is Rome, not Milan and not Edinburgh!' someone shouted, disgusted that she had snubbed the president. To escape being attacked, Maria was taken through an underground passage from the theatre to the Hotel Quirinale, but the mob were waiting outside the hotel and stood under her window, shouting insults throughout the night.

The following morning, a doctor examined her and diagnosed bronchitis and tracheitis, and reporters asked if they could photograph her ill in bed. 'I am a serious artist, not a soubrette, and I do not pose for pictures in bed,' she said.[71] Considered the most scandalous woman in Italy, the newspapers wrote that she had partied too much and her departure before the second act was a capricious whim. Insults were printed:

> This is a second-rate Greek artist. Italian by marriage. Milanese because of the baseless veneration she enjoys from a section of the audience at La Scala … The present episode shows that Callas is, in addition, an ungracious performer without a grain of discipline and propriety.[72]

The English press were among the scandalmongers, with the *Daily Mirror* reporting that Maria locked herself in her dressing room and threw a chair at Titta. The gossip columnist, Henry Fielding sent her a message saying, 'I told you so':

> Maria's explosiveness has already got her into trouble … I warned her then that her tantrums would finally hurt herself. A great singer yes. But she must not treat the public like dirt … Maria is sending apologies everywhere. Too late, I fear. You can't have tantrums at top level all the time.[73]

She had written to the president, and his wife telephoned and said, 'Tell Maria we know she was sick and could not continue.'[74] Unfortunately, Maria noted, the First Lady did not issue a similar statement to the newspapers. Offered no mercy from the government, she was publicly denounced in parliament, and the Teatro dell'Opera was granted an order banning her from the theatre. Later, the opera house tried to sue her for $13,000 in damages.* 'My name was seriously damaged by this incident,' she said, 'and I still find it unjust that an artist who has had great triumphs in Italy for twelve years should have to explain one cold and be condemned for it.'[75]

In Milan, she expected support from Ghiringhelli but found none. Since Edinburgh, he had begun to undermine her and those she trusted, and now revolted against her. At the time, she said, 'I know one thing for sure, that I wonder whether it's worth my while to sing.'[76]

---

* The case was settled in 1971, Maria was found not guilty and awarded $1,600 in lost fees.

11

Submersion

Of all creatures that can feel and think,
we women are the worst treated things alive.

Medea, Euripides

In the aftermath of the Rome scandal, Maria said, 'There is always an inside story to all things … just care about how I sing and the human being that's in me.'[1] Consumed by intrusive thoughts and convinced her career was over, she retreated to her home. 'It's my destiny,' she wrote, 'to be given glory together with continuous beatings and insults.'[2]

Those who were privy to the situation hinted that she had felt suicidal: without her career, the battleground of an opera house in which she destroyed her enemies, what was the point of living? To an outsider, it had the melodrama of a libretto, but for Maria, it was life or death. The public wrote letters, telling her that she was necessary to them, 'that my reason [for] living, that is, for music, isn't wasted. In that way, I knew that I'm really loved, I'm really needed, and it gave me courage to go on and have new faith in myself'.[3] In an interview, she said, 'It is true, life is not easy for me and my path is often strewn with big stones that sometimes menace to fall over me and smash me, but God is so great that I always seem to jump over these obstacles.'[4]

However, the Italian Government proceeded with their order prohibiting her from appearing at state opera houses, and the American Guild of Musical Artists (AGMA) was investigating a complaint made by the San Francisco Opera, stating that she was in breach of her contract and suing her for $35,000. If found guilty, she would be suspended from singing in American opera houses, therefore jeopardising her contract with the Metropolitan. She wrote to Rudolf Bing, asking, 'What in heaven's name shall I do? If others get away with all they did not being ill, and I being ill be condemned, then I really will be sure the world is crazy.'[5]

On 22 January 1958, Maria arrived in Chicago to give a benefit concert for the Allied Française. 'Why has this all come about?' she asked, referring to the AGMA case. 'Contracts are just a matter of … having to sign a contract … but once I say I come, I come.'[6] The *Chicago American* wrote, 'Maria Callas sounds to be in big vocal trouble – how serious only she is equipped to measure. But last night, heard for the first time in twelve months, her voice … seems to have aged ten years.'

Two days later, she appeared on Edward R. Murrow's television show, *Person to Person*, recorded live from her suite at the Waldorf Astoria. Arranged by CBS the month before, they promised, 'There will be no questions other than the ones she wants asked', and her apparent discomfort was mistaken for humility.[7]

In measured tones, she spoke of her American upbringing, 'I was brought up in New York and I'm rather proud of that too'; her temperament, 'You just react as any normal human being, only that I suppose these situations are taken advantage of … shall we say, we're victims of certain situations'; her appearance, 'I usually dress in Europe because I live there … but my under-things are real American'; her hobbies, 'I love shopping, my husband says I'm ruining him'; her lucky charm, a miniature painting of the Madonna – 'it's very precious to me'; her music, 'I've dedicated my life to it'; the Rome scandal, 'I happened to catch a stupid cold'; and her reason for living, 'Being a happy wife … it's the main thing in the life of a woman, I feel.'

After the cameras stopped rolling, she received a telephone call from Litsa's benefactor, Mrs Zarras. 'Guess who is standing here with me, Maria. Your mother!'

'Why is she with you?'

'Because we love her, Maria.'

'Then you can have her. You can keep her.'

'Maria, your mother would like so very much to see you.'

'My mother is mentally ill,' she said, before hanging up.[8]

The scene unnerved Maria, as did all of Litsa's attempts to contact her. Throughout difficult periods in New York, she found solace at Leo Lerman and his partner, Gray Foy's home, asking him, 'Why would they not let me alone? Why, oh why, all this with my mother? What did she ever do for me?'[9]

On 26 January, she appeared before the board of the AGMA, who conducted a four-hour-long interview. They accepted her medical documents as evidence, although she was reprimanded for her absence in San Francisco, which they felt 'was not fully justified'. Thus, she was permitted to appear at the Metropolitan in February and March.

However, Bing found her more elusive than ever. She had reservations about the productions, which included *Macbeth*, *La traviata* and *Tosca*, and was reluctant to commit to their tour in the spring–summer of 1959. Reassured that she would have six days' rest between productions, she agreed to a letter of intent but continued to avoid signing a contract.

Meanwhile, she complained of the conditions at the Metropolitan, which she compared to 'the Middle Ages', particularly the tired scenery and shabby costumes.[10] She felt that her own costume, brought from La Scala, made her look 'as slick as something out of a fashion magazine'.[11]

Due to the budget, she was permitted only one dress rehearsal. She said, 'I sympathise for opera is expensive, but ... it must be rehearsed.'[12] Furthermore, *La traviata* was then a new production, directed the year before by Tyrone Guthrie, whose staging differed from Visconti's. Unfamiliar with the sets, she studied them from photographs and rehearsed on the stage roof with only a table and chair for props and chalk marks on the floor. 'This is not art,' she said. 'In Italy it's called *botteghino* [box office].'[13]

On the opening night of *La traviata*, conducted by Fausto Cleva, she was given an ovation before she sang a note. It was, as the *New Yorker* called it, 'far and away the finest ... at the Metropolitan'. *Time* agreed that 'Miss Callas carried the house from the moment she lifted her first note across the orchestra pit'. But although the *New York Times* found her in a better voice than last season, 'there were places where Miss Callas's singing was not worthy of her station in the operatic world'.

In *Lucia di Lammermoor*, also conducted by Cleva, the Mad Scene stunned the audience, who maintained 'a soundless shriek of frozen terror'.[14] Afterwards, she found a hairpiece in her dressing room, a gift from Marlene Dietrich. Amused, she asked what she could do with it.

'You keep it. You keep it forever. You cherish it,' Leo said.[15]

From the neighbouring state of New Jersey, Litsa read the reviews and passed her own judgement. 'Maria is an instinctive actress. She inherited her talent for make-believe from her father, who has been acting all his life.'[16]

In *Tosca*, Richard Tucker sang the part of Mario and could never entirely warm to her again after their recording of *Aida*; he was jealous when she talked about a young tenor (possibly Franco Corelli), with whom she would have preferred to sing.[17] During their duet, '*O dolci mani*', she whispered, 'Why is it, Richard, that whenever I sing with you, I feel good?'

He responded, 'It's simple, Mary.* When you're singing with me, you're in the big leagues.'[18]

The audience's response was reminiscent of La Scala; the claque roused and began booing, but their catcalls were drowned by cheering and screams of '*Bravo!*', and an elderly man in the front row of the grand tier rattled his ear trumpet on the railings. The *New Yorker* wrote, 'We came away bruised, our musical education complete.'

Between the final *Lucia di Lammermoor* and the opening night of *Tosca*, Maria and George were interviewed by Hy Gardner. Their segment was conducted over the telephone and filmed at the Waldorf Astoria. In his column, Gardner referred to Maria as 'the dizzy dame of opera singers', and live on air, he goaded her into 'documenting the truth … and setting the record straight once and for all'. She would not, however, speak of Litsa:

> Forgive me if I make this quite clear; these are very personal and intimate problems or affairs of the family and I feel it is my privilege and duty to keep them so … To justify myself or to say anything: all I can say is please, let's leave this in the four walls of the family, because anything that happens only makes it worse for any reconciliation.[19]

On a separate occasion, Litsa was also invited onto Gardner's show, to appear with Jolie Gabor. To evoke sympathy, she said:

> I am flat broke. I have lost everything and for nearly ten years I am bitterly separated from Maria. It is heartbreaking not only to be poor but to have a daughter who won't even speak to you. Still, a mother cannot have hate in her heart … It is a tragedy because I love Maria more than her sister. Maria is my baby.[20]

Afterwards, Gabor gave Litsa a job, selling cultured pearls at her boutique on Madison Avenue, and she often ran errands for her daughter, Zsa Zsa, who was living at the Hotel Pierre. Curious patrons bought pearls, thrilled with the prospect of talking to the prima donna's mother, and muckrakers courted her, hoping her exhibitionism would reveal new scandals. Inspired by their interest, she made dolls based on Maria's operatic characters and tried, but failed, to sell them to Bloomingdale's.

---

* Since their engagement in Verona in 1947, Tucker continued to call her Mary, even though she disliked it.

Ignoring her mother's behaviour, Maria flew to Madrid to give a concert at the Cinema Monumental. She then went to Lisbon for two performances of *La traviata* at the Teatro Nacional de São Carlos, which were broadcast over the radio. In what had become a common theme, her celebrity excited the audience, but critics remained unmoved:

> The first sensation that one has when listening to her is of adverse signs. The timbre of the voice does not seduce … The colour of the voice is unequal; it seems to be beginning to be nasal at certain moments. And how then can one speak of an exceptional figure? Because of other things. Because of the temperament, the intelligence, the personality, the stage mastery of unmistakable originality.[21]

In April, Maria returned to Milan and became fixated with Ghiringhelli defending her honour. 'If it had not been for La Scala's treatment of me at Edinburgh, there would have been no San Francisco scandal,' she said.[22] Six months before, he had manipulated her into writing an article for *Oggi*, praising La Scala; however, after its publication, he ignored her. 'La Scala has a great fetish about her pure reputation,' she complained. 'No one must ever say a bad word about La Scala; the blame must always be placed somewhere else.'[23] She failed to understand his aloofness, as for years he offered her gifts: a silver bowl, a silver mirror, a chandelier, costumes and lots of sugared words and compliments.[24]

Both Maria and Titta were convinced the Italian Government had forced Ghiringhelli to dispose of her services, although she was permitted to fulfil her remaining contract. She also learned that her scheduled performance of *Anna Bolena* at the Milan Fair was to be replaced with *Murder in the Cathedral*, thus forcing her into resigning from La Scala. 'I would not leave during the season and give La Scala the opportunity to say that "Callas has walked out – as usual",' she said. 'Not that I lacked provocation.'[25]

Nevertheless, the opening night of *Anna Bolena* was an emotional homecoming for Maria, who had not performed in Italy since the scandal in Rome. As such, La Scala anticipated trouble and 200 policemen were deployed in and around the theatre. However, the only disruption came from the claque who booed, hurled radishes and, after one performance, someone threw a shoe.

Her singing eventually silenced the audience, who then cheered for five minutes, and afterwards she gave five curtain calls. Although Ghiringhelli watched from his box, he never visited her dressing room. Their only communication was through letters: he refused to use her first name and she addressed him as the 'Administration of the Theatre'.

Suffering further hostility, a dead dog was placed inside her car, and hooligans covered the outside walls of her house in graffiti and smeared excrement on the gate and walls. The telephone rang late into the night with anonymous callers delivering insults and sending threatening letters, which she gave to Milan's chief of police, but the matter remained unresolved. 'For my self-defence and dignity, I had no choice but to leave La Scala,' she said. 'La Scala did not "dispense of my services". I resigned.'[26]

Less than a month later, Maria gave her last performance in Bellini's *Il pirata*, an event marred by her ill health, resulting in a gynaecological operation. She channelled her pain into the performance, and singing the words, '*Là vedete il palco funesto* [There, see the fatal scaffold],' she pointed to Ghiringhelli, seated in his box. The audience turned their heads toward him and he rose from his seat and left.

Before her performance, a group of young men had asked for permission to throw flowers onto the stage, but Ghiringhelli forbade them to do so. Regardless, she was given a thirty-minute ovation, with shouts for her to remain at La Scala. Angered by the display, Ghiringhelli lowered the fire curtain. 'I know of no single act in the entire repertoire of operatic insults as brutal as this one,' she later wrote. 'It is a blunt, iron signal that says: "Show's over! Get out!"'[27]

As she walked to her car, she was followed by admirers who threw flowers at her feet. 'I am hurt, I wish I could go back,' she said. 'But I cannot return while Ghiringhelli is there.'[28] However, he would have the final word, and to the state opera board he claimed that Maria's voice was failing and La Scala, therefore, had no interest in her.

She left for London* to sing at a gala concert to mark the centenary of the Royal Opera House. She was disheartened when Queen Elizabeth II spoke to her colleagues and, when presented to her, she smiled and walked away. 'What does one say to Callas?' the queen reputedly asked. Ten days later, on 20 June, she gave the first of five performances in *La traviata*, conducted by Nicola Rescigno. Although the critics found her voice inconsistent, particularly in the death scene, *Opera* wrote, 'At the final performance she rode the orchestra, opened up her voice and achieved the maximum degree of intensity, which aroused the audience to a spontaneous outburst of applause.'

---

* Maria returned to London in September, where she spent five days recording for EMI at Abbey Road Studios.

For the remainder of the summer, Maria stayed at her new villa at Sirmione, Lake Garda. 'It is peaceful,' she wrote to Leo Lerman, 'and thank heavens people have stayed away a bit.'[29] It was a transitional period in her private life: she wanted to retire and have a baby. The latter was an antidote to her unhappy marriage; she could no longer fool herself that Titta loved her, nor could she maintain a happy facade.

Months before, she had given an interview to an English reporter, affording him twenty minutes to ask questions and take photographs. In front of the reporter, Titta undermined her and claimed she had plenty of time. '*You* have,' she hissed, '*you* have!'[30] She was tired of working and wanted to lead 'the usual woman's life, forgetting I am a singer and doing whatever ... anything else but reminding me of being a singer'.[31]

During the summer, she decided not to perform in the Metropolitan's winter season nor participate in their spring tour, though she had not informed Bing.[32] She 'hated the idea' of her forthcoming concert tour.[33] She expected to become pregnant and could, therefore, cancel her later contracts.

Despite being 'most affectionate' to Titta, he did not reciprocate her advances, making it impossible to conceive a child. He accepted no responsibility for this and later claimed that she had fertility problems, particularly early menopause, which occurred before the age of 30. The year before, she had undergone a series of tests to find the cause of her health issues: she had headaches, vertigo and low blood pressure. She was also underweight – she weighed 117lb – and it resulted in irregular periods, which eventually ceased but later resumed when she gained weight, and with it, her longing for a baby 'more than anything'.[34]

Decades later, Titta produced a medical certificate, written (perhaps forged) by his brother-in-law, claiming Maria had a malformed uterus and was, therefore, infertile. In theory, it was a tilted uterus, a common condition affecting one in five women, and posed no threat to her health or her ability to bear children. It must also be noted that studies of women's health and the subsequent treatments were, at times, draconian, and Titta's medical theories were probably invalid. He was not above embellishing the truth, particularly if it meant stripping Maria of her feminine power to protect his fragile ego.

However, Maria confided to a friend that she and Titta rarely had what she called physical love, 'I would have liked to have had children but my husband ... it's no good blaming anyone.'[35] Interestingly, she looked to the future and spoke of remarrying after his death, presuming she would be a young widow and, therefore, still of childbearing age. 'The thought of being alone terrified

her,' Anita Pensotti wrote. 'She would scrutinise the list of possible replace-
ments, some of whom I knew, married and with children.'[36]

Regardless, she continued to play the dutiful wife and praised her husband
in public. The devotion was sincere. 'You love, then you worship, then you
honour. You never say a lie, you do your best to never betray that person.'[37] She
had become an expert at deceiving herself and others, though, as demonstrated
in a letter written at the time, 'But each one of us [has] a destiny … after all,
mine is really wonderful. Especially my husband. That's what counts for me.
Personal happiness which gives great wealth of soul.'[38]

It was rumoured that her marriage to Titta was never consummated, and
Franco Zeffirelli said she confided they had marital relations only once a
year. Both accounts were false. Her friend and confidante, Mary Carter, said,
'[Titta] was crude. The marriage was expedient, but Maria took it very seriously.'[39] Regardless, Maria's unguarded comments, published in *Time*, were
mocked, 'My best hours are in bed, and my best work too, with my dog
cuddling beside me and my husband asleep.' In further satirical tones, the
magazine added, 'She coats [Titta] with twenty-four-carat affection, holds
hands with him [in] the street.'

Sometimes, in front of others, she lost her temper with him, particularly
when he mishandled a contract. 'If you can't be secretary then don't do it!' she
screamed at him, in the presence of Bing. She was beginning to see him for
what he was: grasping, unsophisticated – an opportunist.

At the beginning of October, Maria dined with Bing in New York and delivered a list of complaints. She no longer wanted to do *Lucia di Lammermoor* and
she disliked the sets from *La traviata* and what remained from Guthrie's staging.
He proposed *Macbeth*, a new production for the Metropolitan, but she said it
was a heavy part and she would need several days to recover before opening
in *La traviata* – ideally, she did not want to combine the two operas. Titta disapproved of the tour's conditions: the hotels were below standard, the airlines
would not carry their poodles, the trains were filthy and the schedule was too
demanding. Afterwards, he sent Bing a letter, in Italian, and forged Maria's
signature, asking him to 'call a spade a spade':

> You have told me that Tebaldi, last season, demanded categorically that I
> should not take over her *Traviata*, because if you did not accede to this

request she threatened not to return to the Metropolitan … However, you also told me, a few days ago, that Tebaldi has refused to sing *Traviata* this year, although she was committed to do so, and that you, for the sake of peace, have accepted this. It is therefore logical that I should not perform this role either, since Tebaldi has dared to impose the above-mentioned cancellation on you … It is perhaps because my *Butterfly* disturbed Signorina Tebaldi, who – although in a grave moment – left you completely in the lurch last season, and it is perhaps possible that she has once again imposed on you, as is the case with *Traviata*.[40]

Calling the tone of the letter 'deliberate unfriendliness', Bing did not care to change the programme and told her, 'Maria, if you sing, I can fill every seat with old productions'.[41] She said she was 'delighted to be earning so much money for him';[42] however, she was ashamed of the material he gave her. Their embittered words continued, and he told her, 'Your letter sounds more the Maria Callas of whom I have been warned than the Maria Callas I know, like, and respect.'[43] So, she asked, 'Do you make your judgements with the brain of some little fool?'[44]

Nevertheless, the contract remained unsigned and Titta advised her to free herself from the Metropolitan. She knew if she renounced their letter of intent, she would be held in breach of their contract, thus involving another hearing with the AGMA. Perhaps she would have honoured the performances, but for Titta the matter was urgent: he could earn more money from concerts, but the itinerary would have clashed with the Metropolitan's spring tour. Therefore, his only tactic was to infuriate Bing until he fired her.

In mid October, Maria began the first part of her North American concert tour, presented by the impresario Sol Hurok, beginning in Alabama, followed by Atlanta, then Montreal and Toronto. 'She can look like a pixie or like a devil; she can croon like an angel; she can wail like a banshee,' the *Atlanta Constitution* wrote.

Afterwards, she opened the Dallas opera season with *La traviata*, directed by Franco Zeffirelli, at the State Fair Music Hall. Unlike Visconti's production, Zeffirelli remained true to the original libretto, setting it in 1852, with crinoline gowns made in Rome. In his diary, Leo Lerman wrote, 'The performance was the most extraordinary *Traviata* I have ever seen. It is the only genuinely created *Traviata* … The diva sang better than I have heard her sing in years, and she looked so right.'[45] The *Dallas Morning News* called her the 'rarest of creatures, a genuine artist, by which we mean a musical intelligent first and foremost'.

Several days later, she arrived at a dress rehearsal for *Medea*, directed by Alexis Minotis, and went to her dressing room, clutching a telegram from Bing asking her to confirm her appearance at the Metropolitan. 'I found her in a rage such I had never seen,' Leo recalled.[46] As she entered the stage, 'the eyes were so full of hatred that it became apparent immediately that, if Bing were anywhere about, they would strike him dead'.[47] At four o'clock in the morning, they left the theatre, and like a child, she held Leo's hand in the back of the car.

Several hours later, she received a telegram from Bing:

> Since you have not seen fit to reply to my telegrams November three and November five or furnish confirmation as requested please consider your contract for Metropolitan season 1958–59 cancelled.[48]

Responding in Italian and signing Maria's name, Titta wrote:

> I am utterly amazed about your as usually urgent and unacceptable manner. I repeat and I shall insist that it is absolutely impossible to mix opera such as *Macbeth* and a light opera. I thought I was facilitating your task by eliminating operas which are evidently incompatible and in contrast to each other.[49]

The following afternoon, Bing held a press conference and announced he had fired Maria from the Metropolitan. That evening, she opened in *Medea* to an audience of bejewelled society women and their millionaire husbands listening to the music with one ear and the other listening to the election results coming in over the transistor radios. Backstage, a swarm of reporters filled her dressing room, goading her into answering their questions on Bing. She shrieked:

> I just refused next year's contract because he offered me the old repertoire … and I said, no, I am sorry, I cannot do routine. I want new performances, staged well. You know like here, a little young Dallas is doing, my God. I suppose that made him angry, I don't know. I mean, I can't explain it otherwise … I cannot, excuse me, do those lousy performances. And I cannot change artists every performance … So … I'm sorry, I can't do that, that's not art.[50]

Later, she made a pragmatic statement, 'Our disagreements have been principally artistic ones, and if I must disagree with someone, I much prefer it to be on an artistic rather than personal basis.'[51] Her ego was bolstered by her Dallas patrons who, to spite Bing, offered to finance a production of *Medea* in New York. However, he thought it was an unstable foundation on which to sustain a career:

> In Dallas, Miss Callas was *prima donna assoluta* … an entire opera company had been built around her. Everyone told her that she should never do anything she didn't wholeheartedly want to do. She was Maria Callas, and the world would have to follow her lead.[52]

At Mary Carter's home, she cast Titta to the side and partied until dawn. Her time spent in Dallas was a revelation: she was exposed to flabbergasting richness: private luncheons for 500 and after-parties at the Cipango, Imperial Club and the City Club; billionaires who earned a million dollars a week and their wives who ordered thirty ballgowns from Paris and were displayed like trophies.[53] As a child, when she passed a shop window, she had stared at her father, expecting him to read her mind and indulge her. Now, in a Dallas restaurant, they knew she liked ice cream* and served her fifteen varieties.

The fun was short-lived and Titta looked forward to the fortune he could make from her tour, which she resumed in Cleveland, Detroit, Washington DC, San Francisco and Los Angeles. Tired of the monotony, during a press conference she snapped at reporters, 'You people always ask me the same questions. Why couldn't you have been here when the other paper was, then I could have answered you both at once.'

Someone asked if she was a tempestuous person, and she responded, 'That's what they always ask. It is so boring.'[54] Nevertheless, the *San Francisco Examiner* said of the audience, 'The hypnotic way in which the crowd massed up to the stage … is a subject I recommend to psychologists, sociologists, and students of the occult.'

In December, she went to Paris to sing in a televised concert at the Palais Garnier, on behalf of the Legion d'Honneur, to whom she donated her fee of 5 million francs. Perhaps the most glamorous production given in post-war Europe, Titta took credit for organising the event which, he said, was held in Paris to spite the Italian Government. There seems to be little

---

* Perhaps her favourite food, Maria's love of ice cream was legendary. Leo Lerman wrote in his diary of evenings spent eating ice cream with her, straight from the carton. If friends took her out for dinner, she would ask, 'Won't you buy me an ice cream?'

evidence to support his claim, for the event was sponsored by *Marie Claire*.
Maria said:

> My name bears considerable responsibility, and I feel frightened at times.
> Also, sometimes we wish to do so well, yet feel so small because we are
> human … You have shown so much love and respect for me, a singer who
> has never sung for you, that I feel, as I said before, very small and human. One
> cannot know for sure how the evening of the 19th will go, and I am there-
> fore asking you to understand the way I feel – you understand that – and to
> wish me to sing as I never sang before, for your sake as well as mine, because
> you deserve it. This is the only wish I have now.[55]

Among the celebrities and dignitaries was Aristotle Onassis, who, since their
first encounter in Venice, was intrigued by her fame but had not yet seen her
perform. With his interests in oil, shipping, whaling and an airline, he had
conquered land, sea and air, the way she had dominated the world of opera.
Throughout her stay in Paris, he sent roses to her suite at the Ritz, with messages of admiration written in Greek, although left unsigned. On the last day,
he revealed his identity, signing his name, 'The Other Greek'. She wondered
why Onassis, then 53 and married with two children, would romance her from
afar. 'I approach every woman as a potential mistress,' he remarked to a friend.
Jealousy stirred within Titta: he never imagined that someone could turn her
head. After all, she had begged him to marry her and had always loved him
more than he loved her.

In the New Year of 1959, Maria sang in St Louis, Philadelphia, Washington
DC and New York – the latter two were significant, for she sang *Il pirata* in a
concert format rather than a full-scale opera. 'This wasn't the Met,' the *New
York Times* wrote of the Carnegie Hall engagement, but undoubtedly Bing
noted the sold-out tickets.

Then it was on to Europe, singing in Madrid, Barcelona, Hamburg, Stuttgart,
Munich and Wiesbaden. 'Whoever said I couldn't live without my work!!!' she
said, bemoaning her 'long contracts of years in advance'.[56] She had also written
an article, 'I am not Guilty of all Those Callas Scandals', for *Life*, revealing the
details of her conflicts with opera houses, the estrangement between herself
and Ghiringhelli, and her dismissal from the Metropolitan. 'I take responsibility for the truth I have written here,' she wrote, 'even though the truth always
hurts the pride of some people and infuriates others.' After its publication, she
asked Leo Lerman, 'How did you like my *Life* article? What do people say? Or
don't they care anymore?'[57]

Onassis continued to pursue Maria from afar, and they were to meet again in the spring, in Venice, at Contessa Castelbarco's annual ball. She danced with Onassis, thrilled by 'our hands, the textures of our skin, so pleasing to each other's touch', while his wife, Tina, watched.[58] Accustomed to his philandering, Tina joked that he was facing a midlife crisis; he boasted of his virility, flew into rages and, at times, played the doting husband. Although only 30, Tina was tired of their fast-paced life and moving between their many homes around the world. In contrast, since childhood, Maria had known nothing except a roving life.

As they said goodbye in the early hours of the morning, Tina invited them aboard their yacht, the *Christina*, for scrambled eggs and champagne, but Titta declined: Maria had to rest ahead of *Medea* in London. 'I'll be there,' Onassis announced, even though he hated opera and compared it to Italian chefs shouting risotto recipes at one another.

In his youth, he had had an affair with Claudia Muzio, an Italian prima donna almost twenty years his senior, and he courted a prima ballerina from Anna Pavlova's ballet company. Ahead of Maria's performance, Onassis bought tickets from the black market and arranged to hold a party in her honour at the Dorchester. 'Meneghini's pissed off with the way he thinks you're climbing on Maria's bandwagon,' remarked Onassis's confidante, Johnny Meyer.[59] Calling Titta 'an undertaker', Onassis said, 'He's not servicing the account, so what the hell.'[60]

In London, Onassis did not attempt to hide his attraction to Maria, nor did she make an effort to discourage it. She had experienced glimmers of a hedonistic life in Paris in 1957, when Elsa Maxwell had taken her on a whirlwind tour of the city, stopping for tea with the Duchess of Windsor and introducing her to the nightlife of Maxim's and the Lido. One evening, intoxicated by the glamour of the jet set, she had met Prince Aly Khan and he expressed his desire to have an affair with her. It seemed Maxwell had orchestrated it: she was obsessed with Aly, obsessed with Maria, and together they would fulfil a fantasy she had created.* Nothing became of it; perhaps the intensity of living out the scenarios that existed on the stage was too much, in reality. She ran back to Titta and immersed herself in a traditional role that was unobtainable: there was no devoted husband, no baby, and only the love of her fans.

However, the veil between the two worlds had now been lifted; she was emotionally and spiritually adrift. She, who had chased Titta and initiated his

---

* In her 1957 book, dedicated to Maria, Maxwell wrote of her dream dinner guests (Maria and Aly Khan), and she included seating charts of them placed together.

clumsy attempts at passion, was happy to be pursued by a man 'no longer young, but still predatory, still sexy, still stalking'.[61]

The opening night of *Medea* was the social event of the season, and Onassis appeared with an entourage of thirty-six. 'Fury hot and fury cold,' the *Saturday Review* wrote of her performance. 'Burning passion and intensity,' *Opera* said of her voice.

Arriving at the Dorchester at one o'clock in the morning, Onassis rushed to greet her. The strings of the Hungarian orchestra there had failed to impress her and she was sorry that nobody played tango music any more, so he pushed £50 into the conductor's hand, ordering him to play it non-stop. She danced with Onassis until 3 a.m., and as they parted, he invited her on a cruise, but she was hesitant to accept.

Unbeknownst to her, he had boasted of liaisons at his mews house in Sutton Square and in the back of his Rolls-Royce as they drove down Park Lane. 'One way or another, all ladies do it for money,' he said, alluding that it was a gesture of thanks for the chinchilla coat he had bought her. As they bid one another goodbye, he embraced her, and Titta emerged from behind with a firm hand on his foe and a warning look in his eyes.

At the end of June, they left for her forthcoming concerts in Amsterdam and Brussels. In Amsterdam, Maria was met by reporters as she walked across the runway to meet Peter Diamand, the manager of the Holland Festival. 'I can only say one thing, that I hope to God that everything goes well,' she said.

Behind the scenes, she appeared tense as she was trailed by Titta, whose grasping ways she could no longer tolerate. 'That man of mine would search my wardrobe to find money,' she remarked to her Dutch secretary, Elly Schotte.[62]

One afternoon at the Amstel Hotel, Titta entered Schotte's room through a connecting door and slid his hand up her skirt. 'How would you like to become the chief secretary of my secretaries in Italy?' he asked in broken English. Disgusted by his behaviour, Schotte recalled, 'Slowly, I began to realise that, how should I put it, he was trying to abuse his position. He made advances to me while his wife was staying in the room next to us.'[63]

Before leaving Holland, Maria asked Diamand to hold her fee in escrow until further notice. 'Peter, you have to help me, you have to keep my fee,' she pleaded:

> Don't book the money over to my agent. Don't get fooled by Meneghini. I will need that money myself in the near future. Big things are about to happen in my life. All my instincts tell me so. You'll hear many things … Please stay my friend.

'What melodrama!' he remarked.
'No, not melodrama, Peter – drama.'[64]

In mid July, Maria and Titta went to Sirmione, a place where she felt 'as near as possible a normal human person'.[65] She was restless, and more than ever she argued with Titta and found him unbearable to live with. Their confrontations were interrupted by telephone calls from Onassis, reminding her of his invitation, but she was reluctant to accept. She was ashamed to be accompanied by Titta, whose social gaffes she could no longer ignore: his mumbling in Italian and his inability to converse with her friends. He scolded her if she stayed out late and told her to shut up and mind her own business if she asked about their finances – which were entirely supported by her earnings.

Having broached the subject of retiring, she made the accidental discovery that Titta 'passes for a millionaire when he hasn't got a dime to his name' and had squandered her fortune.[66] 'You can't retire, because you can't afford to,' he said. The Swiss bank account was in his name and he used it to pay off his debts and to make long-term investments. As for the remaining funds, he 'couldn't justify where [they were] or what he had done with [them]'.[67] She asked for her freedom, but he demanded complete financial control over her, or nothing. 'There is a lot of disillusionment in this and I hope I can stand it,' she wrote to a friend.[68] She also said, 'So my eyes were opened to a husband who was a pimp. I've opened my eyes to that.'[69]

A week later, on 21 July, Maria and Titta arrived in Monte Carlo, where they were to board the *Christina*. Although Prince Rainier ruled Monaco, Onassis had economic control of the principality through his ownership of SBM* and the Monte Carlo Casino. Checking into a suite at the Hotel Hermitage, she found a letter from Elsa Maxwell: 'From now on try to enjoy every moment of your life. Take everything (which is a delicate art). Give what you can (which is not delicate but important).'[70]

Since their falling out in 1957, Maxwell had attended similar parties and observed from afar, 'the fat slob was so subdued that one wouldn't have known she was there'.[71] Now Maxwell was in the company of Onassis but was not invited on the cruise, and Titta, who called her a witch, saw her presence in Monte Carlo as a bad omen.

---

* *Société des Bains de Mer et du Cercle des Étrangers à Monaco.*

However, until the last moment, Maria remained undecided: some say she was to holiday with friends in Venice and others claim Titta forced her to go, as he wanted to meet his fellow passenger and guest of honour, Sir Winston Churchill. Perhaps, having been impressed by the social whirl of Dallas, she wanted to experience a luxurious cruise with the man who had lavished her in Paris and London, and whose game of seduction she wanted to play.

On the eve of the cruise, a tense evening was spent dining with Onassis, Tina and Maxwell, the conversation in English excluded Titta, and Maxwell made innuendos about 'dangerous … powerful men' and their peccadilloes.

'When dealing with the wicked, the Gods first deprive them of their senses,' Onassis said, in Greek.

'Are you wicked?' Maria asked in their common language.[72]

Predicting the cruise would change Maria's life, Maxwell said, 'She will learn fast.'

Glimpses of Maria's childhood.

Glimpses of Maria's childhood.

The real Anita Duval/Nina
Foresti photographed in
the 1950s.

Maria in the 1940s.

Maria and Meneghini on their wedding day, 1949.

Candid Callas in the 1950s.

Before and after a
performance.

London and Milan, late 1950s.

Maria and Prince Aly Khan,
Paris, 1958.

Amsterdam, 1959. (Courtesy of Fotocollectie Anefo)

On Edward Murrow's *Small World*, 1958.

Maria and Onassis throughout the years.

At a Milan airfield, going to meet Onassis, 1959.

A lonely figure in Milan, 1960.

At the police station, Milan, 1960.

Candid Callas in the 1960s.

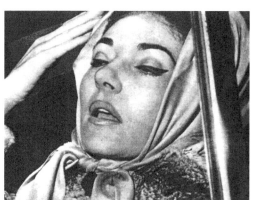

Candid Callas in the 1970s.

With Giuseppe Di Stefano, Milan, 1972.

Jackie and Litsa Callas, Paris, 1978.

12

Falling

I give myself to pleasure, since pleasure
is the best medicine for my ills.

La traviata, Verdi

On 22 July, Maria and Titta boarded the *Christina* in Monte Carlo, the last of the guests to arrive. She was nervous when Onassis introduced her to Sir Winston Churchill and his wife, Clementine, and their daughter and granddaughter, Diana and Celia Sandys. Also travelling with Churchill was his private secretary, Anthony Montague Browne, and his wife, Nonie. The Sandys women claimed they were not musical, and Celia, then 16, found Maria large and awkward, and compared her looks to Tina, who was blonde, petite and sporting a new nose from the London Clinic.

The following morning, they docked in Portofino and the women left for a shopping excursion. Although the men remained behind, Titta insisted on accompanying Maria, whose rose-printed beach pyjamas drew silent criticism from the others. 'We all hated her,' Celia said.

They also considered Titta vulgar, particularly when he whistled to Maria and kissed her. Calling him 'meningitis', they found him 'an absolute pill … he seemed to epitomise the very worst traits of a greedy and selfish Milanese bourgeois'.[1] At dinner, he made clumsy passes at Nonie, whose legs were marked from his white deck shoes.

Feeling excluded, it reminded Maria of the conservatory and how the girls whispered about her appearance: one day, they told her to dress better and lose weight, then the next, they brushed her hair and washed her collar. 'She just looked at us,' one of the girls recalled, 'like a lost soul.'

On the cruise, however, she had a friend in Nonie and offered to paint her nails – she collected nail polish and 'as a manicurist she is just as good as a singer'.[2] She confided her beauty habits: she plucked her legs every morning and showed Nonie the hairpieces she wore, including a short wig. Nonie was among the few who realised that friendship with Maria was uncomplicated and, at times, 'very mundane'.[3] Those who had worshipped her musical genius were unaware that she enjoyed watching cartoons and westerns and playing with her dogs. 'She could be very sweet and almost sisterly,' a friend recalled. 'It depended on how threatened she felt at that moment, or what she had pressing up against her.'[4]

The others, however, found that she complained about everything. 'She has the mien of a goddess, yet she can rage like a spoiled, stupid child,' Elsa Maxwell had once said of her. In his memoirs, Anthony Montague Browne wrote, 'She seemed almost to be trying to parody a stereotypical prima donna in her behaviour.'[5]

She surprised everyone by warning Titta not to turn on the air conditioning in their room, saying, 'Sopranos hate air conditioning even more than they hate other sopranos'. They also took offence at her joke, 'I like travelling with Winston Churchill. It relieves me of some of the burden of my popularity.'[6] Then, she offended Churchill's family by feeding him ice cream from her spoon.

Titta was equally miserable, he muttered to himself and leered at Tina in her bikini, comparing her tiny figure to Maria's body, which inflamed his wife's insecurities.

Maria's strange behaviour was fuelled by something deeper than guilt, as if she had something to hide. She was attracted to Onassis. It had begun in London and, years later, she told friends she knew they would be together. It was her destiny to fall for a powerful man. Others sensed the attraction, even if Maria thought she was being discreet. They saw the secret looks and overheard snippets of conversations in Greek, his hollow laugh responding to her silly jokes.

Every day, she tried to be alone with him, but either her husband or his wife was always in the way. She loved to watch him in action, taking business calls over the radio-telephone and talking in various languages to associates all over the world. To her, he was the epitome of masculinity. Titta remarked that his hairy torso resembled a gorilla's, but she saw it as a sign of his virility. Despite embodying the human form of a satyr, women found him attractive. 'If he hadn't had a dollar he could have snapped a lady's garter anytime he liked,' Ava Gardner said. 'He was a primitive with a yacht. For some ladies, that's an irresistible combination.'[7]

As they sailed along the Amalfi coast, Titta complained of seasickness and retired to their stateroom. Later that evening, Maria and Onassis sat alone, drinking a nightcap. She was unnerved when he said he wanted to sleep with her, for although she felt the same way, she hid behind the respectability of marriage. Nevertheless, he confided that his marriage was in name only and that Tina had a young lover. They had married in 1946, when Tina was 17 and he was 40 – a business arrangement to strengthen his ties to the Greek Establishment, as her father, Stavros Livanos, was a powerful shipping magnate.

The following evening, as the sun was setting, they stood on the deck to look at Stromboli smoking in the distance. 'Come on, show us your face,' Onassis yelled as he sounded the horn. At that moment the volcano erupted and lava plummeted to the sea. He called it a bad omen, and Maria, equally disturbed, crossed herself.

As though solidified by their Hellenic roots, they grew closer as the *Christina* sailed through the Straits of Messina and into the Gulf of Corinth, stopping at Itea for an excursion to Delphi. A believer in the occult, Maria found an array of symbolism in the ruins: the Priestess of Delphi, Pythia was sometimes an aristocrat, sometimes a peasant, both rich and poor, she could be learned or ignorant, and her oracle told the past, present and future.

Their next stop was Nafplion, in the Peloponnese, to visit the Epidaurus, where locals had erected a floral display in honour of Churchill. 'Flowers for me, how kind!' Maria said.

'They are not for you,' Diana replied, 'they are for papa.'

The following night, Maria and Onassis dined alone while the others ate in the formal dining room and gossiped about Maria's shameless behaviour. Aware of their whispering, Onassis asked Nonie to chaperone him and Maria, and, under the guise of stargazing on deck, she swam in the pool while the conspirators spoke in Greek and kissed.

On 4 August, the fates began to turn when, in the early hours of the morning, the *Christina* docked in Onassis's birthplace of Smyrna. As with Maria's maternal forebears, his family were Greek Orthodox and, for several generations, they had lived in Turkey and held Turkish nationality.

He spoke of the night, in 1922, when the port was set ablaze by Turks during the Greco-Turkish War, destroying his father's tobacco warehouses and, along with it, the family's fortune. Several of his family perished and he recalled the sight of bodies floating in the harbour, men brutally executed in the street (including his favourite uncle, Alexander) and women being dragged from their homes and raped. His stepmother and sisters fled to Lesbos, and his father was arrested by the Turks and narrowly avoided the death penalty.

A displaced person, Onassis sailed to Buenos Aires and found a job at a telephone company, and he made extra money by subletting his bed. With the money he earned, he invested in English-Argentine tobacco and founded two cigarette brands, Primeros and Osman, making him a millionaire at the age of 25. He bought tankers (their value had decreased after the stock market crash of 1929) and formed the first Argentine shipping trading company, Astilleros Onassis, used for trafficking heroin disguised inside crates of tobacco.

Speaking in Greek, so the others would not understand, he told Maria of his exploits. As a schoolboy, he seduced his French tutor and the family laundress and, perhaps for bravado, he included the wife of his father's friend. He described the brass beds at the brothels of Demiri Yolu, and she blushed when he confided his favourite scent was civet and *Talk Pudrasi* (talcum powder), which evoked memories of those days.[8] He concluded the tour in English, and four hours later they were at sea.

Inside their room, Maria and Titta argued over her future engagements and she stormed out. Walking the length of the yacht, she found Onassis leaning over the railing of the stern. They stood in silence as the land slipped out of view. He spoke first and told her how, at the age of 6, he lost his mother and, he wondered, had she lived, would his life have been different? Confiding in one another, they discussed their rootless existences, and she viewed them both as victims of their circumstances. Above all else, he said, he admired her resilience.

The next port of call was Istanbul, and while the others went on a sightseeing tour, Maria and Onassis drifted out to the harbour in his Chris-Craft boat. A respite from prying eyes, for aside from their pent-up frustration, they could speak freely. Later that day, they visited Mount Ethos, to be received by the Ecumenical Patriarch Athenagoras, the spiritual leader of the Orthodox Church. All her life she looked for signs: omens, good or bad, were viewed as God's will. She ignored conventionality and saw herself as an entity, a *spirito*, guided by her soul's desires.

At the holy site, Maria and Onassis knelt side by side to receive the Patriarch's blessing, he addressed them as 'the world's greatest singer and the greatest mariner of the modern world, the new Ulysses'. She had tears in her eyes and remained profoundly disturbed.

Later that evening, she rationalised her feelings: in her mind, she and Onassis were man and wife, and hours later they consummated their love. At dawn, she returned to her room and found Titta awake, questioning her whereabouts. Turning on him, she yelled, 'You act like my jailer. You never leave me alone. You control me in everything. You're like some hateful guardian … I'm suffocating!'[9]

It seemed pointless to hide their affair since everyone except Churchill was aware something had taken place. Sometime between midnight and 2 a.m., Tina had gone to the saloon and caught Maria and Onassis in one another's arms, beneath the counterfeit El Greco painting.[10]

Once Tina moved past the humiliation of the shipboard gossip, she used it to her advantage and asked for a divorce. Titta played the scorned husband and, calling Maria an animal, he asked how she could let herself go. 'I love him,' she said.

At the end of the cruise, Onassis gave her a gold bangle; the mark of all his mistresses.

On 13 August, Maria and Titta returned to Milan; neither spoke a word during the flight. Inside their home, she asked, 'What would you do, if I no longer wanted to stay with you?'[11] This was a hypothetical question, for a letter written on Hotel Hermitage stationery to her lawyer indicated that she had been planning to divorce Titta before the cruise: 'As for the reasons, right now I can only say for personal ones and disagreements … Trust me only for I have valid ones,' she wrote. 'Tell me, how can I get a divorce fast and good in the States, being an American. Does that help? Please keep this to yourself. You are the only one I've told it to.'[12]

Observing Maria's behaviour, Titta wrote, 'Maria was now a different person. She seemed to have become the succubus of some hellish demon.'[13] Undoubtedly, it was a reference to the sexual affair she had begun with Onassis. 'Living with a man so much older than I, I became prematurely depressed and old,' she said. 'I couldn't think of anything other than money and my reputation. Now, at last, I am an ordinary woman. Happy.'[14] Interestingly, Onassis was 53-years-old, a decade younger than Titta, but she thought he had the stamina of a young man. She asked Titta to move to their villa at Sirmione, explaining she wanted to be alone.

Forty-eight hours later, Onassis arrived in Milan and they spent a clandestine evening together. The next morning, she told Titta, 'It's all over between us. I have decided to stay with Onassis.' At ten o'clock in the evening, she met with him to discuss their separation and her future contracts.

Before the cruise, she had received an offer of £178,000 from a German production company to star in *The Prima Donna*, but she had declined. She had also been invited by the NBC Opera Company to perform in a televised production of Respighi's *La fiamma*. 'From a superficial look, it would seem a good medium for Callas,' the producer wrote. 'The Ravenna Byzantine background, the heroine who lures her man by witchcraft.'[15]

Given the present situation, the offer was rejected. Titta remarked, 'Maria is too busy with projects that flatter her vanity, her self-love, her taste for the colossal.'[16]

Litsa agreed, 'Maria has no intention of marrying Onassis. Maria is a careerist. She would also pass over my corpse to make a career and I am not surprised that, for the moment, she is getting ready to pass over the corpse of her marriage.'[17] To an Italian tabloid, Litsa added:

> It's painful, because Maria is always unhappy. She carries bad luck inside her, in her inability to love. She's condemned to that. Also, I feel bad for her husband, because he's old and dared to marry her. He dared to touch the Goddess, to walk on her altar. Everything in her has been sacrificed to art.[18]

In future, Maria told Titta, Onassis would manage her career, and he spoke of renovating the Salle Garnier, the opera house in Monte Carlo, 'where she would occupy the number one position under the brightest light of all, the blazing Monaco sun'.[19]

A day later, Maria and Onassis arrived at Sirmione to resume their discussions. However, Titta, whose resentment had been simmering since the cruise, was in no mood to negotiate. The tension was exasperated by Onassis's drinking – he was often unpredictable when drunk – and Maria was in a strange mood and behaved like a petulant child. After dinner, she gave Onassis a tour of the villa and he offended Titta by saying, 'You have a nerve confining a woman like Maria to the edge of a puddle like the lake of Sirmione.'[20] The evening ended with the two men exchanging insults and Maria sobbing uncontrollably. Before retiring, Titta yelled, 'I am placing a curse on you that you never have peace for the rest of your days.'

At four o'clock in the morning, Maria and Onassis left. Her butler, Ferruccio, telephoned Titta and asked him to send her passport, clothing and her miniature of the Madonna, and she asked for access to her accounts. Sending her clothes and passport, he refused to part with the Madonna, her lucky talisman, nor would he surrender control of the accounts. She said goodbye to Onassis on the airfield and he flew to Venice where, unbeknownst to her, he asked Tina to reconsider the divorce, before flying back to Milan. They went to Monte Carlo and checked into the Hotel Hermitage.

'My wife left Milan last Thursday,' Titta wrote in his diary. 'Today is Monday. Where is she?'[21]

A game of cat and mouse began, and on 2 September, Titta went to Malpensa Airport to meet her but she escaped through another exit. She cancelled her meeting with Titta, and later that evening she and Onassis were photographed leaving a nightclub and entering the Principe di Savoia, where they spent the night.

In a statement to the press, Tina said, 'I had hoped that Mr Onassis had loved our children enough and respected our privacy sufficiently to meet with me to straighten out our problems. But that was not to be.' She had known Onassis since she was 14, and during their thirteen-year marriage she would accuse him of emotional and physical abuse. 'A Greek who had spent so much time in Argentina – what would you expect?' her friend said. 'He was raised in two of the most machismo environments in the world.'[22]

Only once in those early days did Maria experience a brief flash of his temper when a photographer spied on them dancing. 'Try that again and I won't break your camera, I'll break your head,' Onassis said, threatening to punch him.[23] She was flattered by his defending her honour. As the rumours gathered momentum and the international newspapers reported on the affair, Titta no longer remained silent:

> At first, Maria sounded nebulous. She hinted that she had arrived at a turning point in her life. She acknowledged loving another man, but would not say who it was, although I urged her to be frank. Then, an hour later, she admitted the man she loved was Onassis. Onassis wants to glamorise his grimy tankers with the name of a great diva. They are in love like children. I created Callas and she repaid me by stabbing me in the back.[24]

In retaliation, Maria planted a dart, 'I am now my own manager. Mr Onassis and I have been very close friends. I even have a professional relationship with him.'

Over the telephone, she screamed at Titta, 'I will come to Sirmione with a gun and kill you!'

'I'll be waiting to machine-gun you down,'[25] he replied.

In the autumn of 1959, Maria spent seven days recording *La Gioconda* at La Scala, a welcome distraction from the maelstrom of publicity that continued to surround her. The return to the opera house, albeit under different circumstances, restored her friendship with Ghiringhelli. She had also spoken to Bing, who telephoned her and was surprised to find a congenial voice on the other end. 'Naturally, I want you back and, if you feel that you would like to reappear in New York … I would certainly be very willing to make an effort,' he said.[26]

The gesture incensed Titta, and he looked for new talent. In September 1960, he signed two young singers, Liubiunka Radosavlievic and Silvana Tumicelli, as his clients. However, his connection to the industry was non-existent and individuals with whom he had negotiated for years turned their backs on him and sided with Maria.

During that period, Maria filed for a legal separation, as divorce was illegal in Italy. In Titta's preliminary statement, he cited adultery and abandonment, as the courts were lenient to a husband who denounced their wife's character. In a hurry to finalise the separation, Maria did not challenge him – the legal system was unsympathetic toward women: it was not illegal for a husband to beat his wife, commit adultery or fail to provide for his family. Agreeing to the division of their assets, she gave him their villa in Sirmione and asked to keep their house in Milan, and he scoffed when she separated their dogs. He then tried to have her arrested for committing adultery – then a criminal offence in Italy. As she was an American citizen, she escaped imprisonment.

Shocked by Titta's deception, Maria joined Onassis on a Greek cruise. 'Our friendship is being put to trial by gossip and poor taste!' she snapped at reporters who gathered at the harbour.[27] Leaning over the railing, Onassis shouted, 'I am a prisoner!'[28] For the sake of respectability, her luggage was placed in the Santorini suite; his elder sister, Artemis, and her husband, Dr Garofalidis, were also on board in the guise of chaperones. Prophesying the Patriarch's blessing, he sounded the horn as they sailed toward Greece: the two most famous Greeks in the world were going home.

A week later, Maria flew to Bilbao for a concert and, surrounded by four bodyguards, a reporter convinced her to give an interview. 'I'll only ask you four questions,' he said. 'I won't touch any topic that might disturb you.'

'Alright, I believe in your graciousness,' she said, surprising him.

'La Callas, is she sad or happy now?'

'So, so.'

'And if I tell you that I see a deep sadness in your eyes, what will you tell me?'

'Yes, I am sad ... Many unexpected things happened, for which I don't have any more remedies.'

'I think you're forcing a smile.'

'You've already asked me four questions.'

The public was reminded by a priest, Father Joaquim de Dios Llserna, that, although she was a talented singer, 'one must not forget she was still a wife' and, therefore, now a sinner.[29] Feeling attacked, she called the concert 'a silly little engagement', resulting in a hostile response: 'Who is Maria Callas? We don't mean the opera singer, we mean the woman who insults her public when it suits her.'[30] They responded coldly to her singing: after the first act the applause was minimal, and she was not called back to the stage.

In her dressing room, she asked, 'Why does this happen to me, at this moment of great responsibility?' Someone responded that she gave a fantastic performance, but she turned on them, yelling, 'How was this fantastic? You made me believe I was alright. You lied to me!'[31]

Maria flew to London for a concert at the Royal Festival Hall and was ambushed by reporters, who asked if she was looking for romance. 'If you were separated as I am, would you not be looking for romance?' she snapped. They mocked her lone appearance: 'Not a sign of that *other* friend, shipping king Onassis'. The Greek tabloids, however, wrote that Onassis was dining with the actress Melina Mercouri at a taverna where, after too many drinks, they smashed plates, and he was billed for the damage. 'Callas is a sister to me and that is all,' he said.[32]

Avoiding the fifty reporters who waited for half an hour to meet her, Maria dined in her suite at the Savoy and spent the afternoon shopping in Oxford Street. Her London agent, Sandor Gorlinsky, told them, 'Rehearsals finished early and the guests weren't there. Madame Callas was standing in the draught from the air-conditioning and couldn't find anywhere else to go. So she decided to leave before she caught a cold.'[33]

Later that night, the audience of 3,000 applauded for twelve minutes and she was called to the stage ten times. One critic thought it was a waste of her talent, due to the small stage, and a violinist had obstructed her path during Lady Macbeth's sleepwalking scene. As she departed, the *Evening News* wrote, 'And the tigress went out like a lamb.'

Returning to Milan, she was surprised to find Titta had moved into her house to gain the right of possession. In her own words, she was left homeless, without clothes and the means to live. He opened the safe and removed their joint will, made in 1954, which appointed him as her sole heir. It seemed she had forgotten about the will, for when the safe was later opened in the presence of a legal witness, she was satisfied with its contents. Within days, Titta returned to Sirmione, and through the press, he addressed Maria, 'I bought and rebuilt this villa for you. It is always your house. If you want to return, the doors are open.'[34]

When she was accused of behaving badly, Maria said, 'I am only fighting for my rights'. She was also given the news that he had filed for a legal separation, despite his previous refusal to surrender her to Onassis, as though she were his property – under Italian law, she more or less was.

The hearing was scheduled for 14 November. She told a reporter, 'It is, in fact, a break, but not for sentimental reasons toward Onassis.'[35] Her Milanese friends treated her like a pariah, for embedded in their psyche was the belief that a woman's honour could not be compromised. Joining the witch hunt was Elsa Maxwell who, wanting to gain favour with Tina, wrote, 'I have not been able to defend [Maria] or explain her as a person since August 1959'. However, Onassis's sister, Artemis, was the first to recognise the trauma she had suffered, 'A woman who is adored by her fans but mistreated by her husband will never be secure.'[36]

At the end of October, Maria flew to New York en route to Kansas City for a concert at the Midland Theatre. There was news of a suspected bomb in the orchestra pit and the audience, which included the former President Harry Truman, had to be evacuated. 'What time is it supposed to go off?' Maria asked. At 9.30 p.m., she was told. 'Then I will go out and sing and let the people know I am here. If I don't they will say, "Well that Maria Callas". I'll take the risk.'[37]

Eventually, the bomb was declared a hoax and she sang to thunderous applause. She returned to her hotel suite and discovered £300 worth of costume jewellery had been stolen, along with £100 in cash. Refusing to discuss it, she told reporters, 'Mind your own business.'[38]

Afterwards, Maria left for Dallas to open the season with *Lucia di Lammermoor*. Due to the company's lack of money, they could not pay her costumier in Italy and substitutes were ordered from Neiman Marcus. She viewed it as a bad omen and her overwrought nerves were being tested by her separation from Onassis. A greeting from Dorle Soria was a reminder of the crossroads she had reached: 'Love for Maria to whom I wish everything her heart and art desire.'[39]

In the opening performance, she failed to reach the E flat in the Mad Scene and, backstage, she sang the note several times to prove she could. The *Dallas Morning News* wrote that her high notes were 'badly aimed attacks which she barely covered by roulades downward into the more comfortable register'. Afterwards, she said, 'I gambled my career tonight, my career ends here.' In her hotel room, she sobbed until three o'clock in the morning.

Interrupting the Dallas season, she went to Italy and appeared with Titta before the judge at the courthouse in Brescia. After a hearing lasting for six hours, he withdrew his original separation order and they agreed to live apart by mutual consent. 'It's pitiful that I wasted twelve years of my life for nothing but a smeared name and not even one-third of my fortune gained!'

she wrote to a friend. 'You would [have] never believed it from that numb face, would you?'[40]

Returning to Dallas, she gave two performances of *Medea* on 19 and 21 November and hurried back to Monte Carlo to join Onassis on the *Christina*. After her arrival, he received a telephone call from his confidante, Costa Gratsos, informing him that Tina, an American citizen, had filed for divorce in the New York Supreme Court on the grounds of adultery and asked for custody of their children. However, Tina did not cite Maria as a co-respondent but instead named an old school friend, Jeanne Rhinelander, in the petition. Surprised by the move, Maria said, 'I have nothing – really, nothing – to hide.'[41]

Regardless, he ordered Maria to disembark and move into the Hotel Hermitage, then he telephoned Tina, begging her to reconsider the divorce. Even then, after the change in his personality, Maria did not realise he was 'a charming psychopath ... bound by absolutely no moral imperatives at all'.[42] Perhaps to make him understand she would be a faithful wife, she told *Gente*, 'I want to live just like a normal person, with a family, a home, a dog.' She changed her appearance to suit his tastes, cutting her long hair at his request, and wearing black, his favourite colour.

The emotional dilemma coincided with a series of health issues: she developed a hernia, a side-effect of her appendectomy, and had inflammation in her jawbone and fluid in her nasal cavity. 'I was like a deaf man shouting,' she said.

Abandoned by Onassis, who moved between London and Monte Carlo, and with no future engagements, Maria returned to Milan and spent her 36th birthday alone. She also spent Christmas by herself. 'I don't like traditional holidays,' she said. 'You're forced to buy presents and be happy and merry when maybe you don't feel like it.'[43] The future remained uncertain: she had no contracts to fulfil, nor did she have the financial security to retire. 'I have closed many chapters this year,' she said, but little by little, she was losing control. 'She has reached the peak,' Litsa observed. 'Now, like a girl with acrophobia, she is afraid of falling.'[44]

13

Detour

To me, a wicked man who is also eloquent seems the most guilty of them all. He'll cut your throat as bold as brass, because he can dress up murder in handsome words.

Medea, Euripides

For years to come, Maria had a reoccurring dream: she and Onassis were in a hotel suite, packing things into suitcases, and from the window they saw a landscape of mud; the sight filled them with hopelessness.[1] Each time she awoke, she had a foreboding sense of despair and knew it was a bad omen: the *fatum*. 'We were doomed,' she said.

In the New Year of 1960, she made the first attempt to divorce Titta, whom she accused of being 'not normal' and, tired of his harassment, she asked for police protection.[2] She wrote to Walter Cummings, asking his legal advice on whether she qualified for a quick divorce in Alabama, which catered to non-residents. 'Is it valid?' she asked him. 'Will I have to stay there for a long time?'[3]

The matter remained unresolved, forcing the status of her relationship with Onassis into limbo. Although, unbeknownst to her, he began an affair with Agnetta Castallanos, Vice President of Olympic Airways, which lasted for two years.

In Paris, Maria took a suite at the Ritz Hotel, ten minutes from Onassis's apartment at Avenue Foch. 'I can't be truly free because [Titta] keeps check on me all the time.' she said.[4] She also gave conflicting information about her private life, vowing to revive her career, and stating, 'There is no love interest in my life at present.'[5] To *France-Soir*, she confided, 'I want to have a baby; I'm thirty-six-years-old, with no one in my life, and I do not even know if I am capable of giving [birth] to a being.' Given society's morals, it was a provocative statement: she knew the father of her child would not be her legal husband. A victim of her circumstances, she remarked:

> The world has condemned me for leaving my husband. But I didn't leave him. He left me because I no longer wanted him to handle my affairs. I believed in love. But Meneghini wasn't a husband, he was a manager. He wanted to take advantage of my glory. And that's why we're not together any more.[6]

Since December 1959, the Italian press had speculated that Maria was pregnant. The rumours were first published in the women's magazine *Annabella*, which reported that she suffered from 'dizziness, sudden sickness and had a more florid than normal appearance'. The gossip columnists bombarded her home with telephone calls, looking for any clues of pregnancy, and wrote that she looked 'pale and worn-out' after her trip to Dallas.[7] In a statement, she said:

> The interference with my privacy has now reached an unprecedented point. The report of my pregnancy is completely groundless. I am now considering legal action against the persons responsible for the publication of this false report.[8]

Knowing of Maria's longing for a family, Onassis had made promises to her in late 1959, which came to fruition in early 1960, when she conceived a child. His words meant nothing, however, because during his marriage to Tina, he wanted only one child: his son and heir, Alexander, born in 1948. Thereafter, he forced Tina to have abortions and, when she became pregnant in 1950, she decided to keep her baby. As she had failed to obey him, Onassis beat Tina, hoping to cause a miscarriage, but it did not. Their second child was a girl, Christina, who, ironically, was a disappointment to her mother. After the birth, Onassis claimed he suffered from sexual dysfunction and explained that he could not, in his words, visit the place from where his children came.

Responding to Maria's news, he ordered her to abort and offered 'any amount of money' for her to do so.[9] A cruel remark, for not only had he rejected their child, but he had exploited her financial situation.[10] Perhaps she thought he would change his mind and marry her when they were both free from their spouses.

So, she met with Titta to discuss an American divorce and asked for his signature on a document. A simple process, in their separation contract, they had negotiated two specific clauses: he could not oppose or hinder her from seeking an American divorce, nor could either party, while still legally married, behave in a way that caused a scandal.

However, someone close to Maria informed Titta of her pregnancy and he took the opportunity to blackmail her into giving him 50 per cent of her recording royalties.[11] She refused, emphasising that she was ruined due to his mishandling of her finances. Furthermore, he kept their investment property, which had been bought with her money. So, he threatened to withhold his signature and reveal her pregnancy, thus creating a scandal and making her in breach of their contract.

As Titta was head of the household and she was legally his wife, he would have rights to her child, despite its paternity. 'The fight is hard and savage,' she wrote to Cummings.[12] Under Italy's patriarchal law, she knew Titta would take everything from her, including her child.

As time progressed, her desperation became evident. 'Tell me how much it will cost and how long it will take, if I need Meneghini's consent or if I can do without it,' she wrote. 'And see if he can obviously prepare everything in secret … Please don't think I'm crazy. I know I am.'[13]

Having a baby with one man while married to another would have ended her career. Marriage to Onassis, albeit outside of Italy, would have made her a bigamist in her adopted country. 'If I married tomorrow and had a child – and like every woman, I want to have many children – by Italian law, I would be imprisoned for two years.'[14]

To Cummings, she wrote, 'Of course, for the Orthodox Church I am not married, but as an Orthodox I am, if you can understand what I mean.'[15] Battling her conscience, she knew her religion viewed her as immoral and that Titta was influencing the public's perception of her. Having longed for a child since 1949, it was, therefore, a cruel irony that her pregnancy made her feel isolated, terrified and trapped. '[Titta] took my love of peace, all that I ever had,' she confided to a friend. 'I think I will soon heal these wounds. Wounds caused by my husband.'[16]

Maria's emotional crisis was heightened by Onassis leaving with Sir Winston Churchill on a month-long cruise. She was not invited, as he explained her presence would embarrass the elderly statesman. Although she found Churchill 'so boring', she was humiliated by the rejection.[17]

In mid April 1960, he returned from the cruise and went to Paris to meet with Tina, to discuss the terms of their divorce: she had since agreed to drop the adultery suit in New York and sought an uncontested divorce in Alabama, on the grounds of mental cruelty. A natural when it came to publicity, he encouraged the rumours that he and Tina would reconcile. 'There was never any romance between Callas and myself,' he said. 'We are just good friends.'

During that period, Maria was hurt by the publication of her mother's ghostwritten memoirs. To a friend, she confided, 'The case of my mother is a thing we cannot avoid. She is in the hands of vulgar, shady agents who earn their money on the simple fact that she is my mother.'[18]

It was a blow to her self-esteem; she had always been ashamed of her mother's behaviour, particularly her parents' marital problems, and now the world knew the intricacies of her upbringing. Publicly, Maria said nothing to fuel Litsa's publicity campaign, which foundered, along with her poorly received book. But in private, she said:

> One day, soon, I'll decide to write my own book – a biography. But I will need someone who does research – statements (real ones) and information, because my memory may lack sometimes. You know how I am precise about everything. At least I try to be as good as I can.[19]

Despite Onassis's treatment, Maria loved him to the point of obsession; the more he rejected her, the more she wanted him. It evoked a new vulnerability, and years later, she wrote, 'If you could read into my feelings, you would feel the most powerful and rich man in the whole world.'[20]

Since his divorce, he had become preoccupied with Tina and her position as the Greek Mother: her breaking away from his dynasty and reverting to her unmarried name, Livanos, threatened his identity as a powerful patriarch. However, Maria was summoned by Onassis to Monte Carlo, where they were photographed dancing at his nightclub, Maona, and she told reporters they would marry as soon as possible. The following day, he dismissed her announcement as a joke.

In mid July 1960, Maria went to London for recordings, and during the first and third sessions, Legge brought her to Ivor Griffiths, a laryngologist, who found her 'vocal apparatus in marvellous condition'.[21] According to Griffiths, 'All she needs is to start work again seriously, and the psychological uplift that only a few public successes could give her.'[22]

The sessions were unproductive, due to Maria having not sung in eight months, and to his colleague, Legge wrote, '[Her] muscles have slackened and the body has become unaccustomed to the physical tensions which are an integral part of the art of singing.'[23] After two hours, she became fatigued and left, leaving him in doubt of their future collaborations. 'I shall be happier in my mind,' he said, 'when I have heard her sing again in public.'[24]

Several days later, Maria went to Brussels to give a concert at the Kursaal in Ostend, a venue which, although popular in the 1920s, was no longer associated with singers of her calibre. Perhaps she viewed it as an easy source of income to tide her over during her pregnancy, for Onassis remained unsupportive.

Now she was in her fourth month and the physiological changes were becoming obvious. Were her various hints of wanting a baby, despite her marital status, a way to gauge the public's reaction? Could she risk the scandal of having a baby and raising it alone? Or had she believed the public would view her as an operatic heroine, like Norma, 'a woman who does not feel bad nor does she feel wronged by unfavourable situations, which, in the end, she has caused herself'.[25]

In Brussels, she attended a rehearsal but cancelled the concert due to tracheitis. A doctor reported that her illness was caused by a sudden change in temperature. 'When the soprano arrived in Ostend, strong gusts of wind blew, and the singer's clothing was very light. The throat was not even protected by a scarf.'[26] She wrote to Leo Lerman, 'I had [to] miss the concert and it really was a pity ... But as you see everything went well – no scandal.'[27]

A short time later, she suffered a miscarriage, whether or not the tracheitis contributed – staphylococcus bacteria can be dangerous to pregnant women – remains unknown. Her close friend and occasional secretary, Giovanna Lomazzi said:

> During the period of 1960, I was in almost daily contact with Maria ... During this time, [she] went to a clinic in Milan, under a false name and had an abortion. What is not known is whether this was a natural abortion [treatment following a miscarriage], or was planned. This is a secret that died with Maria Callas.[28]

As Lomazzi admitted, she was uncertain of how the pregnancy ended but she knew of Maria's admission to a clinic, a natural turn of events, but nothing more. There are contradictory elements. As abortion was illegal and carried a prison sentence, it was unlikely the procedure was performed in a clinical environment. According to an investigative article in the *New York Times*, written before abortion was legalised in Italy, it was accessible to rich women, who were referred by their gynaecologist to whoever carried out the procedure, often in their homes and costing $250. The women returned to their gynaecologist for aftercare as 'the abortionist would never want to set eyes on [them] again'.[29]

The reason for Maria using a false name at the clinic was understandable, as Titta's brother-in-law was a prominent doctor and, given his past conduct, he could have easily obtained her medical records and, therefore, proven her pregnancy and used it to his (legal) advantage. As one of the most famous women in the world, it is doubtful that her alias concealed her physical identity; however, in terms of documentation, it protected her privacy. The ending of her pregnancy, regardless of how it happened, was, perhaps, inevitable: she knew how it felt to be rejected by a parent and did not want a similar fate for her child.

Afterwards, she wrote to Cummings and postponed the divorce proceedings. She said, 'Until the day that I get married, I won't be able to count on anybody but myself and I won't accept help from [Onassis].'[30] It was not a question of accepting help from Onassis – he did not offer any, and left on a cruise without her. 'I was invited, but I had to explain to Mr Onassis that I have to work,' she told reporters. 'I am not so lucky as some of his other friends who have lots of spare time.'[31]

In his diary, Leo Lerman wrote, 'Maria is leading the sort of life any woman lives, her timetable being totally controlled by the whims of her man who is apparently more loved than loving.'[32] Leo added, 'Her new smile – very young, sweet, hurt; her softness; her vulnerability.'[33]

Responding to criticism, she said, 'I'm an Oriental,' and she called Onassis 'my *pasha*'.* Some felt it ran deeper than subservience; he had broken her spirit.

In August, Maria went to Greece to perform in the National Theatre's production of *Norma*, conducted by Serafin and directed by Alexis Minotis. Staged at the Ancient Theatre of Epidaurus, her fee of £15,000 for three performances was controversial, particularly as the National Theatre was state owned, but she donated it to the founding of a Maria Callas Scholarship Fund:

> I want you all to understand one thing: I am grateful to Mr Bastias because, when I was fourteen or fifteen years old, I believe, the National Opera of

---

* A Turkish title for a high-ranking male. Similarly, in 1949, she called Titta 'my master, my man, my consolation, my heart and brain, my food, my everything'.

Greece was being founded and I had an audition with Mr Bastias, when I was just a child then, who agreed with Mme. de Hidalgo to pay me to continue my studies at the disposal of the Opera. This I could never forget.

The first performance on 21 August sold 17,000 tickets but was cancelled due to an unexpected thunderstorm and coachloads of patrons were driven back to Athens. However, superstitious locals viewed it as a bad omen from the Greek gods, who permitted only drama and not opera to be performed at the sacred theatre. Three days later, she appeared on stage and gave a performance that was heralded 'as a landmark in the annals of Greek artistic history'.[34]

Although Onassis was absent from the opening night, he threw a party on the *Christina* and many were surprised to find Maria catering to his guests. Before her second performance two days later, she developed a fever but appeared on stage, preceded by a warning from Bastias that she was unwell. Her final performance was cancelled, for which she lost her £5,000 fee, and she sailed away with Onassis, telling the press she had a 'rapid deterioration of influenza'.[35]

In December 1960, Maria returned to Milan for La Scala's production of *Poliuto*, singing opposite Franco Corelli. At the premiere, the theatre was decorated with thousands of carnations, and outside her admirers hung banners reading, 'Welcome Home, Callas'. Tickets were sold on the black market at ten times their original value, and the guest list resembled a film premiere: along with Onassis, the audience was formed of film stars; the European jet set; Prince Rainier and Princess Grace of Monaco; and the Aga Khan. But the glitterati could not distract from her performance and *High Fidelity* wrote, 'There was an audible hiss of sympathy from the audience when she flattened like a ton of bricks in several high notes.' Her acting was described by the *New York Times* 'as consummate as ever … what actresses uses her hands as Callas does? There were moments when she achieved a poignancy that no other singer can rival.'

At the beginning of 1961,* Maria temporarily moved to Paris and rented a suite at the Hotel Lancaster on the Rue de Berri, a mile from Onassis's apartment.

---

* From 29 March–5 April 1961, Maria recorded her first French recital, conducted by Georges Prêtre, at the Salle Wagram. She was unhappy with her upper register and refused to allow certain arias to be released. At the end of May, she sang in a benefit concert for the Edwina Mountbatten Trust at St James's Palace.

Longing to begin a new life, she burnt her old stage costumes, explaining, 'They belonged to a past I didn't like.'[36] She told reporters, 'I love Onassis. But I could never be his wife, because my husband forbids it.'[37] Nevertheless, they speculated that 'something's not quite right between Callas and Onassis … the clamorous incident with the paparazzi shows that the supposed idyll of the singer and the tycoon is slowly breaking down'.[38] It was claimed that she had driven at full speed into a reporter's car, causing the reporter to remark, 'Everyone is aware of her uncontrollable spirit.'[39]

From the shadows, Titta continued to destroy Maria's reputation and to profit from her income. To the press, he had spoken of their prior negotiations having taken place 'in a serene atmosphere' and that their agreement to separate their assets was 'made with affectionate understanding'.[40] In July, he presented a dossier of newspaper articles to the court in Brescia, asking to annul their mutual agreement to live apart and have it replaced with a separation order naming her as the guilty party. For Maria, it meant more legal fees; however, the judge dismissed his appeal due to insufficient evidence. Embittered, Titta said, 'I will pursue [her] to the end of the world if necessary. She let her career break up after she left me. Now she is drifting around the world in search of happiness.'[41]

In early August 1961, Maria returned to the Epidaurus to perform in *Medea*, donating her £10,000 fee to the Maria Callas Scholarship Fund. On the night of the performance, people gathered outside the theatre, certain of hearing Maria's voice, although they could not see her. Among the audience of 16,000 were dignitaries, foreign royals and film stars. Onassis was absent, having sailed to Egypt on a business trip. 'I began to cry,' Wally Toscanini said. 'She was losing her voice … You could almost see the blood coming out of her vocal cords.'

A week before the opening night, she invited her father, who was living in Athens, and Jackie to dinner at a restaurant in Glyfada. 'I suddenly realised that I didn't know this woman at all. The Maria I had last seen, the Maria I knew, was fat and awkward, ill-tempered and greedy; here was this vision of refined elegance,' Jackie said of the meeting, their first since 1949.[42] Afterwards, she gave her father and sister a tour of the *Christina* and introduced them to Onassis, who was entertaining business colleagues.

'Are you happy?' Jackie asked, overwhelmed by the opulence. Although surprised by the question, Maria admitted she was happy with Onassis but tired of their nomadic life, and she said, 'I'd like to have a baby.'[43]

Their next meeting was tense. She arrived alone, upset by an argument she had had with Onassis, and attacked Jackie when she spoke of her own singing ambitions. 'It was your crazy mother who thought you had a voice. Don't you know how old you are? Don't you know you're too old to train your voice? Singing is for young people, it needs years of study, not just braying like a donkey,' she shouted.

Sensing that Maria wanted to exorcise her repressed anger, perhaps toward Onassis or her own shortcomings, Jackie told her she was wrong. She gave up singing to care for Milton, who was dying of cancer.

'Do you want me to start breaking dishes?'[44] Maria asked, before regaining her composure and settling into polite conversation.

Two days later, Maria sent Jackie a message, inviting her to tea on the *Christina.* When Jackie arrived, Maria was trying on expensive jewellery and deliberating over her outfit. 'I hear you're jealous of me, Jackie,' she said, catching her sister unaware. 'Enough,' she added, 'Tell me what to wear ... which dress, which of these diamonds.'

The insecurities of her youth encouraged her display of extravagance and, like a spectre, the press continued to dwell on her past 'tubby, bespectacled' appearance: 'She had a double chin, a bad complexion, and a curious loping walk which only emphasised her ungainly figure.'[45] Even her trusted confidante, Elvira de Hidalgo, although nameless in print, echoed their views, 'She never flirted. Nobody courted her. She was awkward and ashamed.'[46] Perhaps Maria wanted to instil similar feelings of inadequacy within Jackie for, after their meeting, she pointed her in the direction of a bus stop, and left in a Rolls-Royce.

The remainder of the summer was spent with Onassis, who no longer concealed his changing temperament. During her marriage to Titta, she had said, 'Are you never jealous of me? That's not good, and I'm displeased. I would like to see and feel that you are a little jealous of your woman, even if you trust me.'[47] So she thought Onassis's bursts of anger were a sign of their intimacy and his feelings for her. At times, he reduced her to a nervous wreck: if he left for a business trip, she threatened to commit suicide or warned that she would leave him. Many were struck by how 'defenceless and inappropriate she looked ... like an apprehensive school girl' when she was around him.[48] She accompanied him to strip shows and, at his request, wore nothing but her diamonds to bed.[49]

Often, he embarrassed her. He said she sang like a hummingbird and kissed like a stomach pump. And he compared her to other women, using it as a weapon to attack her self-esteem. He told her, 'You know I prefer women who are tall and a little bit fat like you.'[50] Such remarks both flattered and unnerved her, for she had a phobia of becoming fat (pocrescophobia) and occasionally starved herself and took diuretics to maintain her figure. There was no longer a veil of secrecy: the staff were accustomed to their loud voices, particularly the scenes of verbal abuse – a common theme – which he used as a prelude to sex, often manhandling her and causing her pain. She gave him a licence to hurt her, in every sense of the meaning, telling him, 'I am yours – do with me as you want.'[51]

In December 1961, Maria sang in La Scala's production of *Medea* opposite Giulietta Simionato, who found her in a state of nervous despair. 'It's not my voice that is sick, it's my nerves,' she remarked. Her upper register, described by *Opera News* as a 'bit frayed and wobbly – and takes painfully wrong notes occasionally', cracked during the aria, 'Dei tuoi figli', and the claque began to hiss. Turning to the gallery, she raised her fist and sang, '*Crudel ... Ho dato tutto a te* [Cruel ... I gave everything to you].' The *Corriere della Sera* wrote:

> Speaking of Callas is like walking over burning coals. There are those who adore her with a sort of inclination to fetishism. There are those who detest her on the basis of the gossip, often tendentious, of a certain part of the press enamoured of rumours ... This *Medea* of hers is unique for the psychological penetration of character.

Before the final performance on 20 December, Maria had an operation on her sinuses and awoke to a bouquet of carnations from Onassis, who had left for Monte Carlo. She threw the flowers in the bin; he had let her down when she needed him most. Regardless, she spent Christmas with him in Monaco and became a resident of the principality due to Titta pursuing her in the courts as a resident of Milan, but now the judge was bound to her new territorial jurisdictions.

For the next two months, Maria lived at the Hotel Hermitage, although Onassis's yacht remained moored in the harbour. 'I am trying to fulfil my life as a woman,' she told those who asked of her future engagements. To others, she spoke of sacrificing 'one hell of a career' for the man she loved.[52] Her statements mirrored her inner conflict: she continued to respect music, regardless if she was singing at La Scala or practising alone. Having discovered his favourite piece was Chopin's Nocturne in D flat major Op. 27 No. 2, she taught herself how to play it on the piano. 'I took great liberties,' she said. 'He liked to hear me play it. It soothed him.'[53]

Onassis told friends he wanted her to pursue her career, as it gave her a purpose, but to Maria, when she considered offers, such as *Medea* in Paris, he said, 'What do you want to work for? I have plenty of money.'[54] Once, at a dinner party, a friend engaged Maria in a conversation about composers and referred to Puccini as a seeker of beautiful women and libretto. In response, Onassis banged the table and shouted, 'Son of a bitch, just like me! Only I don't give a damn about the libretto!'

In the summer of 1961, she had met with Rudolf Bing, who asked her to sing at the Metropolitan, and warned her the programme was scheduled eighteen months in advance. Although she eventually declined, she had resorted to playing games with Bing, whether intentional or not, perhaps to prove to herself and to Onassis that she was in demand.

Maria had undertaken a balancing act, submitting to Onassis in their private life and rising to the occasion when he exploited her fame. More than ever he needed her celebrity to support his ego, which had suffered after Tina's marriage to John Spencer-Churchill, the Marquess of Blandford, the son and heir to the Duke of Marlborough.

With his ex-wife now a marchioness, Onassis re-evaluated Maria's importance in his life. 'All you need is one golden apple,' he told a friend, who asked the secret to his success. 'A single apple that somebody else wants, and you have control.'[55] She was his golden apple: a retired singer was unappealing but a career as a film star would, he thought, give her higher status.

The year before, Onassis had persuaded the Hollywood producer, Carl Foreman, to give her the leading female part in *The Guns of Navarone*, a war film starring Gregory Peck, Anthony Quinn and David Niven. 'Give her ten days and if she's no good, okay, dump her, get somebody else – I'll foot the bill,' he told Foreman. Since 1954, Maria had received offers to appear on screen, beginning with Visconti, who asked her to play an opera singer in his film, *Senso*. She was wary of the medium – she called it 'technical manipulation' – or perhaps reluctant to preserve herself on film, as she could be distorted as the director saw fit.[56] The *Tatler* wrote, 'In the theatre she can have her own way, overruling the director or conductor. But she knew that in a film studio even the greatest stars have to obey orders.'[57]

She lost her nerve and declined Foreman's offer. Consumed by rage, Onassis referred to her as a nightclub singer who knew nothing, and she ran from the room in tears. It was reminiscent of a colleague's hurtful remark, '[You're] really rather a dull person, [you're] just a singer.'[58] She understood Onassis's reasoning: she was no longer valuable; there was no reason for him to love her. 'I get up every day of my life to win!' he shouted in her wake. 'I don't know why you bother to get up at all.'

14

Consequences

Weep, o heavy eyes,
While my heart is bleeding.

La Gioconda, Ponchielli

'It's not difficult to be swept off one's feet. Living with the consequences, that's the hard part,' Maria said, as she learned the facets of Onassis's character.[1] He was a man who signed agreements in invisible ink; everything was an illusion. What was fact and what was fiction? Even his very origins were questionable: some believed that his family were not Greek, and documents suggested he was 7 years older than his given age. Were his stories true? His heroic escape from Smyrna on the night of the fire?

The details were inconsistent, as he spoke of swimming across the harbour, his limbs smashing off dead bodies and dodging bullets from the Turks. Maria was haunted by the images he evoked of watching his uncles being executed in the street which, as papers from Washington proved, was actually false. Avoiding the subject, his sister said, 'It was a very confusing time, he had nightmares for years.'

In moments of introspection, Maria might have questioned her own identity. Perhaps Onassis's words haunted her: that without ambition, she had nothing to live for. During her marriage to Titta, she was treated like a child. She could not write a cheque nor access her accounts, and he gave her a meagre amount of money, scarcely enough to pay the hairdresser. The humiliation of having to depend on others made her accept twice as many engagements than in the past two years. 'I have to work,' she said. 'It's for my dignity.'[2]

In February 1962, she embarked on a concert tour, conducted by Georges Prêtre, beginning at the Royal Festival Hall in London. With their usual praise, the British press wrote, 'In London's Savoy Grill, Maria Callas finished her coffee and stood up. And so did most of the sophisticated Savoy set just to get a better look at this thirty-eight-year-old soprano. Callas has that rare quality of feminine magic.'[3]

On the opening night, however, the press accused her of exploiting the public, for although she had 'unfettered showmanship', she failed to give a good performance:[4]

Looking like a Left Bank beatnik in pencil-slim black skirt and sequinned pink jersey, Maria Callas slinked on to the platform last night to make as bad a start as I have heard in a celebrity recital … Good show, Maria, but not great singing.[5]

Proceeding to Germany, she sang in Munich, Hamburg, Essen and Bonn, before going to London to record mezzo arias, but she was unhappy with her voice so only the Rondo-Finale from *La Cenerentola* was released. Underestimating her fragile self-esteem, the *Daily Herald* wrote, 'I doubt if [the] reviews of her performances, ranging from reproachful to quite savage, worried her greatly. What, after all, are the opinions of a handful of critics compared with the adoration of faithful thousands?'

She suffered alone, for Onassis remained in Monte Carlo, facing his own crisis. In recent months, his relationship with Prince Rainier had deteriorated, following President Charles de Gaulle's blockade of Monaco, a retaliation against French citizens using the principality as a tax haven. Therefore, to support its economy, Rainier asked Onassis to invest in two hotels and an apartment block to cater to mass tourism, but Onassis wanted to maintain the resort's exclusivity.

While in London, Maria received word from New York that Litsa, who was living in a bedsit, had attempted suicide by overdosing on barbiturates. Next to her bed, she had left a final letter to the public, detailing how Maria had condemned her to a life of poverty. In other letters, written to relatives, she spoke of her funeral arrangements and entrusted her body to the Institute of Legal Medicine. 'I knew you would want to know the circumstances concerning this situation,' Dr James Ducey from the Roosevelt Hospital wrote to Maria, by way of Onassis's offices in Monte Carlo.[6]

In response to Litsa's condition, she said, 'My mother is not quite sane.'[7] Writing to her godfather, Maria suggested placing her mother in an inexpensive institution. Then, dwelling on her abusive childhood, she decided if Litsa were to '[come] to her senses for one minute she might really commit suicide'.[8]

This troubling period was punctuated by Titta filing a petition with the Civil Tribunal in Milan, stating that their marital break-up was 'detrimental to his prestige', and as compensation, he asked for Maria's house. He exhibited images of Maria and Onassis in various settings – an example of what he called her unseemly and dishonourable demeanour – and asked the judge to consider his appeal. Although the images suggested 'an affectionate attitude', there was no proof of adultery and the case was dismissed.[9] Reflecting on her circumstances, Maria said, 'God has given me two big crosses to carry. One, my mother, who is not quite sane ... And second, my dear husband, who defames me constantly.'[10]

Two days later, Maria left for New York, where she was to sing at President John F. Kennedy's 44th birthday party at Madison Square Garden. It was a gala evening and she was one of many performers. She was photographed talking to Marilyn Monroe, her smile betraying her unhappiness. After forty-eight hours, she departed, having refused to reconcile with her mother and ignoring her friends' invitations to dinner. In moments of despair, she isolated herself from others, perhaps not wanting to hear their criticism or face the reality of her situation.

She went to Milan for two performances of *Medea*. As she sang her first notes, her voice cracked and the hissing from the claque echoed her inner frustration. The critics paid little attention to her. 'La Scala,' she said, 'is the only theatre that's ever seen me sing bad, sing well, has suffered with me.'[11] Aside from being in poor voice, she had fluid on her vocal cords and was in pain from a hernia in her abdomen. 'For the first time ever,' she remarked, 'I submitted to these difficulties and lost all my audacity.'[12]

In times of strife, her body revolted against her, but her doctor found no physical symptoms to suggest illness and diagnosed her ailments as psychosomatic. To justify her frequent bouts of ill health, she frequently complained of dysmenorrhoea, headaches and sinusitis, but she was dismissed as a hypochondriac. In her prime, she spoke of killing her enemies with her voice, but now she spoke of killing herself because of it. 'Unhappy birds cannot sing, she said. 'Only my soul knows how much I suffer.'[13]

After the failure in Milan, she spent the following months living with Onassis at Avenue Foch, where she also had an apartment at No. 44 – he owned the building – and aboard the *Christina*. His issues with Rainier were unresolved and, in his troubled frame of mind, he responded to her love, which was almost maternal. She fussed over his meals and insisted he wore a sweater in case he caught a cold.

Now there was little secrecy surrounding their relationship, and in front of his staff he held her hand and called her 'Maritsa'. More importantly, he viewed her as a buffer between himself and the Monégasque royals, who were fond of her, particularly Princess Grace, with whom she shared a close friendship. Her friends sensed he was using her, because in social circles, particularly in Paris and London, she made 'the ageing Greek bandit'[14] seem respectable. 'He is pretty vulgar,' Richard Burton wrote. 'One suspects him of orgies and other dubious things.'[15]

As though repelled by his feelings for her, Onassis began to vanish for long periods at a time, citing business meetings in London and family commitments in Greece; the latter was an excuse to see his lover, Agnetta Castallanos. Maria suspected he was being unfaithful but he denied it, telling her she was paranoid and that her accusations were pathetic. However, her instincts proved correct: in the spring of 1962, he ended his involvement with Castallanos and began an affair with Lee Radziwill, the 28-year-old wife of Prince Stanislaw 'Stas' Radziwill, and younger sister of the American First Lady, Jacqueline Kennedy.

At first, Onassis and Lee confined their liaisons to the Dorchester in London, but they soon began meeting in Paris and Athens. Speaking of Onassis, with whom she had fallen in love, Lee said, 'He was amusing to be with. And he had charm, a fascinating way with women. He made sure they felt admired and desired. He took note of their slightest whim. He interested himself in them – exclusively and profoundly.'[16] As with Maria, he met Lee when she was at her lowest ebb: she was recovering from postnatal depression, the humiliation of her husband's affair, and moving in her famous sister's shadow. 'Money isn't just luxury, it is power,' he told Lee. 'That power can be yours, too, if you'd like to be by my side.'[17]

Although Maria was unaware of Lee, she discovered that Onassis was a client of Madame Claude's, whose brothel near the Champs Elysée employed 500 prostitutes and catered to the mafia, film stars, tycoons, statesmen and royals. Since his first experience at Fahrie's in Smyrna, he came to view women as transactions and derived pleasure in treating them as such. The décor of his bedroom at Avenue Foch was modelled on a brothel which, in his words, was to remind women of what they were. 'The best girl,' he said, 'is a girl you never have to see again.'[18]

His depraved requests shocked even Madame Claude, and as Maria would soon learn, he preferred emaciated young women for such trysts. 'He's sick …

destructive,' she said of his behaviour, although she never reproached him.[19] Ashamed of her living arrangements, she called it a 'hidden life'.[20]

Perhaps the realisation that Onassis was sexually attracted to women with androgynous figures caused Maria to abuse food, as she had done throughout the years. When alone in Paris, she weighed every morsel of food and followed a regimental menu:

Monday
Breakfast:* coffee or tea with a teaspoon of sugar, and skimmed milk just enough to stain. A slice of toasted bread with a thin veil of jam.
Lunch: fat-free lamb and cooked vegetables, or 40-grams of low-fat cheese, a mandarin.
Dinner: A pound of steak tartar. Coffee.

Tuesday
Lunch: liver and grated carrots, seasoned with lemon.
Dinner: two slices of roast veal, salad, a cooked pear.

Wednesday
Lunch: 1.5-grams of grilled kidneys with parsley and lemon sauce, two spoonfuls of steamed vegetables and a slice of pineapple.
Dinner: escalope with canned beans, natural yoghurt, a slice of dry bread.

Thursday
Lunch: cooked legumes, an apple.
Dinner: a slice of liver and one onion baked in the oven. 22-grams of green salad, half a grapefruit, a slice of dry bread.

Friday
Lunch: baked bread, hide it in the oven, breathe in the smell.
Dinner: scrambled eggs, spinach, 40-grams of mozzarella, 22-grams of green salad, fruit salad, a slice of dry bread.

Saturday
Lunch: rare steak, 30-grams of feta, a slice of dry bread.
Dinner: an omelette of two eggs, a baked apple, a slice of dry bread.

---

* She ate the same breakfast every day.

Sunday
Lunch: a slice of roasted chicken, without sauce; two tablespoons of rice. No
pasta, no drinks except for tea. A mandarin. A slice of dry bread.
Dinner: two slices of lean ham, 22-grams of green salad, a baked pear, a slice
of dry bread.

No salt. Replace salt with lemon juice and vinegar. No cold drinks while
eating, especially no alcoholic or carbonated drinks.[21]

Not only was she afraid of becoming fat, but she also wanted to fit his ideal.
'The fact is that I am always starving,' she said. 'I am ravenous and it wears
me out.'[22]

Nevertheless, Onassis could not resist playing games with her, and when
she was at her thinnest he showed a marked interest in heavier women. 'Look
at her bust, Maria,' he said of a guest, who had borrowed her dress. 'Look how
beautifully her bust fills out that dress of yours.'[23] Still, she rejected food, particularly chocolates and pastries, and asked others to eat in front of her, so she
could witness their pleasure – although, at times, she gave into temptation and
devoured cakes and cartons of ice cream. Her eating habits irritated Onassis,
who berated her for not finishing meals, as it offended his chef. 'Many of [the
staff] did not like her,' Onassis's former secretary recalled. They refused to
assist her more than necessary and often followed their employer's lead and
ignored her.

In Monaco, Onassis continued to behave as though he ruled the principality
and the press mockingly called Maria 'the princess', which she thought was
an affront to Princess Grace who, like Rainier, had come to loathe him. Their
displays of wealth were reported in the newspapers; she partied all night and
slept until noon, and every luxury was at her disposal. At times, the press cast
her, not as his partner, but as a courtesan or his mistress. In a similar tone, the
adjectives to describe Onassis were many, and a former girlfriend asked, 'Why
is it, even when you're wearing a tuxedo, you still look like a gangster?'[24]

As though ashamed of her status and his reputation, Maria accepted engagements in New York and London, only to cancel at the last minute. She had
agreed to and subsequently declined *Il trovatore*, directed by Visconti in London,
and she had learned the German libretto of *Tristan and Isolde*, which also
foundered. There was speculation that she would appear in *La traviata* in Paris
and Moscow, and in *Anna Bolena* in London. However, she agreed to appear in
A Golden Hour from the Royal Opera House, a televised concert conducted by
Prêtre and featuring Giuseppe Di Stefano. The *Daily Mirror* ran a competition,

offering tickets to those who wrote the most amusing telegrams to Maria who, they warned, 'has an international reputation for her fiery, unpredictable temperament … but she also has a great wit and a lively sense a fun'.[25]

Once, Maria had explained that when she was singing she felt as if she were in a glass box and nobody could hurt her. But the moment she stopped singing, the glass shattered. It was a period in which she felt exposed to the world and hunted by reporters, set on her by Onassis. 'Go to hell, we don't need the publicity,' she snapped. It was a vapid existence; all she wanted was 'a real life, a private life'.[26]

A real life never appealed to Onassis: he was not attracted to the woman but had fallen in love with a fantasy, and in turn, she was deceived by his lies. What else could she be except for a piece of iconography: a symbol of his wealth. He sent her to Biki for a new wardrobe of dark clothes and told her not to wear her glasses on the yacht, for he thought they made her look plain. So, she walked around the deck half-blind – perhaps a metaphor for her tolerance of his behaviour. 'Since I own the boat, I get to wear whatever I want,' he said of his casual attire.

Accepting his flaws, she suffered his verbal abuse and remained silent when he called her derogatory names. His tactic kept her in line, abusing her and loving her. More than ever, Maria had become passive to his whims, and friends noticed how she faded into the background, overshadowed by his arrogance. 'But it is her silence that I remember most,' Francis Robinson recalled. 'Sometimes it is wistful to the point of making me sad.'[27]

Knowing how to provoke her, Onassis manipulated Maria into behaving in ways that later embarrassed her. She had always claimed that her fiery temperament belonged in the theatre: a weapon against her colleagues. Now she behaved similarly in public, rising to his goading across the table in nightclubs, screaming at him in front of his friends and business associates.

They spent Christmas in London, where the British press no longer wrote of her talent but hinted that she had become déclassée. 'I have never seen a [mink] coat take up so much of the cloakroom,' they wrote about the symbol of her frivolity.[28] At the Café de Paris, they were joined by the prima ballerina Dame Margot Fonteyn and her husband, Tito Arias, who handled Onassis's Panamanian business interests. Known by Arias as 'the terrible couple', they spent the evening arguing, their loud voices creating a scene. 'Our life then was hell,' Maria said.

At the beginning of 1963, Maria spent a week at the Columbus Clinic, where 'the double doors of the room remain constantly closed'.[29] It was later speculated that she had had an abortion. However, there is no evidence to suggest she terminated a pregnancy. The rumours – although an abortion was never explicitly mentioned – originated in the press, beginning with the French tabloids writing of her weight gain ('Callas is back on the spaghetti'), followed by the Italian newspapers alluding to a secret operation:

> She asked to be left alone … This morning, she learned that the news of her hospitalisation had leaked, the singer had gone on a rampage: she had begged the management to deny her presence and apparently threatened to be transferred to another clinic. Callas's friends and doctors also kept the most scrupulous secret.[30]

In reality, Maria had a hernia operation, something she wanted to keep secret from the public, who she realised would gossip. But she also wanted to protect her privacy, as the hernia contributed to ongoing gynaecological issues, and for that she also sought treatment. 'Now I'm practically as good as new,' she said, 'but it will take a few weeks before I can start singing, so I'm taking it easy.'[31]

During her convalescence, she received an offer to perform in a stadium concert, accompanied by the Philharmonic Orchestra of New York, with a fee of $10,000 plus 50 per cent of the net receipts. She declined, as she preferred 'to take no commitments during the summer season' in case Onassis wanted her by his side.[32]

During that period, she received a letter from the New York City Welfare Department, informing her that Litsa had applied for public assistance of $120 per month. 'In accordance to the law,' the authorities informed her, 'you are responsible for her support to the extent of your ability to contribute.'[33] Furthermore, Litsa had contacted reporters and arranged for them to follow her into the Welfare Office on Amsterdam Avenue.

Learning of the publicity stunt, Maria wrote to her godfather, asking him to act as an intermediary between herself and her mother. It was agreed Litsa would receive a monthly allowance of $200 (her rent was $130) plus $600 for her debts. 'I want no more articles and no more debts,' Maria said.[34] Regardless, Litsa gave an interview to *Gente* magazine. Her insightful remarks about Onassis, albeit from afar, unnerved Maria. In a letter to her godfather, Maria hoped that her mother would 'shut her lovely mouth' and compared her to 'cancer … I'll never get rid of her and the consequences'.[35]

In April 1963, Maria joined Onassis on a cruise of Italy and Greece, in the company of his daughter, Christina, and the Radziwills. The women disliked one another, and Lee, with her gaze fixed on Onassis, made no effort with Maria. In turn, Maria saw Lee as a threat: she, with her tiny frame, embodied everything he looked for when he paid for women. 'I hate Lee. I hate her!'[36] she said.

Christina, not quite 13, might have found a sympathetic ally in Maria if she too was not caught in a power struggle with Onassis. Despite her youth, Christina could relate to Maria's insecurities around Lee, for she was also aware of how her father looked at her with disgust when she ate too much – she had developed an eating disorder – or slapped her across the face for being childish. There were times when Maria was disturbed by Christina's mood swings, described as 'very dark ... very stormy ... she had an aura of doom'.[37] Knowing how the child resented her, all she could say was, 'She's not a nice girl'.

Even the staff chose their sides accordingly and observed Maria's every move, while she watched Onassis, unable to read his behaviour. The senior housemaid, Jeanne, who was privy to most things, was alarmed when Maria asked, 'Jeanne, you can't make the beds and not know the things that go on in them. Is Mr Onassis sleeping with Princess Radziwill?'[38] They both knew the answer, but Jeanne played along and allayed Maria's concerns. No, she answered, Lee never slept in his bed. 'Of course, I knew that he slept with Princess Radziwill elsewhere,' Jeanne later remarked. 'It was a big yacht.'[39]

Among the staff, the affair was old news, and Jeanne, who on several occasions had overheard Maria vomiting, concluded she was secretly pregnant, and that became shipboard gossip. When the physical signs of pregnancy failed to appear, Jeanne reported that Maria had suffered a miscarriage,* and again their sympathies were directed to her.

There was to be further anguish for Maria when, over dinner, Onassis regaled them with tales of the sea. 'You must understand that mermaids are both good and bad luck,' he said, his eyes fixed on Lee, savouring the melodrama. 'Good luck if you find one in the sea. But bad luck if you bring her aboard. Never ever bring a mermaid on board. Remember that.'[40]

Occasionally, Maria and Lee glared at one another as they silently battled for his attention. 'Lee and I are going to be unavailable for the rest of the evening,' he announced.[41] In a pleading tone, Maria asked him to join her at the bar, but

---

* Costa Gratsos and his wife, Anastasia, told Onassis's biographer, Peter Evans, that Maria had become pregnant and miscarried a month later.

he declined, saying he would see her at breakfast. He left the room with Lee, who asked why he had done it, and he explained it was proof that even when Maria was present, he would always choose her. Lee said, 'I am not a mean person … and that was cruel.'[42] The following morning, the yacht docked in Capri and Maria remained in bed, feigning a sore throat. A doctor was sent for and diagnosed 'a boring form of laryngitis'.[43] Showing no concern, Onassis took Lee ashore, and Maria packed her bags and left.

Months before, Onassis had taken Maria to view a château in Versailles, where she hoped they would live together, but her dreams remained unfulfilled. All she had was her career, marred by a vocal crisis and lack of confidence. Onassis had destroyed her self-esteem as a woman, and the public, who she called 'a monster', planted the final dart. So, she periodically forgot about Onassis and returned to the stage, another form of the systematic abuse she sought.

In Paris, she recorded French arias, conducted by Georges Prêtre, and a week later, they went to Germany for a concert tour of Berlin, Düsseldorf and Stuttgart. In their review, *Der Tagesspiegel* wrote: 'What is Maria Callas, the artist, today? What is achievement, what is myth? What is the magic she exerts based on? She is the mistress of the evening. She is simultaneously personality and idol.'

However, the tone changed as she reached her final engagements in Paris and Copenhagen. In Paris, it was reported that she was irritated due to the best seats being reserved for the Knights of Malta, in whose honour the concert was given, instead of her contemporaries from the 'big world'.[44] It was also rumoured that she had purchased fifteen seats in the second gallery for the critics, and a further fifteen seats in the front row for her friends. 'Callas did not have the audience she desired, but her triumph was no less,' *La Stampa* reported. In their review, *Combat* wrote, 'Has Maria Callas retained all her triumphs? No. But she plays the ones she still has in her hand with consummate skill. I do not find her reputation overblown, she offers us a festival of intelligence, charm, and beauty.'

The day before Maria had arrived in Paris, Onassis left on a cruise of the Greek Islands with the Radziwills, the Churchills and the Montague Brownes. 'Why don't you take me on the cruises with Winston Churchill? Am I not good enough for him?' she asked Onassis, who lied and said Anthony Montague Browne told him not to.[45] Later, when she encountered Montague Browne, she said, 'Superficially you are charming, but underneath you are cold and ruthless, and I hate you.'[46] As a form of self-preservation, she confided in no one, but allowed Prêtre to convince her to accept *Tosca* in London and

Norma in Paris, for the 1964 season. 'When she is about to appear on stage in front of thousands of people,' Prêtre said, 'she looks more like a little girl about to take an exam than the best-paid singer in the world.' With the same humility, she retreated from the social scene and devoted herself to music. Criticising her remoteness, the press awarded her a prize for sourness, sending her a miniature gold bottle filled with vinegar.

Sometimes, Maria's mind wandered to the Adriatic, where, from the *Christina*, Onassis informed the press about his liaison with Lee. It placed Lee in an embarrassing predicament, for although she loved him, she was afraid of scandal and berated him for his actions.

'First of all, you do not raise your voice to me,' he said, reducing Lee to tears.[47] It was then Lee realised that he had no intention of marrying her. 'I am not a man you can pressure,' he said, confiding it was impossible to leave Maria, as she had threatened to commit suicide.[48]

Maria's worst fears were confirmed with *Le Parisien*'s headline: 'Callas-Onassis, The End of the Great Love'. Continuing with the theme, *La Stampa* wrote, 'A lot of noise; so many pains, so many joys for nothing Maria now has only one passion: music.' Around that time, she declined an invitation from Jacqueline Kennedy to sing at the White House to commemorate the state visit of Emperor Haile Selassie I of Ethiopia. 'I thank the President and you for your admiration, for which I am deeply touched,' she wrote to Mrs Kennedy.[49] Knowing how the sisters gossiped, she had perhaps wanted to preserve her dignity.

In Copenhagen, she sang in a concert before the Danish royal family and the prime minister. *Aftenavis* wrote, 'The craft, the artistic expression of Callas has barely displayed a voice that lived up to expectations.' A spectator was overheard saying, 'Now we can go home. I'll put some Callas records on the gramophone and realise how much better her voice was five or ten years ago.' In response, Maria said, 'Twenty-six years ... and they take away my confidence.'[45]

After the tour ended, Maria went to Milan, where she was in the process of selling her house to a real estate company who would demolish it and build apartments. In her own words, small enemies, which included Titta, had made it impossible for her to live there. '[They] should leave me in peace ... but also personally, my husband, who I wish would finally leave me alone, so that I can return to Italy which is practically my homeland, at least artistically.'[46] She sold the house for 150 million lire and was charged 20 million lire in corporation tax, as during their marriage, Titta had formed a company (Villa Elena) under which he registered their properties.

The conflict from Maria's private life was now apparent in her career, as it had been during her marriage to Titta. She sensed that, sooner or later, everyone would betray her, and those closest to her would become estranged. 'You know when we have our quarrel,' she told Walter Legge, 'it's going to be hell, because you know how to hurt me, and I know how to hurt you.' In early July, she learned of Legge's long-standing plan to record Verdi's 'Requiem' with his wife, Elisabeth Schwarzkopf. To the general manager of EMI, she wrote, 'I inform you, that through telephone calls and a letter dated January 1, 1962, I have been persuaded to do '*Requiem*' for your company.' Therefore, she added, the news came as 'quite a shock … and the only thing which consoles me and makes the hurt less is that my role was given to Madame Schwarzkopf'.[52]

For some time, Maria's relationship with Legge had been strained and she accused him of exploiting her for publicity reasons, which, she said, 'bothered her the most'.[53] Attempting to protect her pride, she told him, 'If your wife can sing my repertoire then I can sing hers. I intend to record a recital of Mozart arias. Please recommend to me a good Mozart *répétiteur*.'[54]

Months later, Legge was absent from her recording of French arias, produced by Michel Glotz, head of EMI's French division. He introduced her to Janine Reiss, a voice teacher of the French repertoire. 'I need someone who is very strict, who will not let me get away with anything,' Maria said, as she handed Reiss the score of *The Pearl Fishers*, asking her to sing it, to explain how the cadenza was constructed, both rhythmically and harmonically. After their first lesson, Reiss came to respect Maria as a musician, remarking, 'This is a woman who has reinvented music because she reads it … She goes to the source of what is written.'

Although Maria was hurt by Onassis's affair and humiliated by the publicity, she forgave him. 'Men are polygamous,' she remarked, as though to justify his behaviour.[55] Soon after, however, she found a Cartier box and a note to Lee, reading, 'My dearest, my sweetest love'. After an explosive fight, she took an overdose of sleeping pills and he found her unconscious on the floor. Instead of phoning an ambulance, he walked her around the apartment and gave her coffee until she regained consciousness. Only Mary Carter knew of the incident and dismissed it as a cry for help, not a genuine suicide attempt; she sensed Maria had planned for someone to find her. Still, the incident unnerved Onassis: he did not want her blood on his hands, nor the entire world blaming him for her demise. 'In operas,' Maria said, 'I've played heroines who die for love and that's something I can understand.'[56]

They went to Athens and dined with Stas and Lee, who had returned from America following the death of her sister's premature baby. Both Onassis and Maria expressed their sympathy, and she, although remotely interested in her dinner companions, was alarmed when he suggested Jacqueline Kennedy convalesce on the *Christina*, chaperoned by Lee. This was a provocative request – Onassis was a criminal by American standards because, in 1953, he had been indicted by the United States Government for fraud.* However, Jacqueline, grieving for her baby and wounded by her husband's philandering, accepted the invitation.

It seemed Onassis had known the First Lady's weaknesses. In their private moments, he had extracted information from Lee, who was unaware that she was furnishing his desires to infiltrate Washington. The *Christina* was stocked with eight varieties of caviar and vintage champagne; he hired two hairdressers, a French chef, a Swedish masseuse, and an orchestra to join his crew of sixty. Then, as part of his charm offensive, he offered to withdraw, but Jacqueline insisted he should accompany them. 'How can we possibly go without our host?' she asked, her breathless voice enchanting him.

Although Maria had believed that Onassis was not on board, she opened her newspaper and learned otherwise. 'She's the captain; Mrs Kennedy's in charge here,' Onassis told reporters, who gathered at Piraeus, from where the *Christina* departed. It was a bitter blow, for Maria had once moved a stick of furniture on the yacht and was reprimanded for doing so. 'Never forget, my darling,' he had said in measured tones, 'you are not the housewife here, you are only a guest.' The staff watched as he walked away, leaving her crying and shouting in his wake. From afar, Maria followed their itinerary in the newspapers: he had taken Jacqueline and Lee to Smyrna, and the photographs were printed on the front pages around the world.

At the end of the cruise, Onassis gave Jacqueline a diamond and ruby bracelet worth $50,000 and boasted to his friends it was payment for sex, calling her 'a classy coquette'.[57] To Lee, he offered a few bangles, a meagre farewell present – or perhaps a reward for introducing her sister to him. Their old sibling rivalry

---

* At the time, Onassis was negotiating a deal to supply a fleet of oil tankers for the Saudi Arabian Government, giving the country control of their oil industry. It violated an agreement between the American oil industry and the Saudi Arabian King. Washington learned of his deception and repossessed his T2 tankers as they docked in America and seized his profits. In return for pleading guilty and paying $7 million, the criminal charges against him were dropped. See Aristotle Onassis's FBI File, No. 46-17783.

was at play: Lee saw how Onassis looked at Jacqueline, as did Maria, who studied the paparazzi images of him guiding the First Lady through the narrow streets of Smyrna. 'Four years ago, that was me by his side, being seduced by the story of his life,' Maria said. 'I'm sure he makes most of it up. Memories demand too much effort.'[58]

A month later, President Kennedy was assassinated in Dallas, and Maria was surprised when Onassis flew to Washington and checked into the Willard Hotel. It was an embarrassing situation for Lee, as he had arrived unannounced, and Jacqueline felt compelled to host him at the White House – which had been his motive all along. For years, he had wanted to settle a score with Jacqueline's brother-in-law, Bobby Kennedy, the United States Attorney General who, a decade earlier, had exposed the corruption within the Greek shipping industry. Kennedy's investigations led to an enquiry into Onassis's business dealings within the United States, resulting in his indictment for fraud and subsequent arrest in 1953. For this, Onassis never forgave him. The exposé had almost ruined him, and in 1954 it was believed he was on the verge of bankruptcy before eventually gaining control of the SBM in Monte Carlo.

As in business, Onassis saw an opportunity to exploit: Lee was still married to Stas, but Jacqueline was a widow, and therefore, available. Inside the White House, he rode roughshod over the Irish wake, flattered by the women's embarrassed laughter.

As with Maria, Lee was no stranger to his brutality: months before, at the opening of the Athens Hilton, she pulled away when he kissed her on the cheek, so he grabbed her by the neck and kissed her roughly on the mouth. Onlookers were aghast and Lee was visibly shaken, but Maria, her predecessor, had known how to play his games of submission.

After the funeral, he was given a cold reception. The guests mocked him and made jokes at his expense, particularly Bobby Kennedy who, now head of the family, asked how he obtained his fortune. Mortified by his presence, Lee never said a word; she knew she had served her purpose.

Perhaps Onassis realised that only Maria respected him: she never made him feel like an outsider, the way he did among old-money families or political dynasties. He returned to Paris to celebrate her 40th birthday at Maxim's and, despite her cruel disillusions, she said, 'The shepherd when the spring returns thinks no more of the cold that is gone.'[59]

A few days later, Titta submitted papers, which now weighed 40kg, to the Civil Court of Milan, but the hearing was delayed for two months. It did not compromise her happiness or her false sense of security. She and Onassis were once again inseparable as they went from one party to another, in Paris and Monte Carlo, surrounded by the jet set, chatting 'in that corrupt English which is the international language'.[60]

They flew to Port-au-Prince, where he ordered her to sing for Papa Doc, the Haitian president who controlled his citizens through fear, murder and black magic. It was also said that Onassis attended one of Papa Doc's voodoo rituals, sticking pins into a doll of an Irish-American upstart, whom he later revealed was Bobby Kennedy. He wanted to build a resort and brought Maria along to sweeten the deal – or as a friend called it, 'a pimp treating his woman'.[61]

The press reported that marriage was imminent, and others speculated it had taken place in the South of France. But unbeknownst to Maria, he adhered to underhanded tactics which separated his mistresses from a potential wife: he could never marry a woman who had given herself so easily to him.*

Ignoring his duplicity, she pretended she could not think of marriage, as she was preoccupied with her career. In his diary, Leo Lerman wrote, 'Maria C rang from Monte Carlo – long outpouring. Everything is alright – don't believe newspapers – she's working hard – she will do the *Tosca* if everything is perfect … She seems in good spirits, but she does get down.'[62]

One evening, they dined with friends and, in high spirits, Maria said, 'Tell Ari he ought to marry me.'[63] She expected Onassis to respond with a joke, but suddenly his mood changed and his words cut her to the quick. 'Maria, I can't do that,' he said. 'This is a pay as you go arrangement.'[64]

---

* Onassis, who was fascinated by the customs of Ancient Greece, believed in the Solonian Constitution, whereby if a man was caught with a woman who practised some form of prostitution, he could not be accused of adultery. Alas, any woman who offered pre-marital sex placed herself outside of the *Oikos* (the family, the family's property, and the family home).

15

Pendulum

Beware: this is a place of tears.

Tosca, Puccini

In the New Year of 1964, Maria returned to the stage in Zeffirelli's production of *Tosca* at Covent Garden. She said:

> I need to find happiness in my music. If I did not have my work, how would I fill the time between morning and evening? I have no children, no family. I can't just sit around and chat or play cards. I'm not that sort of woman.[1]

As though admitting defeat in her private life, she sought love from a faceless audience and feared their criticism. One form of masochism would replace the other.

Consumed by failure and 'trying to live up to her name',[2] she told her godfather, 'My health does not permit me to work as before … Please tell no one of this.'[3] To her doctor, she complained of overwrought nerves but he ignored her symptoms and diagnosed *grippe morale* (psychological flu).

Tito Gobbi, who played Scarpia, recognised the signs of a breakdown, and every night he escorted her to the wings and held her cold hand, watching the beads of sweat running down her neck and off the edge of her dress. After the first night, the English audience, who had restrained themselves during 'Vissi d'arte', threw ribbons and flowers onto the stage. 'Maria's curtain calls were so like Gypsy Rose Lee's – so naughty,' Leo Lerman observed, unaware of her struggles.[4] The *Daily Mirror* called her 'Callas the Conqueror'.

After a radio broadcast of the second performance, several listeners wrote letters to the critics, questioning their standards and accusing Maria of 'squalling and wobbling'. The second act was recorded for television, and Zeffirelli said, 'Here and there, there is some horrible acting, but no one did anything the music didn't demand'.[5] In a letter to the *Guardian*, the music critic Sir Neville Cardus called Maria's admirers her worst enemies, as they boosted her confidence and led her to the 'brainless roles' of Italian opera. Nevertheless, her performance was considered a success. 'It's fantastic,' she told reporters, 'I've never expected anything quite like this.'[6]

Following the success of *Tosca*, Dorle Soria wrote to Maria, offering her $10,000 for a stadium concert. Her agent, Sandor Gorlinsky, declined on her behalf, 'There is no possibility of her being interested in it because as you know, she never sings in the open air.'[7] In response, Soria wrote:

> As a matter of fact – and as I know – she does sing in the open air … We are old friends and admirers of Maria Callas. We worked with her for many years. We devoted ourselves to promoting her career in this country … It must give you great pleasure to be associated with Mme. Callas.[8]

The offer coincided with Maria's latest vocal crisis and she also cancelled a concert tour of America, saying she would 'rather do opera first'.[9]

Her bravado dissolved when the company sent a London *répétiteur* to Paris to give her weekly lessons, which Peter Andry, an EMI executive, considered a waste of time and money. Although she often sent the *répétiteur* away, she said, 'I studied again, in spite of the fact of knowing full well that the musical world had dug my grave and was waiting for me to throw myself into it.'[10] According to Andry, she was unable to sing the high notes and difficult runs in the arias.

On another occasion, she became hysterical before attempting 'Ritorna vincitor' and, disappointed with the results, she blamed the sound engineer, the conductor, the equipment and the climate. Andry recalled, 'This now became Maria's way of explaining the difficulties we were facing.'[11]

In a letter to her godfather, Maria spoke of facing 'a very delicate moment' in her life.[12] She had become estranged from her father. The final break came in April 1964, after he went to America for medical treatment and sent her a bill for $4,000. 'I hate him for doing this to me,' she said. 'I'm very disappointed in him – maybe worse than my mother.'[13] Furthermore, he had married Alexandra Papajohn and, along with her family, tried to manipulate Maria into giving them money by claiming he was 'dying of cancer in an awful hospital'.[14] Having learned the truth – that he had had minor surgery and that his illness was not life threatening – she wanted nothing more to do with him. 'He chose others. He can keep them,' she warned. 'I'm out for good.'[15]

Despite Maria's feelings, she paid George's hospital bills and sent him $200 a month, so that he 'dies well taken care of because if he dies in bad hands or things like that I alone will be blamed'.[16] To a reporter, she commented, 'I have not reduced my father and my mother to begging – I do not enjoy torturing people!'[17] In response, Litsa wrote to Maria, cursing her with cancer of the throat. Although she was accustomed to her mother's cruelty and her father's deception, she said, 'I'm fed up with my parents' egoism and indifference toward me and the [influences] their conduct has on my career and personal life and feelings.'[18]

During that period, Maria opened in Zeffirelli's production of *Norma* at the Palais Garnier. By then, she had become a gay icon for the intelligentsia who resonated with her transformation, her suffering and her secret life with Onassis. Yves Saint Laurent, who idolised her, attended one of the performances and recalled how half of the audience expected her to fail, while the other half, her ardent fans, wanted her to succeed.

The melodrama created onstage was imitated by the audience who barely applauded her 'Casta diva', which *L'Aurore* called 'uneven … with skirted high notes', and instead cheered for Fiorenza Cossotto, who sang the part of Adalgisa. 'Would Callas accept this setback or would the diva, long famous for her caprices, refuse to appear in the second act?' asked *L'Aurore*. Playing to the drama, Maria advanced toward the audience and pointed to Cossotto, acknowledging their response.

However, Zeffirelli realised the dynamic at play and knew Cossotto had taken advantage of Maria's vocal weaknesses to purposely out-sing the prima donna. Perhaps Maria cared, or perhaps she did not – she had also taken such liberties in her youth. She also recognised cheap tricks – 'rubbish,' she called them – when they were afoot. 'Holding on interminably to long notes and killing the musical phrase by doing so, adding notes that are not written in the score – such things play down to the public not up to them,' she said.[19] Despite this, she could, in her own words, rouse her admirers and destroy her enemies with a single dramatic expression. *L'Aurore* agreed, 'She had definitely won the battle and conquered all of Paris, but the struggle had been close-fought'.

Although Maria could rise to the occasion, she confessed she was 'a bit tired of fighting all my life and especially now when I should be able to enjoy peace and comfort'.[20] Onassis was absent from the opening night but he attended the fourth performance when, in the final scene, her voice broke on a high C, emitting a sound which *The New Yorker* called 'peak peacock cries'. It was a humiliating moment: the audience roared, and the orchestra stopped playing, frozen in disbelief as violence erupted and the police had to be summoned to control the mob. Someone shouted, 'Go dress like a bourgeois and never come back!'; another yelled, 'Get her out!'[21] Among the spectators was Rudolf Bing who, years later, wrote of his sorrow at hearing a sound which Zeffirelli called indescribable, haunting and a reminder that Callas, vocally, had one foot in the grave.

Disturbed by the failure, Maria tried to compose herself and motioned to Prêtre to repeat the scene, and then she reached the top note to a chorus of her admirers fighting with the claque. 'I like challenges, I like to fight,' she had once said,[22] but now she could 'no longer endure this war of nerves'.[23]

Onassis had never been prouder, nor had he expected her to overcome the conflict thundering through the theatre. It was a surreal juxtaposition, for such displays of abuse were his privilege, and his alone. He went backstage and congratulated her, not for her singing, but for her courage. 'I think we need to build some time together,' he said, leading her to believe they had a future.[24]

'Can't you see?' she told Zeffirelli, who detested him. 'He adores me, he can't live without me.'[25]

After the final performance on 24 June 1964, Maria and Onassis spent a week cruising around Corfu, and their reunion was an antidote for her nervous tension. She returned to Paris in good spirits, prepared to record Bizet's *Carmen* for EMI. 'I had to take a tour of the world to get here,' she joked as she negotiated her way around the chairs at the Salle Wagram. In private, she claimed to hate the American reporters, although she granted an interview to *High Fidelity*, who called her 'a sometimes amiable prima donna'.[26]

Carmen was conducted by Prêtre, but some criticised his exaggerated movements and were surprised by his sweat-drenched shirts discarded on a chair and replaced after each take, and how he wore a towel around his neck to mop the 'droplets of sweat [which] rolled off his nose and chin'.[27] There were numerous technical issues, and it took Maria fourteen takes to record the 'Habanera', causing Glotz to become impatient if she left the microphone. 'Enough, Maria,' Glotz ordered. 'Get down there and sing. Time is money.'[28]

Although it was a success, she declined offers to appear in a production directed by Zeffirelli, performing the part of a seductive gypsy, killed by her jealous lover. 'Don't you think I'm too elegant for Carmen?' she asked Leo Lerman. Then, lifting her skirt, she said, 'Look at these legs! Look at these legs! Are they the legs for Carmen?'[29] In his diary, he wrote, 'Oh foolish, foolish, driven Maria, who knew who she was and who wanted to be someone else.'[30]

Being someone else had become second nature to Maria; she repressed her troubles and lived only for Onassis. She thought he had come back to her and was unaware that, since the funeral of President Kennedy, he and Jacqueline had grown close. That spring, he contributed to the purchase of Jacqueline's apartment in New York, thus making clear his intentions. However, the man she loved most was her brother-in-law, Bobby Kennedy.

It made Onassis all the more ardent in his pursuit. He was obsessed with the idea of destroying the Kennedys, but he discovered that she too had a price: $100,000 a year toward her living expenses and a promise to keep their affair a secret. Giving her envelopes of money reminded him of his encounters with Madame Claude's girls and the duplicity excited him. He spent part of the week in New York with Jacqueline and the weekends in Paris with Maria, who was unaware that he was grooming his next consort while biding his time with her.

Nevertheless, he would always gravitate toward Maria, who offered a depth of emotional support that no other woman could. From 1934–46, he had shared a similar dynamic with Ingeborg Dedichen, a Norwegian shipping heiress. He promised marriage and beat her often, lying beside her bruised body and crying tears of remorse which, as with Maria, awakened her maternal instincts. 'Our love affair was wild, tempestuous human bondage, a chemistry of attraction,' Dedichen wrote in her memoir, *Onassis, Mon Amour*.

Like Maria, Dedichen had served a purpose: she taught him how to dress, how to behave in society, and she introduced him to her father's contacts. Ending the relationship when Tina entered the scene, he explained that, unlike Dedichen (who had been divorced twice), he wanted to marry a virgin. In return, he installed Dedichen in an apartment on the Rue Laffitte and continued to give her an allowance of $800 a month. 'With him, I enjoyed the most beautiful and hellish years of my life,' Dedichen said. 'I realised that he was more angel and devil than most men.'[31]

Maria was the echoist to Onassis's narcissist, thus creating a co-dependency which neither could escape. In the summer of 1964, they were each facing watershed moments in their lives: she mourned the breakdown of her relationship with her father, and he was fighting Rainier for financial control of Monaco. 'It will mean blood on the palace walls,' a French investor remarked after Rainier used loans from American investors to create 600,000 non-transferable shares in SBM.

Only Maria knew how the loss of Monaco affected him, although he never revealed his vulnerability to his other women. She thought it gave her power, knowing every intimate detail of his life, but she never exploited his weaknesses as he did hers. By then, she considered herself without a family or roots, belonging only to him. 'You are,' she told him, 'my very breath, my spirit, my pride and my tenderness.'[32]

They went on a cruise of the Greek Islands, dropping anchor in the middle of the sea. Then he took her to Skorpios, a deserted island he had bought in 1963, 10 miles north of Ithaca, the home of his mythical hero, Odysseus. Its 400 acres was barren except for a neoclassical pink house and a stone chapel, and he employed men from the neighbouring island of Lefkada to construct paths, roads, guest cottages, a helicopter pad and a boat quay. He imported white sand from Salamis Island for the stretches of coves and all the trees from the Bible. Shirtless and with his bare hands, he planted the fig trees, vines and snapdragons that Maria had chosen, exerting the primitive masculinity that she found attractive. His buying an island had strengthened her love – she thought he had done it for her, and it would be their fortress from the outside world. 'He offers me everything,' she said. 'Everything I could ever want!'

Even then, he could not resist using her to his advantage. As a token of thanks to the workers of Lefkada, he promised that Maria would sing at their folklore dance festival. She protested that it was bad for her voice and she could not sing in the open air, the idea reducing her to tears. On the evening of the festival, they made the crossing in his Chris-Craft, all the while he nudged her, saying, 'You will sing.' So, the prima donna, with her hair in a ponytail and dressed in a backless sundress, reluctantly climbed onto the small stage and sang from *Cavalleria rusticana*, accompanied by a young pianist from the local music school. Afterwards, the pianist walked home and was stopped by a villager, who asked if he had heard a supernatural echo. In a daze, he said, 'That was Callas.'

The applause could no longer sustain her, artistically nor financially. 'I'm not so young any more,' she confided to her godfather.[33] She carried the burden of supporting her family, for not only did George and Litsa each receive $200 a month, but Jackie also asked for help throughout the years. 'It's high time [Jackie] worked,' she said. 'Everyone wishes to live without working … but life is not like that.'[34]

On another occasion, she could not understand how her sister bought and furnished a home, and yet begged her for a part-time maid.[35] Resentment had set in, and she asked, 'So who is going to think of me one day – God forbid – that I ever be of need?'[36]

That summer, Maria pondered her career prospects or, as she put it, 'to be able to earn money without working very hard'.[37] She asked Onassis to invest her money, particularly in a tanker, perhaps not to put herself on equal footing with him, but to have a mutual interest that was rooted in his identity. Later, Maria would say, under oath, that it was Onassis and his friend, Panaghis Vergottis, who persuaded her to become a shipowner. It was agreed that she would be a stakeholder in their bulk carrier, *Artemision II*. She invested

£60,000 for a 25 per cent share, with Onassis buying 50 per cent, out of which he gave her 26 per cent, thus putting her in control of the vessel to be managed by Vergottis, who also owned 25 per cent. However, the vessel would develop engine trouble on its maiden voyage to Japan, and Maria regretted her initial investment.

Sometime later, it was suggested by Vergottis that she could convert her £60,000 into a loan and, lost in the technical terms, she thought she could turn that loan into an investment should the vessel become profitable. 'Vergottis respected me and loved me,' she said. 'There are quite a few people who do that once they know me.'[38]

In the early months of 1965, Maria was content: she was certain of Onassis's love and the promise of financial security. 'I am quite happy,' she said. 'I try to cherish myself.'[39] That February, she sang in Zeffirelli's production of *Tosca* in Paris, an event so successful that her contract of eight performances was extended to nine. Several days later, she went to New York to appear in *Tosca* at the Metropolitan, in a reproduction of the 1958 staging. This time she did not complain of the tired sets nor the lack of rehearsals.

It seemed incredible to the press and the public that she had returned seven years after Bing had fired her. 'He's a weak man,' she said, although, for the sake of appearances, they embraced and remained cordial.[40] Accompanied by Onassis, she filled his apartment at The Pierre with boxes of his favourite cigars, preoccupied with his happiness instead of her own.

On 19 March, Maria opened in *Tosca*, and from her dressing room, she heard the applause as Jacqueline Kennedy arrived with her entourage. Although she was a patron of the arts, Jacqueline's presence was the type of voyeuristic behaviour that Onassis enjoyed, even if he was absent. Moments later, when the curtain rose and Maria uttered, 'Mario, Mario', the audience applauded, interrupting the scene for four minutes.

'Miss Callas is operating these days with only the remnants of a voice,' the *New York Times* wrote. In his diary, Leo Lerman observed, 'Maria's vocal flaw worked dramatically when she sang-acted *Tosca* ... the ugliness leavened (wrong word) the texture. I mean roughened it, made it more awful ... awesome, like a rough, full-bodied black-red wine, while the full-blown tunes flowed endlessly.'[41]

Despite the public's response, Maria was consumed by nerves and the knowledge that her voice, the main instrument of an opera, had fallen below her standards. 'To me, the art of music is magnificent, and I cannot bear to see it treated in a shabby way,' she said. 'But if music is treated in a shabby way or second-best way, I do not want to be associated with it.'[42] She confessed, 'The world of Maria Callas has become a lonely world of a woman looking for her voice and seeking perfection in her art.'[43]

While she was in New York, she met with Peter Andry to discuss a recording of *La traviata*, which he called a 'can of worms', due to EMI recording it without her in 1955. There had been an offer from Herbert von Karajan to star in a film of the opera, with the soundtrack recorded by EMI's rival, DG; however, it never happened. Therefore, Andry seized the opportunity, and in return, Maria wanted Carlo Maria Giulini to conduct and to have the first refusal on the tenor.

One day, she interrupted a meeting and asked Andry to accompany her to the furriers, on a Saturday, as she wanted a new mink coat. The furriers were Jewish and Saturday was their Sabbath, but he persuaded them to open. She spent hours scrutinising the furs, trying them on and laying them on the floor to inspect their pelts. None met her expectations. She then decided she wanted a radio, but at a discount. So, Andry visited the electrical stores of Manhattan until he found an inexpensive gadget. Naturally – as she expected – the company paid for it. No further along in their discussions and without a tenor engaged, she left for Paris,

In Paris, before opening in *Norma*, she succumbed to the nervous energy that had been stirring within her. 'I have a super-sensitive soul that has a premonition about certain things,' she said. Her pessimism was not unfounded.[44] Titta's petition to change the conditions of their mutual separation, as well as suing her for loss of income, was heard in Milan. 'I didn't want to marry an impresario,' she argued. 'If I had, I would have at least married a good one.'[45]

At the preliminary hearing, she was found guilty but the verdict would not be reached until July. To avoid further upset, she asked her maid to hide letters from her family, as 'I must not have worries of any sort'.[46] Attempting to gain control, she began to diet and lost 11lb, but her doctor tried in vain to make her regain them.[47] To a friend, she wrote, 'This is the only place I can sing, where they know nothing about music and only look at my figure.'[48]

At the first performance of *Norma* on 14 May 1965, Maria's blood pressure was dangerously low; she had a sore throat and complained of period pains, which gave her 'a kind of lumbago'.[49] A doctor declared her unfit to sing, but she asked for an injection of tranquillisers and pain relief. Simionato, who was singing the part of Adalgisa, was accustomed to her histrionics before the curtain rose and ignored her. Backstage, things went from bad to worse when she was given the news that Titta was in the audience and, fearing he would ambush her, security was placed outside her dressing room and at the stage door. Before going on stage, the manager told the audience of her indisposition and asked for their sympathy ahead of the performance. *Arts* reported, 'The fact that the famous singer … had the courage to sing, in that state, demonstrates a rare professional conscience.'

In the third performance, Simionato was replaced by Fiorenza Cossotto who, as in 1964, exploited Maria's vocal inadequacies. For their duet, 'Mira, o Norma', Cossotto held her notes longer than required, leaving Maria breathless. In her dressing room, Maria was injected with Coramine, a drug then given to mountaineers to increase their endurance at high altitudes. Two nights later, Cossotto again dominated the evening and Maria accepted defeat.

On the final night, Maria was injected with stimulants and, at the end of the third act, she collapsed on stage and had to be carried to her dressing room. A doctor tried to revive her with Coramine and massaged her chest to open her airways, but she remained listless on the sofa.

It was announced that she was too ill to continue with the second act and, instead of a violent response, as in Rome in 1958, the audience remained silent until someone shouted, 'Refund!' and everyone laughed. Following another injection, Maria regained consciousness and had been informed of the decision, whereupon she attempted to stand up and get dressed but fell onto the sofa and cried for half an hour. 'I know I've let you down. I'm so sorry,' she told her waiting fans. 'I promise you all that one day I shall return to win your forgiveness and justify your love.'[50] Harassed by the press, who telephoned her apartment day and night, they wrote that she had been murdered by an angry fan.

For three weeks afterwards, Maria and Onassis cruised around the Mediterranean where he, like the public, had grown tired of her despondency. He had neither sympathy nor use for a singer without a voice or a woman in the throes of a nervous breakdown. 'You on your high horse … What are you? Nothing!' he shouted at her. 'You just have a whistle in your throat that no longer works!'

Around that time she began to abuse sleeping pills, taking enough to render her unconscious throughout the day and night, often when Onassis was with other women on the yacht. On one occasion, as they sailed around the coast of Naples, there was a minor fire on board but Maria, heavily sedated, slept through the alarm. There were no boundaries, no facade: he no longer cared how he treated her. His niece recalled a petty row between the couple, which ended with him hitting Maria across the face, leading to a violent scene. 'You're only good for fucking,' he said to her, in front of astonished guests. 'And you're not even good for that anymore.'

Returning to Paris, Maria hid in her apartment and refused to answer telephone calls. She was contracted to give four performances of *Tosca* at Covent Garden, although her doctor advised against it. Then, as the date of the rehearsals grew nearer, she began to panic. Twice she packed for London, and twice she cancelled. 'I admit now,' she said, 'for the first time that for years I have been frightened to go on stage.'[51]

Although Sir David Webster cancelled three of her performances and replaced her with Marie Collier, it was reported he felt betrayed in his trust at the last moment.[52] He did, however, convince her to sing in the third performance, a royal gala in honour of Queen Elizabeth II, for the Royal Opera House Benevolent Fund. 'Many spectators will go to Covent Garden not to listen to the artist,' *La Stampa* reported, 'but to see the worldly character, with the desire perhaps to witness a scandal.'

Hours before the curtain rose, Maria locked herself in her suite at the Savoy. 'Don't Disturb Callas'; 'Maria Callas is Missing', the newspapers mocked, unsympathetic toward the state of her mental health. She practised alone throughout the night, and the following day she arrived at the theatre. 'To do this opera, I disobeyed the doctor's orders,' she told the press, who afforded her little mercy in their reviews, nor were the public enthusiastic in their response.[53] 'I have had the bad fortune to go on stage and feel that the audience does not immediately give me their sympathy,' she remarked. 'Then I am paralysed. My throat closes. The tones, the sounds are there, but all self-confidence has disappeared. Then I feel defeated.'[54]

Echoing the hostility, her contemporary, Renata Scotto, said, 'Callas was a great singer, now she isn't anymore, she's a magazine diva. To sing it takes only one thing: the voice.'[55]

It was to be her last opera. The *Evening Standard* wrote, 'Yesterday only the ashes were seen, the fire was extinguished.'

After London, she said, 'There's a sort of scales in life. You weigh one thing on one side, and another decision on the other.'[56] So, as the public turned on her, she became dependent on Onassis and tolerated his abuse, thinking it was what she deserved. 'If you let me down,' she had once told Titta, 'I would lose faith in all life.'[57]

The warning was now applied to Onassis. At Skorpios, the seclusion of the island only magnified their issues and he acted as if she repulsed him. For most of the time, she stayed in her room and read magazines or walked her dogs.

When she was with him, he ignored her or exploded in an uncontrollable rage if she spoke to him. She remembered when, as an onlooker to his cruelty toward Tina on the cruise in 1959, he saw his wife in a red dress and called her a little French tart. Now, he played on Maria's insecurities and said that her nose was too big and her legs too fat.

A revolving cast of friends arrived and departed. Most were unable to witness his cruelty, although none offered to help. But what could they do? She always leapt to his defence, ready to claim they shared a spiritual bond – 'twins of the same soul' – and accused others of conspiring to spoil their relationship. To an interviewer, two months before, Maria had confessed, 'I'm shy and I need affection so much'.[58]

She relied on Vergottis as a confidante and father figure and accepted his counsel. He advised her to return to her art, that only through work could she restore her self-worth. 'I love you very much,' he told her over dinner at Maxim's.[59] Privately, she told herself, 'These people admire you. Why? You don't deserve it.'[60] Having been privy to her unhappiness, Vergottis often acted as an intermediary for the couple, scolding Onassis for mistreating her and telling her to leave. 'He's black in his heart,' he said.[61]

Sensing Vergottis's influence over Maria, Onassis poisoned her mind against him. It was rumoured that Vergottis had been in love with Maria since 1959 and wanted her for himself. Another rumour, perhaps started by Onassis, was that Vergottis was a homosexual, and they had had an affair in the 1930s. Reading between the lines, Maria understood that Vergottis had taken advantage of Onassis, and she reacted bitterly toward her elderly admirer. Their meetings became strained and, after a quarrel, Vergottis turned her out of his hotel room.

On another occasion, she said something rude to him over the telephone.[62] Later regretting her outburst, she wrote to him, explaining she was under pressure and asked for his forgiveness. There would be no reconciliation, and Vergottis removed her photograph from his mantelpiece.

Around that time, she agreed to star in Zeffirelli's film of *Tosca*, based on the Covent Garden production.* However, the Munich film company, Beta, headed by Herbert von Karajan, bought Puccini's recording rights from Ricordi and asked Zeffirelli to collaborate. Although Zeffirelli agreed,

---

* In 1965, it was rumoured that Maria would star in a remake of *Grand Hotel*. She also received an offer from John Huston to appear as Sara in his film, *The Bible*. Around that time, a French director was planning a Callas biopic, starring Sophia Loren, and focusing on the Rome Scandal of 1958.

Maria did not: she had not forgiven Karajan after he was overheard criticising her performance of *Tosca* in London. So, Onassis gave Zeffirelli £10,000 toward the cost of buying the rights from Karajan and, later, he offered to buy them himself. Confident that a deal could be struck, the cast from the Covent Garden production was flown to the EMI studios in Paris to record the soundtrack. Andry said, 'We knew that if only we could get the whole of this opera properly filmed and directed and in colour, we would own a property worth millions.'[63]

Discussions between Maria and Zeffirelli took place at Skorpios and on the *Christina*, with Onassis acting as her agent and making impossible demands: £500,000 for her film debut with £150,000 payable upon signing the contract. During one of their meetings on the yacht, Maria interrupted Onassis and he yelled, 'Shut your mouth, you know nothing!' She ran from the room in tears, the little confidence she had in the project was shattered by his remark.

On another occasion, they met with two film executives, whereupon he attacked her in Greek and she ran from the deck. Why did she stay with him, Zeffirelli asked her as they gossiped in her suite. 'He was the first to make me feel like a woman; the first to really make love to me,' she explained. 'I can't lose him.'

They continued their negotiations at the Savoy Grill, with Onassis making further contractual demands. Having suffered his rudeness to her colleagues, she was relieved when he signalled the meeting was over. It was a game played in public – he wanted her to succeed, but he also wanted to sabotage her opportunities. Winning and losing the game paralleled with his cycle of love and abuse. She displayed her irritation by ordering him to go outside and fetch a taxi. One of the executives rose from their chair, offering to get it. 'No, no,' she said, motioning for him to sit down. 'Let him go. He will get it.' Andry noted, 'In this rather less important matter she had shown herself to be in charge. But it was poor compensation.'[64]

Given Onassis's demands and Maria's refusal to collaborate with Karajan, who refused to surrender the rights, the film amounted to nothing. She was bitterly disappointed and blamed Zeffirelli, asking him to return the £10,000. Refusing to do so, he told her that Onassis was rich enough; he would not miss the money. 'It's my money!' she exploded. 'He made me pay it back from what little I have. Give it back!' When Zeffirelli ignored her request, she cut all ties and would, thereafter, refer to him as 'that crook'.

It seemed impossible to replenish the loss. She refused all offers from opera houses and her recording sessions had become sporadic. She had also been ordered to pay one-third of Titta's legal fees for the period of 1959–65.

The only solace was that the court had granted a legal separation and found both spouses guilty of misconduct during their marriage.[*]

Perhaps, to salvage something from the relationship with Onassis, she claimed they would have been married had she been able to get a Reno divorce. 'I'm too busy, I should [have] gone this summer ... So, here I am, not yet a free woman!'[65] Even then, she had trouble believing her own lies or, as she called it, the art of being a hypocrite.[66] The qualities she abhorred in others, she accepted in Onassis and, to a degree, herself. She said, 'When slight has followed slight and insult has been added to insult, the love which remains is often illogical, but it is also indestructible. It's a kind of madness but nobody chooses to be mad.'[67]

---

[*] In their verdict, the court ruled against both Maria and Titta. 'It can be seen that Callas and Onassis were now a stable couple, who presented themselves with common life habits. As for Meneghini, his responsibilities stem from the disparaging interviews he gave to newspapers at the time when his separation with the Greek soprano existed as a state of affairs. The ruling, in this regard, hints at a serious injury against Callas.' The court rejected Titta's request asking the courts to prohibit Maria from using the surname Meneghini. The judge observed that, in her artistic activity, she always used her own name. The judge also rejected the request for jurisdictional incompetence put forward by Maria's lawyers, thus she was ordered to pay one-third of the court costs.

16

Malevolence

My love for you
was greater than my wisdom.

Medea, Euripides

At the age of 42, Maria was emotionally adrift and without a purpose in her life. In a letter, she wrote, 'I believe in fate, for I am a creature of destiny. I believe in justice, though I see too little of it around. But if we don't believe, what is there left for us?'[1] Those introspective words cast a shadow over her present situation: she had given up singing and, in her words, had cheated long enough. Slowly, she removed traces of her identity that she felt no longer served her. 'I need to have peace in my personal life, which I, unfortunately, do not have.'[2]

Around that time, she gave up her American citizenship to 'civically liberate me from my husband' and took Greek citizenship.[3] A law passed in 1963 did not recognise marriages outside of the Orthodox Church. In Italy, however, her marriage remained valid – Titta reminded her that she would always be his wife and continued to ask for money.*

So began her meaningless existence that pushed her closer to Onassis, while he resisted her. There were long periods spent alone in Paris, enlivened by snippets of scandal in the newspapers. She had gone to Switzerland, perhaps for cosmetic treatments (as she had done in the 1950s), and the Italian Government was suing her for 6 million lire in unpaid taxes from 1961. It was

---

* During that period, Titta was engaged as President of the Tourist Board of Sirmione and in 1968 he was sued by a troupe of dancers, stage technicians and a dressmaker for unpaid fees during the summer festival season.

also reported that Onassis was having an affair with Elizabeth Taylor and he had removed Maria from the *Christina* to make room for Gina Lollobrigida. Both accounts were false, and Lollobrigida said, 'Maria was quite different than what was known about her. That is, she was sweet; she was gentle as a lamb compared to Onassis, he totally dominated her.'[4]

Interestingly, the women whose reputations he capitalised on were, physically, similar to Maria, as if he enjoyed taunting her. She complained to her friend and neighbour, Maggie van Zuylen, that Onassis was no longer interested in her. 'You lovebirds,' Maggie teased the couple over dinner in Monte Carlo and repeated what Maria had told her. With a predatory smile, Onassis admitted he did not sleep with Maria, but he did with other women, then he verbally abused her in Greek. As lifeless as a caryatid, she remained stoic in the eye of the storm.

At Skorpios, she became good at hiding their lives from the outside world. 'After forty, one no longer has any illusions,' she said of her expectations. 'One knows that that is nothing but a dream.'[5] Despite projecting an image of glamour and self-assurance, inside she felt worthless and her confidence was destroyed by Onassis's insults.

That summer, he was drinking heavily and taking prescription drugs, having become dependent on Nembutal ('Yellow Jackets'), a barbiturate that caused respiratory failure if taken in large quantities. Maria realised he needed help, yet she would not help herself. 'Oh, those Orientals!' she remarked. 'They can't let anything out. It's in the head and they can't let it out. They can't go to a doctor and say, "Help me. I can't sleep. I have anxiety. I am nervous" … The first duty is to cure the brain.'[6]

They were each self-destructing – he openly and she behind closed doors – and together they created a co-dependency which neither could break. As time progressed, she feared he would overdose or have a heart attack. The more she fretted, the more he enjoyed torturing her.

She brought his doctor from Paris, who did an angiogram and advised him to cut down on cigarettes and alcohol. After the doctor left, he increased his intake of Nembutal. He was also receiving injections of live sheep cells from Dr Niehans – sold to him as a powerful aphrodisiac – and injecting himself with amphetamines, steroids and testosterone to boost his stamina. However, it made him unpredictable and violent. 'He knew where to hit you till it hurt,' Maria said, 'and it wouldn't show in the morning.'[7] Justifying his behaviour, he said, 'All Greek men beat their women: he who loves well, beats well.'

Everything he did to Maria paralleled with his treatment of Ingeborg Dedichen. On one occasion, he had attacked Dedichen because he disliked her clothes. 'The more he beat me, the more excited he got,' Dedichen wrote in her memoirs. 'Between the blows which rained down on me, he yelled, "Why do you dress in this abominable fashion? Where did you find these abominable pants? Did you think we were going to a circus? You really want to make me look ridiculous."'

Therefore, it was hardly surprising that Maria changed her clothes several times before dining with him. Many considered it vain, although nobody understood how the wrong choice affected his mood. She was terrified of the consequences; he controlled her every thought, every action.

There was another encounter where he had kicked Dedichen unconscious and, alarmed by her injuries, he locked her in his house until her bruises had healed. A similar incident happened with Maria. When Onassis's physiotherapist found her alone in a room, her hair was dishevelled and her face was pale with dark circles under her eyes. Neither mentioned her appearance but there was an undercurrent of malevolence. After a violent episode with Onassis, in which she feared for her life, Maria said, 'You can kill me ... but you can't break me.'*[8]

In the autumn of 1966, Maria knew her relationship with Onassis was ending, although neither would take the initiative to walk away. In Paris, she followed the social whirl of premieres and galas, and he resumed his feud with Rainier, making him something of a joke in the European tabloids. 'The conflict between the prince and the shipowner is a subtle comedy, not a drama,' *La Stampa* reported, after Onassis appealed to the Supreme Court against Rainier's unconstitutional decision to nationalise the SBM and buy his remaining shares. Night after night, he paced the floors of Avenue Foch, directing his outbursts toward Maria, warning her that Rainier's actions were the result of an inferiority complex.

The remains of their relationship were connected to Panaghis Vergottis and the *Artemision II*. After their argument in 1965, she had asked Vergottis to return the £60,000 she had invested, believing he would protect her investment should the tanker fail. Should it become profitable, she understood that she could reinvest and collect the profits. Vergottis refused. Aside from his

---

* She had sung those same lies in *Carmen*, when Carmen knew her jealous lover would kill her. 'I know that you are going to kill me; but whether I live or die, no, no, I shall not give in to you!'

embittered feelings, he explained, it was not how business worked, but she refused to accept his answer.

Despite the complications arising from hearsay and verbatim, Onassis was thirsting for blood, and having been humiliated by Rainier, he directed his revenge toward Vergottis. However, Vergottis warned both Maria and Onassis that going to court would result in a scandal, particularly as the details of their relationship would be made public. For years, the press had stalked the couple, hoping to capture intimate scenes, but Onassis, a shrewd operator, rarely walked beside her. Driven by a bruised ego and mustering his braggadocio, he engaged his lawyers to sue Vergottis for £1.2 million. Then he convinced Maria that Vergottis 'regretted missing the opportunity' to own the tanker, saying, '[Vergottis] was sorry and was crying over spilt milk and he was trying to save out of that spilt milk as much as he could.'[9] Once, she had said, 'I respect revenge,'[10] and now she would co-operate with his plan to destroy Vergottis.

In the spring of 1967, they stood in the witness stand in the High Court of London, but their answers were contrived and it could be said that neither was entirely honest, despite taking an oath. 'We had not loved but cherished Mr Vergottis,' Maria told the judge, Mr Justice Roskill.[11]

The ailing Vergottis, aged 77, sat with a doctor who monitored his low blood pressure and at intervals announced, 'I can't go on.' The evidence was so convoluted that Sir Peter Bristow QC, defending Vergottis, called their deal 'a very queer business arrangement … if one looks at either story with the cold eye of business, neither makes sense'.[12] Later, it was described as 'a sort of catharsis, a sex case in the end'.[13]

In the stand, Maria said, 'I am here to answer all questions. Ask me anything you want. But please speak louder, I am short-sighted and cannot see what you say.'[14]

Several minutes later, she appeared vexed by Bristow's cross-examination, fidgeted with her glasses and erroneously called him Sir Bristow instead if Sir Peter. She accused Vergottis of being dishonest about the percentage of his shares and tricking her into accepting an annual interest payment of 6.5 per cent on the £60,000 she had invested. 'He did not want to take the risk – because I am a woman who works for a living and coming towards the age where it might not be possible to work – of playing around with my money.'[15] Furthermore, she added that Vergottis – 'a man who literally adored me'[16] – reassured her that in 1967, if she wanted to, she could collect the accumulated interest. The *Artemision II*, he explained, was 'a tragically unfortunate ship: twice the machines had broken down and the telegraph driver was faulty and sending false SOS'.[17] Whereas, its operations turned a profit, the interest of which he did not want to pay to her.

In the witness stand, Vergottis took the opportunity to expose Onassis as 'black in his heart' and spoke of his cruelty to Maria, who had considered leaving him in 1965. 'The things he has done and how he started,' Vergottis raged. 'I have been to Greece and investigated lots of things.'[18] Naturally, Vergottis also denied all of Maria's accusations and said Onassis had wanted to transfer his shares to his nephews; it was only then that he enquired about Maria's money. Vergottis allegedly told Onassis the investment was so meagre that it 'lay in the bank vault … he did not exploit it at all'.[19] Their discord, Vergottis explained, was due to Onassis having sabotaged the film adaptation of *Tosca*, an entirely different matter.

Once more, Maria was called to the stand, and the theatrics continued:

> I had the great joy of considering [Vergottis] more than my father because I never had a father or mother virtually. I was very happy with it and he knew it, and he considered me his greatest joy. He was very proud to travel around and participate in my glory. I am not trying to be funny.

The nature of Maria and Onassis's relationship was exposed, and she said she was both married and single.

'That wasn't quite right, was it?' Bristow demanded.

She stretched out her arms and shrugged, 'Why not?' … I could have married anyone anywhere else, civilly, if I had a divorce in America.'

'These questions have to be asked,' Bristow continued.

'No, they don't!' she snapped. 'We are here because of twenty-five shares for which I paid and not because of my relations with another man.' Admitting they cohabitated and therefore lived as a married couple, she gave their joint address in Paris as proof.

'Do you regard her as being in a position equivalent to being your wife, if she was free?' Bristow asked Onassis.

'No,' Onassis replied. 'If that were the case, I have no problem marrying her, neither has she any problem marrying me.'

'Do you feel any obligation towards her other than those of mere friendship?' Bristow implored.

'None whatsoever.'[20]

Despite winning the case* against Vergottis, for Maria, the loss was much greater.

'Madame Callas is not a vehicle that I drive at will,' Onassis said. 'She has her own brakes and own brain.'[21]

Regardless of Maria's slavish devotion, it was clear that Onassis wanted her to have her own life. He gave her an apartment at Avenue Georges Mandel, purchased through two of his Panamanian companies who paid the monthly charges and household expenses. Nevertheless, she still belonged to him and, given his distorted view of women, he treated her as though she were part of the *hetairai* of the ancient world. Thus, he related to and even practised Apollodorus's philosophy: 'We have courtesans for pleasure, concubines [*hetairai*] for the daily tending of the body, and wives in order to beget legitimate children and have a trustworthy guardian of what is at home.'

The apartment was an example of his generosity – he rewarded those who were loyal – and Maria, battling with her pride, told friends that she had paid for it in cash. The large rooms were filled with antique furniture and oil paintings, and detecting an impersonal touch to the décor, Leo Lerman called it 'one of the least occupied places I have ever been'.[22] She had wanted a house with a garden, but Onassis said she knew nothing about housekeeping.

Detecting a problem in the relationship, the press wrote, 'Callas and Onassis: it's over':

> Many had noticed in recent weeks how in his appearances at the great social events at the beginning of the season, in Paris as in Venice, on his yacht as on the great beaches of the southern Spanish coast, Maria Callas was no longer, as in passing, constantly at the owner's side. It is certain that the long and conflicted mental relationship is now over. But behind this decision is the biggest rival Callas probably ever met. Who?[23]

---

* Vergottis was ordered to transfer the shares to Maria and to pay their legal costs. However, he appealed the decision and a hearing was set for a later date. Likewise, Maria and Onassis also appealed, taking their case to the House of Lords. 'Not many guys your age get two Judgement Days to worry about,' Onassis teased Vergottis.
  'I'll handle the second one,' Vergottis replied. 'The first one you worry about.'
  As before, the case was ruled in their favour.

Having spent several months apart, Maria and Onassis met on Skorpios for a bittersweet reunion. 'The only free people are those who love nobody,' Onassis said, sending a pang to her heart. The melancholy was a contrast to the previous summer, when she was not certain if she would survive from one day to the next.

In Paris, she tried to distract herself by taking voice lessons with Elvira de Hidalgo, but it reminded her of all she had lost. She proceeded with EMI's proposed recording of *La traviata* and began rehearsing with Richard Nunn, a voice teacher from Covent Garden. However, she remained frustrated by her lack of progress. Once more, she asked for Giulini to conduct the recording and he agreed, but felt her voice was 'perilously close to being ruined'.[24] The recording was scheduled for October 1968, giving her more than a year to prepare, although everyone knew she lacked interest. 'The truth is, I wasn't content because I wasn't getting what I wanted,' she said. 'I know what I want, and I know it before others.'[25]

In the autumn, Maria suspected Onassis was being unfaithful after he dismissed his servants and hosted a dinner for Jacqueline Kennedy at Avenue Foch. Ignoring the servants' whispers, she never learned the identity of his 'mystery guest' and continued to delude herself into thinking he loved her – and he seemed content to play along. They entered an idyllic period: he was overly affectionate in public, and to reporters, he announced, 'Callas and I have been married for fifteen days.' *La Stampa* reported:

> Callas and Onassis, who looked happy as two newly-weds on their honeymoon, headed to the apartment they share on Avenue Georges Mandel. They showed neither irritation nor embarrassment by the presence of the weekly correspondent and they let themselves be photographed, smiling, on the doorstep. The Italian journalist also asked Onassis's driver for confirmation of the owner's declarations, who replied: 'If he said so, it is clear that it is true.' 'But it could have been a joke,' insisted the reporter. The driver shook his head: 'I really don't think Onassis has the desire to joke about such important things. Besides, why shouldn't I say it? It is true, they are already married.'

They flew to New York and, still leading the press and their friends astray, Maria wrote to Elvira de Hidalgo, 'I drove you crazy, didn't I?'[26] She admitted it had been a joke, devised by Onassis whom, she said, 'Treats me so lovingly … Don't you find [he] has changed for the better?'[27]

Her judgement was clouded by lust and she could not, or would not, open her eyes to his manipulation. 'When lost in ecstasy of ardent passion, with the language of the heart, he swears eternal love,' she sang in *Lucia di Lammermoor*, the heroine's situation matching her own. She had been submissive to his whims but now she became possessive of their relationship and would protect it at all costs. 'You make of me the Queen of my world,' she told him.[28]

Her love failed to balance the equilibrium, however, and, driven by his ego, he left Maria at The Pierre Hotel and visited Jacqueline's apartment around the corner. 'Everybody here knows three things about Aristotle Onassis,' he said. 'I'm fucking Maria Callas. I'm fucking Jacqueline Kennedy. And I'm fucking rich.'[29]

Soon, photographs of Onassis and Jacqueline appeared in the newspapers and, although they were never alone, Maria understood the significance of the publicity. 'With a woman like Jackie and a man like you, starting something is easy, Aristo. But how do you stop it?'[30] she asked him. Denying their involvement, he explained they were close friends – the same explanation he had used to describe his association with Maria. There was an ounce of truth in his statement, for Jacqueline was involved with Bobby Kennedy, a married man, and she was beholden to the Kennedys; she knew her association with Onassis was a stain on their political dynasty.

Attempting to thwart Maria's suspicions, Onassis proposed marriage and she accepted, unaware that she was a pawn in his game. He was a maverick in the business world, but in private he lacked courage and attempted to push her away to force her to end the relationship. So, in London, where the supposed marriage was to take place, he orchestrated an argument with Maria and she walked out, leaving him, as it were, jilted at the altar. She flew to Paris, where she found no sympathy from her friends; they accused her of behaving badly and pushing him into the arms of another woman. To protect her pride, Maria lied and said she had 'nearly got engaged ... but as the day came close I ran away'.[31] It would have spoiled their relationship, she said, if they were to marry. 'Once you're married, the man takes you for granted and I do not want to be told what to do.'[32]

Alone once more, she returned to her voice lessons and began recording herself with the purpose of listening to the flaws in her singing, although it only depressed her. It was made all the more poignant by the death of Serafin, whose photograph[*] was one of the few displayed in her apartment alongside memorabilia of her heroine, Maria Malibran. She missed his

---

[*] Leo Lerman mistook the photograph of Serafin for Meneghini and it was published in various biographies that Maria kept a photo of her former husband, giving way to speculation that she still loved him. Nothing could be further from the truth.

funeral, as she was recuperating from an operation on her hernia that had troubled her since 1960.

After a previous operation in 1963, she wrote, 'The operation went fine only it's a long recovery on account of the internal plastic.'[33] In recent times, the 'internal plastic', or polypropylene mesh, used for hernia repair has become a controversial practice, owing to its painful side effects. However, doctors did not acknowledge her complaints nor relieve her symptoms, thus it took a physical and psychological toll on her health. She must have felt she had no control over her body or that it had, in some way, betrayed her.

This was particularly true when, around that period, Maria told friends that Onassis forced her to have an abortion, in London, in 1966. 'In fact, I was pregnant but he made me have an abortion,' she later confided to Maria Di Stefano.[34] To others, she said it had taken her four months to make a decision – she had previously miscarried at around four months – and how her life would have been different had she defied him. Even at that time, in 1960, he had told her to abort and showed no remorse when she lost the baby.

Mary Carter, to whom she told everything, never believed the story and sensed it was Maria's way of exorcising her regret at not having children. Others agreed that Maria was too strong to follow Onassis's orders. They did not consider how, in the guise of a traditional Greek wife, she 'feared and obeyed' him. Nor could they fathom his controlling nature and violence, so they dismissed her painful confession. Mrs Di Stefano asked why she never fulfilled her dream of motherhood by adopting. 'A child that isn't mine … doesn't come from me, I don't want one like that.'[35]

Following three months of silence, Onassis asked Maria to join him on a winter cruise of the Caribbean. Why would he, having shirked his promise to marry her and leaving her distraught in Paris, do such a thing? 'Sometimes unhappiness in a woman can be sexy,' he remarked, drawn to the pathos he had created.[36] Perhaps the answer lay in his dynamic with Jacqueline, who was reluctant to marry him. That year, Bobby Kennedy was running for President of the United States and had forbidden Jacqueline to make public her involvement with Onassis, nor would he ever accept 'the Greek' as the husband of his brother's widow. So, as Jacqueline withdrew to support Bobby with his presidential campaign, Onassis turned to Maria for his own mercurial reasons.

At every port, there were people invited onboard and Maria was expected to play hostess, which she often resented, but Onassis knew she was the star attraction. Sometimes she complained and threatened to go ashore, but he forbade it. 'I'm not asking for your permission,' she said, before Onassis slapped her across the face, stifling her bravado.

To outsiders, she spoke of 'many wonderful things'; a smokescreen to distract from the reality that was unfolding.[37]

There had been a time when she had loved to watch him in action, talking on his radio-telephones, striking deals and commanding others from afar. All over the world, people were scrambling around, fixing problems and hiding his money. Recently, there were secret operations with Mahmoud Hamshari, a Palestinian terrorist to whom he paid protection money for Olympic Airways; and Madame Claude's girls were coming and going to wherever he was, joining him in bed while he took his business calls.

She could no longer close her eyes to his behaviour, nor could she reconcile her feelings with a relationship built on a rotten foundation. The worm turned, and she walked out. 'I finished with him in Nassau,' she told Leo Lerman. 'He's sick, destructive. He brainwashed me … If I had stayed with him, he would have killed me or I would have killed him.'[38]

However, there was a motive to Onassis's treatment of Maria, for he wanted her to leave the yacht to make room for Jacqueline, without explicitly telling her so. She left for Paris and filmed a BBC interview with Lord Harewood, focusing on her studies in Athens and the 'big career', as she called it.

Despite the problems with Onassis, she was in a congenial mood when Harewood arrived at her apartment. Sitting at her dressing table, she surprised him by saying, 'You know, George, if we had fallen in love when we first met, our son would now be twenty!'[39]

The first recording lasted for three hours, with Maria beating her hand on a cushion to emphasise her point, but the technicians had to stop her as the sounds were 'coming over the microphones like pistol shots'.[40] After the second recording, Harewood invited her to dinner, but she refused as Onassis was coming home and she did not want to look tired.

Given Maria's remark to Harewood, it seemed she had forgiven Onassis for his past treatment and was ready to resume their lives in Paris. But the following day, he never arrived, and she felt cheated all over again. He had flown to New York and brought Jacqueline in his private plane to Palm Beach, then she joined him for a cruise of the Caribbean, although he was careful to invite his sister, as he had done in 1959, to maintain respectability. When the news reached Maria, she felt as though she 'had been struck by a hammer and I still can't breathe'.[41]

As if afraid of losing Maria, due to Jacqueline's reticence to marriage, he telephoned her three times. Once she ignored his call, but twice she answered, and it ended in their screaming at one another. She told de Hidalgo, 'He's irresponsible and disgusts me', and she wanted to leave Paris 'to get some rest'.[42]

In response, de Hidalgo said, 'Maria, you can't go on fighting with someone who has such a strong personality.'[43]

Once more, Maria began rehearsing for the recording of *La traviata*, practising with Gordon Mackie, an accompanist from Covent Garden. After a poor start, her voice grew stronger and Mackie reported to Peter Andry, 'Madam now has an excellent day.'[44]

Maria was going through the motions of reviving her career. She promised EMI a recording of Verdi arias, as well as considering offers from the San Francisco and Dallas opera companies. 'I am not very strong mentally or psychologically,' she confided to de Hidalgo.

Exploiting her weaknesses, Onassis convinced her to fly to Skorpios and join him on a cruise of the Greek Islands.[45] Unbeknownst to Maria, he had recently spent two weeks with Jacqueline at her family's estate in Newport, before going to the Kennedy compound at Hyannis Port.

Bobby Kennedy had been murdered by Sirhan Sirhan, a Palestinian terrorist, and Jacqueline told Onassis that she feared for her children's lives. 'They're killing Kennedys,' she said, unaware that he had boasted of ordering the assassination himself.* Suggesting they marry, he promised to protect her from the outside world.

As in business, he submitted his offer of $3 million 'for her body', and awaited her response, learning that her brother-in-law, Ted Kennedy, would negotiate the marriage contract.[46] Far from being repelled, it was the type of bargaining that Onassis liked best. 'He doesn't love Jackie,' Maria remarked. 'He just likes to be admired by very important women. So he will change me for another, more important woman. But I am certain he does not love her at all.'[47]

In a submissive mood, she arrived at Skorpios and they set sail on the *Christina*. Earlier in the year, she had written to him, 'Try, oh do try please to keep us together forever, because I need your eternal love and your respect.'[48] She battled with her pride, trying to understand why he had betrayed her, but even then, she could not leave him. They were bound together: like a serum, he had entered her bloodstream and only he could give her life. 'Fate happens,'

---

* Onassis believed the protection money he paid to Mahmoud Hamshari to protect Olympic Airways was actually used to order Sirhan to perform Kennedy's assassination on 6 June 1968.

he liked to say, complementing her philosophy, 'Destiny is destiny … there is no way out.' As someone who looked for divine symbolism, she fuelled his belief that, owing to his initials, he was the Alpha and the Omega: her beginning and end.

Then one day, Onassis shattered her delusions – the 'dreamy side, where everything is loyal, everything is beautiful and pure' – and ordered her to leave the yacht.[49] 'Go back to Paris and wait for me,' he said, informing her that an important guest was expected and she could not be there.

'Paris in August, are you crazy?' she asked him, thinking it was a joke.

He reminded her that she was his concubine and, therefore, without respectability. Even his staff, at his behest, treated her like a whore (his description) and upon seeing them together remarked, 'He's busy doing Greek business'.[50]

The important guest, she learned, was Jacqueline, who was coming with Ted Kennedy to finalise the marriage contract, although she was obviously unaware of the latter details. She went to her room and packed her things and thanked the staff for their assistance, disarming them with her dignity. 'I am beginning the final performance of my life,' she said.[51] Before leaving on the Chris-Craft, she warned Onassis, 'You'll never see me again'.

Perhaps Onassis did, in fact, have misgivings about Maria's departure because, night after night, he sat on the stern of the yacht, drinking heavily and playing her records, her voice drifting across the dark waters of the Ionian. Listening to the cries of *Norma*, *Medea* and *Tosca*, he took the records and broke them in half, throwing the contents out to sea. However, he restored his braggadocio and awaited Jacqueline's arrival.

Jacqueline surprised him by rebuffing his offer of $3 million and asking for $20 million upfront. 'Your client could price herself right out of the market,' he warned her financial adviser, who was brokering the deal.[52] But he hated to lose, so he forged ahead with the marriage contract: it would have 170 clauses, stating their financial arrangement and his sexual demands toward his young wife. Despite the sums of money Jacqueline received, including $1 million for each of her children, she was disappointed by the negotiating skills of Ted, who succumbed to Onassis's intimidation. 'There's one thing you must understand about me, my dear,' Onassis said, 'I am completely fucking ruthless.'[53]

In Paris, Maria retreated to her apartment and wrote cathartic letters to her friends, calling his behaviour 'such bad manners after nine years of hoping and doing sacrifices'.[54] Struggling to accept what had happened, she took an overdose of sleeping pills and was admitted to the American Hospital, but she denied it was a suicide attempt. Thinking it a sin to end her life, she must have wanted clemency for her tortured soul, for she took one pill after the other, until the pain was numbed. In a letter to de Hidalgo, she confided, 'I feel so lost.'[55]

Terrified of falling into 'dark and pessimistic thoughts', she flew to New York with Larry Kelly and spent several days at the apartment of Costa Gratsos and his wife, Anastasia.[56] Before leaving for Dallas to meet Mary Carter and travel across the United States, she told Gratsos she would telephone from each place and leave her number, in case Onassis wanted to contact her. Part of her wanted him back, while the other part travelled further from his reach.

Maria and Larry detoured and flew to Kansas City to stay with his friend, David Stickelber, who invited Sue Blair, a former model, to join them. Inside the walls of Stickelber's mansion, Maria's sadness was oppressive, so they went to Colorado Springs. The private plane was laden down with her luggage, and her excess baggage was stored in the bathroom.

Three days later, they motored to Santa Fe, and Maria surprised a local artist, Ford Ruthling, by attending his exhibition of folk art and spending hours posing for photographs. There, Sue met an old friend, John Ardoin, a music critic for the *Dallas Morning News*, and invited him to lunch. Given Maria's frame of mind, she was upset by Ardoin's presence: he was a stranger and a journalist, and she was on her guard.

During the stay, Maria never mentioned Onassis. Larry spoke of reviving her career and she agreed to his proposals. But Sue thought Maria was just going through the motions of making plans, for when they were together, she was struck by her emptiness. Having known the high life from her modelling days in Paris, Sue was surprised when Maria spoke of her regret at not being a mother. 'What could be more wonderful than having a child?' she asked. Yet, she continued to pine for the man who had deprived her of such dreams, expecting him to telephone and summon her back to Skorpios.

Several days later, Mary Carter joined the party and Sue departed, allowing Maria to speak frankly with her old friend. Her pain was evident, but more astonishing to Mary was Maria's dependence on sleeping pills. They checked into an apartment at the Rancho Encantado, whose facilities did not include a telephone, and so Maria fretted that Onassis might be trying to reach her. They went to La Fonda instead, but there were no available rooms, and having been accustomed to travelling with Onassis, the world of commercial travel and hotel reservations were alien to Maria.

Nevertheless, she announced she wanted to go to Las Vegas, so Mary telephoned Moe Dalitz, a former bootlegger and operator of illegal casinos who was the proprietor of the Desert Inn. Thrilled to have 'real class' staying at the hotel, Dalitz sent a white limousine to collect them at the airport and arranged for Maria to attend several stage shows. After three days in Las Vegas, she became upset when Onassis did not phone. 'I thought I deserved more,' she said of his treatment.[57]

They left for Los Angeles, checked into the Bel-Air Hotel and went to dinner with its owner, Joseph Drown, who stared at Maria's legs through the glass table. Unnerved by the attention, she went to her room and discovered it had been ransacked by an intruder, who stole jewellery and left a belt on her bed. The management explained that the belt was for strangulation purposes. Terrified to sleep, she took several pills and rendered herself unconscious.

Day after day, she occupied herself with excursions. She went to Disneyland and explored Hollywood, surprised that moguls such as Mervyn LeRoy asked her to dinner. In San Francisco, she agreed to an interview with the *San Francisco Chronicle* but was upset when the article's headline called Onassis a rat.

Weeks had passed and Onassis did not call, although she followed the same ritual of phoning Gratsos and updating him with her contact details. 'They care for one day, one month, one year, then what?' she said of Onassis's devotion, perhaps hoping Jacqueline would be another phase.[58]

As though to soften the blow, Gratsos sent flowers to Mary's house in Cuernavaca, Mexico – their latest stop – and Maria pretended they were from Onassis. Each day followed the last, with her weeping and dwelling on the past. Sometimes she walked around with a small radio, listening to jazz – its singers, she said, had 'nobility, never vulgarity'.[59]

One night, they went to El Bohemio, a rundown nightclub in the red light district. Maria had a good time, but her eyes kept wandering to the cubicles where the prostitutes plied their trade. Her stay in Mexico ended when she slipped on tiles and tore the cartilage in her ribs.

In Dallas, Maria received medical treatments for her ribs and was given codeine for the pain, but she had an allergic reaction and became ill. At Mary's house, she received flowers from Gratsos and, once more, Maria pretended they were from Onassis; she also kept a telephone next to her on the bed, still believing he would call.

According to Larry, she became so distressed that she overdosed on pills and was taken to hospital to have her stomach pumped. To distract her, he spoke about her comeback. She agreed to sing *La traviata* and Verdi's 'Requiem' in Dallas in 1969, and an announcement was made to the press. 'I don't have all that much time to get cured,' she said of her emotional state, 'because next year I've got to sing.'[60]

To keep Maria's mind off Onassis, she gave a pre-taped radio interview to John Ardoin, but on the recording she was breathless and unsure of herself, and at the beginning she sounded incoherent before hitting her stride. Afterwards, she burst into tears and excused herself, before emerging several moments later and asking if he had another tape – she wanted to record a confessional.

During the hour-long recording, Maria, in a distressed tone, spoke of her neglectful parents and sister, 'Everybody should be proud of me. My mother, God, how many mothers would have adored a child like me?' And she lamented the underhanded tactics of Titta, who she called 'a pimp', due to his mishandling of her money. The focus of her feelings, however, was Onassis:

> I didn't need this mess lately. I didn't need this kind of kicks. I've had too many kicks in my life … To have what in return? What? This. Nothing … I'm quite sure he did not do it on purpose. Nobody could be that cruel … The hurt's there and I can't get rid of it. I put in nine years … It takes time, when serious, strong people promise or guarantee relative happiness, then you have to live up to that. It's too easy to say, "Well, you know, we did our best to be happy." Well, thank you very much … for nine years … The way things have gone, I can't be friends. How can he be my friend? Humiliating me that way.

Years later, and having become friends with Ardoin, she ended their relationship after he wrote a book and used her recordings without permission. 'You could have, at least, informed me of your intentions and asked me if I could agree with such an idea,' she wrote. 'My feeling is, thus, that John Ardoin never understood and will probably never understand Maria Callas.'[61]

From Dallas, Maria flew to New York and stayed as the guest of Glenn and Dorothy Wallichs, founder of Capitol Records, in their apartment at the Sherry-Netherland. Her arrival coincided with Renata Tebaldi opening in *Adriana Lecouvreur* at the Metropolitan, and she agreed to attend the premiere.[62]

Dressed in a floor-length velvet gown and emeralds from Harry Winston, she made a grand entrance and was applauded by the audience, who called for her to return to the stage. Afterwards, Rudolf Bing escorted her backstage and the enemies, who had not spoken since 1951, fell into one another's arms.

Several days later, Maria learned that Onassis was in New York with Jacqueline and she telephoned his apartment at The Pierre. His voice was cold, and he offered no remorse for his actions, nor did he give her the closure she needed. Nevertheless, Onassis ordered his publicity agent to inform the press that he and Maria had met for drinks at El Morocco, leading the public to believe she was still within his grasp. At the time, she was en route to Paris. 'Frankly, I'm terrified about going home,' she said. 'It's like the beginning of a performance.' She longed for 'medicine to give me strength, mental and physical', as she did not think her 'health could stand so much tension'.[63]

In Paris, she waited by the telephone for Onassis's call, yet she feared hearing his voice. 'I wouldn't want him to phone me and start again torturing me,' she confided. 'It is my only fear. He can be so persuasive and destructive, that man, in spite of all his genius.'[64] She battled with mood swings, 'One moment I am filled with confidence and the other so frail'.[65] To de Hidalgo, she wrote, 'One has to take life as it comes. I am feeling well, in an excellent mood. I am free from that nightmare which is called destructive love in every aspect.'[66]

To friends, Onassis spoke of his regret in proposing to Jacqueline; he wanted to leave her and return to Maria. However, Jacqueline called his bluff when her family leaked the news of their marriage to the *Boston Herald*, thus forcing his hand. Regardless, Maria was the last to know and received the news from Onassis's butler, who felt compelled to tell her. Then she read of his marriage plans and her entire world imploded. 'The worst is that he never told me anything about his marriage,' she said. 'I think he ought to after nine years by his side, at least I shouldn't have had to learn it in the newspapers.'[67]

Days later, she received a call from Onassis, pleading with her to come to Skorpios to 'save him'. He knew that if she were to appear, Jacqueline would be furious and leave – or, so he thought. Gathering all of her strength, she defied him.

On 20 October, Onassis married Jacqueline on Skorpios in front of twenty-five guests. There was torrential rain and the groom looked downcast as he drove his bride to the *Christina* for the reception. 'I consider him to be mad, and as such, I want to erase him from my mind,' Maria said, as she watched the events unfolding with the morbid curiosity of an onlooker at an execution.[68] 'It is cruel, isn't it, but they are paying for it, both of them, they will pay for it, wait and see.'[69]

Emerging from the emotional debris, Maria attempted to put things in order. She had summoned her hairdresser and dressed for the film premiere of *A Flea in Her Ear* at the Théâtre Marigny. Carefully painted and lacquered, her appearance betrayed her heartbreak as she smiled for the cameras. Escorted by Sandy Bertrand, the director of *Vogue*, she was greeted by her friends, Elizabeth Taylor and Richard Burton, who embraced her and called Onassis 'a son of a bitch', and Marie-Hélène de Rothschild, who claimed Onassis and Jacqueline were not welcome at her home.

The following day, Visconti sent her a telegram:

> As always you dominate everyone with your great class of woman and artist and give everyone a lesson in style. I send you my affectionate supportive thoughts and my unaltered admiration. Always count on my great sincere friendship. I always embrace you.

From the beginning, Maria had known Onassis would hurt her and she had become resigned to her fate. 'I am yours,' she said, 'do with me as you want.'[70] The inner conflict contrasted with her submission and, months before on Skorpios, he asked what she wanted most for herself. 'I just want to be on good terms with myself.'[71]

17

Cipher

Everything's finished.
I have never lied;
all's over between us.

Carmen, Bizet

In the wake of Onassis's betrayal, Maria said, 'I only have myself to count on and nobody else, in my past, present and future.'[1] It took all of her willpower not to succumb to him, no matter how persuasive he could be or how many secret doors he could open, for behind every door was a trap. He had wanted to merge his power with hers, and instead of triumph, they created chaos. 'I am a courageous woman, as they say, and I am proud of it,' she told Elvira de Hidalgo. 'But it is no consolation.'[2]

Less than a month after Onassis's marriage, he telephoned Maria, pleading with her to see him. After all, he reminded her, they were in business together. Her anger could not be quelled by his false charm, nor did he express remorse for hurting her. To attract her attention, he stood on the street, whistling under her window. 'He's such a pig,' she said.[3] Having been ignored, he went to a nearby restaurant and phoned her, but she would not speak to him. Eventually, he lost his temper and threatened to drive his Rolls-Royce through the gates of her building. Afraid of a scene, she let him in.

Their first meetings were unsuccessful: she could not forgive him, nor could she understand his reasons for marrying another woman. He claimed Jacqueline meant nothing to him. They had not planned a single day past their wedding and, on their honeymoon, she wrote letters to her former (married) lover, Roswell Gilpatric. Despite their contract stipulating that Jacqueline would spend two nights a week with him, she left for New York, leaving him to entertain his associates alone. 'Of course, affection cannot be bought,' Maria remarked.[4]

In his wife's absence, he expected Maria to submit, as before. Going to her bedroom, he undressed and got into bed, but she threw him out. 'Shame on you! And on the anniversary of your second wife's first husband's death!' she yelled out the window as he walked to his car.[5] Momentarily, she had the strength to resist him. 'As for Daddy O,' she said, 'what is over is over. Sagittarians are like that.'[6]

Turning to her career, her recording of *La traviata* remained in limbo and she was advised to study with Norberto Mola from La Scala. She refused, as Mola knew her from 'the good old days' and would 'make her feel self-conscious every time she didn't quite make a note or two'.[7] Instead, she practised with Gordon Mackie from Covent Garden, which ended after he was killed in a freak car accident at Waterloo Station, having returned that day from Paris. 'But who's going to play for us now?' she asked, viewing Mackie's death as a bad omen.[8]

No longer enthusiastic, she refused to sing with Plácido Domingo and instead, Luciano Pavarotti was engaged as Alfredo. The Accademia Santa Cecilia in Rome was booked for three weeks in September, and the orchestra and choir had been paid. Cancelling the engagement, she said Rome would be too cold, and so the recording was never made.

Furthermore, she reneged on her agreement with Larry Kelly and the Dallas Opera, reminding him that no contract had been signed. 'I have always felt that when an agreement is made,' he wrote, 'a signed contract is not really necessary.'[9] He had changed *Norma* to *La traviata*, 'which seemed logical', although his investors would not budget for a full-length opera. It was rumoured that she could not do *Norma* because Elena Souliotis was cast in the part; it was also reported that she refused to sing opposite Shirley Verrett, as Adalgisa. Only the 'Requiem' was scheduled, and he changed the programme to allow her ten days of uninterrupted rehearsals. 'I know,' he said, 'your nervous system is not strong.'[10]

Having exhausted her reasons to cancel, she criticised him for announcing the programme to the newspapers. She told him her nerves 'couldn't stand the presence of world press',[11] but he assured her, 'Callas is such a magic name that the world press would go to the North Pole to see and hear you when you choose to re-enter the stage.'[12] Nevertheless, she refused his counter-offer of *Tosca*, so 'it would not throw into such a bad light an opera company which has tried in every possible way to accommodate your wishes'.[13] The answer was no, she said, 'I don't want to be compared to myself.'

After cancelling Dallas, she refused an offer from the San Francisco Opera due to Kurt Adler wanting her to give eight performances of *La traviata* over the course of two months. It was too long, she explained, her behaviour reminiscent of their 1957–58 conflict. She also cancelled her verbal agreement with Rudolf Bing, as he wanted her to do two gala performances of *Tosca* but she wanted ten *Medeas*. It was self-sabotage, although she hid it behind a veneer of artistic integrity:

> I have made up my mind that if I can return, I will return. If I cannot, I will not make a tragedy of it. The trouble with returning to the stage is that the public always wants more and more and more. If you give yourself 100 per cent one time, they expect 200 per cent the next time. And then 300 per cent. Already, I myself want 200 per cent of what I do. But the public, when it gives you triumph, demands more and more. They exaggerate their demands. And I can't fight that. I find that terrifying.[14]

Instead, Maria considered an offer she had received the summer before at Skorpios, when Francesco Rossellini and Marina Cicogna asked her to star in Pier Paolo Pasolini's film of *Medea*. 'When Franco Rossellini proposed this one,' she said, 'I had no doubt. I knew immediately this was the occasion I'd been waiting for and I was determined not to let it slip by.'[15]

That was not entirely true, and she had reservations about Pasolini, as did Visconti, who warned that his elements of realism were not suited to her talents. She had expressed her disapproval of Pasolini's *Teorema*, whose male protagonist had relations with his friend's family: the parents, son, daughter and maid. The explicitness of the scenes repelled her, and when she was told the protagonist was a metaphorical Christ figure, she called Pasolini a blasphemer. Before making a decision, she consulted Joëlle de Gravelaine, a Parisian astrologer, who advised her to accept.

Meeting Pasolini in Rome allayed Maria's fears. He explained he wanted her 'for herself', not for her celebrity. 'Here is a woman,' he explained, 'in one sense, the most modern of women, but there lives in her an ancient woman – strange, mysterious, magical, with terrible inner conflicts.'[16] Maria was Medea; Medea was Maria – she envisioned herself not as the operatic character to whom she had given life onstage, but the demi-goddess from Euripides's ancient fable. 'Maria Callas is an extraordinary tragic actress,' Pasolini said, having studied photographs of her with Onassis: her still frame, and her dark, myopic eyes pained from abuse. 'She is the only actress who can express, even without acting and without saying a word, spiritual catastrophe.'[17]

In Turkey, Maria stood against the scorched landscape of Cappadocia, dressed in primitive robes and medallions, exorcising Medea's hurt from Jason's abandonment, and her own pent-up feelings toward Onassis. 'She's a woman, with all the experiences of a woman,' Maria told a BBC reporter. 'Even so, everything's bigger; bigger sacrifice … but the hurt is there, just the same as any other woman.' The heat was gruelling and the hours were long, but she toiled as she had done at La Scala. 'Pasolini is so wonderful to work with. I hope [*Medea*] will be a success,' she said. 'But even if it is not, the atmosphere is so wonderful that it was worth my while.'[18]

Behind the scenes, she and Pasolini discussed everything from art to philosophy. He was the first to worship her mind, instead of her voice, and to treat her as an intellectual. As though they shared a telepathic bond ('my antennas … your antennas'), they knew one another's inner-most thoughts.[19] He told her:

> I saw … very light anxiety, barely more than a shadow, and yet unstoppable. It was the feeling of not having completely controlled yourself, your body, your reality: to have been 'used' (and more with the fatal technical brutality that cinema involves) and therefore of having lost your full freedom in part. You'll often experience this heart clamp during our shoot, and I'll feel it with you too.[20]

As much as she admired him, she disapproved of his Marxism and averted her eyes when he disappeared into the caves with the young male extras. He was always in conflict between his so-called 'saintly' side, and his peccadilloes. 'I am scandalous because I have a cord, an umbilical cord, between the profane and the sacred,' he said. 'I devour my existence with an insatiable appetite. How will all of this end? I don't know.'[21]

She knew how it would end. One day, she was approached by a fortune teller, who asked to read her palm. Her driver translated then fell silent, unwilling to divulge the rest. What did she say? Maria implored. She would die young but would not suffer. 'Destiny is destiny.'

As happy as Maria felt, she was besieged by old problems. At her hotel, Onassis rang occasionally, using the alias Mr Lupoli – the surname of Maria's maid, Bruna – but she refused to speak to him. Her friends also phoned, asking if they could visit her in Turkey, but she declined. Perhaps she was afraid they would undermine her work or derail her stability; for the first time in her career, she was in control of the experience. 'I sang for many years without ever being able to see the conductor. I've been to many countries and I've never seen anything. All I know, they told me.'[22]

One day, her body double's costume caught fire and it was reported in the press that Maria had suffered life-threatening burns. Her mother and sister sent word to the set, asking to be informed of her condition. They were leeches, Maria hissed, knowing they were only concerned about their allowance. Her health was beginning to suffer and, succumbing to the elements and her low blood pressure, she fainted while shooting a scene. When she came round, she apologised for delaying the production, although it continued on schedule.

Throughout filming, Pasolini wrote poems for Maria and, in a trance, he drew her picture, decorating it with debris from the earth. She was flattered but became unnerved, as though she had lost the realism he had once seen in her, and he was now viewing her as a deity who sang from the cosmos. It mirrored the experiences of Medea, when Jason, for whom she abandoned her supernatural world, marries another and leaves her alone in the human realm. Assuming the audience would be familiar with Euripides's tale, Pasolini provided no backstory, although Medea's sorceress roots were shown through symbolism during the love scenes; she kept one eye open, her body and mind disengaged, conveying the physical and metaphysical. A film critic for the *New York Times* wrote, 'And this, I think, is where the film goes awry.'

Knowing of Maria's limits, Pasolini abandoned his idea to film an orgy scene with girls and priests, the live burial of a naked boy and girl and a sacrificial scene with a bull which also included bestiality. Another depicted a king with his seven daughters, nude and vying for his attention. He also cut a scene where Medea kills her brother and cuts him into pieces, smearing his blood onto the surrounding leaves and vegetation. 'It's not a horror movie,' Maria said.[23]

During the rushes, she asked him to cut a scene in which she sang a Greek lullaby to her children, who she later kills, and to revaluate his lingering close-ups, as she disliked the camera angles and how her profile appeared. Most people, however, thought she looked beautiful. She had gone on a strict diet, reducing her weight to 130lb, and had an eye lift.[24] She preferred the English version, which they had also dubbed, but Pasolini used the original Italian cut. 'I hate all those English subtitles cutting across my face.'[25]

They moved from the exterior sets in Turkey and northern Italy to the sound stages in Rome. As she left Ankara, the customs officials seized eighty-seven antiques – vases, lamps, plates and bowls – claiming they were part of the country's heritage and belonged in museums. On the last day of shooting, Pasolini gave her a silver ring inset with an antique coin and she gave him a necklace, and they were photographed kissing on the mouth.

Reporters wrote that an engagement was imminent – despite him being openly homosexual – and she hoped, in her naïve way, it would make Onassis jealous. 'It is terrible to be the one used, but also the one who uses,' Pasolini wrote to her.

Their friendship became a joke for satirists, and an Italian art house staged a scene on a darkened stage with a woman's voice calling from the wings, 'Pier Paolo, Pier Paolo'. From the opposite wing, a male voice responded, 'Maria, Maria'. Their cries grew louder, punctuated by heavy breathing and, finally, '*Che bella chiamata* [what a nice call]'. Another voice, closing the scene, said, 'Well, that's all we can manage.'

It was not romantic love, for Pasolini was involved with Ninetto Davoli, his protégé who appeared in several of his films. As he wrote in a poem dedicated to Maria, he could not accept her love for 'my eyes take into consideration / the unclean loins of a woman, of man's flesh'. Instead, Maria viewed Pasolini as someone who treated her with kindness; a father figure or protector, 'reincarnated and destined to die':

> What counts as him, the Father, yes him …
> You smiling at me, are smiling at him.
> But I can never be him, because I do not know him.
> I swear to you, Maria, I haven't the least experience of this …[26]

Maria was always searching for the love that her parents failed to provide. As with Pasolini and her father, she extracted what she wanted from his devotion and ignored his immorality, as it did not fit her ideal.

There was an intrusive side to his admiration. He took gratification from her problems, warping them into fourteen poems to suit his perversions. In one poem, he wrote that she had incestuous feelings for her father:

> Sinful thoughts about him are rightly dissociated;
> his idealisation has blessed forms;
> even if they seem special to you and can in practice make you suffer,
> and you touch mature sex with your eye or thought.[27]

The patriarchal and incestuous elements were apparent in his love for Ninetto, then 21, and with whom he had begun a sexual relationship when the boy was 15 and he in his mid 40s. He told Maria that Ninetto was the love of his life and his obsession with youth was 'a vice more terrible than cocaine'.[28] Turning to Ninetto, she asked if he, too, was in love with Pasolini, and later recalled the crushing revelation. She told Pasolini, 'When Ninetto said he would never fall in love, I knew he was saying things he was too young to understand.'[29]

Somehow, despite the pederastic undertones with Ninetto and others, he continued to adore Maria, the only woman for whom he claimed he might feel desire. Their worshipping of one another was akin to Medea's dark magic, although he was a self-confessed atheist and she, during that period, seemed preoccupied with the occult.

Their vision of *Medea* did not transmit well on the screen and the film was a commercial failure. The press, who had captured Maria on the set and attempted to break into her hotel room by scaling the building, preferred her in the flesh instead of a static image. Its premiere, on 28 January 1970, at L'Opera was attended by the French First Lady, Claude Pompidou, but the applause was a mark of respect for Callas, not the celluloid figure. 'At any rate,' she said, 'it's the kind of film people will either love or hate.'[30]

Several days later, Maria and Pasolini hosted a free screening for students, followed by a debate.* A student asked if her film debut meant an end to her operatic work, which they considered superior. She thought it was 'a mean question' and, in a low voice, exchanged a few words with Pasolini, before answering, 'No, it is the work that is destined to a bad end. Let me explain: it is an art in decline, but if the work is in decline, I am not. I will wait for it to rise again to start singing again.'[31]

Another student said, 'I do not agree with the choice of Madame Callas to play Medea. Medea is a barbarian and Callas is instead a refined woman, she has too much prestige to put herself in the skin of a barbarian.'

To Pasolini, someone asked, 'What are your religious views?'

'I am a Marxist, but I have a sense of the sacred.'

'We are here to talk about *Medea* and not about Marxism,' Maria interrupted. The audience burst into applause.

At the beginning of 1970, Maria told reporters, 'I had a certain relationship with Onassis but fortunately for me it's all over. It was a period of my life that I want to forget.'[32] He was an addiction for which she had no cure, and she soon

---

* In March, Maria and Pasolini went to Buenos Aires to present *Medea* at the Mar del Plata Film Festival. She was flanked by the paparazzi. The public, as in Europe, were more excited by her appearance in the flesh than in Pasolini's slow-moving drama.

lapsed into her old routine of lying to the press and deceiving herself. 'I want to be dominated on my own accord … I don't like people to command me.'[33]

The narcissist in Onassis changed his tactics and turned himself into the victim, therefore he remained in control of her feelings. He spoke of how unhappy Jacqueline made him, and received Maria's sympathy instead of her scorn. Their dynamic changed, and she thought she had the upper hand and could succeed where his wife had failed. To friends, she called it 'a passionate friendship', but maintained it was platonic, explaining that, as he was married in the Orthodox Church, she would burn in hell if it became sexual. '[It] was too much,' she said of their meetings, but she could not stop herself from falling.[34]

During that period, Maria was being escorted around town by Omar Sharif and Raf Vallone. She had entered a new era in terms of her celebrity; she was an independent woman, in charge of her own affairs – an entirely modern stance. Or, as Violetta sang, 'A poor woman, alone, lost in this crowded desert, which is known to men as Paris. What should I do? Revel in the whirlpool of earthly pleasures.' The press wrote:

> The value of Maria Callas, on the contrary, has risen dramatically. Once upon a time, everyone pitied her; in the Parisian salons she was spoken of as the *Pauvre Marie*. Now she's more desirable and high society names compete in inviting her, her presence is enough to determine the international success of a social evening.[35]

However, her outings with other men served to inflame Onassis's jealousy. By contrast, he had become a pitiful figure – 'another sad sugar daddy' in the newspapers[36] – particularly after Jacqueline's letters to Gilpatric were published. He had grown to hate Jacqueline. She spent too much money; during their first year of marriage she had spent $20 million. He resented her detached personality and compared her body to a corpse. In recent months, he had spoken of divorce and consulted with his lawyers, leading Maria to believe that he wanted to marry her. He spent four nights at her apartment and, from her perspective, he had chosen her and not his wife.

Having spent nine years caught in the cycle of his abuse, part of her craved his attention. She had momentarily relapsed, and admitted to Leo Lerman, 'He almost had me again.'[37]

Their first public outing was to Maxim's, where they dined at their favourite table, and they were photographed smiling in the back of his car. 'How was the love between Callas and Onassis reborn?' the press asked. 'Those who know the couple well maintain that the passion between the two has never died.'[38] Cynics assumed he was using her to force Jacqueline into filing for divorce, although the marriage contract allowed him to take a mistress. Maria's happiness was shattered when, a day later, Onassis took his wife to Maxim's. Humiliated by the turn of events, Maria fell into a deep depression and, three days later, she overdosed on sleeping pills.

Although Maria had overdosed several times throughout the years and would do so in future, she always maintained it was accidental. The night before, she had been agitated and begged her friends not to leave her alone. At seven o'clock in the morning, she was driven to the American Hospital.

Onassis was in Athens with Jacqueline who, having again usurped Maria, was planning a week-long cruise on the *Christina*. He showed no concern and released a statement to the press, dismissing rumours of a divorce. After the event, Pasolini wrote to her:

> He manoeuvred you like one of many creatures; and you, believing yourself free, threw yourself with the impetus of other centuries … Still proud to be a 'city girl' and full of the ancient morality pride of generations and regions … You have naively thrown yourself, like a fearless clown to his duty, possessed of vocation: you had no half measures your feelings were real, great feelings: it was the moment in which he lets go completely free.[39]

In Paris, the news of her alleged suicide attempt was broadcast by Radio Luxembourg. To the press, she said, 'I am literally besieged and I formally deny all the rumours that were spread about me. All this concern moves me, but it embarrasses me at the same time, both for my work and for my private life.'[40] The French tabloid, *Noir et Blanc*, repeated the report, and she sued both the publication and Radio Luxembourg and was awarded 20,000 francs in damages. 'I didn't try to kill myself,' she repeated, 'I'm too full of life.'[41]

In Milan, Titta emerged from the shadows and offered an appraisal of Maria. 'She is a strange woman: uneducated but very intelligent, capable of learning a language in a month, so she spoke several, albeit with some blunders.'[42]

Maria could not, however, see when she was being swindled. The latest parasitical individual in her life was Vasso Devetzi, a Greek pianist and the mistress of Jean Roire, proprietor of a French Communist record company. They were first introduced in Athens in 1957, and a polite exchange grew into something bigger in the imagination of Vasso. In the music circles of Paris in the early 1960s, their paths crossed, and by 1970, Maria, now emotionally redundant, needed a friend who understood her career and celebrity. Vasso filled that void.

In June, Maria invited Vasso to accompany her to Moscow, where she judged the Tchaikovsky Competition. There was nothing remarkable about Vasso's presence, as during that time Maria often travelled with friends and had perhaps chosen her as she was familiar with the USSR. Over the course of several days, Maria's arrival was treated as a state visit. She was received at the Kremlin and was the guest of honour at every function she attended. Flattered as Maria was, it was Vasso who revelled in the attention and cadged the privileges of her celebrity. It was the life Vasso had wanted and, like one of her concertos, she studied the score and instinctively played to the orchestra. In time, she became the friend who Maria thought she needed and, by then, it was too late.

In August, Maria went to Tragonisi, an island owned by her friend Perry Embiricos in the Peloponnese, the place of her ancestors. There, she was surprised by Onassis, who arrived in a helicopter to present her with century-old earrings to mark her name day. From a nearby boat, a paparazzo captured them kissing under a beach umbrella. An hour later, Onassis departed, having set up the paparazzo and the kiss, and knowing that within twenty-four-hours, his wife would be reeling. 'He is my best friend … he is and always will be,' Maria said, defensive of their bond.[43] The earrings had, perhaps, stirred up old memories of the expensive diamonds he had once given her, which she left in his safe after walking out in the summer of 1968 – crystallised objects that traced the ebb and flow of their relationship; cameos of love and violence.

On the island, she was joined by Pasolini, who had taken her to North Africa several months before to scout film locations. As she snorkelled in the Aegean and lazed on the sand, Pasolini sketched her frantically, glueing flowers to the canvases. In 1969, she was drawn in full form, and in 1970, a distant profile.

One night, they were sitting on the small pier, sharing intimacies, when she said, 'Words that have no resonance in reality.' Perhaps it was aimed at Onassis, whose visit weighed on her mind, or at Pasolini, as the intensity of their friendship was fading. In a poem, he wrote, 'the blissful smile of fake security … and her hands clasped to her knees like little girls, hiding the tremor behind a sly fake ease'.

After the publication of his poetry, she did not reproach him, and so her feelings remained unresolved. 'You cannot trust others for long,' she later wrote to him. 'Betrayal was the law of nature.'[44] He wanted to believe she was a barbarian in the guise of Medea, who scorned tradition and broke social taboos. Instead, he realised that her fundamental values were bourgeois and, therefore, the hidden side of his nature repelled those senses. At the end of summer, he returned to his medieval tower north of Rome, and she to her apartment in Paris.

In Paris, she was conflicted by her feelings for Onassis, having realised that he was two different people. In Greece, he had been impulsive and kind, conjuring memories of the man she had fallen in love with. However, in Paris, his games were all too evident, and although she could see through him, she continued to deceive herself. He wanted a divorce but was bound by the contract he had negotiated which, in the end, gave Jacqueline the power to exploit him. Various motives were used to force his wife's hand, but she would not file for divorce, nor would she allow herself to be divorced: there was too much at stake. So, he cut Jacqueline's monthly allowance of $30,000 by a third, and she outsmarted him by purchasing her clothes with his money and selling them to consignment stores, thus creating an income.

Then, he began to treat Jacqueline the way he had Maria and would lose his temper and ignore her for long periods, before summoning her to Paris or Skorpios, using her for sex and publicity, then discarding her at his whim. Whereas Maria lost herself in a bottle of pills, Jacqueline made a life for herself in America; her independence was her revenge and it tormented him.

Although Maria was a sympathetic listener, Onassis's pattern with Jacqueline was all too familiar and it provoked feelings of anger and resentment. She told Leo Lerman, 'I'll never forgive him, for humiliating me in public and taking me away from my music.'[45]

Turning again to music, she agreed to do *La traviata* with Visconti in Paris, but she knew her voice could no longer carry a full opera. They both deserted the project, which was a relief to Maria, who said, '[Modern] opera is no spectacular performance ... It's music's ruin. I don't get it.'[46] In a letter to de Hidalgo, she complained of others 'making progress with such dubious talents'.

Instead, Maria went to La Scala and, as she entered Ghiringhelli's box, the audience erupted into applause and shouted, 'We want Maria! You are La Scala!', overshadowing the production of *I vespri siciliani* with Renata Scotto, who was booed by the claque. Enraged, Scotto said:

Callas hoped to harm me. She no longer sings and perhaps she believed she could revive the success in such an incorrect and even a bit pathetic way. But perhaps Callas needs the stolen applause because she has nothing else left … not a husband, not a man who loves her, not a child … I am so much richer than she, and I can even leave the applause to her! If that's all that's left on the avenue of sunset … poor thing. It certainly wasn't in good taste – Callas didn't behave like a true lady. But what do you expect, when you have nothing left in your life and you've passed your peak … you take gratification at whatever cost, even if it means just a few stolen crumbs and so without value.[47]

The public who had once thrown vegetables at Maria now applauded her, and Onassis, who had humiliated her, tracked her movements, hoping for a stolen kiss. In terms of the latter, her feelings had changed: she wanted 'the world to know' he had wronged her, but the *histoire* would not come from her.[48] To her close friends, she spoke of wanting revenge but insisted she had, at last, learned to live with herself. In a letter, Pasolini wrote:

You are like a precious stone that we violently break into a thousand bursts so that it can then be returned to a matter more sustainable than that of life, that is the matter of poetry. It's just terrible to feel broken, to feel that at a certain point, at a certain hour, in a certain day, you're no longer entirely yourself, but only a radiance of yourself: I know how much that can be humiliating.[49]

As though trapped in a hall of mirrors, she existed outside of herself and was viewed in many variations. Callas had surpassed Maria, who was now a spectator in life. 'To tell you the truth, I do not like being called "La Divina". I resent it,' she said. The private woman enslaved to her legacy. 'I adorn Maria Callas. And I am only a woman.'[50]

18

Intermezzo

I am sacred here.

Medea, Cherubini

In the New Year of 1971, Maria went to Italy and filed for divorce from Titta, as the law had been passed the month before. From her hotel suite in Milan, she spoke to reporters, who asked if she would marry Onassis who, it was rumoured, was also filing for divorce. 'I do not answer questions that somehow concern the cause,' she answered.[1]

When the reporters approached Titta, he complimented Maria's appearance, having followed her in the newspapers, and reminded them that he was responsible for her success.* In response, she said, 'He has a bad case of the blah-blahs.'[2]

A month later, she prepared to teach a two-week masterclass at the Curtis Institute of Music in Philadelphia. 'I want to give what I know to the young people,' she said. 'I haven't sung in five, six years, but look how they come.'[3] Beforehand, she went to New York and participated in a question and answer session at the Juilliard School. 'You must work hard, practise always, learn music

---

* A month later, Titta would take responsibility for the success of Katia Ricciarelli's *Il trovatore* at the Regio di Parma. They met in 1969, when she participated in a concert organised by him in Sirmione, and three months later, they saw one another on a cruise of the Mediterranean. 'Once I went to [Sirmione] and while he drove me home, I saw that he was taking me somewhere else. He stopped in front of the cemetery and called me Maria,' she recalled. She got out of the car and ran away. Still masquerading as a talent scout, he falsely claimed to have opened doors for Ricciarelli and expected recognition (and perhaps payment) in return. 'Everything ended before it began, and on the other hand there was no reason for it to begin,' Ricciarelli said. 'Artistically and sentimentally, therefore, for me it has never represented anything.'

first,' she told the audience, who begged her to return to the stage.[4] Then she assumed her engagement in Philadelphia; the students' talents, however, did not meet her standards, and she abandoned the classes.

During that period, she spent more time in New York, staying in a suite at The Carlyle. It was as though she had forged an identity away from Onassis and the scandals of the opera world. 'Now I'm really free,' she remarked. 'Alone? But I always have been, then as now.'[5] In control of herself, she no longer lived to please a man: she grew her hair long and wore trousers, the opposite of what Onassis found attractive. She joked about her insecurities – perhaps a mechanism against his past cruel remarks – 'My legs are too fat for short dresses,' she informed a reporter:

> Then she raises a booted leg into the air, and pats the leather to show how well it hides her alleged figure problem … She is blind as a bat, but doesn't mind having people see her in her brown horn-rimmed glasses. She takes them off, though, when she's being photographed.[6]

Despite her confidence, she was suspicious of most people. 'I always expect everything, including dishonesty, which always amazes me. I am a supporter of integrity and modesty – do you say so? – which is becoming more and more rare.'[7] She spoke of her career, although she was hesitant to return to the stage:

> I haven't given up singing. I just sort of retired. The last time I sang here, I wasn't exactly pleased with my vocal condition. But now I feel in very good condition, and I'm no doubt far better than I used to be. But I don't like to talk about that.[8]

She continued to receive offers, and rejected each one. 'The cinema? I have had so many offers, I will accept the one that will seem more convenient for my temperament, from an artistic point-of-view … I'm a free artist: no rules, no entourage.'[9]

Declining an offer to perform in Poulenc's *La voix humaine* at the New York State Theatre, she said, 'No, no, no'.[10] There were further offers to appear in films, and the producer, Joseph Wishy, sent her the screenplay to *The Makropulos Secret*, offering her the leading part of Elena. 'Only you can do this film,' Wishy informed her. 'If you decide for some unconscionable reason to reject this project I cannot conceive of doing the film with anyone else.'[11] Another producer, Jed Harris, wanted her to play the Russian diva in *Dark Eyes*. Unsurprisingly, she declined all offers, but claimed she would 'love to [do a film] if it were the right role but no nude scenes'.*[12]

That year, the New York City Opera was producing *The Makropulos Case* using revolutionary techniques, but she declined an invitation to its premiere. 'You know … Callas can go to only a few things,' she said. 'Only to opening nights at the Metropolitan, and to premieres. She cannot go to the New York City Opera at all.'[13]

Despite her remarks, she surprised Jerry Lewis during a live telethon for muscular dystrophy, wearing a dress inspired by a circus tent. 'I wore it just for you,' she said, reminding him of their last meeting at the Gala de l'Union des Artistes at the Cirque d'Hiver – he was the clown and she, serving as présidente, was led around the ring and charged at by a baby elephant. 'Sagittarians are strange people,' she remarked. 'We come and go like mad.'[14] All at once, she was both complicated and simple.

Callas was now commanding Maria, and she was strong enough to resist Onassis, who visited her in New York. 'Someone's been in town, I've been seeing him,' she told Leo Lerman. 'And who wasn't even touched? Me! He's not so young anymore.'[15] Her friends gossiped that she was using witchcraft to win him back – an unnecessary statement, for he was there for the taking. Referring to his involvement with both Lee and Jacqueline, she said, 'Let him have his two whores.'[16]

Although her lifestyle was modern, her views were considered old-fashioned. 'The world is going haywire … what a pity,' she said. 'Things were so nice in the fifties, remember? Music, people, theatre, maybe – now it's all over'.[17] Perplexed by society, she disapproved of radicalism or, more to the point, she disliked its aesthetic. 'I see hippies wearing blue jeans and, really, blue jeans are good for working. I used to wear them, too, but seriously, each thing in its place.'[18]

Furthermore, she disagreed with 'excessive feminism' and feared the dismantling of gender roles, although no man had ever cared enough to indulge her love of tradition. 'I failed to fulfil myself as a woman,' she said, 'because what I always wanted, even more than success, was to be a mother.'[19]

---

* She disliked the concepts of modern films and theatre and had once sat through *Easy Rider* and *Midnight Cowboy* because she thought they were westerns. On a similar note, she attended a Broadway production of *Hair* and left after the first act. Later, she went with Giuseppe Di Stefano to a screening of *Deep Throat*, perhaps unaware it was a pornographic film, and left after ten minutes.

Misunderstanding the feminists' fight for equality, she thought it would strip her of her femininity:

> I am a woman and a very feminine one. That's why I am against feminism in the sense that women should never lose their most beautiful role: being a woman. We have a weapon: femininity. If we take that off, what's left for us women? Slaving away, going to work like a man? God knows I've worked a lot. There is some good in the feminist movement, though; one should always have an objective point-of-view about everything.[20]

Those views offered an insight into her feelings and how her instincts were now reductant. Her style of living was like an opera. Although at times it was unsavoury, the sets were beautiful and everyone played a part. Nothing was sacred to a woman whose inner world existed in the shadows and only fragments were exposed for public consumption. 'I understand only one policy: freedom,' she said. 'I paid for it, now I don't want to lose it.'[21]

In the early months of 1971, Peter Mennin, the director of the Juilliard School, invited Maria to teach twenty-three masterclasses, beginning in October and ending the following March. Ironically, given her past refusal of lucrative offers, she accepted, even though the school could not pay her. She asked only for her expenses to be covered 'because hotels etc. cost too much for me'.[22] However, her expenses included a suite at the Plaza, meals and a driver.

Twenty-five of the best students were chosen, one being Barbara Hendricks, who was surprised when Maria advised her to lose weight. 'Well I haven't been skiing this season so I could be a little bit out of shape,' Hendricks replied.[23] Another student, Cynthia Clarey, whose knowledge of opera scores was limited, sang 'Casta diva', having learned it from Maria's recording. Admitting she did not know another aria, she offered to sing a song.

'Do you want to be an opera singer or a songster?' Maria asked.

'A songster,' Clarey replied.

Maria implied that songs were beneath her, so Clarey lifted her score and walked out. Several weeks later, Clarey was waiting for the elevator when the doors swung open and Maria appeared. 'Well,' she announced, 'here's the young lady who thinks she has the world at her feet!'[24]

The classes were scheduled for Mondays and Thursdays, from 5.30–7.30 p.m., and tickets were sold to the public for $5. At first, they sold poorly as nobody was certain if Maria would show up. After the first class on 11 October, they were sold out, and people queued around the block and were prepared to sit on the floor.

'There will be no comments please, just listen,'* she warned the audience. To an autograph hunter, she said, 'This is supposed to be a masterclass. It's not supposed to be a showcase for me.' She told Mennin not to call her a teacher, 'I don't teach. I advise.'

He replied, 'You illuminate.'

To her students, she said, 'I hate to say the word lesson … I'm just indicating to you according to my impressions, but I want your personality in what I tell you to do.' Realising that her instincts for music were lacking in others, she said, 'You youngsters have to remember that all this is done with great passion.'

Although she could be firm, she was caring in her approach and began each class by asking, 'Who feels like singing?' Aware of their nerves, she added, 'Are you relaxed? What would you be comfortable with?' If a student was anxious, she reminded them, 'Relax, take your time … Don't be afraid of breathing well and supporting every sound'. A student apologised for his informal clothing and she reassured him, 'We're just between each other'. If someone was confused by a piece of music, she said, 'You have to find your own way out.' As much as she criticised, she could be complimentary, 'I must say, you're all improving, young ladies. I am proud of you.'

A reporter from *Life* attended a class and thought Maria looked less like a diva and more 'like a *Town and Country* hostess preparing for a hunt breakfast'. Her gift for intimacy disarmed some of the students who, at first, thought her 'arrogant and silly' and came to realise that 'her vulnerability was so apparent and she seemed not to have any confidence'.[25] Cynthia Clarey, who slipped into the back of the stalls, learned that her haughtiness was self-preservation and found her 'very down to earth, very matter of fact about everything'.[26] However, Barbara Hendricks was puzzled by Maria's European accent, knowing English was her first language and, during private conversations with her accompanist, she spoke in a New York dialect.

At times, her criticism strayed from music and became personal, leaving the audience uncomfortable. She complained that some of the female students were too large and advised them to lose weight. 'You don't have to be so fat … You sing very well, but you should be thinner. The public won't like it.'[27] Her insensitivity was baffling. She was preoccupied with her weight and that of others – her heaviest years were her unhappiest and she experienced periods

---

* See the EMI recording, *Maria Callas at Juilliard – The Masterclasses*. Quotes from her lessons have been taken from the transcript.

of self-loathing, particularly around 1951. Therefore, she was troubled by signs of obesity in others, hence her tactless comments.

There were lighter moments, and her criticism of short hemlines drew laughter from the audience. She warned her female students to wear longer skirts or trousers, 'because the public who looks at you down there sees a little more. Forgive me, eh?' Then, she added, 'Let's uncover when we should, you know, and be careful even then!'

It was rumoured that Maria had accepted the masterclasses as a foundation to relaunch her singing career. She was practising with a voice teacher from the Metropolitan and, in the recordings from Juilliard, her voice was stronger than before, and she often sang along with the students or demonstrated how to perform a note. 'Always give value to each note … Never slur on a note. *Never, never, never.* The Germans were guilty of it. It's a very bad habit.' To remedy bad habits, she advised them to 'brainwash yourself into always keeping your head clear' and to never practise before a mirror, which she called 'frightening … inside is your mirror'.

When a baritone failed to impress her with 'Credo' from Act II of Verdi's *Otello*, she performed the piece herself, singing Iago's part, '*E poi? E poi? La morte è il nulla* [And then? And then? Death is nothingness]'. A member of the audience recalled 'her dark, lower voice had us instantly on the edges of our seats … all the emptiness, blackness, nothingness of Iago's soul were suddenly laid bare, just by the way Callas sang that single word. It ruined me for any other Iago'.[28]

In theory, Maria disliked the techniques of modern singers and was alarmed when John Ardoin compared her to Judy Garland. 'I hope you don't mean I sing like her. To me, Judy Garland always just sounds like she's yelling,' she said. 'But there is one singer I do like. I like that Nancy Sinatra.'[29]

Perhaps recalling her days at the Athens Conservatory, she suggested her students read the lives of the composers, and, in doing so, they would learn to respect the composer:

Initially, we are musicians. We must not forget that. Therefore, servants to people who are much better than us, who are the composers, who died in poverty and frequently were misunderstood. Now we must believe and try to help them, not ourselves. Of course, by helping the composer, we help ourselves automatically. And fame comes automatically if you have the courage to also say no to contracts, also to starve yourself a little bit because, you know, I did quite a bit of that and I am quite sure if you read the history of the composers, they certainly went hungry. So, we cannot have our cake and eat it. You must know what you want to do in life; you cannot do too many things.

On a similar theme, she was surprised when a student did not know a particular score. Drawing on her experiences with Serafin and how she learned scores
in a week, she said, 'When you learn these parts, you think them out before.
If vocally, you're not ready because you haven't been trained into it, you've
already figured it out in your mind and the attitude of the music.'* Immersed
in all of her parts, she seldom broke character and had once visited a Milanese
café, absently carrying the dagger from a *Medea* rehearsal. The advice, however,
was not boastful and she reminded her students that music was 'an everlasting
search … the search within'.

Behind the scenes, there were elements of rivalry between Maria and
the mezzo-soprano, Jennie Tourel, who had taught at Juilliard since 1957.
'We're not friends,' Tourel said. Frustrated by the attention Maria's classes had
attracted, Tourel added, 'She isn't a voice teacher. She should have told them
how to be an artist, not how to open the throat.'[30] At her classes, Tourel lec-
tured on the dangers of Maria's teachings, reminding them she had destroyed
her voice and was not in a position to mentor students.

The most troubling incident, Maria claimed, came from Mennin who,
despite being married, sent her flowers and love letters. It was rumoured they
had begun an affair, but she dismissed it as 'common … it's all baloney'.[31]
Sometimes she complained that his behaviour was intense, but she responded
with flirtatious letters,** asking if he still loved her. 'No one ever wanted to
protect Maria,' Leo said. 'She exuded the strength of certainty, of intense and
positive passion.'[32]

In March 1972, Maria resumed her masterclasses and, after her final lesson,
she said:

> Whether I continue singing or not doesn't matter. What matters is that you
> use whatever you have learned wisely. Think of the expression of the words,

---

* In the 1950s, Maria told Leo Lerman, 'Well, you have to know it all, so that when you go
out on the stage for the first rehearsal, you know who you are. Then I am free to breathe on
stage. You know who that girl Lucrezia Borgia is. You know that what people say about her
is either lies or not lies. You also know that you are Maria Callas.'

** According to Maria's secretary and friend, Nadia Stancioff, Maria asked her to narrate the
love letters to Mennin, in order to let him down gently. 'You dictate and I'll write,' Maria
told Stancioff. (See Stancioff's memoir, *Callas Remembered*, p. 213). In what appeared to be
her final letter, Maria sent a photograph of herself in a bikini and wrote, 'This note is not a
"quickie" but meant to say a lot.' The letters belong to the Mennin family and were shown
to the author.

of good diction, and of your own deep feelings. The only thanks I ask is that you sing properly and honestly. If you do this, I will feel repaid.

In private, however, she thought the masterclasses were unsuccessful. 'Let me give you an example that frightened me a little … I wanted to give some of this art to the young, but I've understood that it's nothing you can give, it's something you're born with, and I was unable to give it. I failed.'[33]

Having considered renewing her contract for the new semester, she claimed Mennin used his authority to turn the faculty against her. To her godfather, she wrote, 'Peter Mennin fell in love with me. So, naturally, as I did not feel so towards him, he is against me. It's a pity that should [have] happened.'[34]

The latter part of Maria's time in New York was lonely. She filled her evenings with re-runs of *I Love Lucy* and occasionally dined with Leo at his home. 'Please bring me to eat chop suey, will you?'[35] she had asked him, early in their friendship. So, when they ate together, he ordered Chinese food from Pearl's and made rice pudding, and they dined with pink tablecloths and pink napkins.

When she was alone, she waited for calls from Onassis, who preyed on her weakness and asked her to reconcile. He continued to promise her that he would divorce Jacqueline, hoping to entice her into a physical relationship. 'I'd be a fool to believe him,' she complained to Mary Carter over drinks at Trader Vic's. She had not forgotten his lies, but she maintained a friendship, saying, 'You should not be cruel or inconsiderate to another person just because that person is cruel or inconsiderate toward you.'[36]

To Maria, Onassis appeared as an old man helplessly watching his life falling apart. Knowing that he could not have her enraged him, and he viewed Jacqueline as the bearer of bad luck. 'All she's ever given me is the Kennedy clap,' he said.[37]

The strength of his abuse had not waned and, to humiliate his wife, he informed a photographer of her whereabouts on Skorpios, and she was photographed sunbathing nude – the images spread around the world and appeared in sleazy rags. 'The woman who disappoints,' an Italian newspaper wrote of the former First Lady, 'a naked figure, not very attractive, stands out in a magazine for single men.'[38]

Onassis also spoke of having Jacqueline murdered to save him money. Having succeeded in shaming both women in the public arena, he deflected responsibility for his actions and convinced Maria he was the victim and Jacqueline was plotting to have him institutionalised. 'She's a gold-digger,' Maria raged, and she claimed to have Lee's letters from 1963, to Onassis, 'in case Mrs O tries to declare Aristo mentally undone'.[39]

Despite being caught in Onassis's melodrama, Maria did not want to lose the momentum of Juilliard. 'I work very hard on my own voice, to try to find back, if I can, the voice I had in the past, before I sacrificed it for a man!'[40] she had written to a friend. A believer in fate, she received flowers from her former colleague and old friend, Giuseppe Di Stefano, viewing it as a sign that singing was the answer. He had performed in concerts in Japan and Korea, and the organiser of the concert invited him to return with a soprano: he was offered $4,000 for Anna Moffo, $6,000 for Renata Tebaldi, and $10,000 for Maria Callas.

Inviting Di Stefano to her suite, she said, 'I know you have always cared about me.'[41] Their reunion was bittersweet: she had loved him in the 1950s and this passion was channelled into her collaborations with him, creating magic on the stage. He symbolised the golden era of her career, and with it, the pressure to meet his expectations and her own. They went to a pianist and she sang for him in full voice, although she was trembling from nerves. Afterwards, she burst into tears and fell into his arms.

Before leaving New York, Maria had dinner with Leo, who commented on her new dental veneers, claiming they made her look fifteen years younger. In measured tones, she spoke pragmatically of her career, realising time was almost spent. 'Let's face it,' she said, 'I'm not gonna hit the road again!' Then, she announced, 'I hate opera, so old-fashioned. I detest it,' she said. 'But … it is what I do – what I can do – what I'm good at.'[42]

Despite her fears, she would find her way back to singing.

19

Lucidity

I'm obliged to write a farce,
and I cannot find a subject!
This one is too sentimental,
this other seems to me insipid.

Il Turco in Italia, Rossini

In the fifties, it was rumoured that Maria and Giuseppe Di Stefano had been lovers; gossip which, perhaps, had flattered her ego during her platonic marriage. 'Since our first meeting in 1952, we'd known we were made for each other,' Di Stefano said. 'It was love at first sight.'[1] Neither was willing to begin an affair, fearing it would ruin their respective marriages and careers, so they became the protagonists of romantic stories on stage. For Maria, the fantasy world never intruded on reality, and neither crossed the line. 'Callas is a child who plays at being a woman,' an acquaintance remarked. 'She doesn't know sex.'[2]

Although seasoned by their life's experiences and the triumphs they once shared, Maria's appraisal had not waned. 'He has lots of brains – he does not show them – he loves to portray the playboy he is absolutely not,' she said. 'He has many human qualities.'[3] Attracted to those human qualities, she accepted an invitation to stay with him at Marina di Capo Pino, Sanremo. An apartment was put at her disposal, and she was accompanied by her maid, although it rained for the duration. 'I am so alone,'[4] Maria told Di Stefano's wife, also named Maria, whose devotion to her family she found alien. They were experiencing a difficult period: their 18-year-old daughter was ill with Hodgkin's disease, so Maria 'stayed with them as much as possible because they truly needed my friendship … it's hard for them, what a pity, for they are truly beautiful people'.[5]

Their renewed closeness developed into an affair.[6] However, Di Stefano would later emphasise that 'my relationship with my wife was merely formal' and both he and Maria were hoping to escape the reality of their lives: his sick daughter, her loneliness.[7]

According to Mrs Di Stefano, her husband was 'a womaniser all his life. I let him do it … but that wasn't a mystery to me.'[8] There was nothing to suggest to her that he and Maria were romantically involved, and of the other women, she said, 'I defeated [them] with an unshakable serenity, I drove them crazy with my kindness. Sooner or later they would give in, and [he] came back to me.'[9] So, the familiar pattern of Maria's life was repeated, and she fell for a man who could never be hers.

During that period, Maria felt displaced and spoke of exerting 'no signs of life'.[10] Instead of accepting an offer to become the artistic director of the Metropolitan, she preferred to stay at home; otherwise, she would lose her '*spirito*'.[11] She explained she had to remain in Paris because her household was thrown into disarray after her butler injured his spine, and she was working on her voice with the pianist, Jean-Claude Ambrosini. Such things provided a screen against the real world and her commitments. 'It's an ugly season,' she said of the summer of 1972.[12]

Her lack of interest was disguised as a carefree approach. 'We think we are here forever and we plan ahead, but you see, you never know. That's why we should never worry. Remind me of that. Not that I worry lately about anything. I've assumed this attitude and I'm so better off.'[13]

In December, Maria and Di Stefano went to London to record duets for Philips, accompanied by the London Symphony Orchestra. A futile venture, she arrived at St Giles Church for the last part of the three-hour sessions. She and Di Stefano sang for twenty minutes and spent the remainder of their time arguing in the control room. Despite their quarrels, she wrote to Leo Lerman, 'I must [say] that working together made my comeback in records less difficult than if I were alone.'[14] However, it was unreleased during her lifetime: she felt she was too loud, although the conductor, Antonio de Almeida, accused her of using the sessions to test her voice before the concert tour. 'If it were other singers, it would be marvellous,' she said. 'But [I] always strive for perfection.'[15]

During the recording, her father died and, after a decade of silence, Jackie telephoned her to deliver the news. 'It's just these recordings. What can I do?' She made her excuses not to go to Greece for the funeral. Making her feelings clear in 1964, she had said, 'I hate him'.[16] As with Litsa, she came to think of George as a source of shame, particularly after he 'came storming' to her friends in Athens, asking for money.[17] It did not stop her from grieving for him, or rather, reliving the conflicted feelings of having idolised him in the past, and then his betrayal. 'She wanted other people to understand what she meant,' Di Stefano said, 'while she hid within her shell.'[18]

A month later, Onassis turned to Maria for sympathy after his son died from injuries sustained in a plane crash. He was obsessed with the crash, believing that Alexander was assassinated by one of his enemies. '[They] would rather see me suffer than kill me,' he said, influenced by heavy drinking and remorse, for he had mistreated his son during his lifetime.[19] Although elements of paranoia and superstition ran through Maria, she told him it was a freak accident, perhaps to allay his guilt. Although she was flattered he had chosen her as a confidante, she was also tired of being used.

In March 1973, she joined Di Stefano and his family in Capo Pino, and the climate was far more pleasing than her previous visit. They were followed by reporters, and an Italian newspaper wrote, 'She has a mad desire to live. In the evening, they go wild. "They eat well," declared Antonio Volpi, owner of the Corsaro di Ventimiglia. And they drink better.'[20]

Afraid of gaining weight, Maria wanted to lose 3kg, and her first meal of the day, after she awoke at noon, was lettuce leaves covered in Greek honey.[21] 'Why can't the doctors find a pill that does no harm but makes you consume <u>all</u> you eat!' she asked. 'We go to the moon … but we can't make our glands work properly!'[22]

Weeks later, Maria made her directorial debut with Di Stefano in *I vespri siciliani* to inaugurate the reopening of the Teatro Regio in Turin. This was an interesting choice of engagement, as she had often criticised modern opera and its singers. 'I went to the opera once,' began her appraisal of the Metropolitan's 'very bad' production of *Otello*, directed by Zeffirelli, with James McCracken and Sherrill Milnes. 'The tenor should <u>not</u> sing and Milnes is swallowing his voice. What in heaven's name is wrong with them? My pupils sang better.'[23]

Her own production was beset with problems, beginning with her reluctance to commit to it. 'They have not respected our agreement,' she said, frustrated by the politics of the opera house.[24] Having asked her agent, Sandor Gorlinsky, to renegotiate her contract with the Teatro Regio, she received a warning from the musician's union, as since 1967, the law prohibited theatrical agencies and any form of mediation in the Italian territory. Realising the publicity that Maria's name would bring to the theatre and afraid she would resign, the manager Giuseppe Erba flattered her with chocolates and flowers.

'If he really wanted to seduce me,' she said, 'he would have sent Piedmontese truffles. I can't resist those.'[25]

Nevertheless, Maria believed, 'A contract is a contract'. A view she also held with their leading soprano, Raina Kabaivanska, who the management wanted to replace with Katia Ricciarelli. Kabaivanska admired Maria, having first seen her in *Medea* at La Scala, saying, 'She's up there and we are down here, on the ground.'[26]

Then, as with her masterclasses, Maria's instincts for music did not translate well into the logistics of an opera and she found the process overwhelming; the conductor, Gianandrea Gavazzeni, resigned and was replaced with Vittorio Gui, who became ill and was then replaced with Fulvio Vernizzi. Finally, Maria twisted her ankle but was able to continue to work.

Despite the production's faults, Erba admired her. 'She did not have any star-like attitude … she was kind, reserved, she stayed at the [Grand Hotel] Sitea, sometimes she went to Baratti, Del Cambio, to the hairdresser, Carlo, and a couple of times she was a guest at Villa Agnelli.'[27]

Before the premiere on 10 April, Maria invited the critics to watch the opera and judge it fairly. However, when someone inquired about the politics of the theatre, she interrupted, 'Have you seen the show? No? Then he has no right to speak. Get out of here immediately.'[28] On the opening night, she received further criticism for her unimaginative direction, which she defended as being anti-pornographic.[29]

With ambitions to direct further productions, she set her sights on the Metropolitan but was dissuaded by her experience at the Teatro Regio and the negative criticism.[30] There was also an offer from Patricia Brooks to teach a masterclass to both herself and her colleagues at the New York City Opera, among them, Sherrill Milnes. 'What an opportunity to really learn our craft,' Brooks wrote. 'There are a handful of us, who, I feel, could really put those gems of hers to use.'[31] Brooks also asked Maria for private lessons, despite having had a long career. She declined.

A month later, Maria and Di Stefano went to Osaka, Japan, to teach a masterclass to the six winners of the *Madama Butterfly* competition. 'A very good contract,' she said, and for the prima donna, nothing but praise.[32]

In August and September, Maria prepared for a year-long concert tour with Di Stefano, beginning in Germany and ending in Japan. 'It is such a great risk that I can't take it seriously,' she told Leo Lerman, channelling the bravado of

Callas.[33] But in a letter to her godfather, she remained humble, 'I'm scared stiff but I hope that I will be calm and well by my first one because the expectation is so great and of course I am not what I was at thirty-five-years.'[34] She repeated the line, as though to overcompensate for all she had lost, and relied on Di Stefano for reassurance. 'She's found in Di Stefano a partner who's a gentleman,' a press release wrote. 'She prefers to work with gentlemen who have good manners.'[35]

During that period, Maria grew frustrated by Di Stefano's obligations to his family, and those feelings exerted themselves as jealousy. She knew that he wanted to tour, and so she had a hold over him – her voice. They practised at her apartment and, filled with insecurity, she doubted her singing abilities and cried with frustration. At almost 50 years old, she was facing the psychological changes that came with her age; she became anxious and had spells of depression, and threatened to cancel the tour. At times, their artistic temperaments clashed and, during imperious moments, she said, 'Nobody teaches Callas.'[36] He demanded she open her throat and, unable to do as he asked, she finally exploded in a rage.

'She's nuts,' Di Stefano said, 'that's one of the things I like about her.'[37]

The tour was to open in London at the Royal Festival Hall, but Maria discovered that Gorlinsky had also engaged Franco Corelli and Renata Tebaldi to give a concert the next day. She felt exploited and accused him of reviving their old feud for financial purposes. Having spent all night sobbing, she threatened to cancel the tour, fire Gorlinsky, and release a press statement explaining how she was betrayed.

The following day, Gorlinsky arrived in Paris and offered £50,000 for her first London concert, and £20,000 per concert afterwards, out of which she had to pay Di Stefano £5,000. Having signed the contract, she asked to postpone London and instead open in Hamburg. She cited her health issues: her low blood pressure and glaucoma, for which she administered eye drops every two hours. In a statement to the press, she said, 'My ophthalmologist has imposed absolute rest on me for at least six weeks.'[38]

On 25 October 1973, the tour began in Hamburg and, by then, the Italian newspapers had reported on their affair, although Di Stefano denied it to his wife.[39] 'Love makes women do strange things', they wrote of Maria's comeback.[40]

But how did she feel about her comeback? 'Actually, it feels like I've never really been away,' she said. 'I have continued studying, teaching.'[41] She trembled backstage, and there was fear in her eyes as Di Stefano led her around the stage, acknowledging the applause. An elemental force, she remained still as she controlled the pandemonium. Elizabeth Taylor had arrived after the first aria, bringing with her an entourage of eight people, and was booed. At the end of the concert, Taylor offered Maria a red rose, and in turn, Maria gave her a white rose from the flowers the public had thrown. The critics, however, were unmoved. 'I don't want to suffer pain,' she told her staff, who spared her feelings by cutting hurtful words from the reviews.[42]

They went to Berlin and Düsseldorf, and by then she knew what to expect from the audience and the critics. 'Everything was fine,' she wrote to her godfather. 'I am quite happy, people love me.'[43] Her mood changed when Mrs Di Stefano joined her husband in Munich and remained for the concerts in Frankfurt and Mannheim.

The tension was apparent backstage: in Munich, the audience heckled Di Stefano, who walked offstage, only to return when they applauded and called for him. After that particular concert, Maria looked at photographs of Onassis in a magazine, reminiscing of their games of cat and mouse with reporters – as with most things in her life, she had enjoyed the chase.

In mid November, Maria returned to Paris before resuming the tour in Madrid, but she could not escape the intrusive thoughts of what the critics had written: 'Should memories and the recordings alone remind us of the greatest operatic singer of our time?'[44]

In London, she was also vexed by the arrival of Mrs Di Stefano who, she complained, would never leave them alone. She was further disappointed by her singing; it was the worst performance of the tour. A critic from the *Observer* called it distressing and, tired of the prolonged applause that greeted each aria, he walked out. The editor of *Opera*, Harold Rosenthal, agreed it 'was one of the saddest evenings I have ever had to spend … I was also cross at the sorry spectacle of Callas being led round the platform by Di Stefano as if he were showing off some prize winner in a ring'.

A week later, she gave a second concert, which coincided with her 50th birthday, and the audience serenaded her. 'They love what I was,' she said, 'not what I am.'[45]

On 7 December, Maria and Di Stefano sang at the Champs-Élysées Theatre in Paris, an engagement that filled her with trepidation. It was her home town, and the theatre was filled with many of the gay intelligentsia who worshipped their tragedienne from afar. Afterwards, she was mobbed by her fans who surrounded her car, shouting, 'Diva … Brava, Maria!'

In Amsterdam she was irritated by the audience, whose flashing cameras distracted her, and she asked them to stop, although she patiently signed their programmes afterwards.

There was a brief respite over Christmas, which she spent alone. 'I'm asked out … but I won't go anywhere,' she said, disguising her loneliness. 'I'll just stay home and listen to some music.'[46] Telephone calls from Onassis filled the lonely days, but she was troubled by his paranoia: he was now convinced God had punished him by killing his only son. He wanted her at his disposal and convinced her that the tour, soon to begin in America, was a bad idea. 'Why do you live like a gypsy when Paris is so beautiful and you have your lovely apartment?' he asked.[47] In a lucid moment, she said, 'Music is the only thing I have in my life.'[48]

In that frame of mind, she began to practise alone, listening to her old live recordings and taping her voice to monitor its progress. 'But what is there in life, if you do not work?' she said in an interview. 'If you do not work there [are] only sensations, and there are only a few sensations – you cannot live on them.'[49]

Although she depended on Di Stefano, she was tired of performing and the negative feelings that had begun to manifest during her concert tours in the early 1960s returned. 'I couldn't sleep tonight, so I mustered up the courage to listen to the [Paris] concert,' she told Di Stefano. 'I was amazed. My voice, as you said, is making progress … I'm on the right road, at last, Jesus!'[50]

However, in Milan, she was nervous as she sang with Di Stefano in a private concert for the institution that was treating his daughter. She purposely did not wear her glasses, for she said the sick children would make her cry. Later, in Stuttgart, thirty minutes before the concert, Di Stefano announced he was ill and could not sing. Someone shouted for Maria to perform, so she sang 'O mio babbino caro' and was greeted by calls for another aria and chose 'Suicidio'. A man in the audience complained about the distance he had travelled and received an apology from her. 'Do you want me to sing?' she asked, as he walked away. Despite the audience encouraging her, she walked off the stage.

In February 1974, Maria and Di Stefano went to New York and gave a press conference at the Stanhope Hotel to launch their North American tour, promoted by Sol Hurok. 'My, I'm applauded' – her announcement betrayed her nerves.[51] A reporter wrote, 'She sits down regally with her hands in her lap, like the queen, grande dame, diva, I've imagined her to be … She is gentle, joking, and very much in control.'[52]

Privately, cracks were beginning to form in her affair with Di Stefano. She was both demanding and vulnerable, the two phases of her nature were battling for supremacy, and perhaps her conscience was too. Furthermore, the

American tabloids were beginning to hint at a romance, which angered his in-laws who lived in the Bronx, and so, to prevent gossip, he telephoned his wife and asked her to come to New York.

It was hardly surprising that Maria reacted badly to Mrs Di Stefano's arrival, particularly when she accompanied them to Philadelphia for their concert. To exert her dominance, Maria and Di Stefano travelled in one limousine and his wife travelled in the other. 'In public, I follow them a few steps away,' Mrs Di Stefano wrote in her diary. 'Nobody asks me to do it, I do it because I feel that they are important. Even in the car, I'm always behind.'[53]

They returned to New York and Maria was disturbed by Mrs Di Stefano taking precedence next to her husband. 'Can't she ever respect my privacy?' she cried, furious that her lover had gone to his wife.[54] Later that night, she overdosed on sleeping pills, and the following afternoon was discovered by her maid, who raised the alarm. Doctor Louis Parrish, a doctor of both medicine and psychiatry, arrived and gave her emetine and slapped her face to bring her round. Her speech was incoherent, and she could not recall how many pills she had taken, except, to a tearful Di Stefano, she delivered a message – his wife would have to leave, or she would cancel the tour.

The concert at Carnegie Hall was cancelled and angry fans filled the foyer, then spilled onto the street where one tore her poster from the wall. A medical certificate was produced, claiming she had the 'flu and a throat infection.

Meanwhile, at the Stanhope, Maria sat in the corner of the room, pale and meek, as the others, including Di Stefano, his wife and in-laws from the Bronx, whispered in the corner. Di Stefano was accustomed to Maria's dependency on sedatives; in Hamburg, he found her unconscious on the bedroom floor, and this was a common theme throughout the tour.

From all perspectives, it was a complicated arrangement, and both women depended on Di Stefano for emotional support. 'She should have understood that it was not the right time to think of divisions, separations, divorce, and the like,' he said. 'We needed to wait for time to heal these tremendous wounds.'[55] In hindsight, it was a mistake to revive their old partnership and her feelings for him. 'Maria and I are too similar. I am a hot-blooded Sicilian with a strong sense of dignity and independence. Maria was Greek, the old-fashioned kind,' he said. 'When she was in love, she was possessive, invasive, jealous.'[56]

Ironically, Maria found an ally in Renata Tebaldi, who was also in New York and had telephoned her. They spent hours chatting, dwelling on their failed relationships, the opera world and their past triumphs, which, in her present frame of mind, seemed overshadowed by misfortune. Her last visit to New York had been a positive experience: she regained her confidence and, in a sense, her stability. Now an old rival had become a confidante, her closest friends were treating her with caution, and the wife of Di Stefano would later call her 'Callas, *nemica mia*'.*

They went to Toronto a day earlier than planned while Mrs Di Stefano remained in New York. At the concert on 21 February, Di Stefano was suffering from a cold but continued to sing, knowing how another cancellation would result in bad publicity. So, he sang only one solo and Maria sang three, inspiring a patron to remark, 'She sang not so well; and not so much … As I left the hall, all I could feel was a deep, deep sadness.' However, another commented:

> Dramatically, you couldn't take your eyes off of her. You *had* to look at her. The programme was so intense. There was no let-up and she gave everything that she had. And while her top notes may have had that characteristic wobble, her voice was so incredibly powerful in the chest, that it made you shiver.[57]

Every day, Maria took calls from Onassis, and that influenced her mood; she spoke of their great love and reminisced about their 'beautiful life' together.[58] In a recorded interview with Barbara Walters, she repeated the same line, calling him her best friend and alluding that his wife was behind their misery.

She had grown moody and was prone to outbursts of anger, directed at Di Stefano, whose temperament matched her own. With her energy spent, she relied on Dr Parrish, who flew to whichever city she was performing, to inject her with vitamin B and amphetamines.

Before the Boston concert, Di Stefano refused to perform and flew to Italy, leaving Maria without a singing partner. At Maria's request, Vasso Devetzi filled the gaps in the programme and was paid Di Stefano's fee, but her baroque pieces clashed with the Italian arias. Regardless, the evening was a success.

Arriving at the Drake Hotel in Chicago, she was warned that dogs were not permitted and, scooping her poodle into her arms, she said, 'Rules? Rules? What do you mean rules? Wherever I stay, I make the rules. Let them talk to me about the rules and then we'll see what Callas is.'[59] Her behaviour was provoked by the news that Di Stefano was in town and had checked into a hotel in the suburbs. 'So childish,' she remarked.

On the night of the concert, they were singing a duet when he abruptly stopped and announced he was too sick to continue, causing Maria and the

---

* 'Callas, my enemy.'

audience to fall silent. 'You go and rest, and I will sing the song,' she said, play-ing to the gallery.[60] After the concert, they returned to their separate hotels.

On 5 March, Maria and Di Stefano sang at Carnegie Hall* in a benefit con-cert for the Metropolitan Opera Guild. Hours before the concert, Sol Hurok died, and Maria was inconsolable. That evening, she demanded a stronger injection from Dr Parrish to help her nerves and emotional fatigue. Some of the audience had anticipated she would cancel and entered the foyer in a hostile mood.

'I heard she never had a cold last time,' a woman said to her companion. 'She stood up the President of the Italians, too.'

'Well, I heard she'd had a fight with Di Stefano,' her friend replied. 'I heard she didn't like the way he sings better than she does.'[61]

Nevertheless, applause greeted her as she walked on stage, although she was in poor voice. 'Her voice always had a flaw – gorgeous, but in the top register, a bit scratchy,' Leo Lerman's partner, Gray, recalled. 'The flaw grew – like a crack in the sidewalk – and by the time she was that age, she just couldn't step over it any longer.'[62] Afterwards, she gave an impromptu speech, attacking the management of modern opera houses. 'The blossom fell apart,' Leo said, 'like wax roses – all crumbled.'[63]

Leaving the theatre, she roused admiration from her fans. 'She's great,' Andy Warhol said. 'We used to play her records in our studio.'

'She is one of the greatest actresses of all time,' Paulette Goddard remarked. 'It's an emotional experience.'

I've never seen a cult before,' Mrs Frederick Winship said, unimpressed. 'It's mass hysteria, and it frightens me. Maybe I shouldn't say it; she's a mag-nificent looking woman and wonderfully expressive … but I also happen to love music.'[64]

Telephoning Leo afterwards, Maria said, 'I want to tell you: I know I looked good, but I can sing better. That wasn't as good as I can do.'[65]

Later that evening, Maria was upset by Di Stefano's news that he and his wife were moving out of the Stanhope and into the Elysee Hotel. Afraid of her reaction to Di Stefano's departure, Dr Parrish stayed with her until she fell asleep, only she remained awake, eating miniature tubs of ice cream and watch-ing television. He was surprised by this image, although he should not have been: she liked 3 Musketeers chocolate bars and reading *Seventeen* magazine, indulging in the juvenile habits she was deprived of in her youth. Sometimes

---

* They gave an additional concert on 15 April at Carnegie Hall; however, it was not to benefit the Metropolitan Opera Guild.

she stole from hotel rooms – 'Why bother to pay for these things when you could just swipe a few from the hotel?' – taking trivial items such as slippers and inexpensive knick-knacks.[66] 'In hotels,' Mrs Di Stefano recalled, 'Callas would always take everything with her that wasn't glued to the wall.'[67]

Until the early hours of the morning, she followed on the well-worn routine of reflecting on her childhood, early career, heartbreaks, and present situation. Exasperated, Dr Parrish injected her with a sedative and made for the door.

'What shall I do?' she called after him.

'Get a life,' he said.[68]

There were further concerts in Detroit, Dallas, Miami Beach, Columbus, Cincinnati, Seattle, Portland, Vancouver, Los Angeles, San Francisco and Montreal. She was applauded by her adoring fans and crucified by the critics, but even in her heyday, she had been criticised. As in the old days, the critics and fans created a professional rivalry, this time pitting her against Di Stefano. The *Times* wrote, 'Unlike the tenor, she remains an artist.'

The drama, however, was reserved for their private lives: their volatility was often the consequence of a careless remark or Maria broaching the subject of Di Stefano's marriage. He was tired of being ordered around and, to restore his authority, he placed his wife in the front row of their Montreal concert.

'I don't need the money, I'm rich!'[69] she screamed and threatened to leave for Paris. In his diary, Leo wrote, 'Do not forget Maria's temper – how this is a nourishment to her – an outlet and absolutely important, for it is the result of her superb genius. She breathes through temper as the earth breathes through volcanoes.'[70]

They fought – each referring to the other as 'the soprano' and 'the tenor' – and then reconciled. Maria, the woman, was drawn to him, but Callas, the artist, thought herself superior. Her mother had treated her father in a similar manner; such emotional schizophrenia ran in the family. But Di Stefano was proud, and he resented being cast aside according to her moods, 'She was jealous, blind, and acted impulsively just like a child, making awful mistakes which I could neither accept nor pretend not to see.'[71]

Maria longed to be loved but Callas wanted to take flight. Only now, Callas, as she once was, had become a myth.

Back in Paris, Maria was in a reflective mood, particularly about Di Stefano and the tour. 'You said our concerts were a circus,' she reproached Gorlinsky.

'I am hurt by that expression.'[72] Still, she could not resist the undercurrents of drama and grew jealous of Di Stefano's recording sessions with Montserrat Caballé, whom she admired, despite her feelings. Each day, Vasso Devetzi called at her apartment and delivered saccharine compliments, which she disliked but came to accept. 'I am outside myself and watch my life from the outside,'[73] Maria said, as though to justify her detachment. It troubled her when Vasso's boyfriend, Jean Roire, made a pass at her, and although she never told Vasso, she was afraid of being alone with him.

During that period, she was upset by Larry Kelly's death from cancer at the age of 45. 'How can fate be so unfair?' she cried. Months before, they had met in Dallas and he asked her to perform in *Carmen*. 'Carmen's a brazen slut!' she replied.

There were daily telephone calls from Onassis, and he gave her an inexpensive watch, which her friends thought was mean, but she treasured it. Unlike 'the gold-digger', she was happy with tokens of his admiration; once, when they were still together, he had given her a mink coat but all she had wanted was a single rose.

At the end of September 1974, Maria and Di Stefano arrived in Seoul for their concert tour of the Far East. Their first engagement was at the Ewha University for Women, and their second, in Tokyo, was filmed for television. However, she was unaware of a hidden camera backstage, capturing the tension as they rehearsed.

From therein, the mood changed: she took calls from Onassis, who was distraught after Tina's death from a suspected drug overdose. Her health began to fail – she developed labyrinth vertigo, which affected her reflexes, and for twelve hours she lost her sight. It terrified her, but she thought it was the consequence of a head cold. Later, on tour, the pain from her hernia, inflamed from exercising her diaphragm, gave her internal bleeding, causing her to lose weight. 'Though I love to be thin,' she wrote to Dr Parrish, 'I got frightened I was so thin and wan.'[74]

Several weeks later, in Osaka, Maria had a throat infection and could not sing. At the last moment, she was persuaded to go on stage, but she forgot the words to 'Sola, perduta, abbandonata' and, despite the audience applauding, she went to her dressing room and burst into tears.

Several days later, they went to Hiroshima and then Sapporo. She received news that Onassis had been admitted to the American Hospital in Paris and had been diagnosed with myasthenia gravis, a neuromuscular disease made worse by a small stroke he had suffered a few months before.

On the eve of her final performance in Sapporo, she announced, 'Well, tomorrow's the last one'.[75] She referred to an opera house as a place of worship and once upon a time she was its deity; perhaps now it would be sacrilegious to command from its altar, the stage.

In her youth, she claimed it would be suicide to sing without her weapon – her voice – and so, before the public, Callas, the artist, had condemned herself to death. 'I don't have the resistance any more,' she wrote to Dr Parrish. She thought of dubbing her performances with her old records, so future audiences could 'see Callas on stage (or nearly) and it will remain for posterity'.[76]

Reflecting on her talent, Leo Lerman called it 'a dybbuk-genius'. In mythological terms, he considered Callas a dybbuk spirit and Maria's body its host. 'When the genius left her, when the dybbuk left her actually, she died. She had the grace not to survive the dybbuk too long.'[77]

20

Fable

The fate which pursues you,
leaves no other means
of escape to you.

Anna Bolena, Donizetti

In Paris, Maria turned to rituals to fill her lonely days: she telephoned Onassis and, to others, she spoke hypothetically about work. The tour, once hailed as a comeback, was now referred to as a farewell: the symbolic death of Callas. As though cyclic, everything from her old life was reaching its natural end, beginning with Di Stefano.

Her common sense told her the affair was over, but she periodically contacted him: one day, she wanted him, the next, she did not. As though to protect her pride, she said Di Stefano was still in love with her and she him, 'to a certain point'.[1] During that time, in late February 1975, his daughter was dying, and he considered their affair over. 'At a certain moment we began to argue seriously; our wonderful understanding became strained and finally snapped,' he said. 'At the end of the long tour, we each went our own way.'[2]

Her trusted confidantes were those from whom she was separated by a continent. In letters to her godfather, she pretended to be in good health – 'I've gained weight' – and spoke of being 'peaceful … no great love on my behalf'.[3] She also told Leo Lerman not to worry about her. 'I try to live in a world of my own. I am very peaceful for the time being.'[4]

This false sense of contentment was shattered when Onassis collapsed and was admitted to the American Hospital. 'I want to walk from this car under my own steam. I don't want those sons of bitches to see me being held up by a couple of women,' he told his wife and daughter.[5] Maria knew the end was near and could not visit his bedside, although Jacqueline, without a backward glance, left for America.

Remaining in her apartment, Maria placed calls to Onassis, whose voice was barely audible due to his muscular degeneration. She pleaded with his close friends for snippets of information. Costa Gratsos kept her informed of Onassis's condition: he was surrounded by tubes and was breathing with the assistance of a ventilator.

Outside the hospital, the paparazzi had begun their death watch, and Maria complained to friends that she could not visit him, as she would have been photographed. It remains doubtful that photographers would have deterred her – she had suffered his public humiliation throughout their relationship and, when it came to him, she had no pride. Nevertheless, it was believed that his daughter Christina, who had a morbid fascination* with Maria, allowed her to visit for half an hour.

Throughout Maria's relationship with Onassis, she had adhered to terms and conditions; it was no different in death. She slipped through a side door and entered the hospital room. The sight of him, underweight, connected to tubes and delirious with morphine startled her. He was a man who had taken pleasure in her suffering, and now he was reduced to a comatose state. As much as the dybbuk spirit inside of her was dead, the demon within Onassis had also departed. 'I don't want to go on living with ghosts,' he had told a close friend. 'Too many ghosts.'[6]

Later, Maria confided that he mustered the strength to tell her, 'I loved you, not always well, but as much and as best as I was capable of. I tried.' His final words were, perhaps, a figment of her imagination, for those who had visited him claimed he struggled to speak and suffered from violent hallucinations. The words she sang as Lady Macbeth come to mind: 'What if he was roused from his sleep before the fatal blow?' It was not lying on her behalf but a longing to offer dignity to the relationship. 'We have the same roots,' she said. 'We're both true Greeks.'[7] She, who understood him like no other, composed the ending to suit herself.

In her apartment, the claustrophobia of the four walls and waiting for the inevitable news was too much to bear. So, she escaped to Palm Beach, Florida, where she rented a house for a month and invited her godfather to stay. She also visited her cousin in Tarpon Springs, a place that had given her the happiest memories of her childhood. Regression was the theme, but she tried also

---

* Christina had begun to ask people who knew both Maria and Onassis, 'What was [Maria] like? What kind of a person was she? Do you really think Maria loved my father?'

to think of the future and made plans to buy the house. To others, she went through the motions of describing the Spanish tiles, the pool, the proximity to the beach. It was a distraction from all that was happening in her private world, for she was slowly disconnecting from life. Even the news of Onassis's death, on 15 March 1975, was met with an eerie stillness. 'It's over,' she sighed. 'It's all over now.'

Days later, letters were forwarded to Maria from friends and strangers all over the world, expressing their condolences. In one particular letter, a friend wrote, 'Despite all the difficulties in your relationship with Ari, I can imagine that his passing leaves you with a mourning feeling.'[8] She spent hours reflecting on the words in the letters, not once recalling the pain Onassis had caused her, nor the years of torment she had endured by his side. In her mind, he was now beyond reproach, and the memories of their latter co-dependency could never bring closure. Once, she was asked how to interpret a difficult piece of music. 'Love it,' she said, perhaps thinking of Onassis.

Back in Paris, the chaos of her thoughts intruded on her surroundings and from her apartment she sent letters to her godfather. Most scenarios were hypothetical or had grown in her imagination, particularly her affair with Di Stefano, whose daughter had recently died. 'He lives for this love of ours,' she wrote. 'I am hoping that destiny will take care of things so as the hurt and shock will not be hard on him.'[9]

In reality, she had often presented Di Stefano with an ultimatum: if he wanted to be with her, he had to leave his wife. Naturally, given the circumstances, he refused. So, to protect her dignity, she claimed he was possessive and, therefore, she had to let him down gently. 'Maybe I might meet someone and that would be the ideal solution,' she remarked. 'This way I would not care whether he gets hurt or not.'[10]

Despite her protests, two months later she remained with Di Stefano, claiming she could not find anyone better. 'Richer maybe but poorer in feelings,' she said. Having set impossible standards, she complained, 'Such men are impossible to find'.[11] In her words, he had to be intelligent, rich, honest, generous, devoted 'and not try to change me like our dead friend'.[12]

Admittedly, she seldom went out and, therefore, could not find her ideal partner, but she claimed modern men were 'superficial and presumptuous' and they only wanted an affair.[13] A good man, she said, would be the cure to her 'psychological problems'.[14]

In October, she and Di Stefano finally parted, as she was 'not the same with him' – she wanted him to be something he was not and realised that neither was willing to compromise.[15] She said, 'I have all these personal problems to solve.'[16]

Her behaviour adopted a cyclic pattern, and she expressed her innermost thoughts to whoever played the part of a silent listener. To herself, she delivered an ultimatum: 'I have to be much better or nothing at all.'[17]

Attempts to work on her voice faltered, and she said, 'I have come to a big decision. I'm stopping singing. I'm fed up with the whole business! My nerves cannot stand the strain anymore.'[18] Any plans she had made to direct and sing in *Tosca* with Di Stefano in Japan were formally cancelled and he proceeded with Montserrat Caballé instead. Without their collaboration, there was no point in their being together. 'Now I have to find something to do to keep active,' she said, her thoughts ricocheting from one scenario to the other.[19]

In a bid to be understood, Maria turned to her godfather for sympathy and advice. 'Please love me as I think I deserve', she asked of him.[20] She sent him letters detailing her health issues. It remains unknown if he responded, for she often implored him to write to her. She told him she had had a nervous breakdown and was upset by the changes to her physical appearance, particularly the slowing down of her metabolism. In her youth, when she sought treatment for unexplainable symptoms, her doctor dismissed her as being overworked and neurotic, and now, at almost 52, she was considered menopausal and therefore her symptoms would pass.

Given her ongoing neurological issues, she consulted with Professor Mario Giacovazzo,* an Italian specialist of neuromuscular disorders, who flew to Paris to see her. He was intrigued by the purple markings on her skin, particularly on her neck, and the swollen appearance of her hands. 'You see, Professor, these are no longer the gentle, gentle and pure hands of Floria Tosca, but those of a worker,' she joked. In her own words, she was suffering from memory problems and insomnia, her body ached, she suffered from rashes on her face, and she had gained weight.

Professor Giacovazzo diagnosed her with dermatomyositis, a disease that causes muscle weakness and, to an extent, affects the central nervous system. It would have been responsible for the ailments – autoimmune disorders – that had bothered her since the 1950s, and for which she was accused of being a hypochondriac.

---

* Professor Giacovazzo's daughter, Isabella, wrote to the author on behalf of her father. These details of Callas's health are derived from the letter.

There was no cure, but she was prescribed prednisone (steroids) to relieve her symptoms. 'Now with his cure, I am much calmer,' she said. 'Pills, of course, but good ones not heavy drugs.'[21] She eventually stopped taking the prednisone as she gained weight – a common side-effect. 'I am angry because it takes a severe diet and still I have not seen one kilo lost.'[22] So, she stopped the treatment and her symptoms returned, causing her to suffer throughout the day and to have difficulty sleeping at night. Hoping to find relief, she sent her sister a cheque for $200 in exchange for Mandrax, as the 'soothing little pill' was available only through medical prescription in France.[23]

Morality comes into question: should Jackie, so far away in Athens, have refused to send the drugs to her sister, who tempted her with money? She had used Mandrax during her years with Onassis, but mostly took his drug of choice, Nembutal, as it helped her to sleep. There were other properties that Onassis might have found appealing, namely using Mandrax as a sex drug – it was commonly abused as such – for while it sedated the nervous system, it promoted hypersensitivity and euphoria. It would have caused Maria to lose her inhibitions and control, therefore enabling Onassis to do things that, she later said, were '[painful] and boring'.[24]

Highly addictive, the drug, formed of methaqualone and antihistamine diphenhydramine, was a powerful sedative, thus providing the user with a hypnotic effect. One pill a day for two months alters the body's chemistry and causes physical and psychological dependency. Withdrawal from Mandrax can cause death if done without medical assistance; the side-effects were headaches, convulsions, kidney failure and stomach haemorrhages. Despite being a potent sedative, long-term use made the body immune to its effects, and insomnia was a common complaint.

Therefore, this explains why it had a counter-effect on her, even when she took as many as five. Other side-effects were mania, irritability and, in some cases, seizures. Even in small doses, it was fatal, particularly if mixed with alcohol. In theory, each time Maria took the drug, she was sentencing herself to death. Perhaps she knew this: she once spoke of life as though it were a losing battle, telling Di Stefano that each day was a step closer to the end. She felt she had nothing to live for. 'I've lost everything. My voice is done, it seems. I don't have a man, I don't have a child. Isn't it funny?'[25]

Desperate to ease her physical pain and escape her intrusive thoughts, Maria believed her answer lay in a bottle of pills. Jackie was happy to receive the money and arranged with Mr Bekas, an Athenian chemist, to supply her with Mandrax, which she sent to Paris. Not once, however, did Jackie ask if there could be another answer to her problems, nor did she encourage her to seek help. But was there deeper malice at play? Signs of jealousy were evident in Jackie's memoirs:

> I remember a party we went to that Christmas where I noticed that [Maria] was interested in a boy a little older than her. Driven by who knows what demon, I suddenly decided to spoil things for her and did everything to make sure he spent the entire evening dancing with me … It had revealed an unpleasant side to my character that I knew I would do better to suppress.[26]

Not only did Jackie resent Maria, but she also enjoyed seeing her suffer. Could this have influenced her to send Maria the Mandrax? Did Jackie thrive on hearing Maria's grovelling voice on the telephone, begging for drugs, as both she and Litsa had been held ransom to the monthly $200 cheques? Or had she simply wanted to ease Maria's burdens?

It was also believed that Litsa was involved in this consortium of quasi drug dealers. In desperation, Maria was offering any amount of money for the precious drugs, and Litsa, fuelled by greed, would not have missed an opportunity to exploit her daughter. That is not to imply that Jackie and Litsa were participating in foul play or plotting to kill Maria, whose $200 they depended on. Under the Greek Civil Law, Litsa was Maria's next of kin and, regardless of if she made a will, she could not disinherit her mother. Therefore, in death, Litsa's money which, to an extent, also meant Jackie's money, would have continued.

Embodying the words from Euripides's *Medea*, Maria might have asked, 'Who can stop grief's avalanche once it starts to roll?' The poison bled into the cracks of her life and Vasso was on hand to offer daily affirmations that suited her moods. Vasso said her mother was at the American Hospital, being treated for cancer, while Onassis was there, and that she often smoked cigarettes with those who tended to him. However, this remains doubtful: the hospital floor on which Onassis resided was surrounded by guards and, given her mother's illness was different from Onassis's, she might have been treated in a separate department of the hospital. Nevertheless, Maria saw it as destiny that Vasso should be stalking those hospital corridors while the man she loved was dying. Now all she thought of was Onassis, and she cleared the obstacles that distracted from this. 'I started dying when I met this man,' she told Giulietta Simionato.[27] As in life, when she said, 'I am yours body and soul', in death, she devoted herself to him.[28]

Seldom leaving her apartment, Maria spent her days watching television and eating ice cream. She had an endless supply of Mandrax, for not only was Jackie sending frequent packages, but Vasso also arranged for them to be sent from Athens. 'If she wants them, let her have them,' Vasso said, when her servants expressed their concerns.[29] Leo Lerman's observation of her murderous scene in *Tosca* now applied to her life – governed by self-destruction and reaching for the bottle of pills, 'Her hands knew, then her whole body knew. She was drawn from the scene of the assassination by a sort of self-hypnosis; a sort of euphoria.'[30]

The following summer, Maria broke her monotonous routine and spent one week in Ibiza and two weeks in Halkidiki, in northern Greece. Her holiday was sabotaged by photographers who hid in the bushes and stalked her with their long-lens cameras, trying to capture her in her bikini. It disturbed her, for she had begun to suffer from lipoedema, an autoimmune disorder that causes an abnormal build-up of fat in the legs. To escape their cruel gaze, she retreated to her hotel room and passed the time watching television.

Although the media remained interested in her celebrity, she had no clear goal in sight. 'I have not decided about my future, but I will only do what I feel like,' she said.[31] She told her godfather that she had declined to buy the house in Palm Beach, and that she had 'stopped seeing you know who'.[32]

There were elements of unfinished business: she had left her belongings at Di Stefano's home; however, she did not ask for them back. 'So I leave things as they are,' Maria said. In reality, he had confessed everything to his wife and, enraged by the betrayal, Mrs Di Stefano packed Maria's things into plastic bags. 'I have a family to defend and the lives of my children,' Mrs Di Stefano said. 'Callas only has two blind dogs.'[33]

To her godfather, Maria wrote, '[He] is no longer in my life, thank God. I really was fed up.' Despite the burst of energy, Maria went to her apartment and decided to remain there for the rest of the year. A glint of optimism remained, and she said, 'Maybe next year will be more exciting.'[34]

The last year of Maria's life was a torturous routine of loneliness, introspection and regret. 'I am useless, completely useless,' she said. 'It's sad to say but that's the way it is.'[35] The position of Vasso was difficult to understand, and her servants were onlookers to the daily charade, but nobody attempted to stop her. Every day, Vasso practised on Maria's piano and invited her to sing, although for malevolent reasons: she knew Maria was humiliated when she could not reach the high notes and their sessions ended in tears. Another of Vasso's tactics was to keep Maria oblivious to the outside world, and if friends telephoned, she diverted their calls. According to Di Stefano, Maria had asked him to come to Paris, but when he arrived at her door, he was sent away. Vasso was an expert at directing the scene and knew when to withdraw, if only to convince Maria that she was in control.

On Bastille Day, Maria received Leo Lerman at her apartment, and he was surprised she remained in Paris in July. She rarely travelled or accepted social invitations, explaining she was comfortable at home. 'It was full of things and emptiness,' Leo said of the place. It was his first visit, despite their long years of friendship.[36]

She appeared in a dressing gown and led him to the salon. As she walked, he sensed something was missing, 'I think it was her spirit. I could no longer hear the sound of applause.'[37] Sitting down, she dashed glaucoma drops into her eyes, and turned to him and smiled. He noted in his diary that her smile reassured him – all at once, she was the old Maria. They spoke of their mutual friends and the old days; the reminiscences offered her no comfort, but she went through the motions of making conversation. There was nothing senti-mental about her life, she told him. 'It's more peaceful this way.'[38]

Each day followed the last and the hours were spent watching television through her myopic gaze – her vision had begun to fail her. She became absorbed in the static images of other people's lives. Her blood pressure was declining: eighty at its highest, fifty at its lowest. At night, she reached for the Mandrax, the pills in the bottle rattling as loud as the death-watch beetle.

When her unnatural sleep came, she had reoccurring dreams about Onassis, but it distressed her. 'I want to help him, but I can't.'[39] It was the same helplessness she had felt when he betrayed her. Particularly when, after his abandonment, they were both in New York on 16 September 1968, and she telephoned him, seeking closure and received none.

'Maria's grief, I will never forget, and I can still hear her,' Mary Carter's daughter recalled. 'It was traumatic.'[40] Her grief had come full circle and when the final death knell sounded, on 16 September 1977, it was mercifully quick.

'Maria did something unexpected … she died,' Leo wrote in his diary.[41]

She had explored every option to stay alive, saying, 'The woman is physi-cally stronger than a man. Not in the sense of working hard labour, but standing victorious in the face of great efforts, strain, stress, difficulties, challenges and breakdowns.'[42] In recent days, however, death had stalked the passages of Georges Mandel, and she experienced a sort of terminal lucidity. She questioned her identity, her place in the world, and the point of continuing:

> I am a person without identity. I was born of Greek parents, yet I have never felt absolutely Greek. I was born in America, yet I am not an American. I lived the most crucial period of my career in Italy, I married an Italian but, of course, I am not an Italian. I now live permanently in Paris, but this doesn't mean I feel French. What the hell am I, after all? What am I? I am alone, always alone.

She belonged everywhere and nowhere.

Epilogue

Power means nothing to the dead;
for them a requiem and eternity.

Macbeth, Verdi

There was no post-mortem to determine Maria's cause of death and it was assumed she died of a heart attack. Or simply, her body had given up fighting the effects of illness and the slow poisoning of Mandrax. Almost fifty-four years before, Litsa had invented a dramatic story to punctuate Maria's arrival into the world. She called her daughter a 'child of the storm' and the events became more dramatic with each retelling.

In the end, Maria only had herself. 'Nobody thought,' Maria once said, '"How is this woman feeling, how is she taking it, is there anybody to hold her hand, it must be hell".'[1]

In death, however, the drama was slow to unfold, as Maria's heirs staked their claim. There was no last will and testament, because she had reputedly wanted to leave her estate to her loyal servants, Bruna* and Ferruccio, and her body to medical research.

In her memoirs, Jackie wrote that the servants were oblivious to the fact that Maria had a mother and sister, recounting Bruna's words, 'Madame told me she had no family. We had no idea about you and your mother.' Evidently, Jackie had suffered a lapse in memory because later, in her book, she wrote of Ferruccio and Bruna diverting her calls to Maria when George was dying, and later, of her calls being accepted.

---

* Maria said, 'You know who takes care of me and who I know will always be there? My maid, who adores me, idolises me, and has been a nurse, sister, and mother to me.'

Assisted by her boyfriend, Jean Roire, Vasso became the self-appointed executor of the estate and took Maria's papers, which she gave to a trusted confidante. The authenticity of the papers is questionable, as Vasso was responsible for inventing the rumour that Maria bore Onassis's son in 1960, which she related to Alfonso Signorini, who used it as a subplot in his novel, *Tan Fiera, Tan Frágil*.*Vasso also claimed that Maria had kept a diary during her last years, writing of her love for Titta, and forged a suicide note, addressed to him, with her signature. As Vasso had suspected, it all distracted from the part she had played.

Within days, Jackie arrived at the scene and viewed Maria's corpse as it lay on the Rococo bed, a vision from *La traviata*; the long hair and grey gown a contrast against the deathly pallor. How did she feel viewing the body that she had helped destroy through her offerings of Mandrax? It did not enter Jackie's conscience, despite having taken money from Mr Bekas, who also paid for her ticket to Paris. Instead, she recounted:

> She had had everything in the end. I had been the beautiful one, I was the sister who would marry. Mary [her childhood nickname], dumpy, fat-legged Mary, would sing. Now, there I was, sixty, unmarried and there was Mary, one of the most famous women in the world.[2]

Litsa had remained in Athens, claiming she was too old and frail to travel to Paris for the funeral. Every night, she spoke to Jackie on the telephone,

---

* The child in question, Omero Lengrini, was born and died on 30 March 1960, at the Clinica Dezza in Milan. It was reported by Nicholas Gage in *Greek Fire* that Maria was seven months into her pregnancy when she demanded a caesarean section, which was at that time reserved for medical emergencies only. Therefore, the surgeon would have broken the law. Furthermore, as photographs have shown, there were no traces of a scar on her abdomen, and in those days the surgeon made a sizeable, vertical cut. The Clinica Dezza was used by a nearby convent for unmarried mothers, and women and girls from affluent families could pay to omit their names from birth certificates. Contrary to belief, Lengrini was not an alias used by Maria, but a surname given by whoever registered him, most likely a nun. During that period, illegitimate children could not use their mother's or father's family names, as that was a status reserved for those born in wedlock or if their mothers were married, regardless of the paternity. Instead, their surnames were a hint to their origins or their birthdays, i.e. the place from where their mothers came, or a feast day. Records show that Lengrini was a small homestead close to the Italian–Swiss border – however, as a surname it was uncommon. Further research proves that Omero's mother was an unmarried teenager, who has had to relive her son's death with every retelling in Callas biographies and the press. Signorini claimed the child in his story, named Angelo, was fictional, and Gage discovered unrelated Milanese records around which he based his theory.

'[Maria] had jewels, she had money … Think about it. Just think about it.'[3] Evidently, Litsa was giddy at the prospect of owning those things – the grandeur she had always craved. It never entered their minds to enquire about the legal technicality surrounding Maria's royalties and, sensing this, Vasso offered to handle the moral and economic rights.

At Vasso's suggestion, both she and Jackie went through Maria's possessions: 200 dresses, 200 blouses, 200 pairs of shoes, with handwritten labels detailing the date of purchase and where they had been worn. Meanwhile, Maria's corpse remained in the room, a silent witness to their intrusion. Were they looking for Mandrax, which was kept in large quantities, and if so, did they dispose of it? In her memoirs, Jackie recalled, 'I thought of Bekas handing me the packets of Mandrax and I wondered who else had joined in this bizarre network of death.'[4]

The funeral and cremation, organised by Vasso, was rushed – a formality before they examined the contents of the estate. Between Vasso and Jackie existed an unspoken agreement that a scandal – the drugs – would threaten Maria's image if the details of her lifestyle were made public. Or perhaps they were avoiding a police investigation? Under French law – the Law of 1970 – supplying illegal drugs carried a prison sentence, and under the Greek Law – decree 1176/72 – the distribution of prescription drugs to an individual which caused either harm or death also warranted a prison sentence.

It was agreed that Litsa and Jackie would receive Maria's clothing and jewellery, although Litsa queried the ownership of the apartment. Vasso explained that Maria was being pursued by the French Government for unpaid taxes on her earnings and outstanding rates on her apartment, and before her death she faced financial ruin and eviction. The women accepted the story, despite Maria having been a resident of Monaco and exempt from paying tax on her earnings, and the apartment having been purchased by Onassis's Panamanian companies, who were responsible for the rates. Until her last days, Onassis's estate paid those expenses, including her utility bills. She also part-owned a tanker worth several million on paper, and the dividends were paid into her Swiss bank account.

Not be outdone, Titta produced a will that Maria had signed in 1954, bequeathing everything to him – he had stolen it from her safe in 1959 – and engaged a lawyer to fight for his share of the estate. As divorce had been repealed in Italy, he argued that he was her legal husband and, therefore, entitled to inherit everything. Now, the three people who Maria loathed stood to inherit everything. Perhaps she had always known that others would cling to her glory:

> Of course, I have many acquaintances, and some of them think they are my friends – and so I let them think that. But, unfortunately, I see right through them. To them, I'm only the famous woman. To them, I'm only La Divina they usually only see the gold that glitters.[5]

In the end, they agreed to settle amongst themselves and the contents of her estate were divided into three. Titta arrived in Paris with several removal trucks, taking the majority of her jewellery and clothing. His percentage of the estate was left to his maid, Emma Roverselli-Brutti. In 2000, the items (including Maria's underwear) were sold at auction. Maria's letters were also sold at separate auctions and are now held in private collections and academic archives.

As for Litsa and Jackie's share of the estate, they took the antique furniture and the remaining clothing and jewels, which they sold at auction less than a year after her death. Incidentally, Titta attended the event and bought more than half of the items. The remaining sticks of furniture were later sold by Jackie to Nicholas Petsalis-Diomidis, the esteemed biographer of *The Unknown Callas: The Greek Years*.

Once more, Vasso offered to handle the legal documents, this time relating to the apartment and tanker. She said it was Maria's wish to form a foundation to help young singers, and Jackie agreed the money should be used to fund it. In the meantime, Litsa and Jackie moved to Paris, into an apartment in Vasso's building, and Litsa hoped to be treated like the Queen Mother among Maria's society friends. However, a frosty welcome greeted them and they soon returned to Athens.

In a bizarre turn of events, Maria's ashes were stolen from a columbarium at the Père Lachaise Cemetery and were later discovered in an alleyway. They were taken to Greece in 1979 and scattered over the Aegean, but a gust of wind blew them into the faces of the spectators. Perhaps this supernatural element was derived from the hand of Euripides, and the scorn from Medea herself: 'Hate is a bottomless cup; I will pour and pour.'

Nothing became of the foundation, despite Vasso having taken almost $800,000 from Litsa and Jackie to establish it. It was interesting that both Jackie and Litsa had agreed to wire it into Vasso's account when they, particularly Litsa, coveted Maria's money.

As early as 1951, Maria wrote to her godfather complaining of Jackie's letters asking for money. 'As for my sister, I tried to do my best but I just was cursed on top, so the heck with it.'[6] In terms of family duty, she 'did and will do my best for them but I will not permit them to exaggerate'.[7] So why would they, having succeeded in getting their hands on her fortune, so readily part with it? Was Vasso blackmailing them over their involvement with Mandrax because, unlike her, they had dealt directly with the supplier?

A decade had passed and, by then, Titta and Litsa had died, and Jackie had married Dr Andreas M. Stathopoulos, a Callas fan and PhD student from the University of Athens. He was also an admirer of Fascism (or *Nazi Kameraden*) and subscribed to the ideology of the International Cultivation of the Nazi Führer Cult. He wrote articles for *Chrysi Avgi* in favour of the 'gifted personality of the great European leader Adolf Hitler'.* His comrade, Nikolaos Michaloliakos, who founded the Golden Dawn, an illegal Greek neo-Nazi organisation, was sentenced to thirteen years imprisonment in 2020. In several articles, Andreas refers to the Golden Dawn, although it remains unknown if he actually subscribed to the party. It is also unknown if Jackie shared his views but, either way, she was complicit.

In 1984, Jackie appointed Andreas her power of attorney, and so he had full control over her inheritance. According to her memoirs, he encouraged her to sue Vasso for moral rights. 'Moral Right is the automatic possession of the immediate family,' Jackie argued.[8]

In a twist of fate, Vasso was dying of cancer and the case was never legally resolved, so Jackie, or rather Andreas, took charge of the rights. In 1997, Jackie threatened to sue Bruno Tosi for slander regarding his claims to *La Repubblica* that Maria worked as a babysitter in New York, despite it being supported by her former charge, Donatella Failoni. 'There is nothing degrading about that,' Tosi argued. In retaliation, Tosi also accused Jackie of slander and took legal action against her alleged threatening letters, which eventually ceased.

---

* See *Chrissi Avgi*, 8 August 2007. A Google search of Andreas's name in Greek (Δρ Ανδρέας Μ. Σταθόπουλος) reveals this.

In terms of Maria's monetary estate – estimated at £4.5 million – nothing was resolved by the courts, despite Vasso's threats of a civil action. Years later, Titta's nephews unsuccessfully challenged his will, so they too might become self-appointed heirs of Maria Callas. Also determined to reserve their status as heirs, both Jackie and Andreas waited until Titta's heir had died before she went to court in Athens to be legally declared 'the sole intestate inheritresses' of Maria Callas. As Andreas was Jackie's power of attorney, her rights effectively became his.

After Jackie died in 2004, Andreas continued to collect the royalty payments from Maria's recordings, although within a few years many of the recordings would fall into the public domain. He also appealed to the courts to be appointed Litsa's sole heir, as she too died intestate. In 2008, he attempted to control Maria's publicity rights and filed a legal case* against Association Maria Callas, a fan club headed by Bruno Tosi who, in 2006, filed an application with the US Patent and Trademark Office to trademark 'Maria Callas' in order to market calendars and memorabilia under MC MC S.R.L (Client Identifier: 591111). Despite the organisation abbreviating its name to M.C., Andreas argued that he was the sole heir of Maria's estate, and as the husband of her sister, he 'therefore owns all right, title and interest in and to the intellectual property rights in her name and likeness'.**[9]

As Maria resided in France at the time of her death, the French law expert Julien Blanchard argued that under French law:

> The only family members who can defend a person's name against abuse are those who have themselves, or whose ancestors have 'borne', or used, that name … [Andreas] therefore cannot defend Maria Callas's name because neither he nor any of his ancestors actually bore the surname Callas.[10]

A Greek law expert, Dr Michael Paroussis, also argued that under Greek law:

> Only close relatives and direct heirs possess their own right to protect the name of a deceased person and that right cannot be transferred through

---

* See *Andreas Stathopoulos vs MC MC SRL,* Trademark Trial and Appeal Board, 21 July 2010. No. 91187914 (T.T.A.B. 2008–2011). To read the complete case, visit: www.uspto.gov/main/sitesearch.htm.

** In a similar vein, Andreas opposed Franco Zeffirelli's film *Callas Forever* and wrote letters to the production companies Vanguard Films and Cattleya. Regardless, Zeffirelli proceeded with the film, which was released in 2002. Likewise, when Nicholas Gage's *Greek Fire* was published in 2000, exploiting the story of Maria and Onassis's alleged son, both Jackie and Andreas distanced themselves from the book, despite Gage having, to an extent, infringed on the alleged rights.

inheritance … [Andreas] is only an indirect heir and thus could not have been the transferee of such right.

Therefore, under French and Greek laws, they both argued the said personality rights did not pass to Andreas but rather 'terminated upon the death of Maria Callas's sister'.[11]

In 2011, Paroussis said, in relation to presumed publicity rights, that Maria Callas had never made use of any such rights, but, 'even if there were such a right on the side of Callas, it surely has weakened 33 years after death, and therefore, the name Callas has become a common historical name'.

During Maria's lifetime, those close to her, including her mother, wrote books bearing her name and detailing her life. Although she disputed the facts, she never acted against them in a legal capacity.

In the mid 2000s, when all presumed heirs had died, Andreas, in his own words, 'sought to exploit the "Maria Callas" rights of personality and publicity that I own in the US and abroad. I have done so both to preserve and strengthen Maria Callas's personal and artistic legacy and in the interests of commercialising that legacy'. Represented by Corbis/GreenLight, among the licensing deals were Dolce & Gabbana and The Dorchester; this would be profitable, no doubt. There was a preliminary agreement between Andreas and luxury goods company Montblanc but, having been confronted with Tosi's trademark information, they retracted their lucrative offer.

However, Paroussis claimed, 'Even beyond that, a ruling that calls into question [Andreas's] rights to protect and exploit Maria Callas's name and likeness would cast a cloud on all of the licensing arrangements (including past royalties paid and received) into which he has already entered.'

After two years of setbacks and delays on Andreas's behalf, he wrote a letter to the US board stating he was:

> … being judged by default … I am a retired medical doctor, citizen of Athens, Greece, a country being at bankruptcy. Therefore, I cannot afford the huge expenses of this trial … I do hope that the Honourable Board shall take under consideration all my grounds of documentation filed in the discovery phase of the opposition and shall not enter judgement against me.

The case was dismissed with prejudice, as he failed to submit substantial evidence, nor did he hire another legal counsel.

❊

There are no descendants: Maria and Jackie's branch of the Callas family tree is now extinct. Today, several individuals connected to Andreas, who refer to themselves as 'the remaining members of her family', continue to propagate the legacy of Maria Callas.[12]

> But the real me doesn't exist anymore.[13]

Maria Callas

Notes

1: Displacement

1   John Ardoin interview tapes, 1968 (from here on abbreviated to Ardoin).
2   The age of George varies. His US naturalisation record lists his DOB as 26/12/1887. US census for 1930 lists it as 1880. See NY Naturalization Records, 1882–1944, No. 5135809.
3   Evangelia claimed she was born on 1/1/1898, thus making her 17 when they married. However, records list 1/1/1894. See NY Naturalization Records, 1882–1944, No. 6904254.
4   Evangelia Callas to Maria Callas (MC), 14/8/1951. Courtesy of Allegri, Renzo and Roberto, *Callas by Callas: The Secret Writings of La Maria* (Berkeley: University of California, 1998).
5   Litsa communicated with her dead father. 'There is no barrier of death between us […] he still comes and talks to me.' Callas, Evangelia, *My Daughter: Maria Callas* (London: Leslie Frewin, 1967) p.12.
6   *The Omaha Daily News*, 31/10/1916.
7   US Department of Labor, Naturalization Service, No. 321381.
8   Recorded as Mary-Anna, her DOB was given as 4/12 in George's petition for US Naturalization, No. 387726.
9   Births Reported, 1923 – Borough of Manhattan.
10 Callas, Evangelia, p.12.
11 *Time*, 29/10/1956.
12 MC to Leonidas Lantzounis, 9/1/1963. Robert Baxter Collection on Maria Callas, ARS-0196. Stanford Archive of Recorded Sound, Stanford University Libraries, Stanford, CA (hereafter abbreviated to Lantzounis, RBC).
13 'But real poison …' MC to Edward Konrad, 8/5/1962.
14 MC TV interview with Pierre Desgraupes, *L'Invite du Dimanche*, 1969 (abbreviated to Desgraupes).
15 'We dreaded the diminishing crescent as a herald of bad days to come.' Callas, Jackie, *Sisters* (London: Pan Books, 1990) p.38.

16 George Callas to MC, 23/2/1957. The Maria Callas Alumni Association of the Music School of Kalamata (abbreviated to Music School of Kalamata).

17 Callas, Jackie, p.50.

18 1930 US census.

19 Hy Gardner interview, 2/2/1958 (abbreviated to Gardner).

20 Stancioff, Nadia, *Callas Remembered* (New York: Dutton, 1987) p.51.

21 'My mother is a bit mad like that, but I have never said so to the newspapers, that's one thing I couldn't tell them.' Sutherland, Robert, *Diaries of a Friendship* (London: Constable, 1999) p.225.

22 *Ibid.*

23 MC, 'My First Thirty Years', *Oggi* (1957).

24 US Census, 1930.

25 Desgraupes, 1969.

26 Ardoin.

27 The Norman Ross Show, 17/11/1957 (abbreviated to Ross).

28 Stancioff, Nadia, p.41.

29 MC to Olive Haddock, 1968.

30 Maria Callas Museum.

31 *Plainfield N.J. Courier-News*, 10 May 1928, p.1. Radio Programs from Nearby Stations (213-WCDA-NEW YORK) *10:15 Nina Foresti soprano.*

32 24/10/1933

33 'She startled me …' Sutherland, p.67.

34 George's height was recorded as 5ft 7in, US Department of Labor, Naturalization Service, No. 321381.

35 *Australian Women's Weekly*, 10/2/1971.

36 MC, 'My First Thirty Years', *Oggi* (1957).

2: Destiny

1 'There was hardly such a thing as an exclusive quarter.' Morris, Jan, *Manhattan '45* (Oxford: Oxford University Press, 1987) p.127.

2 MC to Leo Lerman, 9/3/1971. Leo Lerman Papers (abbreviated to Lerman, LLP), Columbia University Rare Book and Manuscript Library.

3 Petsalis-Diomidis, Nicholas, *The Unknown Callas: The Greek Years* (Portland: Amadeus Press, 2001) p.91.

4 Callas, Evangelia, p. 137.

5 *The Callas Conversations*, BBC, 1968.

6 MC to Philippe Caloni, Radio France Musique, April 1977 (abbreviated to Caloni).

7 MC, 'My First Thirty Years', *Oggi* (1957).

8 Petsalis-Diomidis, p.93.

9 *Ibid.*

10 *Ibid.*, p.91.

11 *Ibid.*, p.547.

12 MC to Lantzounis, RBC.

13 Evangelia Callas to MC, 18/9/1949 – Allegri, Renzo.

14 Petsalis-Diomidis, p.96.

15   *Ibid.*, p.97.
16   MC to Anita Pensotti, *Oggi* (January 1957).
17   Callas, Jackie, p.68.
18   *Ibid.*, p.124.
19   Callas, Evangelia, p.31.
20   Callas, Jackie, p.64.
21   Caloni, April 1977.
22   MC, 'My First Thirty Years', Anita Pensotti, *Oggi* (1957).
23   Callas, Jackie, p.64.
24   Petsalis-Diomidis, p.113.
25   *Ibid.*, p.142.
26   Callas, Evangelia, p.149.
27   Petsalis-Diomidis, p.116.
28   Sutherland, p.162.
29   Gardner interview.
30   Ardoin interview.
31   Lerman, Leo, *The Grand Surprise* (New York: Knopf, 2007) p.431.
32   MC to Bernard Gavoty, ORTF, 18/5/1965 (abbreviated to Gavoty).
33   Yannis Kambanis to MC, 4/9/1950, Music School of Kalamata.
34   MC, 'My First Thirty Years', *Oggi* (1957).
35   *Ibid.*
36   Callas, Evangelia, p.39.
37   *The Observer*, 8–15/2/1970.
38   MC, 'My First Thirty Years', *Oggi* (1957).
39   Maria Trivella, letter to Evangelia Callas.
40   Petsalis-Diomidis, p.478.
41   Desgraupes, 1969.
42   *Ibid.*
43   Petsalis-Diomidis, p.138.
44   *Ibid.*
45   Callas, Evangelia, p.150.
46   MC, 'My First Thirty Years', *Oggi* (1957).
47   The Callas Conversations, April 1968.

3: Survival

1   Callas, Jackie, p.79.
2   Elvira de Hidalgo to MC, March 1949, Music School of Kalamata.
3   Caloni.
4   Elvira de Hidalgo to MC, March 1949. Music School of Kalamata.
5   Petsalis-Diomidis, p.176.
6   Caloni.
7   Letter from Elvira de Hidalgo to MC, 24/6/1968.
8   Gardner interview.
9   Petsalis-Diomidis, p.207.

10 Callas, Evangelia, p.34.

11 *New York Times*, 31/10/1971.

12 Desgraupes, 1969.

13 Letter from De Hidalgo.

14 Caloni.

15 'The problem was [Maria's] size. Mother never seemed to acknowledge that [she] had put on weight and that her clothes needed special thought.' Callas, Jackie, p.73.

16 Petsalis-Diomidis, p.289.

17 MC, 'My First Thirty Years', *Oggi* (1957).

18 Desgraupes, 1969.

19 *Ibid.*

20 Petsalis-Diomidis, p.189.

21 *Ibid.*, p.194.

22 *Maria Callas Magazine,* No. 70 (November 2013).

23 Athens Press Conference, 10/8/1960.

24 MC to Micheline Banzet, interview, February 1969 (hereafter abbreviated to Banzet).

25 Callas, Jackie, p.76.

26 Ardoin tapes.

27 Pretorius, Jamie, *Rape and Infidelity: Threats to the athenian Πόλις and Οἶκος* (Stellenbosch University, 2017).

28 Petsalis-Diomidis, p.116.

29 MC to Harry Fleetwood, interviews, 13 and 27/3/1958.

30 MC, 'My First Thirty Years', *Oggi* (1957).

31 *Ibid.*

32 'Preliminary Report on the Undernourishment of Greece during the Period of Occupation', Greek Government sub-Committee on Undernourishment, August 1945.

33 MC, 'My First Thirty Years', *Oggi* (1957).

34 Evangelia Callas to MC, 18/9/1949, Allegri, Renzo.

35 Callas, Jackie, p.79.

36 *Ibid.*, p.105.

37 Petsalis-Diomidis, p.343.

38 Callas, Evangelia, p.62.

39 MC, 'My First Thirty Years', *Oggi* (1957).

40 It was common knowledge that an Italian officer had an arrangement at a hotel, whereby he paid the manager to supply young women who slept with him in exchange for food.

41 Monti, Jennifer, 'The Contrasting Image of Italian Women Under Fascism in the 1930s' (Syracuse University, 2011) p.25.

42 MC to Lerman, 1/5/1967, LLP.

43 Callas, Jackie, p.82.

44 Callas, Evangelia, p.56.

45 MC press conference, 7/2/1974, LLP.

46 Callas, Evangelia, p.64.

47 Article written by Elvira de Hidalgo for a Greek newspaper.

48   Allegri, Renzo, p.24.
49   Petsalis-Diomidis, p.355.
50   Letter from MC to Evángelos Maglivéras, December 1945.
51   Callas, Evangelia, p.68.
52   MC's written statement to Manolis Kalomiris, 20/7/1944, Greek National Opera
     Archive, no. 6–8.
53   *Ibid.*

4: Liberation

1   *Irish Independent*, 13/7/1998.
2   *Ibid.*
3   Ross.
4   MC, 'My First Thirty Years', *Oggi* (1957).
5   *Ibid.*
6   *Ibid.*
7   Ardoin tapes.
8   Desgraupes interview.
9   MC to Stelios Galatopoulos, *Maria Callas: Sacred Monste*r (London: Simon & Schuster,
     1999) p.490.
10   *The Observer*, 8–15/2/1970.
11   Desgraupes interview.
12   Petsalis-Diomidis, p.471.
13   MC to Evángelos Maglivéras, January 1947.
14   *Ibid.*, 1946.
15   *Ibid.*
16   *Ibid.*
17   Lerman, p.330.
18   Callas, Evangelia, p.84.
19   MC, 'My First Thirty Years', *Oggi* (1957).
20   Gavoty.
21   Elvira de Hidalgo.
22   *Ibid.*
23   Callas, Evangelia, p.81.
24   Romano Romani, Petsalis-Diomidis, p. 504.
25   Petitions for Naturalization, The Southern District Court, No. 6904254.
26   Petsalis-Diomidis, p.479.
27   List of US Citizens for the Immigration Authorities, 'Holds US passport No. 360',
     issued US Embassy, Athens, 4/8/1945.
28   It has been wrongly reported that Callas sailed on the *Stockholm*. The passenger vessel
     Stockholm was not launched until 1946. Shipping registers for 1945 prove otherwise,
     listing Sophie C. Cecilia Kalos on the MS *Gripsholm*, which sailed from Piraeus on
     15/9/1945.
29   MC, 'My First Thirty Years', *Oggi* (1957).
30   *Ibid.*
31   Elvira de Hidalgo.

32   *Ibid.*
33   Letter from MC to Elvira Mataranga, 1945.
34   MC, 'My First Thirty Years', *Oggi* (1957).

5: Rejection

1   MC to Evángelos Maglivéras, 2/1/1946.
2   MC, 'My First Thirty Years', *Oggi* (1957).
3   MC to Sally Lantzounis, circa 1945, RBC.
4   MC, 'My First Thirty Years', *Oggi* (1957).
5   MC to Evángelos Maglivéras, 2/1/1946.
6   MC to Sally Lantzounis circa 1945, RBC.
7   'As you see I am staying at the Times Square Hotel.' MC to Evángelos Maglivéras, 2/1/1946.
8   *Ibid.*
9   *Elle*, 9/2/1970.
10   MC to Evángelos Maglivéras, 2/1/1946.
11   Metropolitan Opera Archives.
12   MC, 'My First Thirty Years', *Oggi* (1957).
13   *Ibid.*
14   *Ibid.*
15   Letter from MC to Eddie Bagarozy, 2/9/1947.
16   Banzet, February 1965.
17   *New York Post*, 1958.
18   *New York Post*, 26/12/1958.
19   MC to Eddy Bagarozy, 20/8/1947.
20   'Do you remember her command for $750?' MC to Lantzounis, [undated] 1951, RBC.
21   *Ibid.*
22   It has been inaccurately reported that Litsa arrived in New York on Christmas Eve. Research proves that she arrived on 27 November. See 'New York Passenger and Crew Lists 1820–1957', Roll 7229, List or Manifest of Alien Passengers for the United States, List 27.
23   Callas, Evangelia, p.87.
24   MC to Lantzounis, [undated] 1951, RBC.
25   MC, 'My First Thirty Years', *Oggi* (1957).
26   MC to Lantzounis, [undated] 1951, RBC.
27   *Ibid.*
28   *Ibid.*
29   Drake, James A., *Richard Tucker: A Biography* (New York: Dutton, 1984) p.95.
30   Meneghini, Battista, *My Wife Maria Callas* (New York: Farrar Straus Giroux, 1982) p.15.
31   In his memoirs, Meneghini claimed Louise Caselotti and Nicola Rossi-Lemeni accompanied them. However, his sister, Pia, called it 'a sneaked trip to Venice [where] an affectionate relationship developed quickly' in Meneghini, Pia, 'Seven Years with Maria'.
32   Gardner.
33   9/7/1947, Allegri, Renzo.

34   *New York Times*, 31/10/1971.

35   *Ibid.*

36   Letter from MC to Renato Ravazzin, July 1947.

37   18/7/1947, Allegri, Renzo.

38   Drake, James A., *Richard Tucker: A Biography*, p.94.

39   Meneghini, Pia, 'Seven Years with Maria'.

40   Drake, James A., *Richard Tucker: A Biography*, p.94.

41   Harewood, George Lascelles, *The Tongs and the Bones: The Memoirs of Lord Harewood* (Weidenfeld and Nicolson, London 1981) p.100.

42   Meneghini, Pia, 'Seven Years with Maria'.

43   Drake, James A., *Richard Tucker: A Biography*, p.94.

44   MC to Eddie Bagarozy, 20/8/1947.

45   *Ibid.*, 2/9/1947.

46   MC to Battista Meneghini, 22/9/1947, Allegri, Renzo.

6: Transition

1   *Time*, 29/10/1956.

2   MC to Meneghini, 22/9/1947, Allegri, Renzo.

3   *Ibid.*

4   In an interview in 1959, Meneghini said he had to pay $80 before the visa was issued, as she owned money on the loan she had taken from the US Government in 1945.

5   MC to Eddie Bagarozy, 20/8/1947.

6   *Ibid.*, 2/9/1947.

7   MC to Meneghini, 22/9/1947, Allegri, Renzo.

8   Meneghini, interview, *Gente* magazine, circa 1959.

9   Isolda Cusinati, daughter.

10   Allegri, Renzo, p.50.

11   Caloni.

12   MC to Meneghini, 29/10/1947, Allegri, Renzo.

13   *Ibid.*

14   *Ibid.*

15   *Ibid.*, 3/11/1947.

16   *Ibid.*, 24/6/1949.

17   *Ibid.*, 1/11/1947.

18   *Ibid.*

19   Caloni.

20   MC to Meneghini, March 1948, Allegri, Renzo.

21   *Ibid.*

22   *Ibid.*, 2/5/1948.

23   *Ibid.*, May 1948.

24   *Ibid.*

25   Joan Sutherland: 'Let's face it,' she said, 'at certain times of the month for a woman, a cloudiness, or a fussiness gets on the voice.' *Life*, 26/6/1970.

26   Davis, C.B., and M.L., 'The Effects of Premenstrual Syndrome (PMS) on the Female Singer', *Journal of Voice*, Vol. 7, No. 4 (1993).

27 MC, 16/12/1958.

28 MC to Elvira de Hidalgo, September 1948, Music School of Kalamata.

29 Elvira de Hidalgo to MC, 6/10/1948, *ibid*.

30 MC to Meneghini, 18/11/1948, Allegri, Renzo.

31 Desgraupes.

32 MC to Meneghini, May 1948, Allegri, Renzo.

33 *Ibid*.

34 *Ibid*., 18/11/1948.

35 *Ibid*.

36 Banzet.

37 Desgraupes.

38 *Ibid*.

39 MC to Meneghini, 11/11/1948. Allegri, Renzo.

40 *Ibid*., 18/11/1948.

41 Meneghini, Pia, 'Seven Years with Maria'.

42 MC to Meneghini, 1948. Allegri, Renzo.

43 MC, 'My First Thirty Years', *Oggi* (1957).

44 Meneghini, Pia, 'Seven Years with Maria'.

45 MC to Meneghini, 28/1/1949. Allegri, Renzo.

46 *Ibid*.

47 *Ibid*., 30/1/1949.

48 Elvira de Hidalgo to MC, 3/1/1949, Music School of Kalamata.

49 MC, 'My First Thirty Years', *Oggi* (1957).

50 Meneghini, Pia, 'Seven Years with Maria'.

51 *Ibid*.

52 Callas, Jackie, p.124.

53 *Ibid*.

54 MC, 'My First Thirty Years', *Oggi* (1957).

55 Letter from George Callas to MC, 18/6/1949, Music School of Kalamata.

56 Evangelia Callas to MC, 18/9/1949. Allegri, Renzo.

57 MC to Meneghini, 14/5/1949, Renzo.

58 *Ibid*.

59 'Why did you marry him?' She leaned over to me and in a whisper answered, 'Who would have known that I was to become Callas?' 'Maria Callas', Anita Pensotti, *Oggi*.

7: Success

1 MC to Meneghini, 24/4/1949, Allegri.

2 *Ibid*.

3 *Ibid*., 27/5/1949.

4 *Ibid*., 14/5/1949.

5 *Ibid*., 13/5/1949.

6 27/6/1949, Music School of Kalamata.

7 MC to Meneghini, 20/6/1949, Allegri.

8 *Ibid*., 15/5/1949.

9 *Ibid*., 6/6/1949.

10   *Ibid.*, 8/6/1949.

11   *Ibid.*

12   *Ibid.*, 17/6/1949.

13   George Callas to MC, 18/6/1949, Music School of Kalamata.

14   MC to Meneghini, 3/7/1949, Allegri.

15   MC, 'My First Thirty Years', *Oggi* (1957).

16   MC to Meneghini, 14/4/1949, Allegri.

17   Evangelia Callas to George Callas, circa 1950, Allegri.

18   MC to Marlyse Schaeffer, *France-Soir*, 13/2/1960.

19   Desgraupes.

20   MC to Meneghini, 20/12/1949, Allegri.

21   *Ibid.*

22   *Ibid.*

23   WNYC, 22/9/1977, The NYPR Archive Collections.

24   Allegri.

25   Evangelia Callas to MC, 18/9/1949, Allegri.

26   *Ibid.*

27   Allegri, Roberto, *Editoriale Gli Olmi*, 2007.

28   Evangelia Callas to MC, 14/8/1951, Allegri.

29   MC to Meneghini, 14/5/1950, Allegri.

30   Callas, Evangelia, p.105.

31   MC to Meneghini, 18/5/1950, Allegri.

32   *Ibid.*

33   *Ibid.*

34   *Ibid.*

35   Allegri, *Editoriale Gli Olmi*, 2007.

36   *Ibid.*

37   Allegri, *Editoriale Gli Olmi*, 2007.

38   MC to Meneghini, 14/5/1950, Allegri.

39   *Ibid.*, 25/5/1950.

40   *Ibid.*

41   *Ibid.*, 1/6/1950.

42   *Ibid.*, 5/6/1950.

43   *Ibid.*

44   *Excelsior*, 23/5/1950.

45   MC to Meneghini, 5/6/1950, Allegri.

46   *Ibid.*

47   *Ibid.*, 1/6/1950

48   Callas, Evangelia, p.106.

49   Evangelia Callas to MC, circa September 1950, Allegri.

50   MC to Meneghini, 12/6/1950, Allegri.

51   Petsalis-Diomidis, p.536.

52   *Ibid.*

53   *Ibid.*

54   Evangelia Callas to MC, circa September 1950, Allegri.

55   Meneghini, p.107.

56   Circa September 1950, Allegri.
57   Allegri.
58   Meneghini, p.138.
59   *Ibid.*, p.139.
60   Weaver, William, 'Some Confessions of a Fan'. *Southwest Review*, vol. 77, no. 4, 1992, pp.480–99.
61   *Ibid.*
62   *Ibid.*
63   *Ibid.*
64   MC, 'My First Thirty Years', *Oggi* (1957).
65   *Evening Express*, 7/8/1959.
66   Sutherland, p.174.
67   *Evening Express*, 7/8/1959.
68   MC to Lantzounis, [undated] 1951, RBC.
69   Evangelia Callas to MC, circa September 1950, Allegri.
70   *Ibid.*
71   'I have told them that to me Maria is dead …' *Ibid.*
72   'It was not long after I met Maria that I realised she was an exceptional artistic property …' Meneghini, p.273.

8: Prima Donna

1   Letter from MC to Herbert Weinstock, 12/3/1960.
2   MC, 'My First Thirty Years', *Oggi* (1957).
3   MC to Lerman, 26 /11/1957, LLP.
4   MC, 'My First Thirty Years', *Oggi* (1957).
5   Seroff, Victor, *Renata Tebaldi: The Woman and the Diva* (New York: Appleton Century Crofts, 1961) p.140.
6   *Ibid.*
7   *Ibid.*, p.141.
8   MC, 'My First Thirty Years', *Oggi* (1957).
9   MC to Dorle Soria, 20/11/1957, the Dorle Soria Collection (hereafter referred to as DSC), New York Public Library for the Performing Arts.
10   MC, 'My First Thirty Years', *Oggi* (1957).
11   Seroff, Victor, p.142.
12   *Ibid.*, p.147.
13   Allegri.
14   *Musical America*, 16 January 1952.
15   Caloni.
16   Bing, Rudolf, *5,000 Nights at the Opera* (New York: Doubleday, 1982) p.232.
17   *Ibid.*
18   *Ibid.*, p.234
19   Renato Ravazzin, July 1947.
20   Gardner.
21   George Callas to MC, 1949.
22   MC to Lantzounis, [undated circa 1951], RBC.

23   Allegri, p.154.

24   DSC.

25   MC to Lantzounis, [undated circa 1951], RBC.

26   Allegri.

27   Callas, Evangelia, p.119.

28   *Ibid.*

29   MC to Lantzounis, August 1975, RBC.

30   Evangelia Callas to George Callas, circa 1952, Allegri.

31   Callas, Jackie, p.131.

32   *Ibid.*

33   MC, 'My First Thirty Years', *Oggi* (1957).

34   Braddon, Russell, *Joan Sutherland* (New York: St Martin's Press, 1962) p.50.

35   *Ibid.*

36   *Ibid.*, p.51.

37   *Musical Times*, January 1953.

38   MC, 'My First Thirty Years', *Oggi* (1957).

39   Legge, Walter, 'Signing up Callas for recordings', *New York Times*, 28/3/1982.

40   Scott, Michael, *Maria Meneghini Callas* (London: Simon & Schuster, 1992) p.84.

41   Langdon, Michael, *Notes from a Low Singer* (London: J. MacRae, 1982) p.54.

42   *New York Times*, 28/3/1982.

43   *Ibid.*

44   *Ibid.*

45   *Ibid.*

46   *Ibid.*

47   DSC.

48   Harewood, George Lascelles, *The Tongs and the Bones: The Memoirs of Lord Harewood*, p.226.

49   Weaver, William, 'Some Confessions of a Fan'.

50   Meneghini, p.208.

51   *Ibid.*, p.210.

52   Caloni.

53   *Ibid.*

54   Kesting, Jurgen, *Maria Callas* (Boston: Northeastern University Press, 1993) p.141.

55   *Ibid.*

56   MC to Jacques Bourgeois, interview, 30/9/1968.

57   Seroff, Victor, p.147.

9: Metamorphosis

1   Martha Graham to Francis Robinson, 11/11/1956. The Francis Robinson Collection of Theatre, Music and Dance, Vanderbilt University.

2   Biki Archive, Milan.

3   'She [had] huge sagging arms', Franco Manino. An image, taken in early 1954, revealed a scar and stitches under each arm.

4   'Biki: the dressmaker of Callas', *La Republica*, 15/9/2011.

5   Allegri.

6   Lowe, David, *Diva Assolula: Life, Art, Legacy*, Ungar, New York, 1986

7   29/10/1956.

8   *Record News: The Magazine for Record Collectors*, Vol. 3 (1958).

9   'Please excuse the change in my nature. Battista doesn't like it when I tell jokes.' MC to Eddie Bagarozy, 2/9/1947.

10   Out-takes from *Viva Maria!*, a 1999 Italian broadcast.

11   *Sunday Times*, 19 and 27/3– 2/4/1961.

12   Osborne, Richard, *Herbert von Karajan: A Life in Music* (Boston: Northeastern University Press, 2000) p.352.

13   7/2/1974. LLP.

14   *Sunday Times*, 19, 27/3–2/4/1961.

15   Harewood, George Lascelles, *The Tongs and the Bones: The Memoirs of Lord Harewood*, p.227.

16   Caloni.

17   *Ibid*.

18   Bing, Rudolf, *5,000 Nights at the Opera*, p.235.

19   *Chicago Tribune*, 1/11/1954.

20   Ross.

21   *Chicago Tribune*, 1/11/1954

22   Desgraupes.

23   Dorle Soria to MC, 3/3/1955, DSC.

24   *Ibid*.

25   Lerman, p.174.

26   'Maria Callas' by Anita Pensotti; Tosi, Bruno (ed.), *The Young Maria Callas* (Toronto: Guernica, 2010) p.93.

27   BBC Interview, 31/1/1957.

28   'Maria Callas' by Anita Pensotti; Tosi, Bruno (ed.), *The Young Maria Callas* (Toronto: Guernica, 2010) p.99.

29   Desgraupes.

30   *Ibid*.

31   Caloni.

32   Meneghini, p.180.

33   *Ibid*., p.177.

34   Bing, Rudolf, *5,000 Nights at the Opera*, p. 238.

35   Lerman, p.173.

36   Kesting, Jurgen, p.154.

37   *Time*, 3/11/1958.

38   Lerman, p.174.

39   Drake, James A., *Richard Tucker: A Biography*, p.144.

40   *Ibid*.

41   Simeone, Nigel (ed.), *The Leonard Bernstein Letters* (Yale University Press, 2013) p.326.

42   Kesting, Jurgen, p.155.

43   Simeone, Nigel (ed.), *The Leonard Bernstein Letters*, p.326.

44   Zeffirelli, Franco, *Franco Zeffirelli: The Autobiography* (London: Arrow Books, 1987) p.131.

45   MC, 'My First Thirty Years', *Oggi* (1957).

46   *Life*, 20/4/1959.
47   A Conversation with Bruce Duffie, 16/11/1988.
48   Banzet.
49   *Chicago American*, 1/11/1955.
50   Banzet.
51   Dorle Soria to Carol Fox, 19/10/1955, DSC.
52   Dario Soria manuscript, DSC.
53   'I knew it was going to happen, and I tipped them off. It's called press agentry.' *Deseret*, 14/5/2001.
54   MC to Dorle Soria, 3/12/1955, DSC.
55   Natalie Cassidy, *Chicago Tribune*.

10: Scandal

1   'In 1947 plaintiff "arranged to launch" the career of defendant Callas as an opera singer and "in furtherance" of her career plaintiff expended about $85,000.' *E. Richard Bagarozy, Appellant vs Maria Caligeropolous Meneghini, Theatrically Known as Maria Callas, and Capitol Records Distributing Corp.*, Appellees. Gen. No. 46,700, Illinois Appellate Court — First District, Third Division, 23/11/1955.
2   *Ibid*.
3   MC, 'My First Thirty Years', *Oggi* (1957).
4   *The Chicago Tribune*, 9/7/1956.
5   Osborne, Richard, *Herbert von Karajan: A Life in Music*, p.355.
6   *Ibid*.
7   Luchino Visconti to Meneghini, 13/8/1956, Allegri.
8   *Ibid*.
9   *Time*, 29/10/1956.
10   Walter Legge to J.D. Bicknell, 23/3/59, EMI archives.
11   'Maria Callas' by Anita Pensotti; Tosi, Bruno (ed.), *The Young Maria Callas*, p.93.
12   Allegri.
13   MC to Rudolf Bing, 19/2/1956, Metropolitan Opera Archives.
14   Meneghini, p.228.
15   MC repeated this comment to Edward Murrow, person to person, January 1958.
16   Callas, Jackie, p.146.
17   *Time*, 29/10/16.
18   23/10/1956, DSC.
19   *Ibid*.
20   Horst, Horst P., *Sixty Years of Photography* (New York: Rizzoli, 1991) p.20.
21   Henry Sell to Dorle Soria, 11/11/1956, DSC.
22   *Saturday Review*, 27/10/1956.
23   Sutherland, p.173.
24   Lerman, p.215.
25   *Ibid*.
26   Sutherland, p.172.

27 Croatian radio interview, 1975.

28 *Life*, 20/4/1959.

29 Martha Graham to Francis Robinson, 11/11/1956, The Francis Robinson Collection of Theatre, Music and Dance, Vanderbilt University.

30 *Musical America*, November 1956.

31 Alfred Lunt to Francis Robinson, The Francis Robinson Collection of Theatre, Music and Dance, Vanderbilt University.

32 Payn, Graham and Sheridan Morley, *The Noël Coward Diaries* (Boston: Little, Brown, 1982).

33 *Ibid.*

34 *Time*, 1956.

35 Constance Hope to Lerman, 16/11/1956, LLP.

36 *Life*, 20/4/1959.

37 Meneghini, p.251.

38 *Chicago Tribune*, 1957.

39 MC to Lerman, 15/3/1957, LLP.

40 *Truth*, 8/2/1957.

41 Ardoin.

42 George Callas to MC, 23/1/1957, Music School of Kalamata.

43 *Time*, 29/10/1956.

44 *Ibid.*

45 See Leo Lerman Papers, Columbia University Rare Book and Manuscript Library.

46 MC to Dorle Soria, 20/11/1957, DSC.

47 Letter from MC to Walter Cummings, 11/11/1957.

48 *Ibid.*

49 *Ibid.*

50 *Ibid.*

51 MC, 'My First Thirty Years', *Oggi* (1957).

52 Allegri, *Editoriale Gli Olmi*, 2007.

53 Petsalis-Diomidis, p.655.

54 George Callas to MC, 23/1/1957, Music School of Kalamata.

55 'Theater Through Microphone', Athens, interview, 4/8/1957.

56 Callas, Evangelia, p.132.

57 'Theater Through Microphone', Athens, 4/8/1957.

58 *Life*, 20/4/1959.

59 'Backstage, she was often wrapped in large silk scarves, thin with huge dark eyes, she looked like a mouse, or a chick thrown out of its nest. She always had such cold hands which she would put under the hot water tap: a great artist who was a victim of tension as we all are.' Fracci, Carla, *Gramilano*, 22/4/2014.

60 *Life*, 20/4/1959.

61 Kurt Adler, 3/9/1957, RBC.

62 Dario Soria to MC, 27/9/1957, DSC.

63 Henry Sell to MC, 22/10/1957, DSC.

64 *Life*, 20/4/1959.

65 MC to Henry Sell, [undated] October 1957, DSC.

66   MC to Josephine Duncan, 1/11/1957, DSC.
67   Staggs, Sam, *Inventing Elsa Maxwell: How an Irrepressible Nobody Conquered High Society* (New York: St Martin's Press, 2012).
68   Meneghini, p.233.
69   MC to Lerman, 26/11/1957, LLP.
70   *Life*, 20 April 1959.
71   *Ibid.*
72   *Il Giorno*, 6/1/1958.
73   *Daily Herald*, 4/1/1958.
74   *Life*, 20/4/1959.
75   *Ibid.*
76   *Ibid.*

11: Submersion

1   Gardner.
2   MC to Charles Johnson, 30/9/1957, Maria Callas Museum.
3   MC to Edward Murrow, person to person, 24/1/1958.
4   Letter from MC to Mrs Binchoff, 2/1/1958.
5   Bing, Rudolf, *5,000 Nights at the Opera*, p.241.
6   Ross.
7   John A. Aaron to Dario Soria, 17/12/1957, DSC.
8   Callas, Evangelia, p.155.
9   Lerman, p.175.
10   *Life*, 20/4/1959.
11   *Ibid.*
12   *Ibid.*
13   *Ibid.*
14   Lerman, p.215.
15   *Ibid.*
16   Callas, Evangelia, p.125.
17   Drake, James A., *Richard Tucker: A Biography*, p.146.
18   *Ibid.*
19   Gardner.
20   Gabor, Jolie, *Jolie Gabor* (New York: Mason/Charter, 1975) p.264.
21   *ABC*, [undated] March 1958.
22   *Life*, 20/4/1959.
23   *Ibid.*
24   *Ibid.*
25   *Ibid.*
26   *Ibid.*
27   *Ibid.*
28   *Ibid.*
29   MC to Lerman, 18/7/1958, LLP.
30   Glanville, Brian, *Football Memories: 50 Years of the Beautiful Game* (London: Robson, 2004) p.270.

31 Cologne interview, July 1957.

32 'I hope *La traviata* will come as I wish. Only it's too bad it's for Texas, not because they don't deserve it but of course N.Y. is N.Y.', MC to Lerman, 18/7/1958, LLP.

33 *Ibid.*, 19/4/1959.

34 'I asked her did she ever want a child: "More than anything."' Lerman, p.363.

35 MC to Giulietta Simionato, Allegri.

36 MC, 'My First Thirty Years', *Oggi* (1957).

37 Ardoin.

38 Letter from MC to Emily Coleman, 2/1/1958.

39 Staggs, Sam, *Inventing Elsa Maxwell*.

40 Metropolitan Opera Archives, 27/10/1958.

41 *Life*, 20/4/1959.

42 *Ibid.*

43 Bing, Rudolf, *5,000 Nights at the Opera*, p.244.

44 MC to Rudolf Bing, 2/11/1958, Metropolitan.

45 Lerman, p.231.

46 *Ibid.*

47 *Ibid.*

48 Metropolitan Opera Archive, 6/11/1958.

49 *Ibid.*

50 *Ibid.*

51 *Life*, 20/4/1959.

52 Bing, Rudolf, *5,000 Nights at the Opera*, p.243.

53 Lerman, p.232.

54 *Belfast Telegraph*, 15/11/1958.

55 Interview, 16/12/1958.

56 MC to Lerman, 19/4/1959, LLP.

57 *Ibid.*

58 Evans, Peter, *Ari: The Life and Times of Aristotle Onassis* (New York: Summit, 1986) p.175.

59 *Ibid.*

60 *Ibid.*

61 *Ibid.*, p.182.

62 Ilibrariana.wordpress.com, 10/2/2017.

63 *Ibid.*

64 *Ibid.*

65 MC to Lerman, 19/4/1959, LLP.

66 MC to Herbert Weinstock, 12/3/1960.

67 MC to Emily Coleman, 15/12/1959.

68 MC to Walter Cummings, [undated] 1959.

69 Ardoin.

70 July 1959.

71 Sutherland, p.231.

72 Evans, Peter, *Ari* …, p.180.

12: Falling

1   Montague Browne, Anthony, *The Long Sunset* (London: Cassell, 1995) p.253.
2   *La Stampa*, 15/4/1992.
3   See parterre.com/ardoin_interview.htm.
4   *Ibid.*
5   Montague Browne, Anthony, p.253.
6   *Ibid.*
7   Evans, Peter, *Ava Gardner: The Secret Conversations* (London: Simon & Schuster, 2013) p.11.
8   Evans, Peter, *Ari …*, p.31.
9   Meneghini, p.293.
10 According to Onassis's biographer, Peter Evans, the art connoisseur, Emery Reeves, challenged its authenticity. Onassis said, 'If people wish to believe it to be genuine, why spoil their pleasure?'
11 Meneghini, p.297.
12 MC to Walter Cummings, [undated] 1959.
13 Meneghini, p.296.
14 *Life*, 30/10/1964.
15 Dario Soria to Peter Herman Adler, 14/7/1959, DSC.
16 *La Stampa*, 9/10/1959.
17 *Ibid.*, 11/9/1959.
18 *Epoca*, 20/9/1959.
19 *Liverpool Echo*, 25/4/1960.
20 Meneghini, p.301.
21 *Ibid.*, p.203.
22 Evans, Peter, *Ari …*, p.97.
23 *Daily Herald*, 17/9/1959.
24 Joesten, Joachim, *Onassis* (London: Abelard-Schuman, 1963) p.177.
25 Meneghini, p.310.
26 Bing, Rudolf, *5,000 Nights at the Opera*, p.98.
27 *Sunday Independent*, 20/9/1959.
28 *Daily Post*, 16/9/1959.
29 *La Stampa*, 17/09/1959.
30 *The Stage*, 8/10/1959.
31 *Il Mondo* [undated].
32 *Daily Mirror*, 10/9/1959.
33 *Daily Herald*, 24/9/1959.
34 *La Stampa*, 16/11/1959.
35 *Canberra Times*, 10/9/1959.
36 Moutsatsos, Kiki Feroudi, *The Onassis Women* (New York: Putnam, 1998) p.71.
37 *Kansas City Banner*, October 1959.
38 *Evening Express*, 3/10/1959.
39 6/11/1959, DSC.
40 MC to Lerman, 31/7/1960, LLP.
41 *Daily Mirror*, 10/9/1959.

42   Yannis Georgakis to Peter Evans, *Nemesis* (New York: William Morrow, 2005) p.16.

43   Sutherland, p.109.

44   Callas, Evangelia, p.156.

13: Detour

1   Lerman, p.431.

2   MC to Walter Cummings, 22/1/1960.

3   *Ibid.*

4   *Life*, 30/10/1964.

5   *Evening Telegraph*, 15/1/1960.

6   *Life*, 30/10/1964.

7   *La Stampa*, 30/11/1959.

8   *Daily Mirror*, 1/12/1959.

9   Giovanna Lomazzi.

10   'I am in very bad financial condition.' *La Stampa*, 23/8/1959.

11   'I wish I had dropped the blackmailer of a husband before!' MC to Lerman, 3/7/1960, LLP.

12   MC to Walter Cummings, 12/3/1960.

13   *Ibid.*, 1/3/1960.

14   *Life*, 30/10/1964.

15   MC to Walter Cummings, 12/3/1960.

16   MC to Herbert Weinstock, 12/3/1960.

17   Lerman, p.240.

18   MC to Herbert Weinstock, 12/3/1960.

19   *Ibid.*

20   Letter from MC to Aristotle Onassis, 30/1/1968.

21   Walter Legge to Mr J.D. Bicknell, 21/7/1960, EMI Archives.

22   *Ibid.*

23   *Ibid.*

24   *Ibid.*

25   *Sunday Times*, 19, 27/3, 2/4/1961.

26   *La Stampa*, 22/7/1960.

27   MC to Lerman, 31/7/1960, LLP.

28   Dr Giampolo Lomi. Copies of correspondence were given to the author by Dr Brigitte Pantis.

29   *New York Times*, 16/1/1973.

30   MC to Walter Cummings, 29/7/1960.

31   *The Canberra Times*, 14/7/1960.

32   Lerman, p.240.

33   *Ibid.*

34   *The Times*, 25/8/1960.

35   Dr Papathanassopoulos found inflammation of the upper respiratory system.

36   Gavoty.

37   *La Stampa*, 4/4/1961.

38   *Ibid.*
39   *Ibid.*
40   *Daily Post*, 16/11/1959.
41   *Daily Herald*, 7/7/1961.
42   Callas, Jackie, p.159.
43   *Ibid.*
44   *Ibid.*, p.164.
45   *Northern Daily Mail*, 26/7/1958.
46   *Evening Express*, 8/8/1959.
47   MC to Meneghini, 5/6/5190, Allegri.
48   Lerman, p.240.
49   'She would go to Crazy Horse and watch, preparing this new role as meticulously as she had always prepared her opera roles', Lerman, p.295.
50   Moutsatsos, Kiki Feroudi, *The Onassis Women*, p.84.
51   Letter from MC to Aristotle Onassis, 30/1/1968.
52   Ardoin.
53   Sutherland, p.215.
54   'What d'ya wanna work for? he asked me … So adolescent', Lerman, p.343.
55   Evans, Peter, *Nemesis*, p.80.
56   *Tatler*, 18/12/1965.
57   *Ibid.*
58   *Evening Express*, 8/8/1959.

14: Consequences

1   Evans, Peter, *Ari* …, p.190.
2   MC to Walter Cummings, 17/7/1960.
3   *Daily Mirror*, 28/2/1962.
4   *Daily Herald*, 28/2/1962.
5   *Ibid.*
6   3/5/1962, RBC.
7   Letter from MC to Edward Konrad, 8/5/1962.
8   MC to Lantzounis, 5/5/1963, RBC.
9   *La Stampa*, 15/5/1962.
10   MC to Edward Konrad, 8/6/1962.
11   Emilio Pozzi, 19/7/1966.
12   *Life*, 30/10/1964.
13   MC to Edward Konrad, 8/5/1962.
14   Burton, Richard, *The Richard Burton Diaries* (Yale University Press, 2012) p.599.
15   *Ibid.*
16   Taraborrelli, J. Randy, *Jackie, Janet and Lee: The Secret Lives of Janet Auchincloss and Her Daughters* (New York: St Martin's Press, 2018) p.133.
17   *Ibid.*
18   Evans, Peter, *Nemesis*, p.126.
19   Lerman, p.353.
20   Ardoin.

21 *La Stampa*, 2/12/1965.

22 *Ici-Paris*, 2/12/1963.

23 Stancioff, Nadia, p.156.

24 Evans, Peter, *Ari* …, p.64.

25 *Daily Mirror*, 29/10/1962.

26 *France-Soir*, 16/2/1960.

27 29/10/1959, Francis Robinson Archives, Vanderbilt University.

28 *Daily Mirror*, 27/12/1962.

29 *La Stampa*, 23/1/1963.

30 *Ibid.*

31 MC to Dorle Soria, 7/1/1963, DSC.

32 Teresa D'Addato to Dorle Soria, 12/1/1963, DSC.

33 MC to Lantzounis, 9/1/1963, RBC.

34 *Ibid.*

35 *Ibid.*

36 Lerman, p.430.

37 Evans, Peter, *Ari* …, p.294.

38 Evans, Peter, *Nemesis*, p.74.

39 *Ibid.*

40 Taraborrelli, J. Randy, p.156.

41 *Ibid.*

42 *Ibid.*

43 *La Stampa*, 18/4/1963.

44 *Ibid.*, 6/6/1963.

45 Montague Browne, Anthony, p.257.

46 *Ibid.*

47 Taraborrelli, J. Randy, p.173.

48 *Ibid.*, p.155.

49 MC to Jacqueline Kennedy, 21/7/1963, JFK Presidential Library and Museum.

50 Lerman, p.265.

51 Emilio Pozzi, 19/7/1966.

52 MC to David Bicknell, 21/7/1963, EMI Archives.

53 *Ibid.*

54 Andry, Peter, Stringer, Robin and Tony Locantro, *Inside the Recording Studio: Working with Callas, Rostropovich, Domingo, and the Classical Elite* (Lanham: Scarecrow Press, 2008) p.50.

55 Desgraupes.

56 Russell, Leonard, *Encore* (M. Joseph, 1962) p.84.

57 Evans, Peter, *Nemesis*, p.126.

58 Evans, Peter, *Ari* …, p.195.

59 *Ibid.*, p.198.

60 *La Stampa*, 23/8/1963.

61 Evans, Peter, *Nemesis*, p.118.

62 Lerman, p.265.

63 Montague Browne, Anthony, p.358.

64 *Ibid.*

15: Pendulum

1   *Life*, 30/10/1964.
2   MC to Walter Cummings, 17/11/1963.
3   MC to Lantzounis, 9/1/1963, RBC.
4   Lerman, p.315.
5   *The Guardian*, 23/7/2012.
6   *Daily Mirror*, 22/1/1964.
7   11/2/64, DSC.
8   21/2/1964, DSC.
9   MC to Walter Cummings, 17/11/1963.
10   *Life*, 30/10/1964.
11   Andry, Stringer, Locantro, p.54.
12   MC to Lantzounis, 29/4/64, RBC.
13   *Ibid*.
14   *Ibid*.
15   *Ibid*.
16   *Ibid*.
17   *La Stampa*, [undated] April 1964.
18   MC to Lantzounis, 29/4/1964, RBC.
19   *Life*, 30/10/1964.
20   MC to Lantzounis, 9/1/1963, RBC.
21   *La Stampa*, 9/5/1964.
22   *Ibid.*, 28/5/1965.
23   *Ibid.*, 9/5/1964.
24   Evans, Peter, *Ari…*, p.200.
25   Allegri, p.140.
26   April Ashley to author.
27   *High Fidelity*, February 1965.
28   *Ibid*.
29   Lerman, p.585.
30   *Ibid*.
31   *San Bernardino Sun*, 20/7/1975.
32   MC to Onassis, 30/1/1968, private collection.
33   MC to Lantzounis, 9/1/1963, RBC.
34   *Ibid.*, [undated, 1950].
35   *Ibid.*, August 1975.
36   *Ibid*.
37   *Onassis and Calogeropoulos vs Vergottis* [1967], 1 Lloyd's Rep. 607.
38   *Ibid*.
39   MC to Lerman, 5/2/1965, LLP.
40   Ardoin.
41   Lerman, p.315.
42   *Life*, 20/4/1959.
43   *Ibid.*, 30/10/1964.
44   MC to Meneghini, 19/5/1949, Allegri.

45   *Life*, 30/10/1964.

46   MC to Lantzounis, 29/4/1964, RBC.

47   *La Stampa*, 1/6/1965.

48   MC to Yannis Tsarouchis, Petsalis-Diomidis [undated] May 1964.

49   *La Stampa*, 1/6/1965.

50   Evans, Peter, *Ari…*, p.203.

51   *Life*, 30/10/1964.

52   *La Stampa*, 5/7/1965.

53   *Ibid.*, 6/7/1965.

54   *Sunday Times*, 19, 27/3, 2/4/1961.

55   *La Stampa*, 30/6/1965.

56   Desgraupes.

57   MC to Meneghini, 5/6/1950, Allegri.

58   *La Stampa* 28/5/1965.

59   *Onassis and Calogeropoulos vs Vergottis* [1967], 1 Lloyd's Rep. 607.

60   *Sunday Times*, 19, 27/3, 2/4/1961.

61   *Onassis and Calogeropoulos vs Vergottis* [1967], 1 Lloyd's Rep. 607.

62   *Ibid.*

63   Andry, Stringer, Locantro, p.53.

64   *Ibid.*

65   MC to Walter Cummings, 17/11/1963.

66   German television interview, 1962.

67   Evans, Peter, *Nemesis*, p.60.

16: Malevolence

1   MC to Mr Bean, 19/9/1966, private collection.

2   MC to Walter Cummings, 29/7/1960.

3   Emilio Pozzi, 19/7/1966.

4   *Novecento*, [undated] 2002.

5   Banzet.

6   Lerman, p.353.

7   Sutherland, p.225.

8   Lerman, p.353.

9   *Onassis and Calogeropoulos vs Vergottis* [1967], 1 Lloyd's Rep. 607.

10   *Time*, 29/10/1956.

11   *Onassis and Calogeropoulos vs Vergottis* [1967], 1 Lloyd's Rep. 607.

12   *Ibid.*

13   Evans, Peter, *Nemesis*, p.144.

14   *Onassis and Calogeropoulos vs Vergottis* [1967], 1 Lloyd's Rep. 607.

15   *Ibid.*

16   *Ibid.*

17   *La Stampa*, 18/4/1967.

18   *Onassis and Calogeropoulos vs Vergottis* [1967], 1 Lloyd's Rep. 607.

19   *Ibid.*

20   *Ibid.*
21   *Ibid.*
22   Lerman, p.430.
23   *La Stampa*, 26/8/1967.
24   Andry, Stringer, Locantro, p.54.
25   *Dimanche.*
26   MC to Elvira de Hidalgo, 11/11/1967, private collection.
27   *Ibid.*
28   MC to Onassis, 30/1/1968, private collection.
29   Evans, Peter, *Nemesis*, p.200.
30   *Ibid.*, p.152.
31   MC to Walter Cummings, 1/5/1975.
32   *Life*, 30/10/1964.
33   RBC.
34   Di Stefano, Maria, *Callas Nemica Mia* (Milan: Rusconi, 1992) p.112.
35   *Ibid.*
36   Evans, Peter, *Nemesis*, p.39.
37   MC to Bruna Lupoli, 19/3/1968.
38   Lerman, p.353.
39   Harewood, George Lascelles, *The Tongs and the Bones: The Memoirs of Lord Harewood*,
     p.234.
40   *Ibid.*
41   MC to Elvira de Hidalgo, 16/6/1968, private collection.
42   *Ibid.*
43   *Ibid.*, 24/6/1968.
44   Andry, Stringer, Locantro, p.52.
45   MC to Elvira de Hidalgo, 24/6/1968.
46   'Teddy was negotiating for Jackie's body …' Joan Thring in Evans, Peter, *Nemesis*
     (William Morrow, New York, 2005) p.203.
47   Moutsatsos, Kiki Feroudi, *The Onassis Women*, p.86.
48   MC to Onassis, 30/1/1968.
49   Banzet.
50   Moutsatsos, Kiki Feroudi, *The Onassis Women*, p.85.
51   *Ibid.*, p.87
52   Evans, Peter, *Nemesis*, p.205.
53   *Ibid.*, p.189.
54   MC to Teresa d'Addato, 10/10/1968, private collection.
55   MC to Elvira de Hidalgo, 16/6/1968.
56   MC to Teresa d'Addato, 10/10/1968.
57   *Ibid.*, 15/8/1968.
58   Ardoin.
59   *Arts*, 10/12/1958.
60   Ardoin.
61   *Ibid.*

62   Peter Andry's letter reveals her attendance was confirmed in advance. 'She will attend the opening of the Met with me ... The [Wallichs] want Maria to join them [in Bermuda] but she has opted for the opening.' 3/9/1968.

63   Ardoin.

64   MC to Teresa d'Adatto, 10/9/1968.

65   MC to John Ardoin, 13/9/1968.

66   MC to Elvira de Hidalgo, 3/10/1968.

67   *Ibid.*

68   *Ibid.*, 29/10/1968.

69   *Ibid.*

70   MC to Onassis, 28/1/1968.

71   Evans, Peter, *Nemesis*, p.152.

17: Cipher

1   MC to John Ardoin, 13/9/1968.

2   MC to Elvira de Hidalgo, 24/4/1969.

3   Lerman, p.340.

4   *New York Times*, 31/10/1971.

5   Lerman, p.295.

6   MC to Dorle Soria, 21/3/1969, DSC.

7   John Coveneny to Peter Andry, 3/9/1968, EMI Archives.

8   Andry, Stringer, Locantro, p.54.

9   Larry Kelly to MC, 28/4/1969, RBC.

10   *Ibid.*

11   *Ibid.*

12   *Ibid.*

13   *Ibid.*

14   *New York Times*, 31/10/1971.

15   Schwartz, Barth David, *Pasolini, Requiem* (New York: Pantheon, 1992) p.553.

16   *Lui*, 1/6/1970.

17   *Ibid.*

18   MC to Dorle Soria, June 1969, DSC.

19   Pier Paolo Pasolini to MC, 1969. Courtesy of Graziella Chiarcossi.

20   *Ibid.*

21   *Lui*, 1/8/1970.

22   *La Stampa*, 1/7/1969.

23   *La Stampa*, 9/1/1970.

24   'Maria has been in the hospital having the bags removed, unpacking the satchels under her eyes.' Lerman, p.296.

25   *New York Times*, 10/10/1971.

26   Pasolini, Pier Paolo, *The Bay of Kingstown* (1970); Ivory, James & Stephen Sartarelli, (eds), *The Selected bay Poetry of Pier Paolo Pasolini: A Bilingual Edition* (Chicago: University of Chicago Press, 2015); Chiarcossi.

27   *Ibid.*

28   *Lui*, 1/6/1970.

29   *Ibid.*
30   *New York Times*, 31/10/1971.
31   *La Stampa*, 1/2/1970.
32   *La Stampa*, 16/3/1970.
33   MC to Barbara Walters, 15/4/1974.
34   Lerman, p.340.
35   *La Stampa*, 3/2/1970.
36   Evans, Peter, *Nemesis*, p.233.
37   *New York Times*, 30/11/1970.
38   *La Stampa*, 3/2/1970.
39   Pier Paolo Pasolini to MC, circa September 1971. Chiarcossi.
40   *La Stampa*, 27/5/1970.
41   *New York Times*, 30/11/1970.
42   *La Stampa*, 25/10/1970.
43   *New York Times*, 30/11/1970.
44   *Ibid.*
45   Lerman, p.343.
46   Caloni.
47   *Stop*, December 1970.
48   Lerman, p.313.
49   Pasolini to MC. Chiarcossi.
50   *New York Times*, 31/10/1971.

18: Intermezzo

1   *La Stampa*, 3/1/1971.
2   *New York Times*, 30/11/1970.
3   Lerman, p.330.
4   *Ibid.*
5   *La Stampa*, 28/9/1972.
6   *New York Times*, 30/11/1970.
7   *La Stampa*, 16/1/1971.
8   *New York Times*, 30/11/1970.
9   *La Stampa*, 16/1/1971.
10   Lerman, p.332.
11   Joseph Wishy to MC, 9/12/1971, LLP.
12   Press conference, 7/2/1974, LLP.
13   csmusic.net, 1/9/2000.
14   MC to Dorle Soria, 21/7/72, DSC.
15   Lerman, p.358.
16   *Ibid.*, p.343.
17   MC to Lerman, 8/1/1975, LLP.
18   Caloni.
19   *Gente*, 1/10/1977.
20   Caloni.
21   *La Stampa*, 28/9/1972.

22   MC to Lantzounis, August 1975, RBC.
23   Hendricks, Barbara, *Lifting My Voice* (Chicago: Chicago Review Press, 2014) p.127.
24   csmusic.net, 1/4/2012.
25   Hendricks, Barbara, *Lifting My Voice*, p.133.
26   csmusic.net, 1/4/2012.
27   Fuller, Albert, *Alice Tully: An Intimate Portrait* (Chicago: University of Illinois, 1999) p.69.
28   *San Francisco Examiner & Chronicle*, 17/8/1997.
29   parterrebox.com.
30   Lerman, p.506.
31   *Ibid.*, p.330.
32   *Ibid.*, p.445.
33   Caloni.
34   MC to Lantzounis, [undated] circa 1975, RBC.
35   MC to Lerman, 26/11/1957, LLP.
36   *New York Times*, 31/10/1971.
37   Evans, Peter, *Nemesis*, p.249.
38   *La Stampa*, 27/11/1972.
39   Lerman, p.353.
40   MC to Helen Arfaras, 18/10/1971, private collection.
41   Allegri, p.140.
42   Lerman, p.361.

19: Lucidity

1   Allegri, p.156.
2   A well-known music critic and friend of Callas and Di Stefano. They wish to remain anonymous.
3   MC to Lantzounis, 26/6/1975, RBC.
4   *La Repubblica*, 23/4/1992.
5   MC to Irving Kolodin, 21/7/1972, private collection.
6   In September 1972, Maria thought she was pregnant and lied that it was Onassis's child. The man in her life, however, was Di Stefano. She was relieved when the results were negative. Many have accused Maria of being a fantasist, claiming that, at almost 49, she was too old to bear children. As her personal papers suggest, this was not true.
7   Allegri, p.157.
8   *La Repubblica*, 23/4/92.
9   *Ibid.*
10   MC to Alberta Masiello, 9/7/1972, private collection.
11   *Ibid.*
12   MC to Irving Kolodin, 21/7/1972.
13   MC to Dorle Soria, 21/7/1972, DSC.
14   MC to Lerman, 14/1/1973, LLP.
15   Press conference, 7/2/1974, LLP.
16   MC to Lantzounis, 29/4/1964, RBC.
17   *Ibid.*, 19/11/1964.
18   Giuseppe Di Stefano, *Oggi*, 1/10/1977.

19   Evans, Peter, *Nemesis*, p.244.
20   *La Stampa*, April 1973.
21   *La Repubblica*, 15/9/2007.
22   MC to Lerman, 14/1/1973, LLP.
23   *Ibid*.
24   *Ibid*.
25   *La Stampa*, April 1973.
26   *Gramiliano*, 16/9/2017.
27   *La Repubblica*, 15/9/2007.
28   *La Stampa*, 12/4/1973.
29   *New York Times*, 13/4/1973.
30   'If I had in the future something to do with the Met would Howard [Talley] help? I'm not saying any more.' LLP.
31   Patricia Brooks Mann to Lerman, 25/1/1972, LLP.
32   MC to Lerman, 14/1/1973, LLP.
33   *Ibid*., 1/9/1973.
34   MC to Lantzounis, 1/9/1973, RBC.
35   Press conference, 7/2/1974, LLP.
36   Sutherland, p.247.
37   *Ibid*., p.232.
38   *La Stampa*, 20/9/1973.
39   'Then came the love and a new kind of love: another singer, Giuseppe Di Stefano.' *La Stampa*, 27/11/1973.
40   *Ibid*.
41   Press conference, 7/2/1974, LLP.
42   Sutherland, p.51.
43   MC to Lantzounis, 9/11/1973, RBC.
44   *The Evening Standard*, 27/11/1973.
45   Sutherland, p.89.
46   *Ibid*., p.109.
47   *Ibid*., p.183.
48   *Ibid*., p.117.
49   *The Observer*, 8,15/2/1970.
50   Allegri, p.157.
51   Press conference, 7/2/1974, LLP.
52   *Ibid*.
53   *La Repubblica*, 23/4/1992.
54   Sutherland, p.137.
55   Allegri, p.157.
56   *Ibid*.
57   *Ludwig Van Toronto*, 15/10/2014.
58   *60 Minutes*, February 1974.
59   Sutherland, p.151.
60   *Ibid*., p.163.
61   *New York Times*, 6/3/1974.
62   Lerman, p.400.

63   *Ibid.*
64   *New York Times*, 6/3/1974.
65   Lerman, p.400.
66   Sutherland, p.261.
67   *La Stampa*, April 23/4/1992.
68   Sutherland, p.158.
69   *Ibid.*, p.178.
70   Lerman, p.233.
71   Allegri, p.157.
72   Sutherland, p.235.
73   *Life*, 30/10/1964.
74   MC to Dr Louis Parrish, 23/1/1975, RBC.
75   Sutherland. p.262.
76   MC to Dr Louis Parrish, 23/1/1975.
77   Lerman, p.563.

20: Fable

1   MC to Lantzounis, 24/2/1975, RBC.
2   Allegri, p.157.
3   MC to Lantzounis 24/2/1975, RBC.
4   MC to Lerman, 8/1/1975, LLP.
5   Evans, Peter, *Nemesis*, p. 288.
6   *Ibid.*, p.290.
7   Petsalis-Diomidis, p.567.
8   Bob Crawford to MC, 21/3/1975.
9   MC to Lantzounis, [undated] circa April 1975, RBC.
10   *Ibid.*
11   *Ibid.*, 26/6/1975.
12   *Ibid.*, 29/10/1975.
13   *Ibid.*
14   *Ibid.*
15   *Ibid.*
16   *Ibid.*
17   *Ibid.*
18   *Ibid.*, 18 /7/1975.
19   *Ibid.*, 1/9/1973.
20   *Ibid.*, 18/7/1975.
21   *Ibid.*, 8/10/1975.
22   *Ibid.*
23   Sutherland, p.203.
24   Lerman, p.295.
25   Werner, Schroeter, *Days of Twilight, Nights of Frenzy* (Chicago: University of Chicago Press, 2017) p.2.
26   Callas, Jackie, p.69.
27   Petsalis-Diomidis, p.570.

28 MC to Onassis, 30/1/1968.
29 Callas, Jackie, p.18.
30 Lerman, p.315.
31 MC to Lantzounis, 22/8/1976, RBC.
32 *Ibid.*
33 *La Stampa*, 15/4/1992.
34 MC to Lantzounis, 11/12/1976, RBC.
35 Caloni.
36 Lerman, p.431.
37 *Ibid.*
38 MC to Lerman, 8/1/1975, LLP.
39 *Ibid.*
40 Lainie Reed to author.
41 Lerman, p.435.
42 *Haolam Hazeh*, 1971.

Epilogue

1   Ardoin.
2   Callas, Jackie, p.4.
3   *Ibid.*, p.21.
4   *Ibid.*, p.18.
5   *New York Times*, 31/10/1971.
6   MC to Lantzounis, [undated] 1950, RBC.
7   *Ibid.*
8   Callas, Jackie, p.229.
9   *Andreas Stathopoulos vs MC MC SRL*, Trademark Trial and Appeal Board, 21 July 2010, No. 91187914 (T.T.A.B. 21/7/2010).
10 *Ibid.*
11 *Ibid.*
12 'The present website is the only one run legitimately by the remaining members of her family and serves the ambition to further propagate her legacy …' (see mariacallasestate.com).
13 Petsalis-Diomidis, p.564.

Select Bibliography

Allegri, Renzo, and Roberto, *Callas by Callas: The Secret Writings of La Maria* (Berkeley: University of California, 1998).

Andry, Peter, Stringer, Robin and Tony Locantro, *Inside the Recording Studio: Working with Callas, Rostropovich, Domingo, and the Classical Elite* (Lanham: Scarecrow Press, 2008).

Bing, Rudolf, *5000 Nights at the Opera* (New York: Doubleday, 1982).

Callas, Evangelia, *My Daughter Maria Callas* (London: Leslie Frewin, 1967).

Callas, Jackie, *Sisters* (London: Pan Books, 1990).

Di Stefano, Maria, *Callas Nemica Mia* (Milan: Rusconi, 1992).

Drake, James A., *Richard Tucker: A Biography* (New York: Dutton, 1984).

Evans, Peter, *Ari: The Life and Times of Aristotle Socratres Onassis* (New York: Summit, 1986).

Evans, Peter, *Nemesis: The True Story of Aristotle Onassis, Jackie O, and the Love Triangle That Brought Down the Kennedys* (New York: William Morrow, 2005).

Harewood, George Lascelles, *The Tongs and the Bones: The Memoirs of Lord Harewood* (London: Weidenfeld and Nicolson, 1981).

Galatopoulos, Stelios, *Maria Callas: Sacred Monster* (London: Simon & Schuster, 1999)

Ivory, James and Stephen Sartarelli (eds), *The Selected Poetry of Pier Paolo Pasolini: A Bilingual Edition* (Chicago: University of Chicago Press, 2015).

Kesting, Jurgen, *Maria Callas* (Boston: Northeastern University Press, 1993).

Lerman, Leo, *The Grand Surprise: The Journals of Leo Lerman* (New York: Knopf, 2007).

Meneghini, Battista, *My Wife Maria Callas* (New York: Farrar Straus Giroux, 1982).

Montague Browne, Anthony, *The Long Sunset* (London: Cassell, 1995).

Pasolini, Pier Paolo, 'The Bay of Kingstown' (1970).

Petsalis-Diomidis, Nicholas, *The Unknown Callas: The Greek Years* (Portland: Amadeus Press, 2001).

Schwartz, Barth David, *Pasolini, Requiem* (New York: Pantheon, 1992).

Scott, Michael, *Maria Meneghini Callas* (London: Simon & Schuster, 1992).

Seroff, Victor, *Renata Tebaldi: The Woman and the Diva* (New York: Appleton Century Crofts, 1961).

Staggs, Sam, *Inventing Elsa Maxwell: How an Irrepressible Nobody Conquered High Society, Hollywood, the Press, and the World* (New York: St Martin's Press, 2012).

Stancioff, Nadia, *Maria Callas Remembered* (New York: Dutton, 1987).

Sutherland, Robert, *Maria Callas: Diaries of a Friendship* (London: Constable, 1999).

Taraborrelli, J. Randy, *Jackie, Janet and Lee: The Secret Lives of Janet Auchincloss and Her Daughters Jacqueline Kennedy Onassis and Lee Radziwill* (New York: St Martin's Press, 2018).

Tosi, Bruno (ed.), *The Young Maria Callas* (Toronto: Guernica, 2010)

Index

The History Press

The destination for history
www.thehistorypress.co.uk